A Main Selection of the Military History Book Club
Featured Alternate of the Literary Guild
A National Book Award Finalist
A *New York Times* Notable Book

"*Black Hawk Down* ranks among the best books ever written about infantry combat . . . A descendant of books like *The Killer Angels* and *We Were Soldiers Once.*"     —Bob Shacochis, *The New York Observer*

"Bowden captures the essence of combat—the sights and sounds, the terror and the determination, the sheer will to survive. If *Black Hawk Down* were fiction, we'd rank it up there with the best war novels, *The Naked and the Dead* by Norman Mailer, or *The Things They Carried* by Tim O'Brien."     —Tom Walker, *The Denver Post*

"Stands in a league with Shelby Foote's stirring Civil War diary, *Shiloh*—rare in its completeness and reverence for the valor of young men cast into extraordinary circumstances."
     —Jim Haner, *The Baltimore Sun*

"One of the most gripping and authoritative accounts of combat ever written."     —Kirk Spitzer, *USA Today*

"Riveting."     —Mark Yost, *The Wall Street Journal*

"I can't remember having read such good reporting of a combat engagement . . . Journalistic writing at its best."
     —Don Murray, *The Boston Globe*

"Mark Bowden . . . has told the story with a driving narrative in a treatment that proceeds with dignity like the measured tread of history, yet glows with the passion of a memoir."
     —*San Antonio Express News*

P9-EJU-263

"Bowden's story has a vitality and freshness usually lacking in accounts of combat. He has written an extraordinary book. It is also a shocking one."    —Brian Urquhart, *The New York Review of Books*

"*Black Hawk Down* has the power of an ambush . . . a suspenseful and gruesome account of modern war that's impossible to put down."    —*Orlando Sentinel*

"*Black Haw Down* is destined to become a military classic."
    —*The Washington Times*

"Amazing . . . one of the most intense, visceral reading experiences imaginable."    —Michael Maren, *The Philadelphia Inquirer*

"*Black Hawk Down* may one day stand as one of the most realistic books ever written about soldiers under fire and, by extension, the role of the American military in a post-superpower, police-action world."    —*Chicago Tribune*

"A vivid, immediate and unsparing narrative that is filled with blood and noise . . . It bears comparison to S.L.A. Marshall's classic account of a battle in Korea, *Pork Chop Hill.*"
    —Jonathan Yardley, *The Washington Post*

"*Black Hawk Down* will occupy an honored place in my personal library."
    —General Henry H. Shelton, Chairman, Joint Chiefs of Staff

# BLACK
# HAWK
# DOWN

*Also by Mark Bowden*

*Doctor Dealer*

*Bringing the Heat*

*Killing Pablo*

*Finders Keepers*

*Road Work*

*Guests of the Ayatollah The*

*Best Game Ever Worm*

*The Finish*

*The Three Battles of Wanat*

*Hue 1968*

*The Last Stone*

# BLACK HAWK DOWN

## A STORY OF MODERN WAR

### MARK BOWDEN

Grove Press
New York

Copyright © 1999 by Mark Bowden

All rights reserved. No part of this book may be reproduced in any form or by any electronic or mechanical means, including information storage and retrieval systems, without permission in writing from the publisher, except by a reviewer, who may quote brief passages in a review. Scanning, uploading, and electronic distribution of this book or the facilitation of such without the permission of the publisher is prohibited. Please purchase only authorized electronic editions, and do not participate in or encourage electronic piracy of copyrighted materials. Your support of the author's rights is appreciated. Any member of educational institutions wishing to photocopy part or all of the work for classroom use, or anthology, should send inquiries to Grove/Atlantic, Inc., 841 Broadway, New York, NY 10003 or permissions@groveatlantic.com

Portions of this book were originally published as a series in *The Philadelphia Inquirer.*

Maps by Matthew Ericson.

*Published simultaneously in Canada*
*Printed in the United States of America*

20th Anniversary Edition

ISBN: 978-0-8021-4473-7
eISBN: 978-1-55584-604-6

Library of Congress Cataloging-in-Publication Data
Bowden, Mark, 1951–
Black Hawk down : a story of modern war / Mark Bowden.
    p.   cm.
"Portions of this book were orginally published as a series in
The Philadelphia inquirer."
1. Operation Restore Hope, 1992–1993. 2. United States. Army.
Task Force Ranger—History.   3. Aideed, Mohammed Farah.   I. Title.
                                    DT407.4.B69   1999
967.7305'3—dc21                                    98-46688
                                                    CIP

The companion *Black Hawk Down* television documentary and CD-ROM are available for order from KR Video at (215) 854-4444. Visit the *Black Hawk Down* website at http://www.blackhawkdown.com.

DESIGN BY LAURA HAMMOND HOUGH

Grove Press
an imprint of Grove/Atlantic, Inc.
841 Broadway
New York, NY 10003

Distributed by Publishers Group West

20 21 22   17 16 15 14 13

For my mother, Rita Lois Bowden,
and in memory of my father,
Richard H. Bowden

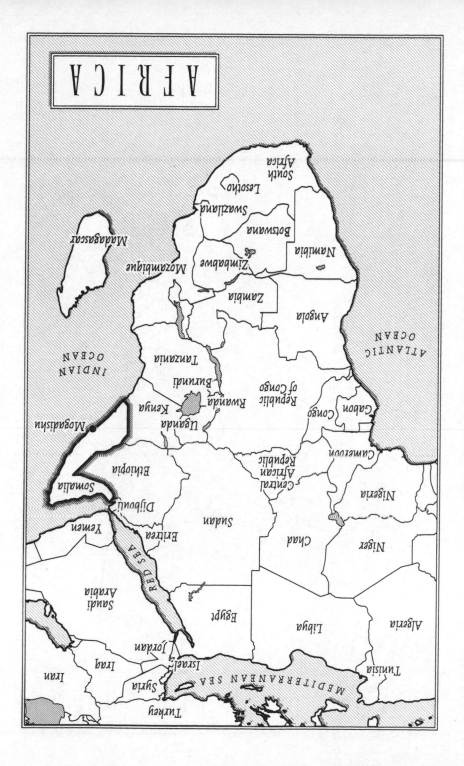

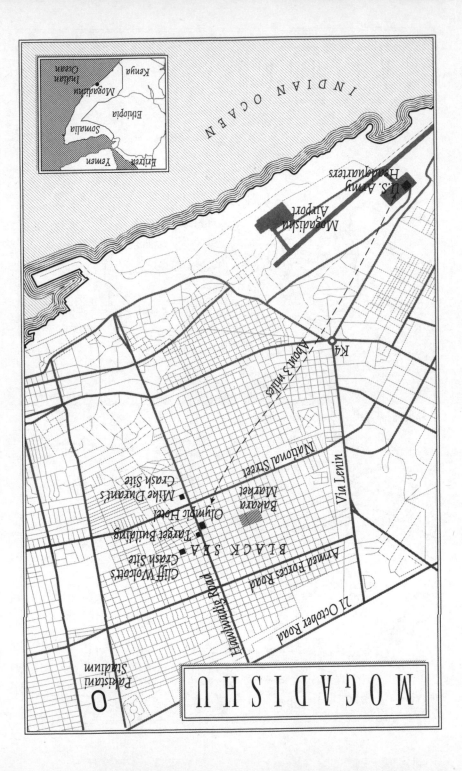

# CONTENTS

It makes no difference what men think of war, said the judge. War endures. As well ask men what they think of stone. War was always here. Before man was, war waited for him. The ultimate trade awaiting the ultimate practitioner.

Cormac McCarthy, *Blood Meridian*

# THE
# ASSAULT

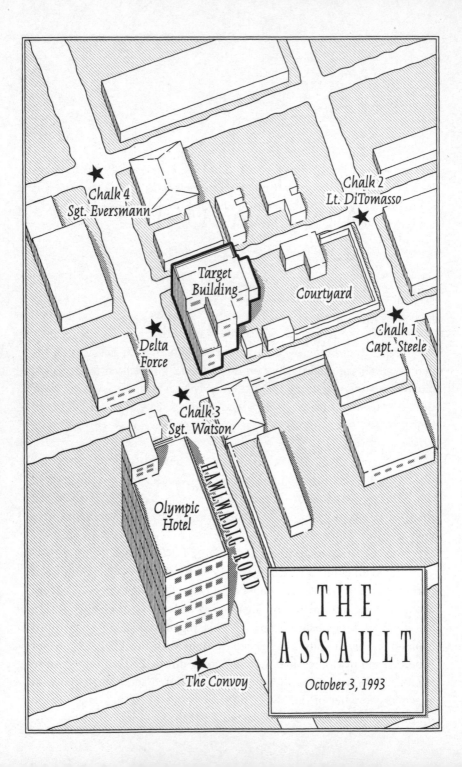

Chalk 4
Sgt. Eversmann

Chalk 2
Lt. DiTomasso

Target
Building

Courtyard

Delta
Force

Chalk 1
Capt. Steele

Chalk 3
Sgt. Watson

HAWLWADIG ROAD

Olympic
Hotel

The Convoy

THE
ASSAULT
October 3, 1993

# 1

At liftoff, Matt Eversmann said a Hail Mary. He was curled into a seat between two helicopter crew chiefs, the knees of his long legs up to his shoulders. Before him, jammed on both sides of the Black Hawk helicopter, was his "chalk," twelve young men in flak vests over tan desert camouflage fatigues.

He knew their faces so well they were like brothers. The older guys on this crew, like Eversmann, a staff sergeant with five years in at age twenty-six, had lived and trained together for years. Some had come up together through basic training, jump school, and Ranger school. They had traveled the world, to Korea, Thailand, Central America . . . they knew each other better than most brothers did. They'd been drunk together, gotten into fights, slept on forest floors, jumped out of airplanes, climbed mountains, shot down foaming rivers with their hearts in their throats, baked and frozen and starved together, passed countless bored hours, teased one another endlessly about girlfriends or lack of same, driven out in the middle of the night from Fort Benning to retrieve each other from some diner or strip club out on Victory Drive after getting drunk and falling asleep or pissing off some barkeep. Through all those things, they had been training for a moment like this. It was the first time the lanky sergeant had been put in charge, and he was nervous about it.

*Pray for us sinners, now, and at the hour of our death, amen.*

It was midafternoon, October 3, 1993. Eversmann's Chalk Four was part of a force of U.S. Army Rangers and Delta Force operators who were about to drop in uninvited on a gathering of Habr Gidr clan leaders in the heart of Mogadishu, Somalia. This ragged clan, led by warlord Mohamed Farrah Aidid, had picked a fight with the United States of America, and it was, without a doubt, going down. Today's targets were two of Aidid's lieutenants. They would be arrested and imprisoned with a growing number of the belligerent clan's bosses on an island off the southern Somali coast city of Kismayo. Chalk Four's piece of this snatch-

and-grab was simple. Each of the four Ranger chalks had a corner of the block around the target house. Eversmann's would rope down to the northwest corner and set up a blocking position. With Rangers on all four corners, no one would enter the zone where Delta was working, and no one would leave.

They had done this dozens of times without difficulty, in practice and on the task force's six previous missions. The pattern was clear in Eversmann's mind. He knew which way to move when he hit the ground, where his soldiers would be. Those out of the left side of the bird would assemble on the left side of the street. Those out of the right side would assemble right. Then they would peel off in both directions, with the medics and the youngest guys in the middle. Private First Class Todd Blackburn was the baby on Eversmann's bird, a kid fresh out of Florida high school who had not yet even been to Ranger school. He'd need watching. Sergeant Scott Galentine was older but also inexperienced here in Mog. He was a replacement, just in from Benning. The burden of responsibility for these young Rangers weighed heavily on Eversmann. This time out they were *his*.

As chalk leader, he was handed headphones when he took his front seat. They were bulky and had a mouthpiece and were connected by a long black cord to a plug on the ceiling. He took his helmet off and settled the phones over his ears.

One of the crew chiefs tapped his shoulder.

"Matt, be sure you remember to take those off before you leave," he said, pointing to the cord.

Then they had stewed on the hot tarmac for what seemed an hour, breathing the pungent diesel fumes and oozing sweat under their body armor and gear, fingering their weapons anxiously, every man figuring this mission would probably be scratched before they got off the ground. That's how it usually went. There were twenty false alarms for every real mission. Back when they'd arrived in Mog five weeks earlier, they were so flush with excitement that cheers went up from Black Hawk to Black Hawk every time they boarded the birds. Now spin-ups like this were routine and usually amounted to nothing.

Waiting for the code word for launch, which today was "Irene," they were a formidable sum of men and machines. There were four of the amazing AH-6 Little Birds, two-seat bubble-front attack helicopters that could fly just about anywhere. The Little Birds were loaded with rockets this time, a first. Two would make the initial sweep over the target and two more would help with rear security. There were four MH-6 Little Birds with benches mounted on both sides for delivering the spearhead of the assault force, Delta's C Squadron, one of three operational elements in the army's top secret commando unit. Following this strike force were eight of the elongated troop-carrying Black Hawks: two carrying Delta assaulters and their ground command, four for delivering the Rangers (Company B, 3rd Battalion of the army's 75th Infantry, the Ranger Regiment out of Fort Benning, Georgia), one carrying a crack CSAR (Combat Search and Rescue) team, and one to fly the two mission commanders—Lieutenant Colonel Tom Matthews, who was coordinating the pilots of the 160th SOAR (Special Operations Aviation Regiment out of Fort Campbell, Kentucky); and Delta Lieutenant Colonel Gary Harrell, who had responsibility for the men on the ground. The ground convoy, which was lined up and idling out by the front gate, consisted of nine wide-body Humvees and three five-ton trucks. The trucks would be used to haul the prisoners and assault forces out. The Humvees were filled with Rangers, Delta operators, and four members of SEAL (Sea, Air, Land) Team Six, part of the navy's special forces branch. Counting the three surveillance birds and the spy plane high overhead, there were nineteen aircraft, twelve vehicles, and about 160 men. It was an eager armada on a taut rope.

There were signs this one would go. The commander of Task Force Ranger, Major General William F. Garrison, had come out to see them off. He had never done that before. A tall, slender, gray-haired man in desert fatigues with half an unlit cigar jutting from the corner of his mouth, Garrison had walked from chopper to chopper and then stooped down by each Humvee.

"Be careful," he said in his Texas drawl.

Then he'd move on to the next man.

"Good luck."

Then the next.

"Be careful."

The swell of all those revving engines made the earth tremble and their pulses race. It was stirring to be part of it, the cocked fist of America's military might. Woe to whatever stood in their way. Bristling with grenades and ammo, gripping the steel of their automatic weapons, their hearts pounding under their flak vests, they waited with a heady mix of hope and dread. They ran through last-minute mental checklists, saying prayers, triple-checking weapons, rehearsing their precise tactical choreography, performing little rituals . . . whatever it was that prepared them for battle. They all knew this mission might get hairy. It was an audacious daylight thrust into the "Black Sea," the very heart of Habr Gidr territory in central Mogadishu and warlord Aidid's stronghold. Their target was a three-story house of whitewashed stone with a flat roof, a modern modular home in one of the city's few remaining clusters of intact large buildings, surrounded by blocks and blocks of tin-roofed dwellings of muddy stone. Hundreds of thousands of clan members lived in this labyrinth of irregular dirt streets and cactus-lined paths. There were no decent maps. Pure Indian country.

The men had watched the rockets being loaded on the AH-6s. Garrison hadn't done that on any of their earlier missions. It meant they were expecting trouble. The men had girded themselves with extra ammo, stuffing magazines and grenades into every available pocket and pouch of their load-bearing harnesses, leaving behind canteens, bayonets, night-vision goggles, and any other gear they felt would be deadweight on a fast daylight raid. The prospect of getting into a scrape didn't worry them. Not at all. They welcomed it. They were predators, heavy metal avengers, unstoppable, *invincible.* The feeling was, after six weeks of diddling around they were finally going in to kick some serious Somali ass.

It was 3:32 P.M. when the chalk leader inside the lead Black Hawk, *Super Six Four,* heard over the intercom the soft voice of the pilot, Chief Warrant Officer Mike Durant, clearly pleased.

Durant announced, "Fuckin' *Irene.*"

And the armada launched, lifting off from the shabby airport by the sea into an embracing blue vista of sky and Indian Ocean. They eased out across a littered strip of white sand and moved low and fast over running breakers that formed faint crests parallel to the shore. In close formation they banked and flew down the coastline southwest. From each bird the booted legs of the eager soldiers dangled from the benches and open doors.

Unrolling toward a hazy desert horizon, Mogadishu in midafternoon sun was so bright it was as if the aperture on the world's lens was stuck one click wide. From a distance the ancient port city had an auburn hue, with its streets of ocher sand and its rooftops of Spanish tile and rusted tin. The only tall structures still standing after years of civil war were the ornate white towers of mosques—Islam being the only thing all Somalia held sacred. There were many scrub trees, the tallest just over the low rooftops, and between them high stone walls with pale traces of yellow and pink and gray, fading remnants of pre–civil war civility. Set there along the coast, framed to the west by desert and the east by gleaming teal ocean, it might have been some sleepy Mediterranean resort.

As the helicopter force swept in over it, gliding back in from the ocean and then banking right and sprinting northeast along the city's western edge, Mogadishu spread beneath them in its awful reality, a catastrophe, the world capital of things-gone-completely-to-hell. It was as if the city had been ravaged by some fatal urban disease. The few paved avenues were crumbling and littered with mountains of trash, debris, and the rusted hulks of burned-out vehicles. Those walls and buildings that had not been reduced to heaps of gray rubble were pockmarked with bullet scars. Telephone poles leaned at ominous angles like voodoo totems topped by stiff sprays of dreadlocks—the stubs of their severed wires (long since stripped for sale on the thriving black market). Public spaces displayed the hulking stone platforms that once held statuary from the heroic old days of dictator Mohamed Siad Barre, the national memory stripped bare not out of revolutionary fervor, but to sell the bronze and copper for scrap. The few proud old government and university buildings that still stood were inhabited now by refugees. Everything of value had been looted, right down to metal window frames, doorknobs, and hinges. At night, campfires glowed from third- and fourth-story windows of the old Polytechnic Institute. Every open space was clotted with the dense makeshift villages of the disinherited, round stick huts covered with layers of rags and shacks made of scavenged scraps of wood and patches of rusted tin. From above they looked like an advanced stage of some festering urban rot.

In his bird, *Super Six Seven*, Eversmann rehearsed the plan in his mind. By the time they reached the street, the D-boys would already be taking down the target house, rounding up Somali prisoners and shooting anyone foolish enough to fight back. Word was there were two big boys in this house, men whom the task force had identified as "Tier One Personalities," Aidid's top men. As the D-boys did their work and the Rangers kept the curious at bay, the ground convoy of trucks and Humvees would roll in through the city, right up to the target house. The prisoners would be herded into the trucks. The assault team and blocking force would jump in behind them and they would all drive back to finish out a nice Sunday afternoon on the beach. It would take about an hour.

To make room for the Rangers in the Black Hawks, the seats in back had been removed. The men who were not in the doorways were squatting on ammo cans or seated on flak-proof Kevlar panels laid out on the floor. They all wore desert camouflage fatigues, with Kevlar vests and helmets and about fifty pounds of equipment and ammo strapped to their load-bearing harnesses, which fit on over the vests. All had goggles and thick leather gloves. Those layers of gear made even the slightest of them look bulky, robotic, and intimidating. Stripped down to their dirt-brown T-shirts and shorts, which is how they spent most of their time in the hangar, most looked like the pimply teenagers they were (average age nineteen). They were immensely proud of their Ranger status. It spared them most of the numbing noncombat-related routine that drove many an army enlistee nuts. The Rangers trained for war full-time. They were fitter, faster, and first—"Rangers lead the way!" was their motto. Each had volunteered at least three times to get where they were, for the army, for airborne, and for the Rangers. They were the cream, the most highly motivated young soldiers of their generation, selected to fit the army's ideal—they were all male and, revealingly, nearly all white (there were only two blacks among the 140-man company). Some were professional soldiers, like Lieutenant Larry Perino, a 1990 West Point graduate. Some were overachievers in search of a different challenge, like Specialist John Waddell on Chalk Two, who had enlisted after finishing high school in Natchez, Mississippi, with a 4.0 GPA. Some were daredevils in search of a physical challenge. Others were self-improvers, young men who had found themselves adrift after high school, or in trouble with drugs, booze, the law, or all three. They were harder-edged than most young men of their generation who, on this Sunday in early autumn, were weeks into their fall college semester. Most of these Rangers had been kicked around some, had tasted failure. But there were no goof-offs. Every man had worked to be here, probably harder than he'd ever worked in his life. Those with troubled pasts had taken harsh measure of themselves. Beneath their best hard-ass act, most were achingly earnest, patriotic, and idealistic. They had literally taken the army up on its offer to "Be All You Can Be."

They held themselves to a higher standard than normal soldiers. With their buff bodies, distinct crew cuts—sides and back of the head completely shaved—and their grunted *Hoo-ah* greeting, they saw themselves as the army at its gung ho best. Many, if they could make it, aspired to join Special Forces, maybe even get picked to try out for Delta, the hale, secret supersoldiers now leading this force in. Only the very best of them would be invited to try out, and only one of every ten invited would make it through selection. In this ancient male hierarchy, the Rangers were a few steps up the ladder, but the D-boys owned the uppermost rung.

Rangers knew the surest path to that height was combat experience. So far, Mog had been mostly a tease. War was always about to happen. *About* to happen. Even the missions, exciting as they'd been, had fallen short. The Somalis—whom they called "Skinnies" or "Sammies"— had taken a few wild shots at them, enough to get the Rangers' blood up and unleash a hellish torrent of return fire, but nothing that qualified as a genuine balls-out firefight.

Which is what they wanted. All of these guys. If there were any hesitant thoughts, they were buttoned tight. A lot of these men had started as afraid of war as anyone, but the fear had been drummed out. Especially in Ranger training. About a fourth of those who volunteered washed out, enough so that those who emerged with their Ranger tab at the end were riding the headiest wave of accomplishment in their young lives. The weak had been weeded out. The strong had stepped up. Then came weeks, months, years of constant training. The *Hoo-ahs* couldn't wait to go to war. They were an all-star football team that had endured bruising, exhausting, dangerous practice sessions twelve hours a day, seven days a week—for *years*—without ever getting to play a game.

They yearned for battle. They passed around the dog-eared paperback memoirs of soldiers from past conflicts, many written by former

Rangers, and savored the affectionate, comradely tone of their stories, feeling bad for the poor suckers who bought it or got crippled or maimed but identifying with the righteous men who survived the experience whole. They studied the old photos, which were the same from every war, young men looking dirty and tired, half dressed in army combat fatigues, dogtags hanging around their skinny necks, posing with arms draped over each other's shoulders in exotic lands. They could see themselves in those snapshots, surrounded by *their* buddies, fighting *their* war. It was THE test, the only one that counted.

Sergeant Mike Goodale had tried to explain this to his mother one time, on leave in Illinois. His mom was a nurse, incredulous at his bravado.

"Why would anybody *want* to go to war?" she asked.

Goodale told her it would be like, as a nurse, after all her training, never getting the chance to work in a hospital. It would be like that.

"You want to find out if you can really do the job," he explained.

Like those guys in books. They'd been tested and proven. It was another generation of Rangers' turn now. Their turn.

It didn't matter that none of the men in these helicopters knew enough to write a high school paper about Somalia. They took the army's line without hesitation. Warlords had so ravaged the nation battling among themselves that their people were starving to death. When the world sent food, the evil warlords hoarded it and killed those who tried to stop them. So the civilized world had decided to lower the hammer, invite the baddest boys on the planet over to clean things up. 'Nuff said. Little the Rangers had seen since arriving at the end of August had altered that perception. Mogadishu was like the postapocalyptic world of Mel Gibson's *Mad Max* movies, a world ruled by roving gangs of armed thugs. They were here to rout the worst of the warlords and restore sanity and civilization.

Eversmann had always just enjoyed being a Ranger. He wasn't sure how he felt about being in charge, even if it was just temporary. He'd won the distinction by default. His platoon sergeant had been summoned home by an illness in his family, and then the guy who replaced him had keeled over with an epileptic seizure. He, too, had been sent home. Eversmann was the senior man in line. He accepted the task hesitantly. That morning at Mass in the mess he'd prayed about it.

Airborne now at last, Eversmann swelled with energy and pride as he looked out over the full armada. It was a state-of-the-art military force.

Already circling high above the target was the slickest intelligence support America had to offer, including satellites, a high-flying P3 Orion spy plane, and three OH-58 observation helicopters, which looked like the bubble-front Little Bird choppers with a five-foot bulbous polyp growing out of the top. The observation birds were equipped with video cameras and radio equipment that would relay the action live to General Garrison and the other senior officers in the Joint Operations Center (JOC) back at the beach. Moviemakers and popular authors might strain to imagine the peak capabilities of the U.S. military, but here was the real thing about to strike. It was a well-oiled, fully equipped, late-twentieth-century fighting machine. America's best were going to war, and Sergeant Matt Eversmann was among them.

# 2

It was only a three-minute flight to the target. With the earphones on, Eversmann could listen to most of the frequencies in use. There was the command net, which linked the commanders on the ground to Matthews and Harrell circling overhead in the Command and Control (or "C2") Black Hawk, and with Garrison and the other brass back in the JOC. The pilots had their own link to air commander Matthews, and Delta and the Rangers each had their own internal radio links. For the duration of the mission all other broadcast frequencies in the city were being jammed. Inside the steady scratch of static, Eversmann heard a confusing overlap of calm voices, all the different elements preparing for the assault.

By the time the Black Hawks had moved down low over the city for their final approach from the north, the advance Little Birds were already closing in on the target. There was still time to abort the mission.

Burning tires on the street near the target triggered momentary alarm. Somalis often set fires to signal trouble and summon militia. Could they be flying into an ambush?

— *Those tires, have they been burning for a pretty good period of time or did they just light them, over?* asked a Little Bird pilot.

— *Those tires were burning this morning when we were up,* answered a pilot on one of the observation birds.

"Two minutes," the *Super Six Seven* pilot alerted Eversmann.

The Little Birds moved into position for their "bump," a sudden climb and then a dive that would sweep them over the target house with their rockets and guns pointing down. One by one, the various units would repeat "Lucy," the code word for the assault to begin: *Romeo Six Four*, Colonel Harrell; *Kilo Six Four*, Captain Scott Miller, the Delta assault-force commander; *Barber Five One*, veteran pilot Chief Warrant Officer Randy Jones in the lead AH-6 gunship; *Juliet Six Four*, Captain Mike Steele, the Ranger commander aboard Durant's bird; and *Uniform Six Four*, Lieutenant Colonel Danny McKnight, who was commanding the ground convoy poised to take them all out. The convoy had rolled up to a spot several blocks away.

— *This is Romeo Six Four to all elements. Lucy. Lucy. Lucy.*

— *This is Kilo Six Four, roger Lucy.*

— *This is Barber Five One, roger Lucy.*

— *Juliet Six Four, roger Lucy.*

— *This is Uniform Six Four, roger Lucy.*

— *All elements, Lucy.*

It was 3:43 P.M. On the screen in the JOC, commanders saw a crowded Mogadishu neighborhood, in much better shape than most. The Olympic Hotel was the most obvious landmark, a five-story white building that looked like stacked rectangular blocks with square balconies at each level. There was another similar large building on the same side of the street one block south. Both cast long shadows over Hawlwadig Road, the wide paved street that ran before them. At the intersections where dirt alleys crossed Hawlwadig, sandy soil drifted across the pavement. The soil was a striking rust-orange in the late afternoon light. There were trees in the courtyards and between some of the smaller houses. The target building was across Hawlwadig from the hotel one block north. It was built in the same stacked-blocks style, L-shaped, with three stories to the rear and a flat roof over the two stories in front. It wrapped around a small southern courtyard toward the rear and was enclosed, as was the whole long block, by a high stone wall. Moving in front, on Hawlwadig, were cars and people and donkey carts. It was a normal Sunday afternoon. The target area was just blocks away from the center of the Bakara Market, the busiest in the city. Conditioned to the helicopters now, people moving below did not even look up as the first two Little Birds came sweeping into the frame from the top, from the north, and then banked sharply east and moved off the screen.

Neither chopper fired a shot.

"One minute," the *Super Six Seven* pilot informed Eversmann.

The Delta operators would go in first to storm the building. The Rangers would come in behind them, roping down from the Black Hawks to form a perimeter around the target block.

Delta rode in on benches outside the bubble frames of the four MH-6 Little Birds, each chopper carrying a four-man team. They wore big black flak vests and plastic hockey helmets over a radio earplug and a wraparound microphone that kept them in constant voice contact with each other. They wore no insignias on their uniforms. Hanging out over the street on their low, fast approach, they scanned the people below, their upturned startled faces, their hands, their demeanor, trying to read what would happen when they hit the street. As the Little Birds came in, the crowd spooked. People and cars began to scatter. Wind from the powerful rotors knocked some people down and tore the colorful robes off some of the women. A few of the Rangers, still high overhead, spotted people below gesturing up at them eagerly, as if inviting them to come down to the streets and fight.

The first two Little Birds landed immediately south of the target building on the narrow rutted alley, blowing up thick clouds of dust. The brownout was so severe that the pilots and men on the side benches could see nothing looking down. One of the choppers found its original landing spot taken by the first chopper in, so it banked right, performed a quick circle to the west, and came down directly in front of the target.

Sergeant First Class Norm Hooten, a team leader on the fourth Little Bird, felt the rotor blade on his chopper actually nick the side of the target building as it came to a hover. Figuring the bird had gone as low as it could, Hooten and his team kicked their fast rope and jumped for it, planning to slide down the rest of the way. It was the world's shortest fast rope. They were only a foot off the ground.

They moved directly toward the house. Taking down a house like this was Delta's specialty. Speed was critical. When a crowded house was filled suddenly with explosions, smoke, and flashes of light, those inside were momentarily frightened and disoriented. Experience showed that most would drop down and move to the corners. So long as Delta caught them in this startled state, most would follow stern simple commands without question. The Rangers had watched the D-boys at work now on several missions, and the operators had moved in with such speed and authority it was hard to imagine anyone having the presence of mind to resist. But just a few seconds made a difference. The more time those inside had to sort out what was happening, the harder they would be to subdue.

The lead assault team that landed on the southern alley, led by Sergeant First Class Matt Rierson, tossed harmless flashbang grenades into the courtyard and pushed open a metal gate leading inside. They raced up some back steps and directly into the house, shouting for those inside to get down. Hooten's four-man team, along with one led by Sergeant First Class Paul Howe, charged toward the west side of the building, facing Hawlwadig Road. Hooten's team entered a shop with colorful cartoons of typewriters, pens, pencils, and other office items painted on the front walls, the Olympic Stationery Store. Inside were six or seven Somalis who promptly dropped to the floor and stretched their arms in front of them in response to the barked commands. Hooten could hear sporadic gunfire outside already, much more than he'd heard on any of the previous missions. Howe's team entered through the next doorway down. The thickly muscled sergeant kicked the legs out from under a stunned Somali man just outside the doorway, dropping him. Howe swept the room with his CAR-15, a black futuristic-looking weapon with a pump-action shotgun attached to the bayonet lug in front. It was important to assert immediate control. All he found was a warehouse filled with sacks and odds and ends.

Both teams knew they were looking for a residence, so they quickly moved back out to the street. They ran south along Hawlwadig and turned left, heading for the courtyard their teammates had already broken into. They rounded the corner in a worsening dust storm. The Black Hawks were moving in.

The first, carrying the Delta ground commander and a support element, flared and hovered about a block north of the target on Hawlwadig as Captain Miller and the other commandos on board roped down. Along with another Black Hawk full of assaulters, they would be the second wave to storm the house. Behind them came the Rangers on four Black Hawks, roping down to positions at the four corners of the block to form the assault's outer perimeter.

As ropes dropped from Black Hawk *Super Six Six,* hovering over the southwest corner, Chalk Three began sliding down to the street in twos, one man from each side of the bird. A crew chief shouted, "No fear!" to each man who exited his side of the aircraft. As Sergeant Keni Thomas reached for the rope, he thought, *Fuck you, pal, you're not the one going in.*

Hovering high over Hawlwadig two blocks north, the *Super Six Seven* pilot told Eversmann, "Prepare to throw the ropes."

Chalk Four was at about seventy feet, higher than they'd ever fast-roped, yet dust from the street was in the open doors. Waiting for the other five Black Hawks to get in position, it seemed to Eversmann that they had held their hover for a dangerously long time. Even over the sound of the rotor and engines the men could hear the pop of gunfire. A Black Hawk hanging in the sky like that made a big target. The three-inch-thick nylon ropes were coiled before the doors on both sides. Specialist Dave Diemer was waiting in the right-side door with Sergeant Casey Joyce. At the head of the line at the left door was the kid, Blackburn. When they kicked out the ropes, at the pilot's command, one dropped down on a car. This delayed things further. The Black Hawk jerked forward trying to drag the rope free.

"We're a little short of our desired position," the pilot informed Eversmann. They were going in about a block north of their corner.

"No problem," he said.

The sergeant felt it would be safer on the ground.

"We're about one hundred meters short," the pilot warned.

Eversmann gave him a thumbs up.

Men started leaping. The door gunners shouted, "Go! Go! Go!"

Eversmann would be the last man out. He removed the head-phones and was momentarily deafened by the noise of the helicopter and the explosions and gunfire below. Ordinarily Eversmann wore ear-plugs on missions, but he'd left them out today because he knew he'd have the headphones. He draped them over his canteen and reached for his goggles. Battling the excitement and confusion, all his movements became deliberate. He would fasten the goggles over his eyes and then, mindful of the crew chief's instruction, would set the headphones on his seat before he left. But the damn strap on his goggles snapped. Eversmann fiddled with it for a moment as the last of his men leapt out, trying to find a way to fix them, saw that it was his turn to hit the rope, chucked the goggles, and jumped, ripping the headset cord from the ceiling and taking the earphones right out of the helicopter with him.

He hadn't realized how high up they were. The slide down was far longer than any they'd done in training. Friction burned through his heavy leather gloves, leaving the palms of his hands raw, and he felt terribly vulnerable, fully extended on the rope for what felt like twice the normal time. As he neared the ground, through the swirling dust below his feet, he saw one of his men stretched out on his back at the bottom of the rope. Eversmann's heart sank. *Somebody's been shot already!* He gripped the rope hard to keep himself from landing right on top of the guy. It was the kid. Eversmann's feet touched the street next to him, and the crew chiefs above released the ropes. They dropped twisting and slapped down across the pavement. As the Black Hawk moved away the noise and dust began to ease, and the city's musky odor bore in like the smell of something overripe.

Blackburn was bleeding from the nose and ears. Private First Class Mark Good, the medic, was already at work on him. The kid had one eye shut and the other open. Blood was coming from his mouth and he was making a gurgling sound. He was unconscious. Good had been through emergency medical training, but this was beyond him. It was the most severe injury the task force had seen in Somalia.

Blackburn hadn't been shot, he'd fallen. He'd somehow missed the rope. Seventy feet straight down to the street. He had just been reassigned as assistant to the chalk's 60 gunner, and he'd been carrying a lot of ammo, so he was heavier than he'd ever been on a fast rope. That, the excitement, the extreme height of the rope-in . . . for whatever reason, he hadn't held on. He looked all busted up inside. Eversmann stepped away. He took a quick count of his chalk.

Hawlwadig was about fifteen yards wide, littered with debris, as was all of Mogadishu. The dust cloud thinned, and he could see his men had peeled off as planned against the mud-stained stone walls on either side of the street. That left Eversmann in the middle of the road with Blackburn and Good. It was hot, and fine sand was caked in his eyes, nose, and ears. They were taking fire, but it wasn't accurate. Oddly, it hadn't even registered with the sergeant at first. You would think bullets flying past would command your attention, but he'd been too preoccupied to notice. Now he did. Passing bullets made a loud snap, like cracking a stick of dry hickory. Eversmann had never been shot at before. *So this is what it's like.* As big a target as he made, he figured he'd better find some cover. He and Good grabbed Blackburn under the arms and head, trying to keep his neck straight, and dragged him to the west side of the intersection. There they squatted behind two parked cars.

Eversmann shouted up the street to his radio operator, Private First Class Jason Moore, and asked him to raise Captain Mike Steele on the company net. Steele and two lieutenants, Larry Perino and Jim Lechner, had roped down with the rest of Chalk One at the southeast corner of the target block. Chalk Four was at the northwest corner. Minutes passed. Moore shouted back down the street to say he couldn't get Steele.

"What do you mean you can't get him?"

Moore just shrugged. The tobacco-chewing roughneck from Princeton, New Jersey, was wearing a headset under his helmet that allowed him to talk without tying up his hands. Before leaving he'd taped the on/off switch for his microphone to his rifle—a nifty touch, he thought. But as he'd roped in, he'd inadvertently clasped the connecting wire against the rope. Friction had burned right through it. Moore hadn't noticed it yet, however, and couldn't figure out why his calls weren't being heard.

Eversmann tried his walkie-talkie. Again Steele didn't answer, but after several tries Lieutenant Perino came on the line. The sergeant knew this was their first time in combat, and his first time in charge, so he made a particular effort to speak slowly and clearly. He explained that Blackburn had fallen and was hurt, bad. He needed to come out. Eversmann tried to convey urgency without alarm.

—*Say again,* said Perino.

The sergeant's voice was fading in and out on his radio. Eversmann repeated himself. There was a delay. Then Perino's voice came back.

—*Say all again, over.*

Eversmann was shouting now. He repeated, "Man down, WE NEED TO EXTRACT HIM ASAP!"

—*Calm down,* Perino said.

That really burned Eversmann. *This is one hell of a time to start sharpshooting me.*

The radio call brought two Delta medics running up Hawlwadig, Sergeants First Class Kurt Schmid and Bart Bullock. The more experienced men quickly began assisting Good. Schmid inserted a tube down Blackburn's throat to help him breathe. Bullock put a needle in the kid's arm and hooked up an IV.

Fire was growing heavier. To the officers watching on screens in the command center, it was like they had poked a stick into a hornet's nest. It was an amazing and unnerving thing, to view a battle in real time. Cameras from high over the fight captured crowds of Somalis throughout the area erecting barricades and lighting tires to summon help. Thousands of people were pouring into the streets, many with weapons. They were racing from all directions toward the Bakara Market, where the mass of helicopters overhead clearly marked the fight throughout the city. Moving in from more distant parts were vehicles overflowing with armed men. The largest number appeared to be coming from the north, directly toward Eversmann's position and that of Chalk Two, which had roped in at the northeast corner.

Eversmann's men had fanned out and were shooting in every direction except back toward the target building. Across the street from where the medics were working on Blackburn, Sergeant Casey Joyce had his M-16 trained on the growing crowd to the north. Somalis approached in groups of a dozen or more from around corners several blocks up, and others, closer, darted in and out of alleys taking shots at them. They were wary of the Americans' guns, but edging in. The Rangers were bound by strict rules of engagement. They were to shoot only at someone who pointed a weapon at them, but already this was unrealistic. It was clear they were being shot at, and down the street they could see Somalis with guns. But those with guns were intermingled with the unarmed, including women and children. The Somalis were strange that way. Most noncombatants who heard gunshots and explosions would flee. Whenever there was a disturbance in Mogadishu, people would throng to the spot. Men, women, children—even the aged and infirm. It was like some national imperative to *bear witness*. Rangers peering down their sights silently begged the gawkers to get the hell out of the way.

Things were not playing out according to the neat script in Eversmann's head. His chalk was still a block north of their position. He'd figured they could just hoof it down once they got on the ground, but

Blackburn falling and the unexpected volume of gunfire had ruled that out. Time played tricks. It would be hard to explain to someone who wasn't there. Events outside him seemed to be happening at a frantic pace, but his own perceptions had slowed; seconds were like minutes. He had no idea how much time had gone by. Two minutes? Five? Ten? It was hard to believe things could have gone so much to hell in such a short time.

He knew the D-boys worked fast. He kept checking behind him to see if the ground convoy had moved up. It was too early for that, but he looked anyway, wishing, because that would be a sign that things were wrapping up. He must have looked a dozen times before he saw the first Humvee round the corner about three blocks down. What a relief! *Maybe the D-boys have finished and we can roll out of here.*

Schmid, the Delta medic, had examined Blackburn more closely, and was alarmed. The kid had a severe head injury at a minimum, and there was a big lump on the back of his neck. It might be a break. He looked up at Eversmann.

"He's litter urgent, Sergeant. We need to extract him right now or he's gonna die."

Eversmann called Perino again.

"Listen, we really need to move this guy or he's gonna die. Can't you send somebody up the street?"

No, the Humvees could not move up. Eversmann relayed this news to the Delta medic.

"Listen, Sergeant, we've got to get him out," said Schmid.

So Eversmann summoned two of the sergeants in his chalk, Casey Joyce and Jeff McLaughlin, who came running. He addressed the more senior of the two, McLaughlin, shouting over the escalating noise of the fight.

"You need to move Blackburn down to those Humvees, toward the target."

They unfolded a compact litter and placed Blackburn on it. Five men took off with him, Joyce and McLaughlin in front, Bullock and Schmid in back, with Good running alongside holding up the IV bag connected to the kid's arm. They ran stooped. McLaughlin didn't think Blackburn was going to make it. On the litter he was deadweight, still bleeding from the nose and mouth. They were all yelling at him, "Hang on! Hang on!" but, by the look of him, he had already let go.

They had to keep setting down the litter to return fire. They would run a few steps, set Blackburn down, shoot, then pick him up and carry him a few more steps, then put him down again.

"We've got to get those Humvees to come to us," said Schmid. "We keep picking him up and putting him down like this and we're going to kill him."

Joyce volunteered to fetch a Humvee. He took off running on his own.

# 3

On the screens and from the speakers in the JOC, everything appeared to be going smoothly. The command center was a whitewashed two-story structure adjacent to the hangar at Task Force Ranger's airport base. A mortar round had fallen on it at some point, and the roof was caved in on one side. It bristled with so many antennae and wires that the men called it the Porcupine. On the first floor, off a long corridor, there were three rooms where senior officers sat wearing headphones and watching TV screens. General Garrison sat in the back of the operations room, chewing his cigar and taking it all in. Color images of the fight were coming from cameras in the Orion spy plane and the observation helicopters, and there were five or six radio frequencies buzzing. Garrison and his staff probably had more instant information about this unfolding battle than any commanders in history, but there wasn't much they could do but watch and listen. So long as things stayed on course, any decisions would be made by the men in the fight. The general's job was to stay on top of the situation and try to think one or two steps ahead. In the event things went wrong he could call across the city to the UN compound, where troops from the 10th Mountain Division waited, three regular army companies in varying degrees of readiness. So far there was no need. Other than one injured Ranger, the mission was clean. At about the same time they learned of Blackburn's fall, the D-boys inside the target building radioed that they'd found the men they were looking for. This was going to be a success.

It had been risky, going into Aidid's Black Sea neighborhood in daylight. The nearby Bakara Market was the center of the Habr Gidr world. Dropping in next door was a thumb in the warlord's eye. The UN forces stationed in Mog, most of them Pakistanis since the U.S. Marines had pulled out in May, wouldn't go near that part of town. It was the one place in the city where Aidid's forces could mount a serious fight on short notice, and Garrison knew the dangers of slugging it out there. Washington's commitment to Somalia wouldn't withstand many American losses. He had warned in a memo just weeks before:

"If we go into the vicinity of the Bakara Market, there's no question we'll win the gunfight, but we might lose the war."

The timing was also risky. Garrison's task force preferred to work at night. Their helicopters were flown by the crack pilots of the 160th SOAR, who had dubbed themselves the Night Stalkers. They were expert at flying totally black. With night-vision devices, they could move around on a moonless night like it was midday. The unit's pilots had been involved in almost every U.S. ground combat operation since Vietnam. When they weren't fighting they were practicing, and their skills were simply amazing. These pilots were fearless, and could fly helicopters in and out of spaces where it would be hard to insert them with a crane. Darkness made the speed and precision of the D-boys and Rangers that much more deadly. Night afforded still another advantage. Many Somali men, particularly the young men who cruised around Mog on "technicals," vehicles with .50-caliber machine guns bolted in back, were addicted to *khat*, a mild amphetamine that looks like watercress. Mid-afternoon was the height of the daily cycle. Most started chewing at about noon, and by late afternoon were wired, jumpy, and raring to go. Late at night it was just the opposite. The *khat* chewers had crashed. So today's mission called for going to the worst place in Mog at the worst possible time.

Still, the chance of bagging two of Aidid's top men at the same time was too good to pass up. They had done three previous missions in daylight without a hitch. Risk was part of the job. They were daring men; that's why they were here.

The Somalis had seen six raids now, so they more or less knew what to expect. The task force had done what it could to keep them guessing. Three times daily, mission or no mission, Garrison would scramble the whole force onto helicopters and send them up over the city. The Rangers loved it at first. You piled into the back end of a Black

Hawk and held on for dear life. The hotshot Nightstalkers would swoop down low and fast and bank so hard it would stack your insides into one half of your body. They'd rocket down streets below the roofline, with walls and people on both sides flashing past in a blur, then climb hundreds of feet and scream back down again. Corporal Jamie Smith wrote to his folks back in Long Valley, New Jersey, that the profile flights were "like a ride on a roller coaster at Six Flags!" But with so many flights, it got old.

Garrison had also been careful to vary their tactics. They usually came in on helicopters and left by vehicles, but sometimes they came in on vehicles and left by helicopters. Sometimes they came and left on choppers, or on vehicles. So the template changed. Above all, the troops were good. They were experienced and well trained.

They had come close to grabbing Aidid several times, but that wasn't their only goal. Their six previous missions had struck fear into the Habr Gidr ranks, and more recently they'd begun to pick off the warlord's top people. Garrison felt they had performed superbly so far, despite press accounts that portrayed them as bumblers. When they'd inadvertently arrested a group of UN employees on their first mission— the "employees" had been nabbed in an off-limits area with piles of black market contraband—the newspapers had dubbed them Keystone Kops. Garrison had the stories copied and posted in the hangar. That sort of thing just fired the guys up more, but to the public, and to Washington officials keenly concerned about how things played on CNN, the task force was so far a bust. They had been handed what seemed like a simple assignment, capture the tinhorn Somali warlord Mohamed Farrah Aidid or, failing that, take down his organization, and for six weeks now they'd had precious little visible success. Patience was wearing thin, and pressure for progress was mounting.

Just that morning Garrison had been stewing about it in his office. It was like trying to hit a curveball blindfolded. Here he had a force of men he could drop on a building—any building—in Mogadishu with just a few minutes' notice. These weren't just any men, they were faster, stronger, smarter, and more experienced than any soldiers in the world.

Point out a target building and the D-boys could take it down so fast that the bad guys inside would be hog-tied before the sound of the flashbang grenades and door charges had stopped ringing in their ears.

They could herd the whole mess of them out by truck or helicopter before the neighborhood militia even had a chance to pull on its pants. Garrison's force could do all this and even videotape the whole operation in color for training purposes (and to show off a little back at the Pentagon), but they couldn't do any of these things unless their spies on the ground pointed them at the right goddamn house.

For three nights running they had geared up to launch at a house where Aidid was either present or about to be (so the general's spies told him). Every time they had failed to nail it down.

Garrison knew from day one that intelligence was going to be a problem. The original plan had called for a daring, well-placed lead Somali spy, the head of the CIA's local operation, to present Aidid an elegant hand-carved cane soon after Task Force Ranger arrived. Embedded in the head of the cane was a homing beacon. It seemed like a sure thing until, on Garrison's first day in-country, Lieutenant Colonel Dave McKnight, his chief of staff, informed him that their lead informant had shot himself in the head playing Russian roulette. It was the kind of idiotic macho thing guys did when they'd lived too long on the edge.

"He's not dead," McKnight told the general, "but we're fucked."

When you worked with the locals there were going to be setbacks. Few people knew this better than Garrison, who was the picture of American military machismo with his gray crew cut, desert camouflage fatigues, and combat boots, a 9 mm pistol strapped to a shoulder holster and that unlit half cigar jammed perpetually in the side of his mouth. Garrison had been living by the sword now for about three decades. He was one of the least known important army officers in America. He had run covert operations all over the world—Asia, the Middle East, Africa, Central America, South America, the Caribbean. One thing all these missions had in common was they required cooperation from the locals.

They also demanded a low threshold for bullshit. The general was a bemused cynic. He had seen just about everything, and didn't expect much—except from his men. His gruff informality suited an officer who had begun his career not as a military academy graduate, but a buck private. He had served two tours in Vietnam, part of it helping to run the infamously brutal Phoenix program, which ferreted out and killed Viet Cong village leaders. That was enough to iron the idealism out of anybody. Garrison had risen to general without exercising the more politic demands of generalship, which called for graceful euphemism and frequent obfuscation. He was a blunt realist who avoided the pomp and pretense of upper-echelon military life. Soldiering was about fighting. It was about killing people before they killed you. It was about having your way by force and guile in a dangerous world, taking a shit in the woods, living in dirty, difficult conditions, enduring hardships and risks that could—and sometimes did—kill you. It was ugly work. Which is not to say that certain men didn't enjoy it, didn't live for it. Garrison was one of those men. He embraced its cruelty. He would say, *this man needs to die.* Just like that. Some people needed to die. It was how the real world worked. Nothing pleased Garrison more than a well-executed hit, and if things went to hell and you had to slug it out, then it was time to summon a dark relish for mayhem. Why be a soldier if you couldn't exult in a heart-pounding, balls-out gunfight? Which is what made him so good.

He inspired loyalty and affection by not taking himself too seriously. If he told a story—and the general was a hilarious storyteller—the punch line was usually at his own expense. He loved to tell about the time he went to great lengths to hire a rock band (with $5,000 out of his own pocket) to entertain his troops, mired for months in the Sinai Desert on a peacekeeping mission, only to have an unsuspecting soldier cheerfully inform him that the band "sucked." He'd shift the cigar stub to the other side of his mouth and grin sheepishly. He could even joke about his own ambition, a rarity in the army. "If you guys keep pulling this shit," he'd whine to his executive staff, "how'm I ever gonna make general?" On his career climb to leadership of JSOC (Joint Special Operations Command) he'd served a stint as Delta commander. When he arrived at Bragg as a newly leafed colonel in the mid-eighties, his crew cut alone invited scorn and suspicion from the D-boys, with their sideburns and facial hair and civilian haircuts down over their ears. But soon after he started, Garrison saved their ass. Some of America's secret supersoldiers were caught double-dipping expenses, billing both the army and the State Department for their covert international travel. The scandal could have brought down the unit, which was despised by the more traditional brass anyway. The new bullet-headed colonel could have scored points and greased his own promotional path by expressing outrage and cleaning house. Instead, Garrison placed his career in jeopardy by defending the unit and focusing punishment on only the worst abusers. He'd salvaged a fair number of professional hides in that caper, and the men hadn't forgotten. In time, his insouciant Lone Star style and understated confidence rubbed off on the whole unit. There were guys from suburban New Jersey who after weeks with Delta were wearing pointy boots, dipping tobacco, and drawling like a cowpoke.

Garrison had been living for six weeks now in the JOC, mostly in a small private office off the operations room where he could stretch his long legs and prop his boots up on the desk and shut out all the noise. Noise was one of the biggest problems in a deal like this. You had to separate out signals from the noise. There was nothing of the general's in this private space, no family photos or memorabilia. It was the way he lived. He could walk out of that building at a moment's notice and leave behind no personal trace.

The idea was to finish the job and vanish. Until then, it was an around-the-clock operation. The general had a trailer out back where he retreated at irregular intervals to grab about five hours of sleep, but usually he was camped in this command post, poised, ready to pounce.

Take the previous night, for instance. First they were informed that Aidid, who had been code-named "Yogi the Bear," was paying a visit to the Sheik Aden Adere compound, up the Black Sea. A local spy had been told this by a servant who worked there. So powerful cameras zoomed in from the Orion, the fat old four-prop navy spy plane that flew circles high over the city almost continually, and Garrison's two little observation birds spun up. The troops pulled on their gear. The Aden Adere compound was one of their preplanned targets, so the workup time was nil. But they couldn't commit—or at least Garrison refused to commit—without firmer intelligence. The task force had been embarrassed too often already. Before he launched, Garrison wanted two of the Somali spies to enter the compound and actually *see* Aidid. Then he wanted them to drop an infrared strobe by the target building. Two informants managed to get in the compound, but then exited without accomplishing either task. There were more guards than usual, they explained, maybe forty. They continued to insist that Aidid was in the compound, so why didn't the Rangers just move? Garrison demanded that one of them return with the strobe, find Yogi the fucking Bear, and mark the damn spot. Only now the informants said they couldn't get back in. It was dark, past 9 P.M., and the gates had been locked for the night. The guards wanted a password the spies didn't know.

Which was all just bad luck, perhaps. Garrison reluctantly scratched another mission. The pilots and crews shut down their helicopters and the soldiers all stripped back down and went back to their cots.

Then came a late bulletin. The same Somali spies said Aidid had now left the compound in a three-vehicle convoy with lights out. One of their number had followed the convoy west, they said, toward the Olympic Hotel, but lost it when the vehicles turned north toward October 21st Road. All of which sounded significant except that the two OH-58s were still in place, equipped with night-vision cameras that lit up the view like green-tinted noon, and neither they nor anyone watching the screens back at the command center were seeing any of this!

"As a result of this, we have experienced some weariness between [the local spy ring] and the Task Force," Garrison wrote out longhand that morning at his desk in his operations center, venting a little of the frustration that had built up over forty-three days. The memo was addressed to Marine General Joseph Hoar, his commander at CENTCOM (U.S. Central Command, located at MacDill Air Force Base in Tampa, Florida).

"Generally, [the local spy ring] appears to believe that a second-hand report from an individual who is not a member of the team should be sufficient to constitute current intelligence. I do not. Furthermore, when a [local spy ring] team member is reporting something that is totally different than what our helicopters are seeing (which we watch here back at the JOC), I naturally weigh the launch decision toward what we actually see versus what is being reported. Events such as last night, with Team 2 stating that Aidid had just left the compound in a three-vehicle convoy, when we know for a fact that no vehicles left the compound ... tends to lower our confidence level even more."

There had been too many close calls and near misses. Too much time between missions. In six weeks they'd launched exactly six times. And several of these missions had been less than bang-up successes. After that first raid, when they'd arrested the nine UN employees at the Lig Ligato compound, Washington had been very upset. Joint Chiefs of Staff Chairman Colin Powell would later say, "I had to screw myself off the ceiling." The United States apologized and all the captives were promptly released.

On September 14, the assault force had stormed what turned out to be the residence of Somali General Ahmen Jilao, a close ally of the UN and the man being groomed to lead the projected Somali police force. The troops were restless and just wanted to hit something, *anything*. In this frame of mind, it didn't take much of an excuse to launch. When one of the Rangers thought he'd spotted Aidid in a convoy of cars outside the Italian embassy, the assault force was rallied and a duly startled General Jilao was arrested along with thirty-eight others. Again an apology. All of the "suspects" were released. In a cable detailing the debacle for officials in Washington the next day, U.S. envoy Robert Gosende wrote, "We understand that some damages to the premises took place. . . . Gen. Jilao has received apologies from all concerned. We don't know if the person mistaken for Gen. Aidid was Gen. Jilao. It would be hard to confuse him with Aidid. Jilao is approximately ten inches taller than Aidid. Aidid is very dark. Jilao has a much lighter complexion. Aidid is slim and has sharp, Semitic-like features. Jilao is overweight and round-faced. . . . We are very concerned that this episode might find its way into the press."

That episode didn't, but among official circles the task force again looked like Keystone Kops. Never mind that every one of these missions was a masterpiece of coordination and execution, difficult and dangerous as hell. So far none of his men had been seriously hurt. Never mind that their latest outing had netted Osman Atto, Aidid's moneyman and one of his inner circle. Washington was impatient. Congress wanted American soldiers home, and the Clinton administration wanted to remove Aidid as a player in Somalia. August had turned to September had turned to October. One more day was one day too long for the wishes of America and the world to be stymied by this Mogadishu warlord, this man America's UN Ambassador Madeleine K. Albright had labeled a "thug."

Garrison could ill afford another misstep, even though caution could mean missing opportunities. He knew that his superiors and even some people on his own staff thought he was being too tentative about choosing missions. With such shaky work on the ground, what could you expect?

"As a rule, we will launch if [a member of the local spy ring] reports he has seen Aidid or his lieutenants, our RECCE [reconnaissance] helo picture approximates what is being reported, and the report is current enough to be actionable," Garrison wrote in his memo to Hoar. "There is no place in Mogadishu we cannot go and be successful in a fight. There are plenty of places we can go and be stupid."

And just that morning, like manna, the general's rigid criteria had been met.

Every Sunday morning the Habr Gidr held a rally out by the reviewing stand on Via Lenin, where they hurled insults at the UN and its American enforcers. One of the main speakers that morning was Omar Salad, Aidid's top political adviser. The clan had not caught on yet that the Rangers had targeted the entire top rung of Aidid's gang, so Salad wasn't even trying to hide.

He was one of the UN's "Tier One Personalities." When the rally broke up, his white Toyota Land Cruiser and some cars were watched from on high as they drove north toward the Bakara Market. Salad was observed entering a house one block north of the Olympic Hotel. At about 1:30 P.M. came confirmation from a Somali spy who radioed that Salad was meeting with Abdi "Qeybdid" Hassan Awale, Aidid's ostensible interior minister. Two major targets! Aidid might also be there, but, again, nobody had actually seen him.

High above, the Orion zoomed its cameras in on the neighborhood, and the observation choppers took off. They moved up over the Black Sea to watch the same street. The TV screens in the JOC showed many people and cars on the streets, a typical weekend afternoon at the market.

To mark the precise location where Salad and Qeybdid were meeting, a Somali informant had been instructed to drive his car, a small silver sedan with red stripes on its doors, to the front of the hotel, get out, lift the hood, and peer into it as if he were having engine trouble. This would give the helicopter cameras a chance to lock on him. He was then to drive north and stop directly in front of the target house where the clan leaders had convened. The informant did as instructed, but performed the check under his hood so quickly that the helicopters failed to fix on him.

So he was told to do it again. This time he was to drive directly to the target building, get out, and open the car hood. Garrison and his staff watched this little drama unfold on their screens. The helicopter cameras provided a clear color view of the busy scene as the informant's car entered the picture driving north on Hawlwadig Road.

It stopped before a building alongside the hotel. The informant got out and opened the hood. There was no mistaking the spot.

Word passed quietly to the hangar and the Rangers and D-boys started kitting up. The Delta team leaders met and planned out their attack, using instant photo maps relayed from the observation birds to plan exactly how they would storm the building, and where the Ranger blocking positions would be. Copies of the plan were handed out to all the chalk leaders, and the helicopters were readied. Just as Garrison was preparing to launch, however, everything was placed on hold.

The spy had stopped his car short. He was on the right street, but he'd chickened out. Nervous about moving so close to the target house, he'd stopped down the street a ways and opened the hood there. Despite Garrison's finicky precautions, the task force had been minutes away from launching an assault on the wrong house.

The commanders all hustled back into the JOC to regroup. The informant, who wore a small two-way radio strapped to his leg, was instructed to go back around the block and this time stop in front of the right goddamn house. They watched on the screens as the car came back up Hawlwadig Road. This time it went past the Olympic Hotel and stopped one block north, on the other side of the street. This was the same building the observation choppers had observed Salad entering earlier.

It was now three o'clock. Garrison's staff informed General Thomas Montgomery, second in command of all UN troops in Somalia (and direct commander of the 10th Mountain Division's "Quick Reaction Force" [QRF]), that they were about to launch. Then Garrison sought confirmation that there were no UN or charitable organizations (Non-Governmental Organizations, or NGOs) in the vicinity—a safeguard instituted after the arrests of the UN employees in the Lig Ligato raid. All aircraft were ordered out of the airspace over the target. The commanders of the 10th Mountain Division were told to keep one company on standby alert. Intelligence forces began jamming all radios and cellular phones—Mog had no regular working phone system.

The general made a last-minute decision to upload rockets on the Little Birds. Lieutenant Jim Lechner, the Ranger company's fire support officer, had been pushing for it. Lechner knew that if things got bad on the ground, he'd love to be able to call in those rockets—the two pods on the AH-6s each carried six missiles.

In the quick planning session, Lechner asked again, "Are we getting rockets today?"

Garrison told him, "Roger."

# 4

Ali Hassan Mohamed ran to the front door of his father's hamburger and candy shop when the choppers came down and the shooting started. He was a student, a tall and slender teenager with prominent cheekbones and a sparse goatee. He studied English and business in the mornings and afternoons manned the store, which was just up from the Olympic Hotel. The front door was across Hawlwadig Road diagonal from the house of Hobdurahman Yusef Galle, where the Rangers seemed to be attacking.

Peering out the doorway, Ali saw American soldiers sliding down on ropes to the alley that ran west off Hawlwadig. His shop was on the corner of that street and the gate to his family's home was just down from there. The Americans were shooting as soon as they hit the ground, shooting at everything. There were also Somalis shooting at them. These soldiers, Ali knew, were different than the ones who had come to feed Somalis. These were Rangers. They were cruel men who wore body armor and strapped their weapons to their chests and when they came at night they painted their faces to look fierce. Further up Hawlwadig, to his left about two blocks over, another group of Rangers were in pitched battle. He saw two of them drag another who looked dead out of the street.

The Rangers across the street entered a courtyard there and were shooting out. Then a helicopter came down low and blasted streams of fire from a gun on its side. The gun just pulverized his side of the street. Ali's youngest brother, Abdulahi Hassan Mohamed, fell dead by the gate to the family's house, bleeding from the head. Abdulahi was fifteen. Ali saw it happen. Then the Rangers ran out of the courtyard and across Hawlwadig toward the house of Hobdurahman Yusef Galle, where most of the other soldiers were.

Ali ran. He stopped to see his brother and saw his head broken open like a melon. Then he took off as fast as he could. He ran to his left, down the street away from the Rangers and the house they were attacking. At the end of the dirt alley he turned left and ran behind the Olympic Hotel. The streets were crowded with screaming women and children. People were scrambling everywhere, racing around dead people and dead animals. Some who were running went toward the fight and others ran away from it. Some did not seem to know which way to go. He saw a woman running naked, waving her arms and screaming. Above was the din of the helicopters and all around the crisp popping of gunfire.

Out in the streets there were already Aidid militiamen with megaphones shouting, *"Kasoobaxa guryaha oo iska celsa cadowga!"* ("Come out and defend your homes!")

Ali was not a fighter. There were gunmen, they called them *mooryan,* who lived for rice and *khat* and belonged to the private armies of rich men. Ali was just a student and part-time shopkeeper who joined the neighborhood militia to protect its shops from the *mooryan.* But these Rangers were invading his home and had just killed his brother. He ran with rage and terror behind the hotel and then, turning left again, back across Hawlwadig Road to the house of his friend Ahmed, where his AK-47 was hidden. Once he had retrieved the gun he met up with several of his friends. They ran back behind the Olympic Hotel, through all the chaos. Ali told them about his brother and led them back to his house and shop, determined to exact revenge.

Hiding behind a wall behind the hotel, they fired their first shots at the Rangers on the corner. Then they moved north, ducking behind cars and buildings. Ali would jump out and spray bullets toward the Rangers, then run for cover. Then one of his friends would do the same. Sometimes they just pushed the barrels of their guns around the corners and sprayed bullets without looking. None of them was an experienced fighter.

The Rangers were better shots. Ali's friend Adan Warsawe stepped out to shoot and was hit in the stomach by a Ranger bullet that knocked

him flat on his back. Ali and another friend risked the shooting to drag
Adan to cover. The bullet had punched a hole in Adan's gut and made
a gaping wound out his back that had sprayed blood on the dirt. When
they dragged him it left a smear of blood on the street. Adan looked
both alive and dead, as though he were someplace in between.

Ali moved on to the next street, leaving Adan with two friends.
He would shoot a Ranger or die trying. Why were they doing this? Who
were these Americans who came to his neighborhood spraying bullets
and spreading death?

# 5

After bursting into the storehouse off Hawlwadig, Sergeant Paul Howe
and the three other men on his Delta team rounded the corner and entered the target building from the southern courtyard door. They were
the last of the assault forces to enter the house. A team led by Howe's
buddy Matt Rierson had already rounded up twenty-four Somali men
on the first floor, among them two prizes: Omar Salad, the primary target,
and Mohamed Hassan Awale, Aidid's chief spokesman (not Abdi "Qeybdid"
Hassan Awale, as reported, but a clan leader of equal stature).

They were prone and docile and Rierson's team was locking their
wrists together with plastic cuffs.

Howe asked Sergeant Mike Foreman if anyone had gone upstairs.

"Not yet," Foreman said.

So Howe took his four men up to the second floor.

It was a big house by Somali standards, whitewashed cinder-block
walls and windows with no glass in them. At the top step Howe called
for one of his men to toss a flashbang grenade into the first room. It exploded and the team burst in as they were trained to do, each man covering a different firing lane. They found only a mattress on the floor. As
they moved around the room, a volley of machine-gun fire slammed
into the ceiling and wall, just missing the head of one of Howe's men.
They all dropped down. The rounds had come through the southeast
window, and had clearly come from the Ranger blocking position just
below the window. One of the younger soldiers outside had evidently

seen someone moving in the window and fired. Obviously some of these guys weren't clear which building was the target.

It was what he had feared. Howe was disappointed in the Rangers. These were supposed to be the army's crack infantry? Despite all the hype and *Hoo-ah* horseshit, he saw the younger men as poorly trained and potentially dangerous in combat. Most were fresh out of high school! During training exercises, he had the impression that they were always craning their necks to watch him and his men instead of paying attention to their own very important part of the job.

And the job demanded more. It demanded all you had, and more . . . because the price of failure was often death. That's why Howe and the rest of these D-boys loved it. It separated them from other men. War was ugly and evil, for sure, but it was still the way things got done on most of the planet. Civilized states had nonviolent ways of resolving disputes, but that depended on the willingness of everyone involved to *back down*. Here in the raw Third World, people hadn't learned to back down, at least not until after a lot of blood flowed. Victory was for those willing to fight and die. Intellectuals could theorize until they sucked their thumbs right off their hands, but in the real world, power still flowed from the barrel of a gun. If you wanted the starving masses in Somalia to eat, then you had to outmuscle men like this Aidid, for whom starvation *worked*. You could send in your bleeding-heart do-gooders, you could hold hands and pray and sing hootenanny songs and invoke the great gods CNN and BBC, but the only way to finally open the roads to the big-eyed babies was to show up with more guns. And in this real world, nobody had more or better guns than America. If the good-hearted ideals of humankind were to prevail, then they needed men who could make it happen. Delta made it happen.

They operated strictly in secret. The army would not even speak the word "Delta." If you had to refer to them, they were "operators," or "The Dreaded D." The Rangers, who worshiped them, called them D-boys. Secrecy, or at least the show of it, was central to their purpose. It allowed the dreamers and the politicians to have it both ways. They could stay on the high road while the dirty work happened offstage. If some Third World terrorist or Columbian drug lord needed to die, and then suddenly just turned up dead, why, what a happy coincidence! The dark soldiers would melt back into shadow. If you asked them about how they made it happen, they wouldn't tell. They didn't even *exist*, see? They were noble, silent, and invisible. They did America's most important work, yet shunned recognition, fame, and fortune. They were modern knights and true.

Howe did little to disguise his scorn for lower orders of soldiering, which pretty much included the whole regular U.S. Army. He and the rest of the operators lived like civilians, and that's what they told you they were if you asked—although spotting them down at Fort Bragg wasn't hard. You'd meet this guy hanging out at bar around Bragg, deeply tanned, biceps rippling, neck wide as a fireplug, with a giant Casio watch and a plug of chaw under his lip, and he'd tell you he worked as a computer programmer for some army contract agency. They called each other by their nicknames and eschewed salutes and all the other traditional trappings of military life. Officers and noncoms in Delta treated each other as equals. Disdain for normal displays of army status was the unit's signature. They simply *transcended* rank. They wore their hair longer than army regs. They needed to pose as civilians on some missions and it was easier to do that if they had normal haircuts, but it was also a point of pride with them, one of their perks. A cartoon drawn by a unit wit showed the typical D-boy dressed for battle with his hip holster stuffed, not with a gun, but a hair dryer. Every year they were obliged to pose for an official army portrait, and for it they had to get Ranger-style haircuts. They hated it. They'd had to sit for buzzes before this trip to better blend in with the *Hoo-ahs*, and the haircuts had just made them stick out even more; the sides and backs of their heads were as white as frog bellies. They were allowed a degree of personal freedom and initiative unheard of in the military, particularly in battle. The price they paid for all this, of course, was that they lived with danger and were expected to do what normal soldiers could not.

Howe wasn't impressed with a lot of things about the regular army. He and others in his unit had complained to Captain Steele, the Ranger commander, about his men's readiness. They hadn't gotten anywhere. Steele had his own way of doing things, and that was the traditional army way. Howe found the spit-and-polish captain, a massive former University of Georgia football lineman, to be an arrogant and incompetent buffoon. Howe had been through Ranger school and earned the tab himself, but had skipped straight over the Rangers when he qualified for

Delta. He disdained the Rangers in part because he believed hard, realistic, stair-stepped training made good soldiers, not the bullshit macho attitude epitomized by the whole *Hoo-ah* esprit. Out of the 120 men who tried out for Delta in his class (these were 120 highly motivated, exceptional soldiers), only 13 had made it through selection and training. Howe had the massive frame of a serious bodybuilder, and a fine, if impatient, analytical mind. Many of the Rangers found him scary. His contempt for their ways colored relationships between the two units in the hangar.

Now Howe's misgivings about the younger support troops were confirmed. They were shooting at their own men! Howe and his team left the room with the mattress and then moved out to clear the flat roof over the front of the house. It was enclosed by a three-foot concrete wall with decorative vertical slats. As the Delta team fanned out into sunlight, they saw the small orange fireball of an AK-47 erupt from a rooftop one block north. Two of Howe's team returned fire as they ducked behind the low wall for cover.

Then another burst of machine-gun rounds erupted. There were inch-wide slits in the perimeter wall. Howe and his men crouched and prayed a round didn't pass through an opening or ricochet back off the outside of the house. There were several long bursts. They could tell by the sound and impact of the rounds that the shots were being fired by an M-249, or SAW (Squad Automatic Weapon), this time from the northeast Ranger blocking position. The Rangers were under fire, they were overeager and scared, so when they saw men with weapons, they fired. Howe was furious.

He radioed Captain Scott Miller, the Delta ground commander down in the courtyard. He told him to get Steele on the radio immediately and tell him to stop his men from shooting at their own people!

# 6

Specialist John Stebbins ran as soon as his feet hit the ground. Just before boarding the helicopter, Captain Steele had tapped him on the shoulder.

"Stebbins, you know the rules of engagement?"

"Yeah, roger, sir. I know 'em."

"Okay. I want you to know I'm going to be on the fast rope right after you, so you better keep moving."

The prospect of the broad-beamed commander fully laden with battle gear bearing down on his helmet had haunted Stebbins the whole flight in. After roping down, he scrambled so fast from the bottom of the rope that he collided with Chalk One's M-60 gunner, and they both fell down. Stebbins lay there for a moment, waiting for the dust to clear, and then spotted the rest of his team up against a wall to his right.

He was scared, but thrilled. He couldn't shake the feeling that this was all too good to be true. Here he was, an old-timer in the Ranger company at age twenty-eight, having spent the last four years of his life trying to get into combat, to do *something* interesting or important, and now, somehow, through an incredible chain of pleading, wheedling, and freakish breaks, he was actually in combat—him, stubby Johnny Stebbins, the company's chief coffee maker and training room paper-pusher, at war!

His trip to this Mogadishu back alley had started in a bagel shop at home in Ithaca, New York. Stebbins was a short, stocky kid with pale blue eyes and blond hair and skin so white and freckly it never turned even the faintest shade darker in the sun. Here in Mog it had just burned bright pink. He had gone to Saint Bonaventure University, majoring in communications and hoping to work as a radio journalist, which he had in fact done for minimum wages at a few mom-and-pop stations in up-state New York. When the bagel shop offered to make him head baker, the hourly wage was enough to chuck his infant broadcasting career. So he made bagels and dreamed of adventure. Those "Be All You Can Be" commercials that came on during football games spoke straight to his soul. Stebbins had gone to college on an ROTC scholarship, but the army was so flooded with second lieutenants when he got out that he couldn't get assigned to active duty. When Desert Storm blew up in 1990, as his luck would have it, his National Guard contract was up. He started look-ing for a way out of the kitchen and into the fire. He put his name on three volunteer lists for Gulf service and never even got a response. Then he got married, and his wife had a baby, and suddenly the hourly wage at the bagel shop no longer covered expenses. What he needed was a medical plan. That, and some action. The army offered both. So he enlisted as a private.

"What do you want to do in the army?" the recruiter asked him. Stebbins told him, "I want to jump out of airplanes, shoot a lot of ammo, and shop at the PX."

They put him through basic training again—he'd done it once in the ROTC program. Then he had to do RIP (the Ranger Indoctrination Program) twice because he got injured on one of the jumps toward the end and had to be completely recycled. When he graduated he figured he'd be out there jumping and training and roping out of helicopters with the younger guys, except somebody higher up noticed that his personnel form listed a college degree and, more importantly, typing ability. He was routed instead to a desk in the Bravo company training room. Stebbins became the company clerk.

They told him it would just be for six months. He got stuck in it for two years. He became known as a good "training room" Ranger, and fell prey to all the temptations of office work. While the other Rangers were out scaling cliffs and jumping out of planes and trying to break their records for forced marches through dense cover, old man Stebby sat behind a desk chain-smoking cigarettes, eating donuts, and practically inhaling coffee. He was the company's most avid coffee drinker. The other guys would make jokes: "Oh yeah, Specialist Stebbins, he'll throw hot coffee at the enemy." Ha, ha. When the company got tapped for Somalia, no one was surprised when ol' Stebby was one of those left behind at Fort Benning.

"I want you to know it's nothing personal," his sergeant told him, although there was no way to disguise the implied insult. "We just can't take you. We have a limited number of spots on the bird and we need you here." How more clearly could he have stated that, when it came to war, Stebbins was the least valuable Ranger in the regiment?

It was just like Desert Storm all over again. Somebody up there did not want John Stebbins to go to war. He helped his friends pack, and when it was announced the next day that the force had arrived in Mogadishu, he felt even more left out than he had two years before as he watched nightly updates of the Gulf action on CNN. At least he had company. Sergeant Scott Galentine had been left behind, too. They moped around for a few days. Then came a fax from Somalia.

"Stebby, you better grab your stuff," his commanding officer told him. "You're going to war."

Galentine got the same news. Some Rangers had received minor injuries in a mortar attack and they needed to be replaced.

On his way to the airport Stebbins stopped by his house to say a quick good-bye to his wife. It was the tearful scene you'd expect. Then when he got to the airport they told him he could go home, they wouldn't be leaving until the next day. A half hour after their emotional parting, Mr. and Mrs. Stebbins were reunited. He spent the night dreading a phone call that would change the order.

But it didn't come. A little more than a day later, he and Galentine were standing on the runway in Mogadishu. In honor of their arrival they were ordered to drop for fifty push-ups, a ritual greeting upon entering a combat zone. Stebby was thrilled. He'd made it!

There weren't enough Kevlar vests (Ranger body armor) to go around so he got one of the big bulky black vests the D-boys wore. When he put it on he felt like a turtle. He was warned not to go outside the fence without his weapon. His buddies briefed him on the setup. They told him not to sweat the mortars. Sammy rarely hit anything. They had been on five missions at that point, and they were all a piece of cake. We go in force, they told him, we move quickly, the choppers basically blow everybody away from the scene, we let the D-boys go in and do their thing. All we do is provide security. They told him to watch out for Somalis who hid behind women and children. Rocks were a hazard. Stebbins was nervous and excited.

Then he got the news. See, they were glad to have him there and all, but he wouldn't actually be going out with the rest of the guys on missions. His job would be to stay back at the hangar and stand guard. *Maintain perimeter security.* It was essential. Somebody had to do it.

Who else?

Stebbins took out his ire on the folks trying to get past the front gate. He took the guard job as seriously as it was possible to be taken. He was a major pain in the ass. Every Somali got searched from head to toe, every time, in and out. He searched trucks and trunks and carts and climbed up under vehicles and had them open their hoods. It annoyed him that he couldn't figure out a way to search the big tanks on the back of the water trucks. Intel had said the Skinnies were smuggling heavy weapons across the border from Ethiopia. They were told that the Ethiopians checked out all trucks. Stebbins doubted they were checking the water trucks. You could put a lot of RPGs (rocket-propelled grenades) in the back of one of those things.

He finagled his way onto the helicopters for the profile flights, fastening the chin strap on his helmet tight as they zoomed low and fast over the city, cheering like kids on a carnival ride. He figured that was about as close to action as he was going to get . . . and compared to manning the coffeemaker in the training room back at Benning, it wasn't bad.

Then, this morning, just as the runner from the JOC showed up to shout, "Get it on!" one of the squad leaders strode up with news.

"Stebbins, Specialist Sizemore has an infected elbow. He just came back from the doc's office. You're taking his place."

He would be the assistant for 60-gunner Private First Class Brian Heard. Stebbins ran through the hangar, trading in his bulky tortoise-shell vest for a Kevlar one. He'd stuffed extra ammo in his pouches, and gathered up some frag grenades. Watching the more experienced guys, he discarded his canteen—they would only be out an hour or so—and stuffed its pouch with still more M-16 magazines. He picked up a belt with three hundred rounds of M-60 ammo, and debated trying to stuff more in his butt pack, where he kept the goggles and the gloves he needed for sliding down the rope. He decided against that. He'd need someplace to put them when he took them off. He was trying to think through everything. Trying to stay calm. But damn! it was exciting.

"Talk to me, Steb. What you got? What's on your mind?" prodded Staff Sergeant Ken Boorn, whose cot was alongside his. Boorn could see his friend was in a state. He told him to relax. Keep it simple. His job was to secure whatever sector they asked him to point his rifle at, and give ammo to the 60 gunners when they needed it. They probably wouldn't even need it.

"Okay, fine," said Stebbins.

Just before heading out to the Black Hawk, Stebbins was by the front door of the hangar sucking on a last cigarette, trying to get his nerves under control. This was finally it, what he'd been aiming for all this time. The guys all knew this was a particularly bad part of town, too. This was likely to be their nastiest mission yet, and it was his first! He had the same feeling in his gut that was there before his first jump at airborne school. *I'm gonna live through this,* he told himself. *I'm not gonna die.* One of the D-boys told him, "Look, for the first ten minutes or so you're gonna be scared shitless. After that you're going to get really mad that they have the balls to shoot at you." Stebbins had heard the stories about the other missions, how the Somalis were hit-and-run fighters. There was no way they'd get in a real shitfight. Up on the profile flights, they'd never seen any big weapons. This was going to be an urban small-arms deal. *I'm surrounded by guys who know what they're doing. I'm gonna be okay.*

Now, hitting the street outside the target building and hearing the pop of distant gunfire, he knew he was in it for real. After untangling himself from the 60 gunner, he ran to the wall. He was assigned a corner pointing south, guarding an alley that appeared empty. It was just a narrow dirt path, barely wide enough for a car, that sloped down on both sides from mud-stained stone walls to a footpath at the center. There were the usual piles of random debris and rusted metal parts strewn along the way, in between outcroppings of cactus. He heard occasional snapping sounds in the air around him and assumed it was the sound of gunfire a few blocks away, even though the noise was close. Maybe the air was playing tricks on him. He also heard a peculiar noise, a *tchew . . . tchew . . . tchew,* and it dawned on him that this was the sound of rounds whistling down the street. That snapping noise? That was bullets passing close enough for him to hear the little sonic boomlet as they zipped past.

Up the street from Stebbins, Captain Steele spotted a likely source for most of the rounds coming through their position. There was a sniper one block west on top of the Olympic Hotel. It was the tallest structure around.

Steele bellowed, "Smith!"

Corporal Jamie Smith came running. He was the best marksman in the chalk. Steele pointed out the shooter and slapped Smith's back encouragingly. Both men took aim. Their target was a long shot away, more than 150 yards. They couldn't see if they hit him, but after they fired the Somali on the rooftop was not seen again.

Across the alley, hiding behind the inverted frame of a burned-out vehicle, squatted Sergeants Mike Goodale and Aaron Williamson. They were resting their weapons on the hulk, which sloped down from them toward the center of the alley. All the alleys rose from the center in uneven sandy berms to stone courtyard walls and small stone houses on both sides. There were small trees behind some of the walls, and just to the north was the boxy shape of the three-story back side of the target house. The thick rope they had come down on now lay stretched across the alley. The earth had that slightly orange color, which stained the walls and imparted a rusty tint to the air close to the ground. Goodale could smell and taste the dust mixed with the odor of gunpowder. He heard the shooting at the other side of the block, but their corner was still relatively quiet.

Goodale had never felt farther from home in his life, and had a quiet moment or two crouched at that position to wonder how he'd gotten there. Just before leaving for Somalia he'd gotten engaged to a girl named Kira he'd met in a feckless freshman year at the University of Iowa. They had both escaped little Pekin, Illinois, for one of the great party campuses of the Midwest, promptly flunked out, and then determined to straighten up. For Mike that had meant joining the army; for Kira it was taking a low-level job with an advertising agency. They saw each other frequently when Mike was at Benning, but since the Rangers had been away on a training exercise in Texas before getting the summons for Somalia, they had been apart now for more than two months, since the day they'd decided to spend their lives together. The day before he'd gotten his first chance to phone home since leaving Fort Benning, and he'd gotten the answering machine. He would get another chance to call tonight, and he'd told her on the answering machine to expect it. He knew she'd be waiting by the phone.

"Kira, I love you so very much it hurts," he had written her that morning. "I'm reluctant to call again because I know it will just make me miss you that much more. On the other hand, I really want to hear your voice."

A Somali about one hundred yards down the street to their left stuck his head out from behind a wall and rattled a burst with an AK-47. Dirt popped up around Goodale and Williamson. Williamson stepped around to the north side of the hulk. Goodale, who was closest to the shooter, panicked momentarily, thinking the shots were coming from the south. He leapt up and ran from the wreck, hopping as rounds kicked up around him, trying to find someplace better to hide. There was no cover. He dove down behind a pipe sticking up from the road. It was only about seven inches wide and six inches high and he felt ridiculous cowering behind it but there was no place else. When the shooting stopped momentarily he jumped up and rejoined Williamson behind the hulk, just as the Somali started shooting again.

Goodale saw the spray of bullets walk up the side of the car, right down the side of Williamson's rifle, and take off the end of his friend's finger. Blood splashed up on Williamson's face and he screamed and cursed. Goodale leaned over, checking the blood on Williamson's face first and then his hand.

Despite the blood and pain, Williamson seemed more angry than hurt.

"If he sticks his head out again I'm taking him," he said.

Severed fingertip and all, Williamson coolly leveled his M-16 and waited, motionless, for what seemed like minutes.

When the man down the alley leaned out, Williamson fired, and the man's head seemed to explode and he fell over hard. With his un-injured hand, Williamson and Goodale exchanged a high five and some victory whoops.

Moments later, they shot and killed another Somali. The man darted out into their alley and sprinted away from them. As he ran his loose shirt billowed back to reveal an AK, so they shot him. About five Rangers squeezed off rounds at the same time. The man lay on the street only a half block away and Goodale wondered if they had killed him. He asked the medic if they should check him out, help him if he was just injured, and the medic just shook his head and said, "No, he's dead." It startled Goodale. He had killed a man, or helped anyway. It troubled him. The man had not actually been trying to kill him when he fired, so in the purest sense it wasn't self-defense. So how could he justify what he had just done? He watched the man in the dirt, his clothes tangled around him, splayed awkwardly where the bullets had felled him. A life, like his, ended. *Was this the right thing?*


At his corner, about ten yards east of Goodale and Williamson, Lieu-tenant Perino watched Somali children walking up the street toward his men, pointing out their positions for a shooter hidden around a corner further down. His men threw flashbang grenades and the children scattered.

"Hey, sir, they're coming back up," called machine gunner Sergeant Chuck Elliot.

Perino was on the radio talking to Sergeant Eversmann about Blackburn, the Ranger who had fallen from the helicopter. The lieutenant was relaying Eversmann's information and questions to Captain Steele, who was across the street from him. Perino told Eversmann to hold for a second, stepped out, and sprayed a burst from his M-16 toward the children, aiming at their feet. They ran away again.

Moments later, a woman began creeping up the alley directly toward the machine gun.

"Hey, sir, I can see there's a guy behind this woman with a weapon under her arm," shouted Elliot.

Perino told him to shoot. The 60 gun made a low, blatting sound. The men called the gun a "pig."

Both the man and woman fell dead.

# 7

As he roped in at the northeast corner of the target block, Specialist John Waddell delayed his descent long enough to avoid piling into Specialist Shawn Nelson, Chalk Two's 60 gunner, who usually took a second or two longer to untangle himself and his big gun. On a training mission one time Waddell had plowed into the guy beneath him, and then they'd both been hit by the guy coming after them. That time he'd bitten his tongue right through.

This time it went well. Waddell got both feet on the ground and then hurried to a wall on the right side of the street, just the way that Lieutenant Tom DiTomasso had drawn it up. Chalk Two was one long block east of where Sergeant Eversmann's Chalk Four was supposed to have roped down. The lieutenant was concerned because he couldn't see Chalk Four. He managed to reach the embattled sergeant on the radio, and Eversmann explained how they'd roped in a block north of their position. DiTomasso sent a team one block north to see if they could spot Chalk Four from that alley, but they hustled back to report a large crowd of Somalis was massing in that direction.

As he ran to take a position against the north wall, Waddell was surprised to find that all his gear, weapons, and ammo weren't slowing him down. There was a lot of it, and it was bulky and heavy, including a SAW. It was a prestige item, a highly portable machine gun that could deal death at seven hundred rounds per minute. Normally, fully kitted up like that, it felt like gravity had doubled. But Waddell was surprised to find, as he scrambled for a wall, that his arms and legs felt a little numb, but that was it. He figured this was adrenaline, from the excitement and fear, and regarded it with his usual calm detachment.

Waddell was a bit of a loner, a precise young man whose dark hair looked especially stark in the standard Ranger buzzcut. After a month of equatorial sun only his face, neck, and arms were tan. The stupid regs required T-shirts at all times. He was a newcomer to the rifle company, another of Bravo's babies, just eighteen years old. Despite a perfect grade point average in high school back in Natchez, Mississippi, he had decided, to his parents' horror, to temporarily forgo college and enlist in the army, to jump out of airplanes and climb cliffs and engage in the other high-risk behavior of an elite infantry unit.

Rangering had met his expectations so far, but it whetted his appetite for real action. On this deployment to Mog he had spent most of his time waiting around and reading. He went through pulp fiction by the box load. Just today he'd read through to the last chapter of a John Grisham novel that really had him hooked. He'd found a quiet spot on top of a Conex container and had planned to finish it. But then they were called to suit up for a possible mission. They'd sat out in the bird ready to ride out, only to have the mission scrubbed. So he'd stripped down and taken the book back up on the Conex, only to be called back down again to go on a profile flight. He'd suited up again, taken the ride, stripped back down, and was back into the last chapter when they were called for this mission. It felt like the world was conspiring against his finishing that novel.

When everybody was down, the rope jettisoned, and the Black Hawk gone, Waddell's team was ordered by the lieutenant to set up to help cover Nelson, who had placed his "pig" on a bipod at the crest of a slight rise in the road and was already shooting steadily. The chalk's two machine gunners tended to draw most of the fire.

Nelson had been working his gun hard before he'd even left the helicopter. Looking down from the open doorway he'd seen a man with an AK step out to the middle of the street and shoot up through the dust cloud at the bird. Nelson got off six rounds at the guy and didn't notice if he'd hit him until he saw him splayed out where he'd been standing. He figured either he'd hit him or the crew chief alongside him had scored with the minigun.

Rounds had been snapping around his head when Nelson came down the rope. Not many, but one bullet coming at you is too many. It made him mad. It was always hard to slow his drop down the rope with that big 60 gun strapped on, and Nelson fell over at the bottom. Staff Sergeant Ed Yurek had run out to help him to his feet and guide him to a wall.

"Man, this is getting hairy fast," Nelson said.

Nelson had set up near the center of the road facing west. Up to his right was an alley, where he could see Somalis aiming guns his way. Nelson's gun scattered them, all but one, an old man with a bushy white Afro, further down, who seemed so intent on shooting west that he was unaware of the big gun down the alley to his left. He was still a little too far away to shoot, but Nelson could see the man maneuvering in his direction. The 60 gunner knew what the old man was trying to do. DiTomasso had spread the word that Chalk Four was stuck one block northwest of their position. The old man was obviously looking for a better vantage point to shoot at Eversmann and his men.

"Shoot him, shoot him," urged his assistant.

"No, watch," Nelson said. "He'll come right to us."

And, sure enough, the man with the white Afro practically walked right up to them. He ducked behind a big tree about fifty yards off, hiding from Eversmann's Rangers, but oblivious to the threat off his left shoulder. He was loading a new magazine in his weapon when Nelson blasted about a dozen rounds into him. They were "slap" rounds, plastic-coated titanium bullets that could penetrate armor, and he saw the rounds go right through the man, but the guy still got up, retrieved his weapon, and even got off a shot or two in Nelson's direction. The machine gunner was shocked. He shot another twelve rounds at the man, who nevertheless managed to crawl behind the tree. This time he didn't shoot back.

"I think you got him," said the assistant gunner.

But Nelson could still see the Afro moving behind the tree. The man was kneeling and evidently still alive. Nelson squeezed off another long burst and saw bark splintering off the bottom of the tree. The Afro slumped sideways to the street. His body quivered but he seemed to have at last expired. Nelson was surprised how hard it could be to kill a man.

As this was going on, Waddell crept up the rise cautiously alongside Nelson. Both men lay prone. Alongside them, Waddell saw the body of the Somali who had been shot from the helicopter. Looking for a better spot to cover Nelson, Waddell moved over to a wall on the south side of the alley. As he did, he saw another Somali step out from behind a corner to the west and shoot at Nelson, who was absorbed by his duel with the white Afro. Waddell shot the man. In books and the movies when a soldier shot a man for the first time he went through a moment of soul searching. Waddell didn't give it a second thought. He just reacted. He thought the man was dead. He had just folded. Startled by Waddell's shot, Nelson hadn't seen the man drop. Waddell pointed to where he had fallen and the machine gunner stood up, lifted his big gun, and pumped a few more rounds into the man's body to make sure. Then they both ran for better cover.

They found it behind a burned-out car. Peering out from underneath toward the north now, Nelson saw a Somali with a gun lying prone on the street between two kneeling women. The shooter had the barrel of his weapon between the women's legs, and there were four children actually *sitting* on him. He was completely shielded in noncombatants, taking full cynical advantage of the Americans' decency.

"Check this out, John," he told Waddell, who scooted over for a look.

"What do you want to do?" Waddell asked.

"I can't get to that guy through those people."

So Nelson threw a flashbang, and the group fled so fast the man left his gun in the dirt.

Several grenades plopped into the alley. They were of the old Soviet style, which looked like soup cans on a wooden stick. Some didn't
explode, but one or two did. The blasts were far enough away that none
of the Rangers was hit. Nelson screamed to DiTomasso and pointed at
the brick wall on the east side of the road.

He watched the lieutenant and three other Rangers cross over to
a half-open gate, which opened on a parking lot. DiTomasso lobbed a
grenade into the space, and then he and the other Rangers burst in. They
found and took prisoner four Somalis who had been standing on car roofs
shooting down over the top of the wall.

The fire was not yet intense, but Sergeant Yurek was amazed at it. At
twenty-six, Yurek was a crusty veteran with a grim sense of humor and
a big soft spot for animals, especially cats. He had a small pride of cats
back home in Georgia, and had adopted a litter of kittens he'd found in
the hangar here in Mog. When the D-boys complained about the kittens crying and meowing through the night, and threatened to silence
them, Yurek had taken a stand. Nobody touched the kittens without
going through him.

He didn't like the idea of shooting anything or anybody, but accepted the necessity of it. When people were shooting at him, then it
became necessary. So far in Mog, the Skinnies would just fire off a wild
burst and then run away, which suited Yurek fine. But this shooting today,
right from the start, was more stubborn. It was also picking up. Yurek
figured this target must really house some high-priority people. Maybe
Aidid himself. Chalk Two was shooting in three directions at once, west,
east, and especially north. Yurek had picked off a man who had been
firing from a low tower to the northeast. Then one of the squad's medics shouted from across the street, pointing to a flimsy tin shed just east
of their perimeter at the intersection.

"Hey, we've got people in the shed!"

Which was very bad news. Yurek sprinted across the street, and,
with the medic, plunged into the front door.

He just about trampled a huddled crowd of terrified children and
a woman who was evidently their teacher.

"Everyone down!" Yurek shouted, his weapon still up and ready.

The children began to wail with fright, and Yurek quickly realized he needed to throttle things down a notch. Tiger in the kitten den.

"Settle down," he pleaded. "Settle down!"

But the wailing continued. So, slowly and carefully, Yurek bent over and placed his weapon on the ground. He motioned for the teacher to approach him. He guessed she was about sixteen years old.

"Lay down," he told her, speaking evenly. "Lay down," gesturing with his hands.

The young woman was hesitant, but she did as told.

Yurek pointed to the children now, gesturing for them to do the same. They did. Yurek picked up his weapon and spoke to the teacher, enunciating every word in the way people will when vainly trying to communicate through a language barrier.

"Now, you need to stay here. No matter what you see or hear, stay here."

She shook her head, and Yurek hoped that meant yes. As he left, Yurek told the medic to stay by the door to the shed and make sure nobody else decided to check it out and enter blasting.


From his position behind the car, peering down one of the streets at their intersection, Nelson saw a man with a weapon ride out into the road on a cow. There were about eight other men around the cow, some with weapons, some without. It was the strangest battle party he'd ever seen. He didn't know whether to laugh or shoot at it. He and the rest of the Rangers at once started shooting. The man on the cow fell off, and the others ran. The cow just stood there.

And at that moment, a Black Hawk slid overhead and opened fire with a minigun. The cow literally came apart. Great chunks of flesh flew up in splashes of blood. When the minigun stopped and the chopper's shadow passed, what had been the cow lay in steaming pieces on the road.

As horrific as that was, the presence of those guns overhead was deeply reassuring to all the men on the streets. Here they were in a strange and hostile city with people trying to kill them, riding at them on animals with automatic weapons, massing from all directions, bullets snapping past their ears, sights of horror and the smell of blood and burned flesh mingled with the odor of dust and dung ... and the calm approach of a big Black Hawk with the rhythmic beat of its rotors and the terrible power of its guns was a reminder of the invincible force behind them, a reminder of their imminent release, of home.

Somalis continued to mass to the north. In the distance it looked like thousands. Smaller groups would probe south toward Chalk Two's position. One group moved down to just a block and a half away. Maybe fifteen people. Nelson tried to direct his machine gun only at those with weapons, but there were so many people, and those with guns kept stepping from the crowd to take shots, so that he knew he either had to just let the gunmen shoot or lay into the crowd. After a few moments of debate, he chose the latter. That group dispersed, leaving bodies on the street, and another larger one appeared. They seemed to be coming now in swarms from the north, as though chased from somewhere else. They were closing in, just forty or fifty feet up the road, some of them shooting. This time Nelson didn't have time to weigh alternatives. He cut loose with the 60 and his rounds tore through the crowd like a scythe. A Little Bird swooped in and threw a flaming wall of lead at it. Those who didn't fall, fled. One minute there was a crowd, the next minute it was just a bleeding heap of dead and injured.

"Goddamn, Nelson!" said Waddell. *"Goddamn!"*

# 8

At the front door of the target house, Staff Sergeant Jeff Bray, an air force CCT (Combat Control Technician), shot a Somali man who came running at him wildly firing an AK-47. Bray was part of a four-man air force special operations unit made up of experts at coordinating ground/ air communications, like himself, and parajumpers (PJs), daredevil medics who specialized in rescuing downed pilots. The other CCT in the unit, Sergeant Dan Schilling, was with the ground convoy. The two PJs were aboard the CSAR Black Hawk, along with about a dozen Rangers and D-boys. Bray was assigned to the Delta command element that had roped in from a Black Hawk about a block west of the target house. The man he shot had just come blazing straight at him from up an alley. What was he thinking? How could anybody be such a bad shot?

Behind Bray in the target house, the Delta assaulters were assembling the Somali prisoners. They were laid out prone in the courtyard and were being flex-cuffed. In addition to the two primary targets, in the group was Abdi Yusef Herse, an Aidid lieutenant. It was an even better haul than they had hoped for. Checking out other rooms in the house, Sergeant Paul Howe pumped a shotgun blast into a computer on the first floor. Sergeant Matt Rierson, whose men had taken the prisoners, would be responsible for moving them out to the vehicles. Howe, Sergeant Norm Hooten, and their teams went back up to the second floor to help provide cover from the windows and roof.

Back at the JOC, watching images from the aerial cameras, General Garrison and his staff knew the D-boys' work was done when they saw Howe's team move back out on the roof. Other than the Ranger who had fallen, things had gone like clockwork. The Rangers were holding their own at the blocking positions. It was 3:50 P.M. The whole force would be on their way back inside of ten minutes.

# 9

After the helicopters had lifted off from the Ranger compound, Sergeant Jeff Struecker had waited several minutes in his Humvee with the rest of the ground convoy, engines idling just inside the main gate. His was the lead in a column of twelve vehicles, nine Humvees and three five-ton trucks. They were to drive to a point behind the Olympic Hotel and wait for the D-boys to wrap things up in the target house.

Struecker, a born-again Christian from Fort Dodge, Iowa, had more experience with the city than most of the guys. His vehicle platoon had gone on water runs and other details daily. He had been in on the invasion of Panama, so he thought he'd seen the Third World. But nothing prepared him for Somalia. Garbage was strewn everywhere. They burned it on the streets, that and tires. They were always burning tires. It was just one of the mysterious things they did. They also burned animal dung for fuel. It made for a potent olfactory stew. The people here, it seemed to Stuecker, just lounged, doing nothing, watching the world go by outside their shabby round rag huts and tin shacks, women with gold teeth dressed in brightly colored robes, old men wearing loose cotton skirts and worn plastic sandals. Those dressed in Western clothes wore items that looked like Salvation Army handouts from the disco era. When the Rangers stopped and searched the men they'd usually find a thick wad of *khat* stuffed in their back pockets. When they grinned their teeth were stained black and orange from chewing the weed. It made them look savage, or deranged. To Struecker it was disgusting. It seemed like such a purposeless existence. The abject poverty was shocking.

There were places in the city where charitable organizations handed out food daily, and the Rangers had been warned not to drive near those places during business hours. Struecker had come close enough to see why. There were not just thousands but *tens of thousands* of people, throngs who would mob those feeding stations, waiting for handouts. These were not people who looked like they were starving. Some of the Somalis fished, but most had apparently forgotten how to work. Most seemed friendly. Women and children would approach the Rangers' vehicles with smiles and their hands out, but in some parts of town the men would shake their fists at them. A lot of the guys would throw an MRE (Meal Ready to Eat) to kids. They all felt sorry for the kids. For the adults they felt contempt.

It was hard to imagine what interest the United States of America had in such a place. But Struecker was just twenty-four, and he was a soldier, so it wasn't his place to question such things. His job today was to roll up in force on Hawlwadig Road, load up prisoners and the assault and blocking forces, and bring them back out. Directly behind him was the second Humvee of his team, driven by Sergeant Danny Mitchell. Behind that was a cargo Humvee manned by D-boys and SEALs, who would proceed straight to the target building to reinforce the assault team already there. Behind the SEAL vehicle was another Humvee, three trucks, and then five more Humvees, including one carrying Lieutenant Colonel Danny McKnight, who was commanding the convoy. In the front seat of the Humvee with Struecker was driver Private First Class Jeremy Kerr. In back were machine gunner Sergeant Dominick Pilla, a company favorite; Private First Class Brad Paulson, who was manning the .50-caliber machine gun up in the turret; and Specialist Tim Moynihan, an assistant gunner.

Dom Pilla was a big, powerful kid from New Jersey—he had that *Joy-zee* accent—who used his hands a lot when he talked and was just born funny. He loved practical jokes. He had bought these tiny charges that he stuck in guys' cigarettes that would explode halfway through a smoke with a startling *pop!* Pilla would just crack up. Some people who tried that kind of thing were annoying, but not Pilla. People laughed *with* Pilla. The most famous outlet for his comedic gifts were the little skits he and Nelson put on, poking fun at their commanding officers. The skits had become such a big hit that Nelson and Pilla found themselves pressed into repeat performances on just about every deployment. One of the running favorites was their spoof of "Coach" Steele.

Like any tough commanding officer, Steele had a complex relationship with his men. They respected him, but sometimes he annoyed the hell out of them. Steele had been a blocker, an offensive guard, on a national championship Georgia Bulldog team under Coach Vince Dooley in 1980. Football had been the shaping experience in the thirty-two-year-old officer's life. Some of the guys were bugged by his outspoken Christian fervor and fondness for the football metaphor. He'd call the big guys in his platoon his "defensive tackles," and the little skinny guys were his "wide receivers" or "running backs." He was fond of huddling up the guys and having them all put their hands to the center for a bonding cheer, and would quote from the pregame speeches of great NFL coaches. He'd also been infected with the fervent jock Christianity so much a part of the football subculture. Steele would stop guys and ask them, "You go to church on Sundays, son?" Some of the guys found it all a bit much. They never called him Coach to his face, except during the skits. Then it was no-holds-barred.

Nelson was the writer, but Pilla was the star. He was tall and had a weightlifter's build, but he still needed a few layers of extra undershirts to approximate Steele's girth. They would improvise something goofy for the helmet and paint it with a Bulldog, and Pilla would take it from there. He had a natural comic presence. The skit would open with Pilla/Steele alone in his office practicing his blocking and tackling, and go downhill from there. Steele laughed along good-naturedly most of the time. But in one of the skits Nelson and Pilla had suggested, with gratuitous locker-room hilarity, that there might be something of a *don't-ask-don't-tell* thing going on between the captain and his ever loyal second-in-command, Lieutenant Perino. That had the guys rolling in the aisle, but this time Coach didn't laugh. He later chewed out Nelson and Pilla for "portraying alternative lifestyles." It was so funny, in retrospect, Nelson and Pilla thought, that it might make a perfect scene for their next skit.

Struecker and the rest of the column timed their departure so they wouldn't arrive out behind the Olympic Hotel before the assault had begun. They had watched the armada move out over the ocean, and left the base only after the helicopters radioed that they had turned back inland. Struecker, who was supposed to lead the convoy, took a wrong turn. He had studied the photomap back in the hangar, and thought he had it down, but once out in the city things tended to get confusing. Every street looked the same, and there were no signs to help. They were moving fast. They went northeast on Via Gesira to the K-4 circle and then north on Via Lenin to the old reviewing stand. There they would turn right on National Street, proceed east, and then turn north on a street that paralleled Hawlwadig heading toward the target house. But when Struecker took an early left and Mitchell's vehicle followed, the rest of the convoy didn't.

— *Hey, where the hell are you guys?* came the voice of Platoon Sergeant Bob Gallagher over the radio.

"We're coming," assured Struecker. "We turned wrong. We're on our way."

It was embarrassing. Struecker managed to steer his and Mitchell's Humvees back through the maze of streets, and rejoined the rest of the convoy at the hotel.

Before the convoy reached the holding point, Signalman Chief John Gay, a SEAL in the left rear seat of the third Humvee, heard a shot and felt a hard impact on his right hip. Stunned and in pain, he shouted that he'd been hit. They drove straight on, as planned, to the target building, where Master Sergeant Tim "Griz" Martin, the Delta operator who was sitting beside Gay, jumped out and came around to have a look. The remainder of the team fanned out around the vehicles. Martin tore open Gay's pants and examined his hip, then gave Gay good news. The round had hit smack on the SEAL's Randall knife. It had shattered the blade, but the knife had deflected the bullet. Martin pulled several bloody fragments of blade out of Gay's hip and quickly bandaged it. Gay limped out of the vehicle, took cover, and began returning fire.

Struecker was assigned to evacuate Blackburn, the Ranger who had fallen from the helicopter. Sergeant Joyce had fetched help for Blackburn and the men carrying his litter. The SEAL Humvee, driven by Master Sergeant Chuck Esswein, had driven up Hawlwadig and the wounded Ranger was lifted in through the back hatch. Two medics climbed in with him. Delta Sergeant John Macejunas took the shotgun seat alongside Esswein. Struecker's Humvee, with its .50 cal in the turret, took the lead, and Mitchell's Humvee, which had a Mark-19 rapid-fire grenade launcher in the turret, brought up the rear.

— *This is Uniform Six Four,* McKnight radioed up to the command bird. *I've got a critical casualty. I am going to send three out, with one in the cargo that has a casualty in it.*

Struecker told McKnight, "I'll have him back there in five minutes."

The lieutenant colonel said the rest of them would be coming along soon. The mission was almost over.

The three vehicles began racing back to base through streets now alive with gunfire and explosions. This time Struecker knew which way to go. He had mapped a return route that was simple. Several blocks over was National Street. They could follow that all the way back down to the K-4 traffic circle, and from there they would bear right back to the beach.

Except things had gotten a lot worse. Roadblocks and barricades began to appear. They drove around and through them. One of the medics, Private Good, was holding up the IV bag for Blackburn with one hand while shooting his CAR-15 with the other. Up in Struecker's Humvee, turret gunner Paulson was frantically trying to swivel his .50 cal to engage shooters firing from both sides. So Struecker instructed his M-60 gunner, Pilla, to concentrate all his fire to the right, and leave everything on the left to Paulson. They didn't want to drive too fast, because a violently bumpy ride couldn't do Blackburn any good.

Pilla was shot as they turned on National. He was killed instantly. The bullet entered his forehead and the exit wound blew out the back of his skull. His body flopped over into the lap of Moynihan, who cried out in horror, covered with his friend's blood and brain.

"Pilla's hit!" he screamed.

Just then, over the radio, came the voice of Sergeant Gallagher.

— *How things going?*

Struecker ignored the radio, and shouted back over his shoulder at Moynihan.

"Calm down! What's wrong with him?" He couldn't see all the way to the back hatch.

"He's dead!"

Moynihan was freaking out.

"How do *you* know he's dead? Are you a medic?"

Struecker turned for a quick look over his shoulder and the whole rear of his vehicle was covered with blood. Pilla was in Moynihan's lap.

"He's shot in the head! He's dead!" Moynihan said.

"Just calm down," Struecker pleaded. "We've got to keep fighting until we get back."

To hell with driving carefully. Struecker told his driver to step on it, and hoped Esswein would follow. He could see RPGs flying across the street now. It seemed like the whole city was shooting at them.

Then Gallagher's voice came across again.

— *How's it going?*

"I don't want to talk about it."

Gallagher didn't like that answer.

— *You got any casualties?*

"Yeah, one."

Struecker tried to leave it at that. Nobody on their side had gotten killed, so far as he knew, and he didn't want to be the one to put news like that on the air. He knew radio operators all over the battlefield could hear their conversation. There were speaker boxes in some of the vehicles and the birds could all listen in. The radio operators on the ground monitored all the bands. Men in battle drink up information like water—it becomes more important than water. Unlike most of these guys, Struecker had been to war before, in Panama and the Persian Gulf, and he knew soldiers fought better when things were going their way. Once things turned, it was hard to reassert control. People panicked. It was happening to Moynihan right now. Panic was a virus in combat, a deadly one.

— *Who is he and what's his status?* Gallagher demanded.

"It's Pilla."

— *What's his status?*

Struecker held the microphone for a moment, debating with himself, and then reluctantly answered:

"He's dead."

At the sound of that word all the radio traffic, which was busy, stopped. Long seconds of silence followed.

# 10

Ali Hussein was minding the Labadhagal Bulal Pharmacy, well south of all the shooting.

He went to the front steps of the store and saw many men with guns, Aidid militia, running toward the fight. Some were militia and some were just neighbors who had fetched their own guns.

Hussein wanted to see what was happening, but he was afraid the shop would be looted if he left it untended. He just stood and listened as the sound of shooting crept down closer and closer to his street.

Then American army vehicles, three of them, came racing down his street. The big guns in the back were shooting. He jumped into the shop and slammed shut the metal door just as bullets rang off it. He rolled against a side wall that he knew from previous fighting was the safest place in the house, and bullets sprayed through windows into the shop as the vehicles raced past.

Then they were gone and the shooting stopped.

# 11

The little convoy sped out to the main road and for a stretch the firing abated and in the distance was the ocean. But as they approached the port area, there were thousands of Somalis in the streets. Struecker's heart sank. They were no longer taking heavy fire, but how was he going to get his three vehicles through that?

His driver slowed down to a crawl and leaned on the horn as they entered the throng. Struecker told the driver not to stop moving. He threw flashbangs out in front of his vehicle, which chased some of the people away, and then told his .50-cal gunner to open up over the crowd's head. The ocean was on the other side.

Struecker tried to raise the doctors on the radio, and couldn't get anyone to pick up, so he broke in on the command radio net.

"I need the doc right away," he said.

The sound of the big gun scattered most of the people and the vehicles sped up again. The Humvee may have run over some people. It was either that or stones and debris in the road. Struecker didn't look back to see. He then came up on a slow-moving pickup truck with people hanging off the back. It would not get out of their way and there wasn't enough room to go around it, so Struecker told his driver to ram it. A man with his leg hanging off the back screamed with pain as the Humvee hit, and then rolled into the back of the truck, which finally steered off the road.

Struecker radioed, "Can you have the doc waiting for us out there by the gate, over?"

They entered the compound with a tremendous sense of relief and exhaustion. They had run the gauntlet. Several of the Rangers in his and the other Humvees had been injured. Pilla was dead. But, for them, at least, it was over.

His bloodstained crew piled out looking dazed. Struecker was startled by what he saw at the base. He had expected to step out into calm and safety. Instead, everyone around him seemed frantic.

He heard a commander's voice on the speaker box, shouting at someone, "Pay attention to what's going on and *listen* to my orders!"

Something had happened.

The medical crews descended on their vehicles. One of the doctors reached in and started to turn Pilla over.

"Don't worry about him," Struecker said. "He's dead."

So the doctor moved on to Esswein's Humvee to get Blackburn. Struecker grabbed one of the orderlies as he went past.

"Look, there's a dead in the back of my vehicle. You need to get him off."

The sergeant watched as they pulled Pilla from the back of the Humvee. The top of his head was gone. His face was white and distorted and puffed up so bad it looked round. It didn't look anything like Pilla any more.

# 12

Private Clay Othic shot a chicken. When it was time for all the vehicles to move up and start loading prisoners, all hell broke loose on Hawlwadig. There were people racing in all directions, men with AK-47s shooting at them, RPGs zipping smoke trails through the air and detonating with ear-popping explosions ... and in the midst of all this a panicked flock of chickens came hurtling out in front of Othic's gun. One of the birds turned to a puff of feathers when hit by a round from his .50 cal. "Little Hunter" had bagged yet another species.

Othic was the smallest guy in the company, and looked about thirteen, so he was assigned (per standard operating procedure) to the biggest gun, a "Ma-Deuce," the Browning M-2 .50-caliber machine gun, which was mounted in the roof turret of his Humvee. Othic had made a bit of a name for himself early on in the deployment by inadvertently stealing General Garrison's personal Humvee. The turret on his own kept sticking and his sergeant told him to trade it in for another one "over there," pointing toward the motor pool. So Othic had just picked out the one that looked cleanest. They got it back before the general found out.

They called him "Little Hunter" because back home while other guys would head for the bars of Auburn and Atlanta when they had time off, sometimes during hunting season Othic, a country boy from Missouri, would vanish into the woods around Fort Benning with his rifle and come back with wild turkey or deer, which he would clean right there in the barracks and deliver up to the mess. He had that rare capacity of being able to enjoy himself anywhere. He even enjoyed standing guard duty out front of the compound, where the most interesting thing was confiscating film from the bozos who ignored signs forbidding them to take pictures, which turned out to be just about everybody with a camera. He had a collection of unrolled strips of it on the razor wire outside, draped like brown tinsel.

Othic had been keeping track of the days in Mog in a small journal he had stashed in his rucksack. He addressed each entry to his parents, and planned to just give it to them when he got back. In regard to confiscating film, he wrote this entry, borrowing some atmospherics from *Star Trek:*

"Log Entry, Star Date 3 Sept. 1993 1700 hours. Just got off guard duty at the main gate again, it was a pretty interesting one though. We confiscated 1 videotape & three rolls of film in 2 hrs., people aren't allowed to take pictures of the stuff we have & boy do they have a case of the ass when they do have it taken away. It's funny 'cause we have signs up, but they try to be sneaky about it anyway. Ha! You lose, sucker!"

Othic's fondness for writing made it particularly galling that he didn't get as many letters as the other guys, and, most particularly, that he didn't have a girlfriend to correspond with. Guys without girlfriends were so forlorn they looked forward to reading the letters their buddies got from women. Not that all woman letters were good. Sergeant Raleigh Cash, this guy from Oregon, had gotten a Dear John letter while he was in Mog. It was a crusher. The girl sent him a shoebox filled with his stuff, CDs, tapes, pictures, and other detritus of a dead relationship, a real double-barreled dump, right there in the hangar. They teased Cash about it mercilessly, but in a way that made it easier to take. Still, the feeling was that any letter from a woman was better than none. Specialist Eric Spalding, a guy from Missouri who was his best buddy, got some good ones and let Othic read them. This was nice, but it made Othic feel pathetic. He was thinking about getting his sister to write him a real sexy letter just so he'd have something of his own to show off.

He and Spalding had become good buddies and made a plan to drive back to Missouri together in Othic's pickup truck when they got home. Othic's dad worked as an agent for the Immigration and Naturalization Service, and he planned to try for a job there when he got out of the army. He told Spalding his dad might help fix him up, too. They were hoping to get back to Missouri in time for fall deer season.

Both were jealous of the D-boys. The Rangers had spent their down time in Mog flying out to shooting ranges, going on five-mile "fun" runs, pulling guard duty, etc., while the operators had serious fun. Take the pigeons. When the force had first moved in, the pigeons had owned the hangar, crapping at will all over people, cots, and equipment. When one of the D-boys got nailed while sitting on his cot cleaning his weapon, the elite force declared war. They ordered up pellet guns. The birds didn't have a prayer. The D-boys would triangulate fire and send a mess of blood and feathers plopping down on somebody's cot. Did these guys know how to kill time on a deployment or what? They all had custom-built weapons with hand-rifled barrels and such. Gun manufacturers outfitted them the way Nike supplies pro athletes. Some days Delta would commandeer a Black Hawk and roar off to hunt wild boar, baboons, antelope, and gazelles in the Somali bush. They brought back trophy tusks and game meat and held cookouts. They called it "realistic training." Now there was a fucking deal and a half. One of them, Brad Hallings, had been strutting around the hangar with a necklace made of boar's teeth. Stocky little Earl Fillmore had taken the tusks and glued them to a helmet, and he'd strutted around naked striking poses like some Mongolian warlord.

There was no big game on the horizon for Othic and Spalding, so they had found something of their own to hunt. Spalding was a sharpshooter, and most nights his job was to squat up in a hide high in the rafters, peering out over the city with a night-vision scope through a grapefruit-sized hole in the wall. Othic would spend time up there with him, talking to pass the time. Up in the hide they'd gotten a closer look than most of the guys at the rats that were always scampering across the rafters. Mogadishu was rat heaven; there hadn't been a regular trash pickup in recorded history. Othic and Spalding rigged an ingenious snare out of two Evian water bottles, some trip wire from their booby traps, and the contents of an MRE. Othic recorded success in his journal:

"... Good news, The Great White Hunters (me & Spalding) caught a big nasty ole rat in one of our traps (his really, but this is a joint operation). The capture of the rat brought cheers from all."

What Othic wanted most, more even than to go home, were more missions. They had come to fight. There had been a flurry of action in the beginning, but by late September the pace had slacked off. Othic wrote:

"1830 hours. Another day without a mission & I'm starting to get pissed. We did go out to the range & shoot though, as if that's any kind of consolation for us. We also blew more demo, so I'm starting to become pretty adept at making different charges & firing systems.... We get mail tomorrow (knock on wood!). I know these entries have been getting more & more boring, but everything is starting to get too familiar, which is bad because it will lead to laxness that can be dangerous. It's hard to keep sharp when everything gets routine, you know?"

On the night of September 25, the Skinnies shot down a 101st Division Black Hawk. Three crew members were killed when the downed chopper burst into flames, but the pilot and copilot escaped. They exchanged fire with gunmen on the street until friendly Somalis steered them to a vehicle and got them out.

Othic had been on guard duty that night.

"When I came on guard duty at 2 am me & another guy saw a flaming orange ball moving across the sky, it went down & there was a big explosion & there was a secondary explosion," he wrote. "Today the flag was at half mast for 3 101st pilots who died in the crash, they were shot down by an RPG.... Later they had a ceremony for our fallen comrades as they loaded their bodies on the bird home, makes you realize your mortality."

Eight days later, in a Humvee turret behind his .50 cal, Othic didn't have time to ponder his mortality. He was waiting around the corner a block south of the target building, listening to the escalating gunfire and itching to get his big gun into the fight. But his vehicle was the last one in the ground convoy, so he was pulling rear security, with his gun facing down the road away from everything. He was mostly worried about missing out on the shooting. Then the convoy started moving. As his Humvee made the turn onto Hawlwadig, he bagged the chicken.

There was so much confusion it was hard for Othic to orient himself. There were lots of unarmed people in the streets, so he started off trying to be careful. He hit a Somali with a gun in the doorway to the hotel. He blasted another down the alley looking west from the hotel. The man stopped in the middle of the street and looked over his shoulder, locking eyes momentarily with Othic. The big .50 cal rounds, which could punch head-size holes in cinder block, tore the man apart. Othic aimed a few more rounds at the man's gun in the dirt, trying to disable it. Down the street to the south he saw people dragging out tires and debris for a roadblock, so he swung his turret and put a few rounds down there. They ran.

There was just too much shooting from all directions for Othic to sort out what was going on. Bullets were zinging around him and RPGs had started to fly. He would see a cloud of smoke and a flash and then track the fat arc of the grenade as it rocketed home. Brass shell casings were piling up around him in the turret. A Somali round hit the pile and one of the casings flipped up and stung him in the face. When two more rounds hit ammo boxes right next to him, Othic was alarmed. Somebody had a bead on him. He began shooting everywhere. There was a Ranger saying that went, "When the going gets tough, the tough go cyclic."


Othic's Missouri buddy Eric Spalding was in one of the five-ton trucks farther up the line. The truck had sandbags on the floor in back to shield those riding back there from mines, but other than that it wasn't armored. In the passenger seat, Spalding figured his best defense was a good offense, so he started shooting as soon as the convoy rounded the corner toward the target building. He shot a man with a gun on the steps of the Olympic Hotel, and after that targets just kept on coming as fast as he could line them up and shoot. There wasn't any time to reflect on what was happening. The gunfight started fast and accelerated.

For Sergeant John Burns, riding in a Humvee behind Spalding's truck, it was hard at first to grasp the severity of the fight. He and the rest of the Rangers had expected what they usually found on these missions, a Somali gunman or two taking potshots and running. So when he saw a Somali man fire an RPG from behind a crowd of women, Burns leapt from the Humvee to give chase, catching his foot on the lip of the door and falling flat on his face in the dirt. He scrambled up and ran after the man with the RPG tube, and when he had a clear bead on him he dropped to one knee and shot him. The Somali fell and Burns, completely caught up in his own little chase, ran out and grabbed the wounded man by the shirt, figuring they'd haul him back with the other prisoners. But as he began dragging the man he became aware of how much shooting was going on, and then, to his horror, spotted ten armed Somalis around the corner of the hotel.

It dawned on Burns that he was in the middle of a much bigger fight. He released the wounded man's shirt and sprinted back to his Humvee, where the rest of the men, hunkered down and firing, eyed him with amazement.

One Humvee back, Private Ed Kallman felt a rush of adrenaline as he drove around the corner into the melee. He had joined the army searching for excitement after getting bored with high school in Gainesville, Florida. You started off in the army dreading the prospect of actual combat, but little by little the hard training and discipline of Rangering made you start wishing for it. And here it was. War. The real thing. From behind the wheel, watching through the windshield, Kallman had to remind himself that this wasn't a movie, and the realization filled him initially with a dark boyish glee. The smoke trail of an RPG caught the corner of his eye, and he followed it as it zipped past his vehicle and exploded into one of the five-tons in front. When the smoke cleared he saw Staff Sergeant Dave Wilson, one of the only two black guys in the Ranger company, propped against the wall of a house alongside the truck. Wilson's legs were stretched stiff in front of him and were splashed with bright red blood. Kallman was horrified. One of his guys! He gripped the steering wheel and focused on the vehicle in front of his, suddenly eager to get moving again.

From his turret in the rear Humvee, Othic had seen the flash of the RPG tube. He swung his .50 cal around and blasted the spot, mowing down a small crowd that had been standing in front of the shooter.

Then what felt like a baseball bat came down on his right forearm. It felt just like that. He heard the *crack!* and felt the blow and looked down to see a small hole in his arm. The bone was broken.

He shouted, "I'm hit! I'm hit!"

He really did go cyclic on the .50 cal then, just fired continually for maybe as long as a minute, taking down trees and walls and anyone in, around, or behind them, before Sergeant Lorenzo Ruiz stood up in the turret and took the gun.

# 13

At Sergeant Eversmann's intersection, things continued to go badly for Chalk Four. First Blackburn had fallen out of the helicopter, then they'd roped in well off target, then they'd been pinned down so they couldn't get in the right position. He had sent five guys with the litter carrying Blackburn, and none of them had come back yet.

Then Sergeant Galentine got hit.

Galentine was a kid from Xenia, Ohio, who had spent six months operating a press at a rubber-molding plant after high school before deciding there was more that he could be. He'd enlisted on the day the Gulf War started and it was over before he was out of basic training. He'd been waiting for a chance at a real fight ever since. He'd been crushed when he and Stebbins had gotten left back on this deployment. But now, here he was, finally in battle. It had a strange effect on him. He turned giddy. He and his buddy, Specialist Jim Telscher, sat behind two cars as rounds kicked up dirt between them. Telscher had been smacked in the face by his own rifle coming down the rope and had blood all over his mouth. Gunfire methodically shattered the windows on both cars and blew out the tires. Galentine and Telscher sat behind the rear bumpers making stupid faces at one another.

Galentine did not feel frightened. It didn't register that he could get killed. He just pointed his M-16 at someone down the street, aimed at center mass, and squeezed off rounds. The man would drop. Just like target practice, only cooler.

When they started catching rounds from a different direction, he and Telscher ran to an alley. There, Galentine came face-to-face with a Somali woman. She had chosen that moment to dash across the alley, and now stood staring in horror at Galentine and trying to open a door to get inside. His first instinct had been to shoot her, but he hadn't. The woman's eyes were wide. It startled him, that moment. It cut through his silliness. This wasn't a game. He had come very close to killing this woman. She got the door open and stepped inside.

He had next taken cover behind another car on the main road, his rifle braced against his shoulder, the strap slung around his body. He was picking targets out of a crowd of hundreds that had massed up the road and was moving toward their position. As he fired, he felt a painful slap on his left hand that knocked his weapon so hard it spun completely around him. His first thought was to right his gun, but when he reached he saw his thumb flopped on his forearm, attached only by a strip of skin.

He picked up the thumb and pressed it back to his hand.

"You all right, Scotty? You all right?" asked Telscher.

Eversmann had seen it, the M-16 spinning and a splash of pink by Galentine's left hand. He saw Galentine reach for the hand, then look across the road at him.

"Don't come across!" Eversmann shouted. There was withering fire coming down the road. "Don't come across!"

Galentine heard the sergeant but started running anyway. For some reason, the lanky chalk leader across the road meant safety. He ran but seemed to be getting nowhere, like in a dream. His feet were heavy and slow and if there were bullets flying around him he didn't hear or see them. He dove the last few feet, rolled over, and leaned up against the wall alongside Eversmann.

The sergeant was still contending with the crowd. Down the street behind him there were Humvees in front of the target building. Up ahead it looked like half the city of Mogadishu was massing and closing in on them. Men would dart out into the street and shoot off bursts from their AKs and then take cover. He could see the telltale flash and puff of RPGs being launched their way. The grenades would smoke on in and explode with a long splash of flame and a pounding concussion. From across the street the heat of the blast would wash over and leave a trace of acrid powder smell in his mouth and nose. At one point so many rounds came flying down the road, kicking up dirt and chipping the sides of buildings, they created a wave of noise and energy that the sergeant could actually see coming. One of the Black Hawks flew over and Eversmann stood and stretched his long arm in the direction of the fire. He watched the crew chief in back sitting behind his minigun and then saw the gun spout lines of flame at targets up the street and, for a short time, all shooting from that direction stopped. *That's our guys.*

To Eversmann's left, Private Anton Berendsen was lying out on the ground firing his M-203, a grenade-launcher mounted under the barrel of his M-16. Berendsen was aiming east at Somalis who would pop out and spray bullets from behind the rusty tin shacks that protruded at intervals from the stone walls. Seconds after Galentine dove in, Berendsen grabbed his shoulder.

"Oh, my God, I'm hit," he said. He looked up at Eversmann.

Berendsen scooted over against the wall next to Galentine with one arm limp at his side, picking small chunks of debris from his face.

Eversmann squatted down next to both men, turning first to Berendsen, who was still preoccupied, looking down the alley east.

"Ber, tell me where you're hurt," Eversmann said.

"I think I got one in the arm."

Berendsen began fumbling with his good hand with the breech of his grenade launcher. He couldn't get it open with one hand. Eversmann impatiently opened the breech for him.

"There's a guy right down there," Berendsen said.

Eversmann was too busy with the wound to look. As he struggled to lift up Berendsen's vest and open his shirt to assess the wound, the private shot off a 203 round one-handed. The sergeant turned to look. It occurred to him he probably should have fired the round, instead of having Berendsen attempt it one-handed. He watched the fist-sized shell spiral through the air toward a shack about forty meters away. It flattened it in a great flash of light, noise, and smoke. The shooting from that place stopped.

Berendsen's injury did not look severe. Eversmann turned to Galentine, who was wide-eyed, like he might be lapsing into shock. His thumb was hanging down below his hand.

The sergeant grabbed it and placed it in the palm of Galentine's hand.

"Scott, hold this," he said. "Just put your hand up and hold it, buddy."

Galentine gripped the thumb with his other fingers.

"Hold it up. You'll be all right."

A medic came running up to tend the wound. When he saw the severed thumb he dropped the field dressing to the road. Galentine reached into the medic's kit with his good hand, removed a clean dressing, and handed it to him. The injured hand stung. It felt the way it did on a cold day when you hit a baseball wrong.

"Don't worry, Sergeant Galentine, you're gonna be okay," said Berendsen, bleeding beside him.

Now Eversmann had only Specialist Dave Diemer, a SAW gunner, facing east. Diemer was doing the work of three men, so the sergeant moved over to help him. Eversmann lifted his M-16, found an armed Somali down the street, and squeezed off a round. It occurred to him that this was the first shot he'd fired since roping in.

It was hectic, Eversmann thought, but things were not too bad just yet. He wrestled to stay calm, keep track of all these events piling in on him. He took a knee behind a vehicle alongside Diemer. His mind raced.

He had three Rangers injured, only one critically, and he'd managed to get him out. Galentine's was not life-threatening, nor was Berendsen's.

Glass shattered, showering bits over him and Diemer. A Somali had run out to the middle of the street just a few yards away and blasted the car. Diemer dropped behind the rear wheel on the passenger side and shot him with a quick burst. The Somali was thrown backward hard to the street and lay in a rumpled heap.

Eversmann radioed to Lieutenant Perino that he had taken two more casualties, but they weren't urgently in need of evacuation.

"Sergeant Eversmann," called Telscher, who was across the road. "Snodgrass has been shot."

Specialist Kevin Snodgrass, the machine gunner, had been crouched behind a car and a round had evidently skipped off the chassis or ricocheted up from the road. Eversmann saw Telscher stoop over Snodgrass. The machine gunner was not screaming. It didn't look dire.

Then Diemer tapped his shoulder.

"Sergeant?"

Eversmann turned wearily. Diemer wore a panicked expression.

"I think I just saw a helicopter get hit."

# BLACK
# HAWK
# DOWN

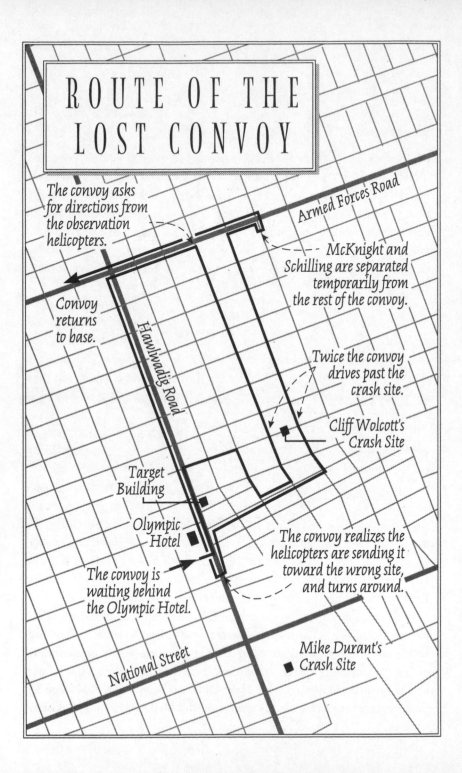

# ROUTE OF THE LOST CONVOY

The convoy asks for directions from the observation helicopters.

Armed Forces Road

McKnight and Schilling are separated temporarily from the rest of the convoy.

Convoy returns to base.

Hawlwadig Road

Twice the convoy drives past the crash site.

Cliff Wolcott's Crash Site

Target Building

Olympic Hotel

The convoy realizes the helicopters are sending it toward the wrong site, and turns around.

The convoy is waiting behind the Olympic Hotel.

National Street

Mike Durant's Crash Site

# 1

Mohamed Hassan Farah heard the helicopters approaching from the north. They came as always, low and loud. Usually they came at night. You would hear only the thrum of their rotors. You never saw them unless they stopped over your block. Then they would come down so low the noise beat at your ears and the wash from their rotors pulled trees out of the sandy ground and sucked tin roofs right off houses, sending them flipping and groaning through the air. Even then you could see the helicopters only in dim outline against a dark sky. They flew black on black, like death.

This time was different. It was daylight, midafternoon. At the sound of them, Farah felt a twinge of panic and anger. He walked outside and watched them pass swiftly overhead, stirring the trees and quaking the rooftops. He knew they were Rangers because Rangers always dangled their boots from the open doorways. He counted about a dozen, but they moved too fast for him to be sure. The soft dry earth under his sandals vibrated.

He had deep wounds that were still healing from an American helicopter attack three months earlier, on July 12—months before the Rangers had come. Farah and the others in his clan had welcomed the UN intervention the previous December. It promised to bring stability and hope. But the mission had gradually deteriorated into hatred and bloodshed. Farah believed the Americans had been duped into providing the muscle for UN Secretary General Boutros Boutros-Ghali, a longtime enemy of the Habr Gidr and clan leader General Mohamed Farrah Aidid. He believed Boutros-Ghali was trying to restore the Darod, a rival clan. Ever since July 12, the Habr Gidr had been at war with America.

On that morning, the American QRF helicopters, seventeen in all, had encircled the house of Abdi Hassan Awale, who was called Qeybdid. Inside the house, in a large second-floor room, were nearly one hundred of his clansmen, intellectuals, elders, and militia leaders. There was urgent business to discuss. The Habr Gidr had been under UN siege for four weeks, ever since a bloody clan ambush killed twenty-four Pakistani soldiers.

Life had grown hard for the clan, but they were used to that. The Habr Gidr was an age-old rival of the Darod, the clan of former dictator Mohamed Siad Barre, who had ruled Somalia with terror for twenty years. As an Egyptian diplomat, Boutros-Ghali had worked against Aidid's revolutionary forces. Barre had been overthrown in 1991, but the Habr Gidr had been unable to consolidate political power. Now the same Boutros-Ghali, through the UN, was again trying to defeat them. This is how they saw it. So they were living as they had for many years, hiding from those in power, biding time, and looking for chances to strike.

That day in July, the leadership had gathered to discuss how to respond to a peace initiative from Jonathan Howe, the retired American admiral who was then leading the UN mission in Mogadishu. Men of middle age were seated at the center of the room on rugs. Elders took chairs and sofas that had been arranged around the perimeter. Among the elders present were religious leaders, former judges, professors, the poet Moallim Soyan, and the clan's most senior leader, Sheik Haji Mohamed Iman Aden, who was over ninety years old. Behind the elders, standing against the walls, were the youngest men. Many of those present wore Western clothing, shirts and pants, but most wore the colorful traditional Somali wraparound cotton skirts called *ma-awis*.

They were the best-educated members of the clan. Ever since the collapse of order and government in Somalia there was little work for intellectuals. So a meeting like this was a big event, a chance to argue over the direction of things. Aidid himself was not present. In the weeks since the UN searched and leveled most of the buildings in his residential compound, he had been in hiding. Qeybdid and some of the others present were his close advisers, hard-liners, men with blood on their hands. Some were responsible for attacks on UN troops, including the massacre of the Pakistanis. There were also moderates in the crowd, men who saw themselves as realists. Ruling impoverished Somalia meant little without friendly ties with the larger world. The Habr Gidr were enthusiastic capitalists. Many of the men in this room were businessmen, eager to resume the flood of international aid and trading ties with America and European powers. They were troubled by the obstructionist and increasingly dangerous game Aidid was playing with the UN. In Mogadishu's present atmosphere of confrontation, their arguments were unlikely to prevail, but some in the crowd at Abdi House were there to argue for peace.

Farah was one of the moderates, a garrulous balding man in his thirties. He was eager for some kind of normalcy in his country, and for friendly ties with nations that could help Somalia. Farah was an engineer, educated in part in Germany. He saw opportunity in the terrible ruins of Mogadishu. Before him lay a lifetime of important and lucrative rebuilding. But he also believed the man who deserved to lead the country—and the only one who would steer valuable engineering contracts his way—was his clansman Aidid. The UN wanted to treat all the warlords and clans as equals when they were not equal.

Farah was on the perimeter of the room with the younger men, but instead of standing, he had set himself down on one knee between two sofas, which probably saved his life.

The TOW missile is designed to penetrate the armored hull of a tank. It is a two-stage forty-pound projectile with fins at the middle and back that trails a copper wire as thin as a human hair. The wire allows the TOW to be steered in flight so that it will follow precisely the path of a targeting laser. Equipped with a shaped charge inside its rounded tip, on impact it spurts a jet of plasma, molten copper, which burns through the outer layer of its target, allowing the missile to penetrate and deliver its full explosive charge within. The explosion is powerful enough to dismember anyone standing near it, and hurls deadly sharp metal fragments in all directions.

What Farah saw and heard was a flash of light and a violent crack. He stood and took one step forward and heard the *whooosh!* of a second missile. There was another flash and explosion. He was thrown to the floor. Thick smoke filled the room. He tried to move forward but his way was blocked by bodies, a bloody pile of men and parts of men a meter high. Among those killed instantly was the eldest, Sheik Haji Iman. Through the smoke, Farah was startled to see Qeybdid, bloody and burned, but still standing at the center of the carnage.

At another part of the room, Abdullahi Ossoble Barre was momentarily dazed by the blasts. To him, it looked liked the men closest to the flash had just evaporated. As soon as he recovered his wits, he began looking for his son.

Those who had survived the first blast were feeling along the wall, groping for the door, when the second missile exploded. The air was thick with dark smoke and smelled of powder, blood, and burned flesh. Farah found the stairs, stood, and had taken one step down when a third missile exploded, disintegrating the staircase. He tumbled to the first floor. He sat up stunned, and felt himself for broken bones and wet spots. He saw he was bleeding from a thick gash in his right forearm. He felt a burning there and on his back, which had been punctured in several places with shrapnel. He crawled forward. There was another explosion above him. Then another and another. Sixteen missiles were fired in all.

Still trapped upstairs, Barre found his son alive beneath a pile of mangled bodies. He began pulling men off, and parts of their bodies came off in his hands. After a great struggle he managed to free his son, who was semiconscious, jerking him free by the legs. Then they heard Americans from the helicopters storming the house, so he and his son lay still among the bleeding and played dead.

Farah crawled until he found a door to the outside. He saw one of his clansmen running from the house, and in the sky he saw the helicopters, Cobras mostly, but also some Black Hawks. The sky was full of them. Red streams poured from the Cobras' miniguns. The men with Farah in the doorway had a quick decision to make. Some had blood running from their mouths and ears. They could stay in the burning house or brave the helicopters' guns outside.

"Let's go out together," one of the men said. "Some of us will live and some will die."

His wounds had nearly healed in the three months since. Now, as the armada of American helicopters roared overhead he was reminded of the shock, pain, and terror. The sight filled him and his friends with rage. It was one thing for the world to intervene to feed the starving, and even for the UN to help Somalia form a peaceful government. But this business of sending U.S. Rangers swooping down into their city killing and kidnapping their leaders, this was too much.


Bashir Haji Yusuf heard the helicopters as he relaxed with friends at his house, chewing *khat* and embroiled in *fadikudirir,* the traditional Somali afternoon hours of male discussion and argument and laughter. Today they had been talking about The Situation, which is about all they ever discussed anymore. With no government, no courts, no law, and no university there was no work for lawyers in Mogadishu, but Yusuf never wanted for argument.

They all stepped out to see. Yusuf, too, saw the legs dangling and knew it was the Rangers. They all despised the Rangers, and the Black Hawks, which seemed now to be over the city continually. They flew in groups, at all hours of day and night, swooping down so low they destroyed whole neighborhoods, blew down market stalls, and terrorized cattle. Women walking the streets would have their colorful robes blown off. Some had infants torn from their arms by the powerful updraft. On one raid, a mother screamed frantically in flex cuffs for nearly a half hour before a translator arrived to listen and to explain that her infant had been blown down the road by the landing helicopters. The residents complained that pilots would deliberately hover over their roofless outdoor showers and toilets. Black Hawks would flare down on busy traffic circles, creating havoc, then power off leaving the crowd below choking on dust and exhaust. Mogadishu felt brutalized and harassed.

Yusuf was disappointed in the Americans. He had been partly educated in the United States, and had many friends there. What troubled him most was, he knew they meant well. He knew his friends back in South Carolina, where he had attended the university, saw this mission to Somalia as an effort to end starving and bloodshed. They never saw what their soldiers were actually doing here in the city. How could these bloody Ranger raids alter things? The Situation was as old and as complicated as his life. Civil war had destroyed all semblance of the old order of things. In this new chaotic Somalia, the shifting alliances and feuds of the clans and subclans were like the patterns wind carved in the sand. Often Yusuf himself didn't understand what was going on. And yet these Americans, with their helicopters and laser-guided weapons and shock-troop Rangers were going to somehow sort it out in a few weeks? Arrest Aidid and make it all better? They were trying to take down a clan, the most ancient and efficient social organization known to man. Didn't the Americans realize that for every leader they arrested there were dozens of brothers, cousins, sons, and nephews to take his place? Setbacks just strengthened the clan's resolve. Even if the Habr Gidr were somehow crippled or destroyed, wouldn't that just elevate the next most powerful clan? Or did the Americans expect Somalia to suddenly sprout full-fledged Jeffersonian democracy?

Yusuf knew the bile on Aidid's radio station was nonsense, about how the UN and the Americans had come to colonize Somalia and wanted to burn the Koran. But in the months since the Abdi House attack he had come to share the popular anger toward American forces. On September 19, after a bulldozer crew of engineers from the 10th Mountain Division was attacked by a band of Somalis, Cobra helicopters attached to the QRF launched TOW missiles and cannon fire into the crowd that came to see the shooting, killing nearly one hundred people. The helicopters had become an evil presence over the city. Yusuf remembered lying in bed one night with his wife, who was pregnant, when Black Hawks had come. One hovered directly over their house. The walls shook and the noise was deafening and he was afraid his roof, like others in the village, would be sucked off. In the racket his wife reached over and placed his hand on her belly.

"Can you feel it?" she asked.

He felt his son kicking in her womb, as if thrashing with fright.

As a lawyer who spoke fluent English, Yusuf had led a group of his villagers to the UN compound to complain. They were told nothing could be done about the Rangers. They were not under UN command. Soon every death associated with the fighting was blamed on the Rangers. Somalis joked bitterly that the United States had come to feed them just to fatten them up for slaughter.

Yusuf saw the armada slow about two kilometers away to the north, over by the Bakara Market. If they were going into Bakara, there would be big trouble. The helicopters circled around the Olympic Hotel.

Right away, he heard the shooting start.

# 2

Most of the Rangers saw *Super Six One* going down.

Chalk Two's SAW gunner, Specialist John Waddell, had started to relax, more or less on, the northeast corner. He could hear the pop of gunfire at the other chalk locations around the target block, but after 60-gunner Nelson had cut down that crowd of Somalis things had quieted at their position. Waddell heard Lieutenant DiTomasso say over the radio that they were getting ready to move to the vehicles, which meant the D-boys must be finished in the target house. He'd be back at the hangar with an hour or two of sunlight left, enough time for him to find a sunny spot on top of a Conex and finish that Grisham novel.

Then there was an explosion overhead. Waddell looked up to see a Black Hawk twisting oddly as it flew.

"Hey, that bird's going down!" shouted one of the men across the street.

Nelson screamed, "A bird's been hit! A bird's been hit!"

Nelson had seen the whole thing. He had seen the flash of the RPG launcher and had followed the smoke trail of the grenade as it rose up at the tail of Black Hawk *Super Six One*, which was directly overhead.

They all heard the thunderclap. The tail boom of the bird cracked in the flash and its rotor stopped spinning with a horrible grinding sound, followed by a coughing *chug-chug-chug*. The chopper kept moving forward but shuddered and started to spin. First slowly, then picking up speed.

# 3

Ray Dowdy felt a jolt, nothing too dramatic, but hard enough to make him bounce in his seat behind the minigun on the left side of *Super Six One*. Dowdy had been maintaining and flying in army choppers for a third of his life. He knew the Black Hawk about as well as anybody in the world, and the hit didn't sound or feel too bad.

It was probably an RPG. Ever since they roped in their load of D-boys, the air had been thick with smoke trails. This had been a growing concern. The QRF Black Hawk that had gone down the week before had been hit by an RPG. It had burst into flames on impact. That incident started everybody rethinking the way they'd been doing things, even though the task force's six missions had gone without a hitch. Some of the pilots began agitating for more flexibility, but their commanders wanted them to stick with the template.

Chief Warrant Officer Cliff Wolcott, the pilot of *Super Six One*, was not one to complain about anything. His unflappable cool had earned him the nickname "Elvis," that and his dead-on impression of the late rock idol. There was a crude cartoon profile of Presley painted on his cockpit door, with the words "Velvet Elvis" underneath. He was a popular pilot. It was his Black Hawk and crew that had decided to go on several unauthorized aerial safaris, and after killing and butchering a two-hundred-pound boar (Wolcott helped hide the carcass from the commanders), they went back out and killed about a dozen more to hold a surprise barbecue for the task force. The shooting got so furious on that hunt that one of the snipers put a hole through the Black Hawk's rotor. Wolcott took the heat, which was mild, because the pig roast was a huge hit with the men, who had been eating MREs and cafeteria food for more than a month. Wolcott brought back a two-hundred-pound kudu that he himself bagged from the seat of his Black Hawk—he planned to have the trophy head mounted. Wolcott was the kind of pilot who would complain to his crew chiefs that he wished he could change places with them—"I have to fly the helicopter while you guys in back get to have all the fun."

His exploits were legendary. He had flown secret missions hundreds of miles behind enemy lines into Iraq during the Gulf War, refueling in flight, to infiltrate troops searching for Saddam Hussein's SCUD missile sites.

When the grenade hit, *Super Six One* was in a low orbit over the target area, varying speed between fifty and seventy knots, trying to avoid moving over the same streets on every pass.

In back were Dowdy and the other crew chief, Staff Sergeant Charlie Warren, and four Delta snipers seated on ammo cans. They were busy selecting targets below, the crew chiefs with their miniguns and the snipers with their custom rifles. At first they shot only at armed Somalis who were moving toward the target area, but as the volume of fire intensified they'd begun targeting anyone with a weapon. Since many of the armed men stayed in crowds, pretty soon Dowdy was mowing down whole crowds of Sammies.

He felt justified. When the QRF's Black Hawk had gone down, Somali mobs had mutilated the corpses of the dead crew chiefs. This being the first mission since then, as a fellow Black Hawk crewman, Dowdy was in full payback mode. Whenever he saw a Somali fall under his guns he'd scream the name of one of the men killed in the crash, something he had vowed to do. The D-boys in back kept looking up at him, wondering what he was doing. Dowdy wasn't being choosey about his targets. He figured anybody moving toward the fight at that point wasn't bringing flowers.

He dropped one Somali with the best shot he'd ever made. One round hit the man in the left buttock and another splashed into his right upper torso. The man ran but then stumbled, dropped his gun, and then collapsed in the road.

"Nice shot, Ray," said pilot Wolcott over the intercom.

When he was close to using the last of his own ammunition, after expending thousands of rounds, Dowdy reached across to the right side of the aircraft where Warren sat, fishing for one of his partner's ammo cans.

"Hey, I've got a guy with an RPG," said Warren. "He's five o'clock moving to six o'clock," which meant, since the chopper was in a left-turning orbit, the guy ought to be showing up on Dowdy's side any second.

He couldn't spot him.

"Is he by a building or something you can describe?"

Warren started to answer when they felt the jolt. Dowdy had that second or two of feeling all right about it, but when the chopper started its spin, he knew they were in trouble. He gripped his seat and looked forward to the cockpit. Dowdy knew that the correct emergency procedure for a tail rotor hit was to pull back on the power control levers, taking the engines off line. This eliminated torque, which was what caused the craft to spin counter to the direction of the rotors.

He heard Elvis ask his copilot, Chief Warrant Officer Donovan "Bull" Briley:

"Hey, Bull, you gonna pull the PCLs off line or what?"

Wolcott delivered this line in his typically teasing fashion. Briley was already pulling the levers. He yanked them back so hard the whole aircraft shook.

The spin continued. The second turnabout was more violent. This was all happening in seconds but to Dowdy it seemed much longer.

Elvis made a last radio transmission.

—*Six One going down.*

Dowdy and Warren shouted at the D-boys in back to get down and to hold on. The crew chiefs were on seats that could absorb at least some of the impact, but the snipers were sitting upright in back without protection. The impact could crush their spines. The operators scrambled off the ammo cans and spread-eagled—the better to spread the impact out over their bodies. As the spin accelerated, they reached for something to hold on to. One of them, Sergeant First Class Jim Smith, grabbed hold with one hand to a bar behind Warren's seat, and just then the accelerating spin sent his feet flying out the side door. Smith's shoulder wrenched with pain but he hung on.

Dowdy glanced down and noticed he hadn't fastened his seat belt.

The helicopter clipped the top of a house; then it flipped over hard and slammed into the alley nose first and tilted on its left side.

# 4

Nelson watched dumbstruck as the chopper fell.

"Oh, my God, you guys, look at this," he shouted. "Look at this!"

Waddell gasped, "Oh, Jesus," and fought the urge to just stand and watch the bird go down. He turned away to keep his eyes on his corner.

Nelson shouted, "It just went down! It just crashed!"

"What happened?" called Lieutenant DiTomasso, who came running.

"A bird just went down!" Nelson said. "We've gotta go. We've gotta go right now!"

Word spread wildly over the radio, voices overlapping with the bad news. There was no pretense now of the deadpan military cool, that mandatory monotone that conveyed *everything under control.* Voices rose with surprise and fear:

—*We got a Black Hawk going down! We got a Black Hawk going down!*

—*We got a Black Hawk crashed in the city! Six One!*

—*He took an RPG!*

—*Six One down!*

—*We got a bird down, northeast of the target. I need you to move on out and secure that location!*

—*Roger, bird down!*

It was more than a helicopter crash. It cracked the task force's sense of righteous invulnerability. The Black Hawks and Little Birds were their trump card in this God-forsaken place. The choppers, more than their rifles and machine guns, were what kept the savage mobs at a distance. The Somalis *couldn't* shoot them down!

But they had seen it, the chopper spinning, falling, one of the D-boys hanging on with one hand, both feet in the air, riding it down.

# 5

*Super Six One* had clipped the roof of Abdiaziz Ali Aden's house as it crashed. Aden was a slip of a teenager with thick bushy hair and glossy black skin, one of eleven children, eight of whom still lived in the house about six blocks east of the Bakara Market. That Sunday afternoon most of them were at home, napping or relaxing after a late lunch, staying out of the hot sun.

Aden had heard the helicopters coming in low, so low that the big tree that stood in the central courtyard of his stone house was uprooted. Then he heard shooting to the west, near Hawlwadig, the big road that passed before the Olympic Hotel three blocks over. He ran toward the noise, crossing Marehan Road outside the door and then Wadigley Road, keeping to the north walls of the alley. The sky was dark with smoke. As he neared the hotel, the air around him sizzled and cracked with gunfire. Above him were helicopters, some with lines of flame coming from their guns. He ran two blocks with his head down, staying against the wall, until he saw American trucks and Humvees, with machine guns mounted on them, shooting everywhere.

The Rangers wore body armor and helmets with goggles. Aden could see no part of them that looked human. They were like futuristic warriors from an American movie. People were running madly, hiding. There was a line of Somali men in handcuffs being loaded onto big trucks. On the street were dead people and a donkey dead on its side, its water cart still attached and upended.

It terrified him. As he started back toward his house, one of the Black Hawks flew over him at rooftop level. It made a rackety blast, and wash from its rotors swept over the dirt alley like a violent storm. Through this dust, Aden saw a Somali militiaman with an RPG tube step into the alley and drop to one knee.

The militiaman waited until the helicopter had passed overhead. Then he leaned the tube up and fired at the aircraft from behind. Aden saw a great flash from the back end of the tube and then saw the grenade climb and explode into the rear of the helicopter, cracking the tail. It began turning, so close that Aden could see the pilot inside struggling at the controls. It was tilted slightly toward Aden when it hit the roof of his house with a loud crunch, and then slammed on its side into the alley with a great scraping crash in a thick cloud of dust.

Fearing it had crushed his house and killed his family, he ran back. He found his parents and brothers and sisters trapped under a broad sheet of tin roof. They had stepped outside and had been standing against the west wall when the helicopter hit and the roof came down on them. They were not badly hurt. Aden worked his way past the huge black body of the

crashed helicopter, which had fallen sideways so that the bottom faced him.
He helped pull the roof off his family. Afraid that the helicopter would
explode, they all ran across Marehan Road, the wide, rutted dirt road just
out their front door, to a friend's house three doors up.

When a few minutes passed with no flames and no explosion, Aden
came back to guard his house. In Mogadishu, if you left your house open
and undefended it would be looted. He entered through the front door and
stood in the courtyard by the uprooted tree. The wall that faced the alley
where the helicopter had fallen was now just a heap of stones and dusty
mortar. Aden saw an American soldier climb out of the hulk, and then
another with an M-16. He turned and ran back out the door to a green
Volkswagen parked against the wall across the same alley where the helicopter had fallen. He crawled under it, curling himself up into a ball.

When the American soldier with the gun rounded the corner he saw
Aden, peered at him closely, probably looking for a weapon, and then moved
on. He stopped near the front end of the car—Aden could have reached out
and touched the soldier's boots—and pointed his gun at a Somali man with
an M-16 across the wide street. The two men fired at the same time but
neither fell. Then the Somali man's gun jammed and the American didn't
shoot. He ran over to the wall across Marehan Road, closer, and shot him.
The bullet went in the Somali man's forehead. Then the American ran over
and shot him three more times where he lay on the road.

As he did this a big Somali woman came running from a narrow alley
beside the house, right in front of the soldier. Startled, he quickly fired his
weapon. The woman fell face forward, dropping like a sack, without putting out her arms to break the fall.

More Somalis came now, with guns, shooting at the American. He
dropped to one knee and shot them, many of them, but the Somalis' bullets also hit him.

Others came out from hiding then, and moved toward the crash. Then
a helicopter landed right on Marehan Road and these Somalis scattered.
It seemed impossible that a helicopter could fit in such a small space. It
was one of the little ones. The roar of the helicopter was deafening and
dust swirled around. Aden couldn't breathe. Then the shooting got worse.

One of the pilots was leaning out of the helicopter aiming his weapon
south, toward the crest of the hill. Another ran from the helicopter toward
the one that had crashed. The shooting was even worse then. It was so loud

that the sound of the helicopter and the guns was just one ongoing explosion. Bullets hit and rocked the old car. Aden curled himself up tight and wished he was someplace else.

# 6

Cameras on the three observation choppers captured the disaster close-up and in color. General Garrison and his staff watched on screens at the JOC. They saw Wolcott's Black Hawk moving smoothly, then a shudder and puff of smoke near the tail rotor, then an awkward counterrotation as *Super Six One* fell, making two slow turns clockwise, nose up, until its belly bit the top of a stone building and its front end was cast down violently. On impact, its main rotors snapped and went flying. The body of the Black Hawk came to rest in a narrow alley on its side against a stone wall in a cloud of dust.

There wasn't enough time for anyone to consider all the ramifications of that crash, but the sick sinking feeling that came over officers watching on screen went way beyond the immediate fate of the men on board.

They had lost the initiative. The only way to regain it now would be to bolster strength at the crash site, but that would take time and movement, which meant casualties. There were already casualties on the downed bird. There was no time to reflect on causes or consequences. If Elvis's chopper had gone down in flames, the general could just pull everybody out with the prisoners as planned and mount a second mission to retrieve the bodies and make sure the chopper was completely destroyed—there were sensitive items on the bird that the army didn't want just anybody to have.

But seeing men climb out of the wreckage, and watching as the unscripted battle now joined around it, the ground shifted beneath Garrison's feet. The next moves were part of a contingency they had rehearsed. Another Black Hawk would take *Super Six One*'s place over the target area, and the CSAR bird would move in and drop its team. Those fifteen men would give emergency medical treatment and provide some protection for the crash survivors, but they couldn't hold out long. Already mobs of Somalis were moving toward the crash site from all directions. Securing it would take all of the men on the ground. The mission had been

designed for speed: swiftly in, swiftly out. Now they were stuck. The entire force at the target building and on the convoy would have to fight their
way to the crash site. They had to move fast, before Aidid's forces surrounded it and cut it off. If that happened, the crash survivors and the CSAR
team would have no hope. Delta Force and the Rangers were the best the
army had to offer. Now they were going to be tested.

It was hard to imagine any other force of 150 men trapped in a hostile city, besieged on all sides by a heavily armed populace, who had a rea-
sonable chance of surviving. They were at the eye of a terrible storm. The
observation birds showed burning tires sending tall black columns of smoke
around the perimeter of the contested blocks. Many thousands of armed
Somalis were thronging toward those plumes from all directions, on vehicles and on foot. People were erecting barricades and digging trenches
across roads, laying traps for American vehicles, trying to seal them in. The
streets surrounding the target house and crash site were already mobbed.
You could see the ring closing.

Word was sent to the 10th Mountain Division troops across the city
to mobilize immediately. This was going to be one hell of a gunfight.

# 7

"We gotta go," Nelson told Lieutenant DiTomasso. "We gotta go right now."

From Chalk Two's position at the target block's northeast corner,
Nelson had gotten a pretty good fix on where *Super Six One* had crashed.
He could see crowds of Somalis already running that way.

"No, we've got to stay here," said the lieutenant.

"There's a crowd over there," argued Nelson, the impending disaster overcoming his deference for rank.

"Stand fast," DiTomasso said.

"I'm going," said Nelson.

Guns poked out of a window across the street, and just then he spotted two Somali boys running, one with something in his hand. Nelson
dropped to a knee and fired a burst with the M-60. Both boys fell. One
had been holding a stick. The other got up and limped for cover.

Specialist Waddell was feeling the same urge to run toward the crash.
They had all heard about the way the Somalis had mutilated the remains

of the men who died in the previous Black Hawk crash. In the hangar they had talked it over. They resolved that such a thing would never happen to *their* guys.

DiTomasso held Nelson back. He raised Captain Steele on the radio.

"I know where it is. I'm leaving," the lieutenant said.

"No, wait," said Steele. He could understand the urge to go help, but if Chalk Two just took off, the target building perimeter would break down. He tried to get on the command net, but the airwaves were so busy he couldn't be heard.

He waited fifteen seconds.

"We need to go!" Nelson was shouting at DiTomasso. "Now!"

As he started running, Steele called back.

"Okay, go," he told DiTomasso. "But I want somebody to stay."

DiTomasso shouted, "All right, Nelson. Make it happen."

With some of the men already in pursuit of Nelson, the lieutenant ran down the street to Sergeant Yurek. He would leave half the chalk.

"You keep the fight here," he told Yurek.

Eight Rangers moved at a trot. DiTomasso caught up with Nelson and his M-60 in front. Waddell was in the rear with his SAW. They moved with their weapons up and ready. Somalis took wild shots at them from windows and doorways as they moved, but no one was hit. Twice on their way east, Nelson dropped to a knee and opened fire on the crowd moving parallel to them one block north.

When they rounded the corner three blocks over, there was a wide sand road that sloped down to the intersection of the alley where *Super Six One* lay. Straight in front of them—and this just astonished Nelson— one of the Little Birds had landed. Its rotors were turning in a space so small the tips were just inches from the stone walls.

# 8

Piloting the Little Bird *Star Four One*, Chief Warrant Officers Keith Jones and Karl Maier searched for and found the fallen Black Hawk minutes after it went down. They could tell by the way the front end of the bird had crumpled that Elvis and Bull were probably dead. Jones saw one soldier, Staff Sergeant Daniel Busch, on the ground propped against a wall bleeding from the stomach with several Somalis splayed on the ground around him.

Landing in the big intersection near Busch would have been easier, but Jones didn't want to be a fat target from four different directions. He eased the bird up the street between two stone houses and set it down on a slope. He and Maier felt themselves rock back when they touched down.

As soon as they landed, Sammies came at them. Both pilots opened fire with handguns. Then Sergeant Smith, the operator who had hung on with one hand as the Black Hawk fell, and the second of the two soldiers Abdiaziz Ali Aden had seen climb out of the wreckage (Busch had been the first), appeared alongside Jones's window.

Over the din he mouthed to Jones, "I need help." His one arm hung limp. Jones hopped out and followed Smith back to the intersection, leaving Maier to control the bird and provide cover up the alley.

Just then, Lieutenant DiTomasso and his men rounded the corner and came face-to-face with the Little Bird. Maier nearly shot the lieutenant. When the pilot lowered his weapon, the startled DiTomasso tapped his helmet, indicating he wanted a head count on casualties.

Maier gestured that he didn't know.

Nelson and the other Rangers hurried down the slope, ducking under the blades of the Little Bird. Nelson saw Busch leaning against a wall one block down with a bad gut wound. The Delta sniper had his SAW on his lap and a .45 pistol on the ground in front of him. There were two Somali bodies nearby. Busch, a devoutly religious man, had told his mother before leaving for Somalia, "A good Christian soldier is just a click away from heaven." Nelson recognized him as the guy who beat all comers in the hangar at Scrabble. One poor guy had lost forty-one straight games to him. There was a mass of blood in his lap now. Busch looked ghostly white, gone.

Nelson shot one of the Somalis on the ground who was still breathing and then lay behind the bodies for cover. He picked up Busch's .45 handgun and stuck it in his pocket. The hulking frame of the Black Hawk was across the wide road to his right in the alley. Somalis climbing on the wreckage fled when they saw the Rangers round the corner.

As the rest of the squad fanned out to form a perimeter, Jones and Smith dragged Busch's limp body toward the Little Bird. Jones helped Smith into the small space behind the cockpit, and then stooped and lifted Busch to the doorway, setting him in Smith's lap. Smith wrapped his arms around the more badly wounded Delta sniper as Jones tried to apply first aid.

Busch had been shot just under the steel belly plate of his body armor. His eyes were gray and rolled up in his head. Jones knew there was nothing he could do for him.

The pilot stepped out and climbed back into his seat. On the radio he heard air commander Matthews in the C2 bird.

—*Four One, come on out. Come out now.*

Jones grabbed the stick and told Maier, "I have it."

He told the command net:

—*Four One is coming out.*

# 9

Under the steady drone of his rotors, layered deep in the overlap of urgent calls in his headphones, Chief Warrant Officer Mike Durant had picked out the voice of his friend Cliff.

—*Six One going down.*

Just like that. Elvis's voice was oddly calm, matter-of-fact.

Durant and his copilot, Chief Warrant Officer Ray Frank, were circling barren land north of Mogadishu in *Super Six Four,* a Black Hawk just like the one Elvis had been flying. They had two crew chiefs in back, Staff Sergeant Bill Cleveland and Sergeant Tommie Field, waiting behind silent guns. For years they had done little but prepare rigorously for battle, but here they were stuck in this calm oval flight pattern over sand, a good four-minute flight from the action.

The shadow of their chopper glided over the flat, empty landscape. Mogadishu ended abruptly and turned to sand and scrub brush north of October 21st Road. From there to the blazing horizon was little but stubby thorn trees, cactus, goats, and camels in a hazy ocean of sand.

Durant thought about his friends, Elvis and Bull. They were skilled, veteran warriors. It didn't seem possible that a motley rabble of Somalis had managed to shoot them out of the air. Bull Briley had seen action from Korea to the invasion of Panama. Durant remembered seeing Bull angry the night before. He'd gotten a chance to phone home, the first chance in months, and had gotten the damned answering machine. God, wouldn't it be sad if . . .

Durant continued his methodical turns. Every time he banked west it felt like he was flying straight into the sun.

Going down over Mog was bad news but not catastrophic. It was a contingency. They had practiced it since their arrival, with Elvis's own helicopter, in fact—which was weird. It wasn't even that shocking, at least not to the pilots, who had a finer sense of the risks they ran than most of the men they flew. Most of the Rangers were practically kids. They had grown up in the most powerful nation on earth, and saw these techno-laden, state-of-the-art choppers as symbols of America's vast military might, all but invulnerable over a Third World dump like Mog.

It was a myth that had survived the downing of the QRF's Black Hawk. That was chalked up as a lucky shot. RPGs were meant for ground fighting. It was difficult and dangerous, almost suicidal, to point one skyward. The violent back blast could kill the shooter, and the grenade would only fly up a thousand feet or so, with a whoosh and a telltale trail of smoke pointing back to the shooter. So if the back blast didn't get him one of the quick guns of the Little Birds surely would. They were all but useless against a fast-moving, low-flying helicopter, so the logic went. And the Black Hawk was damn near indestructible. It could take a hammering without even changing course. It was designed to stay in the air no matter what.

So most of the foot soldiers who rode in the birds regarded the downing of a Black Hawk as a one-in-a-million event. Not the pilots. Since that first Black Hawk had gone down they'd seen more and more of those climbing smoke trails and sudden airbursts. Going down was suddenly notched from possible to probable and entered their nightmares. Not that it deterred Durant and the other pilots in the least. Taking risks was what they did. The 160th SOAR, the Night Stalkers, chauffeured the most elite soldiers in the U.S. military into some of the most dangerous spots on the planet.

Durant was a compact man. He was short, fit, dark-haired, and had this way of standing ramrod straight, feet set slightly wider than his shoulders, as if daring someone to knock him down. If he looked better rested than most of the guys back at the hangar it was because Durant had searched out a sleeping space in the small cooking area of a trailer behind the JOC. All the pilots slept in the trailers, which were relatively luxurious compared to the cots in the hangar. Given the precision and alertness flying demanded, not to mention the responsibility for their crew and their multi-million-dollar high-tech flying machines, Garrison considered well-rested pilots a priority. Durant had done better than most. The cooking trailer was air-conditioned. His part of the deal was he had to break down his bunk every night and clear the space for the cooks, but it was well worth the hassle.

Durant had been with the Night Stalkers long enough to be a veteran of dangerous low-flying night missions in the Persian Gulf War and the invasion of Panama. He had grown up in Berlin, New Hampshire, with a reputation for being a cutup and an athlete, a football and hockey player. Age and experience had changed him. Many of the people in his neighborhood in Tennessee, just over the state line from the Night Stalkers' base at Fort Campbell, Kentucky, didn't even know what he did for a living. His own family often didn't know where he was.

It was hard to keep track. If Durant wasn't on a real mission like this one, he was off somewhere in the world practicing for one. Practice defined the lives of the Night Stalkers. They practiced everything, even crashing. When they were done they flew off someplace new and practiced it again, again, and again. Their moves in the electronic maze of their cockpits were so well rehearsed they had become instinctive.

On the day Durant's unit was dispatched to Somalia they had gotten only two hours' notice. Enough time to drive home and spend fifteen minutes with his wife, Lorrie, and year-old son, Joey. Never mind that his parents were due in town the next day for a long-planned, weeklong visit, that Joey's first birthday was in three days, and Lorrie was due to resume schoolteaching in a week, or that the house they were building was only half finished (with Durant playing subcontractor). Lorrie knew better than to protest. She had just pitched in to help him pack. It wasn't immediately apparent, but Durant was also an emotional man. He fit in with his daring aviation unit, men whose allegiance was as much to action as flag, but the sentiment he felt for his wife and baby son, who had just started to crawl, was closer to the surface than with some of these guys. There were men in his unit who made a show of how hard it was to leave but who secretly lived for missions and weren't happy unless in danger. Durant wasn't that way. It was hard to leave Lorrie and his baby boy, to miss his parents and the birthday party. He had been looking forward to it. He phoned his folks to tell them, and to say how sorry he was. He was not allowed to say where he was going. There was no time even to write out a list of the things that needed doing on the new house (he would send that via E-mail from Mogadishu, way overusing his allotted number of bytes in the batch-mailing). Durant stood with his travel bag in the doorway of their home with that stiff posture of his, kissed Lorrie good-bye, and went off to war. Even his leavings were well practiced.

After Elvis crashed, Durant knew three things would happen quickly. The ground forces would begin moving to the crash site. *Super Six Eight,* the CSAR bird, one of the Black Hawks in the holding pattern with Durant, would be summoned to deliver a team of medics and snipers. His bird, *Super Six Four,* would be asked to fill Elvis's vacant slot flying a low orbit over the action providing covering fire.

For now, they waited and circled. On a mission like this one, with so many birds in the air, breaking discipline meant becoming a greater hazard than the enemy. For Durant, the most harrowing part of his mission was done. Inserting Chalk One, his fifteen-man portion of the ground force, had meant descending into an opaque cloud of dust to rooftop level over the target building, avoiding poles and wires and squinting down through the Black Hawk's chin bubble into the brown swirl to stay lined up while the men slid down ropes to the ground. All Durant could do was hold blind and steady, and pray that none of the other birds flitting around him in the cloud got thrown off schedule or bumped off course. A complex mission like this one was choreographed as carefully as a ballet, only dangerous as hell. Guys got killed all the time just training for exercises like this, much less ducking RPGs and small-arms fire. Durant had inserted Chalk One without incident. The rest was supposed to be easy.

Now nothing was going to be easy.

# 10

Admiral Jonathan Howe's first inkling that something was amiss in Mogadishu came when air traffic controllers at the UN compound forced his plane to circle out over the ocean for a time before landing.

Howe was returning from meetings in Djibouti and Addis Ababa, exploring a plan for bringing Aidid peacefully to heel. When they were cleared to land, Howe saw attack helicopters refueling and uploading ammo on the tarmac by the Task Force Ranger hangar. When he landed, Howe telephoned his chief of staff. He was told about the Ranger raid and the downed helicopter. The aide told him there was a big fight going on in the city and he would probably be stuck for a while at the airport.

Howe was a slender, white-haired man whose pale complexion hadn't even pinked after seven months in Mogadishu. His staff joked that it was from all those years aboard submarines, although in Howe's distinguished naval career he had commanded his share of surface vessels, everything from battleships to aircraft carriers. Whatever the cause, he seemed immune to sunlight, even Somalia's. Aidid's propaganda sheets had dubbed him "Animal Howe," but the envoy's calm, polite manner belied the nickname. He had served as deputy national security adviser for President Bush and had helped with the transition in the White House to the Clinton administration, so impressing the new team that he had been talked out of a comfortable Florida retirement to assume the unenviable task of supervising an even trickier transition in Somalia. He was Boutros-Ghali's top man in Mog, effectively running the mission on the ground.

It was not an easy assignment. Howe had slept for months on a cot in his office on the first floor of the old U.S. embassy building, which was falling apart. For some of the time he had a tin-roofed cabin, but regular shellings generally drove him and the other civilians at the compound inside the stone walls of the main building. There were no toilets in the embassy, and so few portable ones outside, that the men toted plastic bottles to relieve themselves. They ate three meals a day out of a cafeteria on the grounds. A story in *The Washington Post* that suggested the UN staff enjoyed luxurious accommodations had provoked bitter laughter.

More than anyone, Howe had been responsible for bringing the Rangers to Mogadishu. He had pushed his friends in the White House and Pentagon so hard that summer for a force to snag Aidid that in Washington they were calling him "Jonathan Ahab." He was convinced that getting rid of the warlord—not killing him, but arresting him and trying him as a war criminal—would cut through the tangle of tribal hatred that sustained war, anarchy, and famine.

The state of the city had shocked him when he arrived eight months earlier. It was a savage place. Everything had been shot up, nothing worked, everything of value had been looted, and nobody was in charge. Here was a country not just at ground zero, but *below* zero. The very means of recovery had been destroyed. The hobbled predicament of the place was reflected in the number of land-mine victims, men, women, and children pulling themselves around on crutches. The UN intervention had ended the famine, but where would Somalia go from there? Efforts to build a coalition government out of the nation's feuding clans were still far from successful. Nine out of ten Somalis were unemployed, and most of those who did work were employed by the UN and the United States. The factional fighting had gone beyond anything rational or even understandable from the admiral's perspective. He felt contempt for the men responsible, for men like Aidid, Ali Mahdi, and the other warlords, the very leaders needed to set Somalia back on its feet.

It soon became clear to Howe that power sharing was not in the plans of Aidid and his Somalia National Alliance (SNA), the political/military arm of the Habr Gidr. Having been the principal engine of Barre's defeat two years earlier, Aidid and his clan felt it was their turn to rule. They had purchased that right with blood, the ancient currency of power. Ali Mahdi and all the other lesser faction leaders were enthusiastic about nation-building plans. Why wouldn't they be? The UN was offering them a share of power they could never wrest from Aidid on their own.

With the 38,000-strong military force of UNITAF (Unified Task Force) in the country, the backbone being U.S. Marines and the army's 10th Mountain Division, the warlords had stopped fighting. But when the last of the Marines pulled out on May 4 and the 10th was relegated to backup duties as the QRF, the situation predictably deteriorated. The worst incident had been the June 5 slaughter of twenty-four Pakistanis. The next day the UN had pronounced the SNA an outlaw faction. Aidid was officially dealt out of the nation-building process. Over the next few weeks, Howe had authorized a $25,000 bounty for the warlord as gunships flattened Aidid's Radio Mogadishu and UN troops invaded the warlord's residential compound. To no avail. The Habr Gidr was insulted by the paltry sum being offered for its leader. They countered with a defiant $1 million reward for the capture of "Animal" Howe. Radio Mogadishu continued broadcasting its propaganda with mobile antennae, and the wily old general just melted into his city.

Aidid had kept up the pressure. From his southern stronghold, mortar rounds were lobbed daily into UN compounds. Somali employees of the UN mission were terrorized and executed. The warlord proved to be a formidable adversary. His name, Aidid, meant "one who tolerates no insult." He had been schooled in Italy and the old Soviet Union and had served as army chief of staff and then ambassador to India for Siad Barre before turning on the dictator and routing him. Aidid was a slender, fragile-looking man with Semitic features, a bald head, and small black eyes. He could be charming, but was also ruthless. Howe believed Aidid had two distinct personalities. One day he was all smiles, a warm, engaging, modern, educated man fluent in several languages with an open mind and a sense of humor. Aidid had fourteen children who lived in America. (One, a son named Hussein, was a Marine reservist who had come to Somalia with UNITAF forces in the December intervention.) It was this cosmopolitan side of Aidid that had encouraged earlier hopes for success. But the next day, without apparent reason, Aidid's black eyes would show nothing but hatred. There were times when even his closest aides avoided him. This was Aidid the son of a Somali camel herder who had risen to success as a clever and ruthless killer. He thought nothing of ordering people killed, even his own people. Howe had evidence that Aidid's henchmen were inciting demonstrations, then gunning down their own supporters in order to accuse the UN of genocide. Aidid had certainly used starvation as a weapon against rival clans, hijacking and withholding world food shipments. The warlord also knew the value of terror—some of the dead Pakistani soldiers had been disemboweled and skinned.

Howe was outraged, and adamant that Aidid be stopped. The admiral was accustomed to having his way. He wasn't a screamer, but once he bit into something he held on. Many old Africa hands regarded this trait as ill-suited to this part of the world. In Somalia, warlords who feuded one day could be warm old friends the next. Howe was unyielding. If he lacked the means to remove Aidid, he would get the means. He still had friends, friends in very high places, friends who owed him, who had talked him into this job. One of them was Anthony Lake, President Clinton's national security adviser. Another was Madeleine Albright, America's emissary to the UN, who was an unabashed enthusiast of New World Ordering. Flush with success against Saddam Hussein and the collapse of the Soviet Union, there were plenty of politicians, diplomats, and journalists with bright hopes for a new millennium of worldwide capitalist free markets. America's unrivaled big stick could right the world's wrongs, feed the hungry, democratize the planet. But the generals, most notably outgoing Chairman of the Joint Chiefs of Staff Colin Powell, demanded more solid reasons for getting their soldiers killed. Howe found some allies in the administration, but strict opposition from the Pentagon brass.

When Washington denied Howe's request for Delta in June, he began a fruitless effort to catch Aidid with the forces already in place. At first, to avoid harming innocent people, helicopters with loudspeakers broadcast warnings of impending UN action, a gesture thought ridiculous by most Somalis. After administering such a warning, a multinational force descended on Aidid's compound on June 17. A house-to-house search was conducted by Italian, French, Moroccan, and Pakistani troops, and an armored cordon was thrown around the site by the French and Moroccans. Aidid easily slipped away. Legend on the streets had the general rolling out under the noses of UN troops on a donkey cart, wrapped up in a sheet like a dead body. The UN was not only incapable of capturing Aidid, they were turning him into a folk hero.

The decision to attack the Abdi House on July 12 reflected mounting UN frustration. After the Pakistani ambush, the clan escalated its sniping and mortar attacks. The Turkish commander of UN troops, General Cevik Bir, and his second, U.S. Army Major General Thomas Montgomery, wanted to take the kid gloves off. This would be an attack without warning, a chance to chop off the SNA's head. The clan leadership had taken to meeting regularly at the Abdi House. The plan called for helicopters to encircle it from the air, fire TOW missiles and cannons into it, then raid the house to arrest survivors.

Howe opposed it. Why, he asked, couldn't troops simply surround the place and order those inside to come out, or why not just storm the house and arrest everybody? Such approaches would subject the UN forces to too much risk, he was told. None of the units in-country were capable of policing a "sanitized" cordon, so issuing a warning would be self-defeating. The officials would just flee—as Aidid had earlier. And the force lacked the capability to perform the kind of lightning snatch-and-grab tactics used by Delta. When the Pentagon and White House signed off on the attack, Howe relented.

The number of Somalis killed in the attack was disputed. Mohamed Hassan Farah, Abdullahi Ossoble Barre, Qeybdid, and others present claimed 73 dead, including women and children who had been on the building's first floor. They said hundreds were wounded. The reports Howe got after the attack placed the number of dead at 20, all men. The International Committee of the Red Cross set the number of dead at 54, with total casualties at 250. But the dispute over the number of dead Somalis was quickly eclipsed by the deaths of 4 Western journalists who rushed to the Abdi House to report on the attack, only to be killed by an enraged Somali mob.

The journalists' deaths focused worldwide anger on the Somalis, but in Mogadishu the shock and outrage was over the surprise attack. The massacre bolstered Aidid's status, and badly undercut the UN's humanitarian image. Moderates opposed to Aidid now rallied behind him. From the Habr Gidr's perspective, the UN and, in particular, the United States, had declared war.

Howe kept pushing for Delta. It was the clearest way out he could see. At Fort Bragg, teams of Night Stalker pilots and Delta officers worked up a plan in June that would require only about twenty men. They would slip into the country surreptitiously and use the QRF's helicopters and equipment. An intelligence assessment found Aidid still making public appearances and moving around Mogadishu with his conspicuous escort of technicals. But through July and most of August there was no green light from Washington.

Howe's pleas won out finally in August, when remote-controlled land mines first killed four American soldiers and then, two weeks later, injured seven more. Vacationing on Martha's Vineyard, President Clinton assented. Delta would go. Aidid became America's white whale.

Task Force Ranger arrived on August 23 with a three-phase mission. Phase One, which would last until the thirtieth, was just to get the force up and running. Phase Two, which would last until September 7, would concentrate exclusively on finding and capturing Aidid. The command staff already suspected this would be futile, since widespread publicity about the Rangers' intentions quickly drove Aidid underground. Phase Three would target Aidid's command structure. This was the meat of Task Force Ranger's mission. If the D-boys couldn't catch the warlord, they were going to put him out of business.

Howe had initially envisioned a small unit of stealthy operators, but he was delighted to get the whole 450-man task force. He weathered with patience its early missteps. As September rolled on, despite the glitches, the force achieved mounting success. Howe was especially pleased on September 21 when a surprise daylight assault on a convoy of cars resulted in the capture of Osman Atto, the arms dealer and Aidid's chief banker, who was now imprisoned with a growing number of other SNA captives on an island off the coast of the southern port city of Kismayo, in pup tents surrounded by razor wire.

Aidid was feeling the heat. A Habr Gidr leader cooperating with U.S. forces told them, "He [Aidid] is very tense. The situation out there is very tense." In late August the Somali warlord sent a letter to former president Jimmy Carter pleading for him to intervene with President Clinton. The general wanted an independent commission "composed of internationally known statesmen, scholars and jurists from different countries," to investigate the allegations that he was responsible for the June 5 incident—Aidid claimed it had been a spontaneous uprising of Mogadishu citizens who feared the UN was attacking Radio Mogadishu. He also called for a negotiated solution to his standoff with the UN.

Carter had taken this message to the White House, and the suggestion was received warmly by Clinton, who directed that efforts to resolve matters peacefully be renewed. The State Department began quietly working on a plan to intercede through the governments of Ethiopia and Eritrea. The plan called for an immediate cease-fire, and for Aidid to remove himself from Somalia until the international inquiry was done. It set a new round of nation-building talks in November. There were other feelers being put out in Mogadishu by Howe through Habr Gidr elders alarmed at the recent turn of events. Howe and his supporters in Washington were convinced that Aidid's sudden flexibility was a direct result of Garrison's pressure.

Peace had been the reason for Howe's journey this weekend. On his long flight over the dry wasteland, watching the shadow of his plane racing ahead of it across the dunes, he felt like the UN at last was dealing from a position of strength.

\* \* \*

After circling out over the water for nearly an hour, Howe's plane was finally cleared to land at the Ranger base late Sunday afternoon. He knew there was a battle raging, but he didn't get the full picture until he returned to the UN compound early that evening. General Montgomery was at work there piecing together an enormous international convoy to go in and rescue the downed Rangers and pilots.

There was little for Howe to do but find a place to sit and observe. Montgomery had his hands full. The Malaysians and Pakistanis, who had the necessary armor, wanted no part of the Bakara Market. These were the same troops that had effectively backed out of the city streets after the Marines had left. They did want to help, but were balking at the idea of sending big armored vehicles into the hornet's nest. In those densely populated neighborhoods, moving slowly through narrow streets, armor was highly vulnerable.

The Italians, whose loyalties had been at best suspect throughout the intervention, were nevertheless ready to commit, as were the Indians, who had tanks of their own they could throw into the fight. It would take longer to get the Italians and Indians into position, so Montgomery was pushing the Malays and Pakis hard.

Howe couldn't help but wonder what would have happened if such a determined international response had greeted the June 5 slaughter of the Pakistani troops, as he had urged. Still, he was pleased to see it now. It was a shame the task force had gotten stung, but once the bleeding stopped, maybe there would be more of an appetite in Washington to get rid of this upstart warlord once and for all.

# 11

Word that there was big trouble in the city spread quickly through the Somali staff at the U.S. embassy compound. Abdi Karim Mohamud worked as a secretary for Brown & Root, one of the American companies providing support services to the international military force. He had been a twenty-one-year-old college student when the Barre regime was toppled. He had furthered his education on his own ever since. He wore wire-rimmed glasses, spoke fluent English, wore neatly pressed oxford blue shirts, and had about him an air of eager, cheerful efficiency that won him increasing responsibility. He was also a pair of smart eyes and ears for the Habr Gidr, his clan.

Abdi had been hopeful about the UN when the humanitarian mission began. He'd found a job and the effort seemed good for his country. But when the attacks began on his clan and General Aidid, and every week there was a mounting toll of Somali dead and injured, he saw it as an unwarranted assault on his country. On July 12, the day of the Abdi House attack, he had seen victims of the bombing who were brought to the U.S. embassy compound. The Somali men, elders of his clan, were bloody and dazed and in need of a doctor. Instead the Americans photographed them and interrogated them and then put them in jail. Abdi kept his job but for a different reason.

He could hear waves of gunfire crackling over the city, and heard the fight was at the Bakara Market.

At Brown & Root, all Somali employees were sent home.

"Something has happened," Abdi was told.

Abdi lived with his family between the market and the K-4 traffic circle, which was just north of the Ranger base. The rickety jitneys, so crammed with passengers that the American soldiers called them "Kling-on Cruisers" (a nod to *Star Trek*), were still running up Via Lenin. The sounds of gunfire increased and the sky was thick with helicopters speeding low over the rooftops, flying great looping orbits over the market area. There were bullets snapping over his head when he got home. He found his father there with his two brothers and sister. They were in the courtyard of their home with their backs against a concrete wall, which was the place they always went when bullets flew.

It seemed to Abdi that there were a hundred helicopters in the sky. The shooting was continual and seemed to be directed everywhere. Aidid's militia would fight from hundreds of places in the densely populated neighborhood, not in any one place. So the fight raged in all directions. As bad as it was, Abdi found that he grew accustomed to the shooting after a while. It all seemed to be passing overhead anyway. After waiting an hour or so with his family against the wall, he grew restless and began moving around the house, looking out windows. Then he ventured outside.

Some of his neighbors said the Rangers had taken Aidid. Many people were running toward the fight. Abdi wanted to see for himself, so he joined the crowds moving that way. He had relatives who lived just a few blocks from the Olympic Hotel and he was eager for news of them. With all the bullets and blasts it was hard to believe anyone in the market area had not been hit.

When he got close to the shooting there was terrible confusion on the streets. There were dead people on the road, men, women, children. Abdi saw an American soldier up one alley, lying by the road, bleeding from the leg and trying to hide himself. When a woman ran out in front of Abdi, the American fired. The woman was hit but got off the street. Abdi ran around a corner just as one of the Little Birds zoomed down that alley. He pressed himself against a stone wall and saw bullets kick up in a line at the alley's center toward and then past him. Venturing out like this had been a bad idea. He could not have imagined such madness. After the helicopter passed, a group of Somali men with rifles ran to the corner, trying to find a better angle to shoot at the American.

Abdi ran then to the house of a friend. They let him in and he got on the floor with everyone else.

# 12

In the minutes before *Super Six One* was shot down, the Rangers and Delta operators back at the target house had been preparing to leave. It was taking longer than it should have. First, they had the wounded Ranger, Blackburn, who had fallen from a Black Hawk. Three Humvees had been separated from the ground convoy to return Blackburn to base—Sergeant Pilla had been killed on that ride. After those three vehicles departed, the convoy just sat.

All of the men had heard veterans talk about "the fog of war," which was shorthand for how even the best-laid plans went to hell fast once shooting started, but it was shocking nevertheless to see how hard it was to get even the simplest things done. Staff Sergeant Dan Schilling, the air force CCT in the convoy's lead Humvee, finally got fed up waiting and went looking for what was holding things up. It turned out the D-boys had been waiting with the prisoners for some signal from the convoy, while the convoy had been waiting for the D-boys to come out. Schilling ran back and forth a few times and finally got things moving.

Schilling was a laconic man from southern California, a lean, athletic former army reservist who, eight years earlier, had gambled his pay grade and rank to join the air force and see if he could get past the rigorous selection process for combat controllers. It was a quicker path into special ops than any the army offered, and it sounded like fun. CCTs specialized in dropping into dangerous places and directing pinpoint air strikes from the ground. Since this mission called for close coordination between forces on the ground and in the air, Schilling had been assigned to ride with the convoy commander, Lieutenant Colonel Danny McKnight. It was exactly the kind of adventure Schilling had sought. He was now thirty, a six-year veteran of special ops, and he was earning his danger pay today. He fidgeted while the flex-cuffed Somalis were packed into one of the flatbeds. The rest of the assault force had set off on foot for the crash site. The longer the convoy waited like this out on the street, the more vulnerable they were. Every minute of delay gave Aidid's militia and the armed mob time to amass. There was a noticeably steady increase in the volume of fire. From the outset they'd assumed a thirty-minute window. If they could get in and out in that time, they'd probably be okay. Schilling looked at his watch. They'd been on the ground now for thirty-seven minutes.

Then *Super Six One* went down and everything changed. They were ordered to move to the crash site, pronto.

There were already wounded men in nearly every vehicle. Thick smoke was in the air and there was the odor of gunpowder and flames, and up alleys and in the main road and before some of the buildings along Hawlwadig there were Somali bodies and parts of bodies. There were upended carts and burning riddled hulks of automobiles. One of the convoy's three flatbed five-ton trucks was hugely aflame. It had been hit and disabled by an RPG, and a thermite grenade had been ignited to completely destroy it. Big holes had been blasted in the whitewashed cinderblock walls of the Olympic Hotel and surrounding buildings. Trees had been leveled with gunfire. In the alleyways and at intersections the sandy soil had soaked up pools of blood and turned brown. The noise was deafening, but had increased gradually enough that the men had grown accustomed to it. A loud snap or the chip of nearby stone would signal alarm, but the mere sound of gunfire no longer stopped anyone. They moved cautiously but without fear in the din. McKnight seemed particularly heedless of the danger. He strode confidently across streets and up to men crouched behind cover as though nothing was out of the ordinary. Shortly he began waving Rangers into the vehicles.

—*This is Uniform Six Four* [McKnight]. *I am ready for exfil . . . I am loaded with everything I can get here and I am ready to move to the crash site, over.*

—*Roger, go ahead and move* [this from Lieutenant Colonel Gary Harrell, the Delta squadron commander in the C2 Black Hawk]. *The streets are fairly clear. We have been getting reports of sniper fire from the north of the crash site.*

—*Roger. We'll take a right out of here and we'll head down to the crash site to the east, over.*

It sounded simple enough. Two blocks north, three blocks east. The convoy started rolling, six Humvees and the two remaining flatbed trucks. There were three Humvees in front of the trucks and three behind them. The trucks had big fluorescent orange panels on top to help the surveillance birds track them. The helicopters would be their eyes in the sky, guiding them through the city.

They were driving into the bloodiest phase of the battle.

# 13

Black Hawk pilot Mike Durant had seen a Little Bird ascend from the crash site as he swung *Super Six Four* back south on its holding pattern. Straight ahead was the bright white front of the Olympic Hotel, one of the city's few tall buildings, which was across the street from the target building. In the far distance was the darkening green of the Indian Ocean. Smoke rose and drifted over the rooftops around the hotel, marking the fight. Black Hawks and Little Birds moved through the dark haze like predatory insects, darting and firing down into the fray.

Then he heard the expected radio call for *Super Six Eight,* the CSAR Black Hawk. He watched it swing away south.

His own summons from Lieutenant Colonel Matthews in the command bird came moments later.

—*Super Six Four, this is Alpha Five One, over.*

—*This is Super Six Four. Go ahead.*

—*Roger, Six Four, come up and join Six Two in his orbit.*

—*Six Four is inbound.*

Moving in fast and low over the city, Durant caught glimpses of the action beneath his chopper's chin bubble through the swirling clouds of smoke and dust. The neat box-structure they had outlined earlier, with Rangers positioned on all four corners of the target block, had completely broken down. It was hard to make sense of the action below. He could see the general area where Elvis's bird had gone in, a dense neighborhood of small stone houses with tin roofs in a crosshatch of dirt alleyways and wide cross streets, but the crashed Black Hawk was in such a tight spot between houses he couldn't spot it. He caught glimpses of small Ranger columns moving up the dusty alleys, crouched defensively, rifles up and ready, taking cover, exchanging fire with the swarms of Somalis who were also running in that direction. Durant flipped a switch in the cockpit to arm his crew chiefs' guns, two six-barreled 7.62 mm miniguns capable of firing four thousand rounds per minute, but warned them to hold fire until they figured out where all the friendlies were. Durant fell into Elvis's vacant place in a circular pattern opposite *Super Six Two,* the Black Hawk piloted by Chief Warrant Officer Mike Goffena and Captain Jim Yacone, and began trying to get in sync with them.

—*Six Four, say location,* Goffena asked.

—*We are about a mile and a half to your north.*

—*Six Four, keep a good eye on the west side.*

—*Roger.*

The idea was to maintain a "low cap," a sweeping circle over the battle area. On the radio Durant heard that the CSAR bird had been hit, but had managed to rope in the rescue team and was still flying. On the radio Goffena and Yacone were already pointing out targets for Durant's gunners, but it was hard to get visually oriented. Durant's seat was on the right side of the airframe, and he was flying counterclockwise, banking left, so mostly he was seeing sky. It was maddening. When he leveled off, he was flying so low and fast that the view down through the chin bubble was like peering down through a tube. Flashing fast beneath his feet were rusty tin roofs, trees, burning cars and tires. There were Rangers and darting Somalis everywhere. He couldn't tell if he was being shot at. What with the roar of his engines and the radio din Durant could never tell for sure if he was being shot at. He assumed he was. Two birds had been hit already. He was doing all this and listening and also varying his airspeed and altitude, trying to make his Black Hawk a more challenging target.

It was on his fourth or fifth circle, just as things were starting to make sense below, that he felt his chopper hit something hard.

Like an invisible speed bump.

# 14

After they had delivered Private Blackburn, the Ranger who had fallen from the helicopter, to the small rescue column that would return him to base, Sergeants Jeff McLaughlin and Casey Joyce had set off north on Hawlwadig to rejoin their element, Chalk Four. They hadn't gotten far. They were distracted by a gunman down an alley who would pop out to shoot and then duck back before they could return fire. McLaughlin covered the alley so Joyce could scamper across. Then they both got down on one knee at opposite sides of it waiting to nail this guy. From a distance, all the Somali fighters looked the same, skinny black guys with dusty bushes of hair, long baggy pants, and loose, oversized shirts. While most of them would wildly spray bullets and then run, some were fiercely persistent. Occasionally one would run right out into the open, blazing away, and invariably be mowed down. This one was smart. He would lean out just long enough to take aim and shoot, then duck back behind the corner. McLaughlin tried to anticipate him. The shooter's head would appear, the sergeant would squeeze off a well-aimed round, and the man would duck away again.

McLaughlin was determined to get him. He stayed down on one knee around a corner trying to hold his M-16 perfectly steady, drawing a bead on the spot down the alley where the shooter would briefly appear. Sweat stung the sergeant's eyes. He grew so absorbed in this fruitless duel that he lost track of time and place and was startled when a platoon sergeant yelled his name.

"Hey, Mac! Come on!"

The convoy was moving on the street behind him, rolling north on Hawlwadig. Everybody seemed to be on it except him. He looked over for Joyce and he was gone, too. He had already climbed into a vehicle. McLaughlin crossed the road and trotted along on the far side of one Humvee, past the contested alley. The Humvee was full.

"Jump on the hood!" shouted one of the men inside.

McLaughlin got one long leg up before it occurred to him that this was a bad idea. Vehicles were bullet magnets. He pictured himself threading through this deadly madness spread-eagled on top of a Humvee. It was bad enough to be in one of these streets, and quite another to be a six-five Ranger bull's-eye mounted on top. He ran around the vehicle and opened the door and insisted that Private Tory Carlson shove over. Carlson did, and McLaughlin crawled on the seat and set his M-16 on the rim of the open right rear window.

About a hundred yards farther up, the convoy came upon the remainder of Sergeant Eversmann's beleaguered Chalk Four. Eversmann and his men had been pinned down ever since Blackburn fell from the chopper. They had seen the helicopter crash. When he pulled himself up to his considerable height, Eversmann could see the wreckage of *Super Six One* from one of the angled alleys leading east. Captain Steele had radioed with orders for the sergeant to move his chalk down to it on foot.

"Roger," Eversmann had said . . . meaning, like, *yeah, right.* There was little chance of their moving anywhere. In the distance he could already see men in helmets and flak vests and desert uniforms around the wreckage, so he knew Americans had gotten there. They were near enough for him to instruct his men to hold their fire in that direction. He was down to only about four or five men who could still fight.

The convoy arrived like an answer to his liftoff Hail Mary. Eversmann saw his friend Sergeant Mike Pringle in the turret of McKnight's lead Humvee, working the .50 cal hard with his head down so far he was actually peering out *under* the gun. It brought a smile to Eversmann's face in spite of everything.

"Hey, Sergeant, get in! We're driving to the crash site," shouted McKnight.

"Captain Steele wants us to move over on foot; it's right down there," said Eversmann, pointing.

"I know," said McKnight. "Get in. We're driving over."

Schilling provided covering fire up Hawlwadig as Eversmann and his men moved across the road. The chalk leader herded his men aboard the crowded vehicles, loading the wounded first, literally piling them in the back on top of other guys, then finding room for the others. He was the last man standing on the street as McKnight shouted for him to hurry up. Eversmann checked off the list of names in his head, determined to account for every man in his chalk. He'd lost track of McLaughlin and Joyce and the medics he'd sent off with Blackburn, but they were not at his intersection or anywhere down the block. The column was rolling again. There was nothing for him to do but leap on the back of one. He landed on somebody, and found himself flat on his back looking up at the sky, moving through the streets with Somalis still shooting at them, realizing what a terrific target he was and that he couldn't even return fire. *I'm going to get shot and there isn't a damn thing I can do about it.* As helpless as he felt, he was relieved to be back with the others and moving. If they were together and rolling it meant the end was near. The crash site was just blocks away. Then he would position himself better for the ride out.

While Eversmann had been loading his men, Schilling ran out to the middle of the road to gather up Chalk Four's two fast ropes, which were still stretched across Hawlwadig. The task force had been drilled to recover the three-inch-thick ropes, which were hard to replace. Despite the gunfire, he fetched one. It was hard work hauling it back and he was already sweaty and dirty and tired, so Schilling asked John Gay, a SEAL in the Humvee behind his, if he'd help him with the other. Gay was crouched behind cover returning fire. He gave Schilling a shocked stare and then rolled his eyes.

"Forget the fucking ropes!" he shouted.

It dawned on Schilling that he'd just risked his life for a long strand of braided nylon. He got back into the Humvee wondering at himself. As the convoy started up again, the gunfire was heavier than ever. Rounds pinged off the armored sides of the vehicles, and every few minutes the wobbly smoke trail of an RPG would zip past. Schilling spotted a donkey tied to an olive tree in an alleyway. The animal stood perfectly still in the maelstrom, clearly distressed, long ears folded back and tail pointing straight down. He'd seen the donkey when they first pulled up and assumed it would eventually be hit. As they pulled away he caught another glimpse of it, still standing stock still, unscathed.

Nobody in the rear vehicles knew where they were going. Many of the men didn't know that a helicopter had been shot down. One who did not was Eric Spalding, the Ranger who had designed the successful rat trap back in the hangar. Spalding was in the passenger seat in the cab of the second truck, the one with the prisoners. He assumed when they began moving, that was it. The mission was over. They were on their way home. Driving was Specialist John Maddox. They had the front windshield flipped up and out so Spalding could shoot forward.

He leaned his M-16 out the truck window. Although an expert marksman, he was no longer just squeezing off one careful round after the next. There were too many targets, too many people shooting at him. It was as if "Kill-an-American Day" had been declared in Mog. It seemed like every man, woman, and child in the city was out trying to get them. There were people in alleyways, in windows, on rooftops. Spalding kept shooting his rifle dry. Then he would shoot with his 9 mm Beretta pistol with one hand while he replaced the rifle magazine with the other. He just wanted to get the hell out of there. When the column took a turn to the right, he wondered what was up. *The mission is over. Why aren't we going back?* There wasn't enough time to find somebody to ask.

After going two blocks east, the convoy made another right turn. They'd lost track of the men moving to the crash site on foot. Now the convoy was bearing south, heading toward the back end of the target house and toward National Street, the paved road they'd come in on. At least Spalding thought that was where they were headed. Most of the streets in Mogadishu looked the same, rutted orange sand with big gouges in the middle and treacherous mounds of debris, shabbily mortared stone walls on both sides, stubby olive trees and cactus bushes and crisscrossing dirt alleys. The intersections were the problem. Every time the truck approached an alley Spalding would lie out across the warm hood and just open up as they rolled through. He could hear nothing but the sound of automatic weapons fire and bullets snapping around him and pinging off the truck.

A woman in a flowing purple robe darted past on the driver's side of the truck. Maddox had his pistol resting on his left arm, pretty much shooting at whatever moved.

"Don't shoot," Spalding shouted. "She's got a kid!"

The woman abruptly turned. Holding the baby in one arm, she raised a pistol with her free hand. Spalding shot her where she stood. He shot four more rounds into her before she fell. He hoped he hadn't hit the baby. They were moving and he couldn't see if he had or not. He thought he probably had. She had been carrying the baby on her arm right in front.

*Why would a mother do something like that with a kid on her arm? What was she thinking?* Spalding couldn't get over it. Maybe she was just trying to get away, saw the truck, panicked, and raised the gun.

There wasn't time to fret over it.

# 15

Black Hawk pilot Mike Goffena was coming up behind Mike Durant's *Super Six Four* when the grenade hit. It blew a chunk off the tail rotor. Goffena saw all the oil dump out of it in a fine mist, but the mechanism stayed intact and everything seemed to still be functioning.

—*Six Four, are you okay?* Goffena asked.

The Black Hawk is a heavy aircraft. Durant's weighed about sixteen thousand pounds at that point, and the tail rotor was a long way from where he sat. The question came before he had even figured out what happened. Goffena explained that he had been hit by an RPG and that there was damage to the tail area.

"Roger," Durant radioed back, coolly.

Nothing felt abnormal about the bird at first. He did a quick check of all his instruments and the readings were all okay. His crew chiefs, Cleveland and Field, were unhurt in the back. So after the initial shock, Durant felt relief. Everything was fine. Goffena told him he had lost his oil and part of the gearbox on the tail rotor, but the sturdy Black Hawk was built to run without oil for a time if necessary, and it was still holding steady. Matthews, the air mission commander, had also seen the hit from his seat in the orbiting C2 bird. He told Durant to put the Black Hawk on the ground, so the pilot of the stricken chopper pulled out of his left-turning orbit and pointed back to the airfield, about a four-minute flight southwest. Durant could see the base off in the distance against the coastline. He noted, just to be safe, that there was a big green open area about halfway there, so if he had to land sooner he had a place to put it. But the bird was flying fine.

Goffena followed Durant for about a mile, to a point where he felt confident *Super Six Four* would make it back. He had just started to turn around when Durant's tail rotor, the whole thing, the gearbox and two or three feet of the vertical fin assembly, just turned into a blur and evaporated.

Inside *Super Six Four*, Durant and copilot Ray Frank felt the airframe begin to vibrate. They heard the accelerating high-speed whine of the dry gear shaft in its death throes. Then came a very loud bang as it blew apart. With the top half of the tail fin gone, a big weight was suddenly dropped off the airframe's back end. Its center of gravity pitched violently forward, and the bird began to spin. After a decade of flying, both Durant's and Frank's reactions were instinctive. To make the airframe swing left meant pushing gently on the left foot pedal. Durant now noticed he had already jammed his left pedal all the way to the floor and his craft was still spinning rapidly to the right—with no tail rotor there was no way to stop it. The spin was faster than Durant ever imagined it could be. Details of earth and sky blurred like patterns on a spinning top. Out the windshield he saw just blue sky and brown earth.

Durant tried to do something with the flight controls. Frank, in the seat next to him, had the presence of mind to do exactly the right thing. The power control levers for the engines were on the ceiling of the cockpit. Frank had to fight the spin's strong centrifugal force to raise his arms. In those frantic seconds he somehow managed to pull one lever back, shutting off one engine, and to pull the other one halfway back. Durant shouted into his radio.

—*Going in hard! Going down! Raaaay!*

The plummeting helicopter's spin rate suddenly slowed. Just before impact its nose pulled up. Whether for some aerodynamic reason or something Durant or Frank did inside the cockpit, the falling chopper leveled off. With the spin rate down to half what it had been, and with the craft fairly level, the Black Hawk made a hard, but flat landing.

Flat was critical. It meant there was a chance the men in the helicopter were still alive.

# 16

Yousuf Dahir Mo'alim was near the man who fired the grenade. Mo'alim was behind a tree in an alley that went behind the Bar Bakin Hotel, a smaller white stone building that was one block south of the Olympic Hotel. He ducked behind the tree to hide from the Black Hawk overhead. As he did one of his men, part of a group of twenty-six militia who had come running from the neighboring village of Hawlwadigli, dropped to one knee in the middle of the alley and pointed up his Russian antitank weapon. The tube had been fitted with a metal funnel, which was welded on the back end at an angle to direct the back blast away from the shooter's body.

"If you miss, I've got another round!" Mo'alim shouted.

They were veteran fighters, guns for hire, mostly, although everybody was now fighting the Americans for free. Mo'alim's father had died in 1984 in fighting between Somalia and Ethiopia, and at age fifteen the son was recruited to take his place. He was a skeletal young man, lost in oversized shirt and pants, with deep hollow cheeks and a goatee that filled out his narrow chin. He had fought for two years as one of Siad Barre's soldiers, but as the tide of that insurrection changed, he had slipped away from his unit to join Aidid's rebel troops. He was a veteran of many street fights, but none as fierce as this.

He had organized the men in his village, a labyrinth of twisting cactus-lined dirt paths around rag huts and tin-roofed shanties just south of the Bakara Market area, into an irregular militia for hire. They remained primarily allied to Aidid, because they belonged, as he did, to the Habr Gidr clan. Mainly they defended their village from other marauding bands of young fighters. They provided security for anybody willing to pay, including, at times, the UN and other international organizations. Occasionally they went looking for loot themselves. Men like Mo'alim and his crew were called *mooryan*, or bandits. They lived by the gun, mostly M-16s and the Russian AK-47s that could be bought at the market for a million Somali shillings, or about two hundred dollars. They also carried antitank weapons, everything from World War II–era bazookas to the more reliable and accurate Russian-made RPGs. They took payment for their services in rice or *khat*. The drug took its toll. Another word for the *mooryan* was *dai-dai*, or "quick-quick," for their jumpy ways and nervous tics. They were fearless fighters, and they often died young. But these days all the *mooryan* in southern Mogadishu had a common enemy. Some had begun calling themselves, in a play on the word "Rangers," Revengers.

They knew the best way to hurt the Americans was to shoot down a helicopter. The helicopters were a symbol of UN power and Somali helplessness. When the Rangers arrived they had seemed invincible. The Black Hawks and Little Birds were all but invulnerable to the small arms that made up most of the Somali arsenal. They were designed to punish with impunity from a distance. The Rangers, when they came, descended from helicopters quickly, grabbed their captives, and were gone before a significant force could be formed to fight them. When they traveled on the ground, it was in armed convoys that moved fast. But every enemy advertises his weakness in the way he fights. To Aidid's fighters, the Rangers' weakness was apparent. They were not willing to die.

Somalis were famous for braving enemy fire, for almost suicidal, frontal assaults. They were brought up in clans and named for their fathers and grandfathers. They entered a fight with cunning and courage and gave themselves over to the savage emotion of it. Retreat, even before overwhelming enemy fire, was considered unmanly. For the clan, they were always ready to die.

To kill Rangers, you had to make them stand and fight. The answer was to bring down a helicopter. Part of the Americans' false superiority, their unwillingness to die, meant they would do anything to protect each other, things that were courageous but also sometimes foolhardy. Aidid and his lieutenants knew that if they could bring down a chopper, the Rangers would move to protect its crew. They would establish a perimeter and wait for help. They would probably not be overrun, but they could be made to bleed and die.

Aidid's men received some expert guidance in shooting down helicopters from fundamentalist Islamic soldiers, smuggled in from Sudan, who had experience fighting Russian helicopters in Afghanistan. In the effort they had resolved to focus their entire arsenal of RPGs, the most powerful weaponry left Aidid after the summer's air attacks on his tanks and big guns. This was problematic. The grenades burst on impact, but it was hard to hit a moving target with one, so the detonators on many were replaced with timing devices to make them explode in midair. That way they wouldn't need a direct hit to cripple a chopper. Their fundamentalist advisers taught them that the helicopter's tail rotor was its most vulnerable spot. So they learned to wait until it passed over, and to shoot up at it from behind. It was awkward and dangerous to point the tubes at the sky, and suicidal to aim from rooftops. The helicopters spotted an armed man on a rooftop quickly, usually before he had a chance to aim his weapon and fire. So Aidid's fighters devised methods to safely shoot up from the ground. They dug deep holes in the dirt streets. The shooter would lie supine with the back of the tube pointed down into the hole. Sometimes he would cut down a small tree and lean it into the hole, then cover himself with a green robe so he could lie under the tree waiting for one to fly over.

They hit their first Black Hawk in the dark early morning of September 25, but it wasn't part of a Ranger mission. The success heartened them. The next time the Rangers came out in force, they would be ready. They would only have to hit one.

When Mo'alim heard the helicopters come in low on October 3 he grabbed his M-16 and rounded up his gang. They ran north, fanning out into groups of seven or eight up past National Street and around behind the Olympic Hotel, moving through neighborhoods they knew well. The sky was infested with helicopters. Mo'alim's smaller groups tried to stay together in the crowds of people moving that way. Surrounded by unarmed civilians, they knew the Americans would be less likely to shoot at them even if they were spotted. They wore sheets and towels thrown over their shoulders to cover their weapons and carried their automatic rifles stiffly at their sides. They were one of many militia gangs moving quickly to the fight.

Mo'alim's group first encountered Rangers at an intersection in a Humvee just south of the hotel on Hawlwadig Road. As they crept up and fired on the Americans, a helicopter appeared and opened fire, killing the eldest of Mo'alim's squad, a portly middle-aged man they called "Alcohol." Mo'alim dragged Alcohol's limp body off the street, and his squad regrouped a block further south, behind the Bar Bakin Hotel.

It was there that they watched the first helicopter go down. The men cheered wildly. They continued moving and shooting, staying about two blocks away from the Rangers. They were still south of the target building when one of Mo'alim's group knelt in the road, took aim at another Black Hawk, and fired. The grenade hit the rear rotor and big chunks of it flew off in the explosion. And then, for a few instants, nothing happened.

It seemed to Mo'alim that the helicopter crashed very slowly. It flew on for a while like it had not been damaged, and then abruptly tilted forward and started to spin. It fell in Wadigley, a crowded neighborhood just south of his own. The crash brought cries of exaltation from the crowd. All around him Mo'alim saw people reverse direction. Moments before, the crowd and the fighters had been moving north, toward the Olympic Hotel and to where the first Black Hawk had crashed. Now everyone around him was racing south. He ran with them, back through his own neighborhood of Hawlwadigli, a goateed veteran soldier waving his weapon and shouting: "Turn back! Stop! There are still men inside who can shoot!"

Some listened to him and fell in behind Mo'alim and his men. Others ran on ahead. Ali Hussein, who managed a pharmacy near where the helicopter crashed, saw many of his neighbors grab guns and run toward it. He caught hold of the arm of his friend Ali Mohamed Cawale, who owned the Black Sea restaurant. Cawale had a rifle. Hussein grabbed him by both shoulders.

"It's dangerous. Don't go!" he shouted at him.

But the smell of blood was in the air. Cawale wrestled away from Hussein and joined the running crowd.

# 17

In ordinary circumstances, as close to the first crash as they were, the convoy would have just barreled over to it, running over and shooting through anything in its path. But with all the help overhead, Task Force Ranger was about to demonstrate how too much information can hurt soldiers on a battlefield.

High in the C2 Black Hawk, Harrell and Matthews could see one group of about fifteen gunmen racing along streets that paralleled the eight-vehicle convoy. The running Somalis could keep pace with the vehicles because the trucks and Humvees stacked up at every intersection. Each driver waited until the vehicle in front completely cleared the cross fire before sprinting through it himself. To get stuck in the open was suicidal. Every time the convoy stalled, it gave the bands of shooters time to reach the next street and set up an ambush for each vehicle as it gunned through. The convoy was getting riddled. From above, Harrell and Matthews could see roadblocks and places where Somalis had massed to ambush. So they steered the convoy away from those places.

There was an added complication. Flying about a thousand feet over the C2 helicopter was the navy Orion spy plane, which had surveillance cameras that gave them a clear picture of the convoy's predicament. But the Orion pilots were handicapped. They were not allowed to communicate directly with the convoy. Their directions were relayed to the commander at the JOC, who would then radio Harrell in the command bird.

Only then was the plane's advice relayed down to the convoy. This built in a maddening delay. The Orion pilots would see a direct line to the crash site. They'd say, "Turn left!" But by the time that instruction reached McKnight in the lead Humvee, he had passed the turn. Heeding the belated direction, they'd then turn down the wrong street. High above the fight, commanders watching out their windows or on screens couldn't hear the gunfire and screaming of wounded men, or feel the impact of the explosions. From above, the convoy's progress seemed orderly. The visual image didn't always convey how desperate the situation really was.

Eversmann, still lying helplessly on his back toward the rear of the column, had felt the vehicle turn right after leaving his blocking position, which he expected. He knew the crash site was just a few blocks that way. But when the Humvee made the second right-hand turn, it surprised him. Why were they headed south? It was easy to get lost in Mog. The streets weren't laid out like some urban planner's neat grid. Roads you thought were taking you one place would suddenly slant off in a different direction. There were more turns. Soon, the crash site that had been close enough for Eversmann to see from his spot on Hawlwadig Road was lost somewhere back in the hornets' nest.

The convoy was bearing south when Durant's helicopter crashed. Up in the lead Humvee, McKnight got the word on the radio from Lieutenant Colonel Harrell.

—*Danny, we just had another Hawk go down to RPG fire south of the Olympic Hotel. We need you to get everybody in that first crash site. Need QRF to give us some help, over.*

—*This is Uniform. Understand. Aircraft down south of Olympic Hotel. Recon and see what we can do after that.*

—*We are going to try to get the QRF to give us some help. Try to get everyone off that crash site* [Super Six One] *and let's get out of here down to the other Hawk and secure it, over.*

It wasn't going to be easy. McKnight was supposed to take this convoy, with the prisoners and the wounded, move to the first crash site, and link up with the bulk of the force there. There was not enough room on the packed Humvees and trucks for the men he already had. Yet the immediate plan called for the convoy to load everyone and proceed south to the second crash site, covering the same treacherous ground they were rolling through now. They pushed on.

Heavy fire and mounting casualties took their toll on the men in the vehicles. Some of the slightly wounded men in Eversmann's vehicle seemed to be in varying degrees of paralysis, as if their role in the mission had ended. Others were moaning and crying with pain. They were still a long way from the base.

The state of things infuriated Sergeant Matt Rierson, leader of the Delta team that had taken the prisoners. Rierson's team was with the prisoners on the second truck. Rierson didn't know where the convoy was going. It was standard operating procedure for every vehicle in a convoy to know its destination. That way, if the lead vehicle got hit, or took a wrong turn, the whole convoy could continue. But McKnight, a lieutenant colonel more used to commanding a battalion than a line of vehicles, hadn't told anyone! Rierson watched as inexperienced Ranger Humvee drivers would stop after crossing an intersection, trapping the vehicles behind them in the cross fire. Whenever the convoy stopped, Rierson would hop down and move from vehicle to vehicle, trying to square things away.

As they passed back behind the target house, an RPG scored a direct hit on the third Humvee in the column, the one McLaughlin had squeezed into. Private Carlson, who had moved over to make room for the sergeant, heard the pop of a grenade being launched nearby. Then came a blinding flash and ear-shattering *BOOM!* The inside of the Humvee filled with black smoke. The goggles Carlson had pinned to the top of his helmet were blown off.

The grenade had cut straight through the steel skin of the vehicle in front of the gas cap and gone off inside, blowing the three men in back right out to the street. It tore the hand guards off McLaughlin's weapon and pierced his left forearm with a chunk of shrapnel. He felt no pain, just some numbness in his hand. He told himself to wait until the smoke cleared to check it out. The shrapnel had fractured a bone in his forearm, severed a tendon, and broken a bone in his hand. It wasn't bleeding much and he could still shoot.

Holding his breath in the dark cloud, his ears ringing, Carlson felt himself for wet spots. His left arm was bloody. Shrapnel had pierced it in several places. His boots were on fire. A drum of .50 cal ammo had been hit, and he heard people screaming for him to kick it out, *kick it out!* which he did, then stooped to pat out the flames on his feet.

Two of the three men blown out the back were severely injured. One, Delta Master Sergeant Tim "Griz" Martin, had absorbed the brunt of the blast. The grenade had poked a football-sized hole right through the skin of the Humvee, blew on through the sandbags, through Martin, and penetrated the ammo can. It had blown off the lower half of Martin's body. The explosion also tore off the back end of one of Private Adalberto Rodriguez's thighs. Rodriguez had tumbled about ten yards before coming to rest. His legs were a mass of blood and gore. He began struggling to his feet, only to see one of the five-ton trucks bearing straight for him. Its driver, Private Maddox, momentarily disoriented by another grenade blast, rolled the truck right over him.

The convoy stopped and soldiers scrambled to pick up the wounded. Medics did what they could for Rodriguez and Martin, who both looked mortally wounded. The wounded were lifted back into the vehicles, while Rangers spilled out to cover the surrounding streets and alleys. At one, Specialist Aaron Hand and Sergeant Casey Joyce became engaged in a furious firefight. They were positioned at opposite sides of an alley. From just outside his truck, Spalding watched rounds shatter the wall over Hand's head.

Hand was shooting down the alley, too preoccupied to notice that shots were now coming at him from a different angle. Spalding screamed for Hand to get back to the vehicles, but there was too much noise for him to be heard. From where Spalding stood, it looked like Hand was going to be shot for sure. He was doing everything wrong. He was fighting bravely, but he had not sought cover and he was changing magazines with his back exposed. Spalding knew he should go help cover him and pull him back, but that meant crossing the alley where all the lead was flying. He hesitated. *Hell no, I'm not going to cross that alley.* As he debated with himself, SEAL John Gay ran out to help. Gay was still limping from where his knife had deflected an AK-47 round at his hip. He put several rounds up the alley and herded Hand back to the convoy.

Across the alley, Joyce was on one knee facing north, doing things right. He had found cover and was returning disciplined fire, just the way he'd been taught, when a gun barrel poked from a window above and behind him and let off a quick burst. Carlson saw it happen. There wasn't even time to shout a warning, even if Joyce had been able to hear him.

There was just a *blaaaap!* and a spurt of fire from the barrel and the sergeant went straight down in the dirt on his face.

One of the .50 cals promptly blasted gaping holes in the wall around the window where the gun had appeared, and Sergeant Jim Telscher, ignoring the heavy fire, sprinted out to Joyce, grabbed him by the shirt and vest, and, without even slowing down, dragged him back to the column.

Joyce's skin was already gray and his eyes were open wide and rolled back so you could only see the whites. He had been hit in the upper back where the Rangers' new Kevlar flak vests had no protective plate. The round had pierced his heart and passed through his torso, exiting and lodging in the vest's frontispiece, which did have an armored plate. They loaded him in on the back of Gay's Humvee, where a Delta medic went to work on him frantically, holding an IV bag up high with one hand, despairing, "We've got to get him back in a hurry! We've got to get him back in a hurry or he's gonna die!"

The convoy lurched forward again, turning left (bearing east) and then left again, so they were now heading back toward the north. They were moving up a road one block west of the crash site. To get there, all they had to do was drive two blocks north and turn right. But the gunfire was relentless. Up in the lead Humvee, Lieutenant Colonel McKnight was hit. Shrapnel cut into his right arm and the left side of his neck.

At the rear of the convoy, Sergeant Lorenzo Ruiz, the tough little boxer from El Paso who had taken over Private Clay Othic's .50-caliber machine gun after Othic had been hit in the arm, slumped and slid down limp into the laps of the men inside the Humvee.

"He got shot! He got shot!" shouted the driver, who raced the Humvee frantically up the column with the .50 cal just spinning in the empty turret.

"Get the fifty up!" screamed one of the sergeants. "Get the fifty up ASAP!"

Packed in the way they were, with Ruiz now slumped in on top of them, no one could climb into the turret from inside, so Specialist Dave Ritchie got out and jumped up on the turret from the outside. He couldn't lower himself into it because Ruiz's limp body was blocking it, so he leaned in from the outside as they began moving again, swiveling and shooting the big gun, hanging on to avoid being thrown to the street.

Inside, they pulled Ruiz down to let Ritchie get behind the gun. Staff Sergeant John Burns tore off the wounded man's vest and shirt.

"I'm hit! I'm hit!" Ruiz gasped and then began to cough up blood.

Burns found an entrance wound under Ruiz's right arm, but couldn't locate an exit wound. They propped him against a radio and a Delta medic went to work. Ruiz was in shock. Like many of the men in the vehicles, he had taken the ceramic plate out of his flak vest.

Up in a Humvee turret behind a Mark-19, a machine gun–like grenade launcher, Corporal Jim Cavaco was pumping one 40 mm round after another into the windows of a building from which they were taking fire. Cavaco was dropping grenades neatly into the second-story windows one after another—*Bang!* . . . *Bang!* . . . *Bang!* . . . *Bang!*

From his seat in the second truck, Spalding shouted, "Yeah! Get 'em, Vaco!" and then saw his friend slump forward. Cavaco had been hit by a round in the back of his head and killed instantly. The convoy stopped again, and Spalding leapt out to help pull Cavaco out of the turret. They carried him to the back of Spalding's truck and swung his body in. It landed on the legs of an injured Ranger who shrieked with pain.

The volume of fire was terrifying. Yet Somalis seemed to be darting across streets everywhere. Up in the lead Humvee, Schilling watched the runners with bewilderment. *Why would anybody be running around on the streets with all this lead flying?* He found that by rolling grenades down the alley it kept the shooters from sticking their weapons out. He tried to conserve ammo by shooting only at the Somalis who were closest. When he ran out of ammo, a wounded Ranger in back fed Schilling magazines from his own pouches.

# 18

Over the radio came a hopeful inquiry from the command helicopter, which didn't seem to understand how desperate the convoy's plight had become.

—*Uniform Six Four, you got everybody out of the crash site, over?*

—*We have no positive contact with them yet,* McKnight answered. *We took a lot of rounds as we were clearing out of the area. Quite a few wounded, including me, over.*

—*Roger, want you to try to go to the first crash site and consolidate on that. Once we get everybody out of there we'll go to the second crash site and try to do an exfil, over.*

This was, of course, out of the question, but McKnight wasn't giving up.

—*Roger, understand. Can you give me some . . . we just need a direction and distance from where I'm at, over.*

There was no answer at first. The radio net was filled with calls related to Durant's crash. When he did hear from his commanders again, McKnight was asked to report the number of Rangers he had picked up from Eversmann's Chalk Four. He ignored that request.

—*Romeo Six Four* [Harrell], *this is Uniform Six Four. From the crash site, where am I now? How far over?*

—*Standby. Have good visual on you now. . . . Danny, are you still on that main hardball* [paved road]*?*

—*I'm on the exfil road. Down toward National.*

Harrell apparently misunderstood. He gave McKnight directions as if he were still on Hawlwadig Road, out in front of the target house.

—*Turn east. Go about three blocks east and two blocks north. They're popping smoke, over.*

—*Understand. From my location I have to go east further about three blocks and then head north, over.*

—*Roger, that's from the hardball road the Olympic Hotel is on, over.*

But McKnight was already three blocks east of that road.

—*I'm at the hardball road east of the Olympic Hotel. Do I just need to turn around on it and head north?*

—*Negative. They are about three blocks east, one block north of building one* [the target building], *over.*

# 19

In the convoy's second-to-last Humvee, where Ruiz was fighting for his life, Sergeant Burns couldn't get through to McKnight on the radio so he took off on foot. He feared if they didn't get Ruiz back to base immediately the young Texan was going to die. Burns noticed that the gunfire that had hurt his ears initially now sounded muffled, distant. His ears had adjusted to it. As he neared the front of the line he saw Joyce stretched out bloody and pale, with a medic working over him furiously on the back of a crowded Humvee. He was about to reach the front when a D-boy grabbed him.

"You've been hit," the Delta operator said.

"No I haven't."

Burns hadn't felt a thing. The D-boy slid his hand inside Burns's vest at his right shoulder and the sergeant felt a vicious stab of pain.

"Having trouble breathing?" the D-boy asked.

"No."

"Any tightness in your chest?"

"I feel all right," Burns said. "I didn't even know I was hit."

"You keep an eye on it," the D-boy said.

Burns made it up to McKnight, who was also bloody, and busy on the radio. So Burns told Sergeant Bob Gallagher about Ruiz. Burns thought they should allow a Humvee or two to speed right back to the base with Ruiz, as they had done earlier with Blackburn. But Gallagher knew the convoy could not afford to lose any more vehicles and firepower now. They still had roughly a hundred men waiting for them around the first crash site, then there was the second crash site. . . . Gallagher was already kicking himself for sending those three vehicles back with Blackburn. While he knew this might be a death sentence for Ruiz, he told Burns there was no way anybody was leaving.

"We have to move to the crash site and consolidate forces," he said.

Disgusted, Burns began to make his way back down the column to his vehicle. He had only gone a few steps when the convoy started rolling again. He jumped on the back of a Humvee. It was already jammed. The rear of the vehicle was slick and sticky with blood. Moaning rose from the pile of Rangers. Beside him, Joyce looked dead, even though a medic was still working on him. Sergeant Galentine was screaming, "My thumb's shot off! My thumb's shot off!" Burns did not want to be on that Humvee.


They were still pointed north. Some of the men were at the breaking point. In the same Humvee with Burns, Private Jason Moore saw some of his Ranger buddies just burying their heads behind the sandbags. Some of the unit's most boisterous chest-beaters were among them. A burly kid from Princeton, New Jersey, Moore had a dip of snuff stuffed under his lower lip and brown spittle on his unshaved chin. He was sweating and terrified. One RPG had passed over the vehicle and exploded with an ear-smarting crack against a wall alongside. Bullets were snapping around him. He fought the urge to lie down. *Either way I'm going to get shot.*

Moore figured if he stayed up and kept on shooting, at least he'd get shot trying to save himself and the guys. It was a defining moment for him, a point of clarity in the midst of chaos. He would go down fighting. He would not consider lying down again.

Not long after he saw Joyce shot, which really shook him up, Private Carlson felt a sudden blow and sharp pain in his right knee. It felt like someone had taken a knife and held it to his knee and then driven it in with a sledgehammer. He glanced down to see blood rapidly staining his pants. He said a prayer and kept shooting. He had been wildly scared for longer than he had ever felt that way in his life, and now he thought he might literally die of fright. His heart banged in his chest and he found it hard to breathe. His head was filled with the sounds of shooting and explosions and visions of his friends, one by one, going down, and blood splashed everywhere oily and sticky with its dank, coppery smell and he figured, *This is it for me.* And then, in that moment of maximum terror, he felt it all abruptly, inexplicably fall away. One second he was paralyzed with fear and pain and the next . . . he had stopped caring about himself.

He would think about this a lot later, and the best he could explain it was, his own life no longer mattered. All that did matter were his buddies, his brothers, that *they* not get hurt, that *they* not get killed. These men around him, some of whom he had only known for months, were more important to him than life itself. It was like when Telscher ran out on the road to pull Joyce back in. Carlson understood that now, and it was heroic, but it also *wasn't* heroic. At a certain level he knew Telscher had made no choice, just as he was not choosing to be unafraid. It had just happened to him, like he had passed through some barrier. He *had* to keep fighting, because the other guys needed him.

In the second of the three Humvees behind the trucks, Private Ed Kallman sat behind the wheel amazed and alarmed by what he was seeing. He saw a line of trees on the sidewalk up ahead begin to explode, one after the other, as if someone had placed charges in each and was detonating them at about five-second intervals. Either that or somebody with a big gun was systematically taking out the trees, each about two stories high, thinking that they might be hiding snipers. He found it strange, anyway, the blasts walking their way toward him splintering the trees one by one.

Kallman, who had felt such a rush of excitement an hour earlier as he encountered battle for the first time, now felt nothing but nauseating dread. So far neither he nor anyone in his vehicle had been hit, but it seemed like just a matter of time. He watched with horror as the convoy disintegrated before him. He was a soldier for the most powerful nation on earth. If they were having this much trouble, shouldn't somebody have stepped in? Where was a stronger show of force? Somehow it didn't seem right that they could be reduced to this, battling on these narrow dirt streets, bleeding, dying! This wasn't supposed to happen. He saw men he knew and liked and respected bellowing in pain on the street with gunshot wounds that exposed great crimson flaps of glistening muscle, men wandering in the smoke bleeding, dazed and seemingly unconscious, their clothing torn off. American soldiers. Those who were not injured were covered with the blood of others. Kallman was young and new to the unit. If these more-veteran soldiers were all getting hit, sooner or later he was going to get hit. Oddly, the surprise he felt overshadowed the fear. He kept telling himself, *This is not supposed to happen!*

And Kallman's turn did come. As he slowed down before another intersection he looked out the open window to his left and saw a smoke trail coming straight at him. It all happened in a second. He knew it was an RPG and he knew it was going to hit him. Then it did. He awoke lying on his right side on the front seat with his ears ringing. He opened his eyes and was looking directly at the radio mounted under the dash. He sat up and floored the accelerator. Up ahead he saw the convoy making a left turn and he raced to catch them.

Later, when he'd had a chance to inspect his Humvee, he saw that the RPG had hit his door, deeply denting it and poking a hole through the steel. He and the others inside had evidently been spared by the bulletproof glass panel behind the door—Kallman had the window rolled down. The brunt of the grenade's force had been absorbed by the Humvee's outer shell, and the glass barrier had been thick enough to stop it. Kallman's left arm began to swell and discolor, but otherwise he was fine.

* * *

Dan Schilling felt better whenever they were moving. But the convoy seemed to inch along, stopping, starting, stopping, starting. Whenever they stopped the volume of fire would surge, so many rounds that at times it looked like the stone walls on both sides of the alley were being sand-blasted. There were plenty of targets to shoot at. Up in the turret, Pringle unloosed the .50 cal on a group of armed Somalis. Schilling watched as one of them, a tall, skinny man wearing a bright yellow shirt and carry-ing an AK-47, came apart as the big rounds tore through him. Deep red blotches appeared on the yellow shirt. First an arm came off. Then the man's head and chest exploded. The rest of the Somalis scattered, mov-ing around the next corner, where Schilling knew they'd again be wait-ing for them to cross.

As the Humvee came abreast of the alley Schilling didn't bother to use his sights, the men were that close. The first man he shot was just ten yards away. He was crouched down and had a painful grimace on his face. Maybe Pringle had hit him earlier. Schilling put two rounds in his chest. He shot the man next to him twice in the chest and as he did he felt a slam and a dull pain in his right foot. When they were through the intersection, Schilling inspected his boot. The door had taken two bullets. One had passed through the outer steel and been stopped by the bullet-proof glass window inside it. The second had hit lower, and had passed right through the door. The door, which was guaranteed to stop the AK-47's 7.62 mm round, had not stopped either bullet. The glass got the first, and the sec-ond had been slowed enough so that it hit with enough force to hurt, but not enough to penetrate the boot.

Pringle had just put doors on the vehicle earlier that day. They'd done the previous six missions without them, and these had just arrived in a shipment from the States. Schilling had mixed feelings about them. He liked the protection, but the doors made it a lot harder to move. When he had checked them out that morning, he couldn't get his window to roll down, so he'd started to remove the door. Pringle stopped him.

"Hey, I just put those on!" he shouted.

Schilling had showed him how the window stuck, and Pringle had fetched a hammer and simply whacked the frame until the window dropped down. Now, Schilling was glad they'd kept the door, but some of the sense of invulnerability he'd felt was gone. Both bullets had gone completely through.

They continued north for about nine blocks, all the way up to Armed Forces Road, one of the main paved roads in Mogadishu. They'd gone past the crash site, only a block west of it, without stopping. The helicopters had directed them to turn right, but the alleyways looked too narrow to Schilling and the others in the lead Humvee. If the trucks got stuck they'd probably all be killed. So they continued on. Some of the men in the convoy saw the downed Black Hawk just a block over as they went past, but no one had told them that it was their objective. Many of the men in the vehicles still thought they were heading back to base. As they approached Armed Forces Street, they stopped again.

Schilling fought back feelings of futility. McKnight seemed dazed and overwhelmed. He was bleeding from the arm and the neck, and not his usual decisive self. Schilling muttered to himself, "We're going to keep driving around until we're all fucking dead."

He then decided to do something himself, since McKnight seemed stymied. Using a frequency he knew helicopter pilots used to talk among themselves, he bypassed the C2 Black Hawk and contacted the observation helicopters flying orbits higher up. Coordinating communications between the air and ground was Schilling's specialty. He asked them to vector him to the crash site. The choppers were eager to oblige. They told him to steer the convoy west on Armed Forces Road, and then hang another left. McKnight gave permission for Schilling to direct them, and the convoy was moving once again.

They made the left turn off Armed Forces and drove through the storm of gunfire for about seven blocks before Schilling saw up ahead the smoldering remains of the five-ton they had torched in front of the target building. They'd come full circle. Schilling hadn't told the observation bird pilots *which* crash site he wanted. The pilots could see how desperate things were around Durant's crash, where Somali mobs had begun to encircle the unprotected downed Black Hawk, and had taken it upon themselves to direct the convoy there. Schilling hadn't realized it until he saw the target house and the Olympic Hotel again.

"We're headed for the second crash site," he told McKnight.

The lieutenant colonel knew only what his orders were. He reiterated that they were to proceed to the *first* crash site.

On the command net, their wanderings had turned to black comedy. Matters were now complicated by the fact that a second vehicle convoy had been dispatched from the base to attempt a rescue at Durant's crash site.

—*Danny, I think you've gone too far west trying to look at the second crash. You seem to have gone about four blocks west and five blocks south, over.*

—*Romeo Six Four* [Harrell], *this is Uniform Six Four* [McKnight]. *Give me a right turn, right turn! Right turn!*

—*Uniform Six Four, this is Romeo Six Four. . . . You need to go about four blocks south, turn east. There is green smoke marking the site south. Keep coming south.*

A voice came over the busy command frequency pleading for order.

—*Stop giving directions! . . . I think you're talking to the wrong convoy!*

—*This is Uniform Six Four, you've got me back in front of the Olympic Hotel.*

— *Uniform Six Four, this is Romeo Six Four. You need to turn east.*

So the convoy now made a U-turn. They had just driven through a vicious ambush in front of the target house and were now turning around to drive right back through it. Men in the vehicles behind could not understand. It was insane! They seemed to be *trying* to get killed.

Things had deteriorated so badly that up in the C2 bird Harrell was considering just releasing the prisoners, their prize, the supposed point of this mission and of all this carnage. He instructed the Delta units on foot now closing in on the first crash site:

—*As soon as we get you linked up with the Uniform element throw all the precious cargo. We're going to try and get force down to the second crash site.*

The voices from various helicopters now trying to steer poor McKnight recorded the frustration of his fruitless twists and turns.

—*Uniform Six Four, this is Romeo Six Four. Next right. Next right! Alleyway! Alleyway!*

—*They just missed their turn.*

—*Take the next available right, Uniform.*

—*Be advised they are coming under heavy fire.*

—*Uniform Six Four, this is Romeo Six Four.*

—*God damn it, stop! God damn it, stop!*

—*Right turn! Right turn! You're taking fire! Hurry up!*

In this terrible confusion the men on the convoy saw strange things. They passed an old woman carrying two plastic grocery bags, walking along calmly through the barrage. As the convoy approached, she set both bags down gently, stuck fingers in her ears, and kept on walking. Minutes later, heading in the opposite direction, they saw the same woman. She had the bags again. She set them down, stuck fingers in her ears, and walked away as she had before.

At every intersection now Somalis just lined up, on both sides of the street, and fired at every vehicle that came across. Since they had men on both sides of the street, any rounds that missed the vehicle as it flashed past would certainly have hit the men on the other side of the road. Sergeant Eversmann, who had found some better cover for himself in the back end of his Humvee, watched with amazement. What a strategy! He felt these people must have no regard for even their own lives! They just *did not care!*

The city was shredding them block by block. No place was safe. The air was alive with hurtling chunks of hot metal. They heard the awful slap of bullets into flesh and heard the screams and saw the insides of men's bodies spill out and watched the gray blank pallor rise in the faces of their friends, and the best of the men fought back despair. They were America's elite fighters and they were going to die here, outnumbered by this determined rabble. Their future was setting with this sun on this day and in this place.

Schilling felt disbelief, and now some guilt. He had steered the convoy the wrong way for at least part of this calamity. Stunned by the confusion, he struggled to convince himself this was all really happening. Over and over he muttered, "We're going to keep driving around until we're all fucking dead."

# 20

Specialist Spalding was still behind the passenger door in the first truck with his rifle out the window, turned in the seat so he could line up his shots, when he was startled by a flash of light down by his legs. It looked like a laser beam shot through the door and up into his right leg. A bullet had pierced the steel of the door and the window, which was rolled down, and had poked itself and fragments of glass and steel straight up his leg from just above his knee all the way up to his hip. He had been stabbed by the shaft of light that poked through the door. He squealed.

"What's wrong, you hit?" shouted Maddox.

"Yes!"

And then another laser poked through, this one into his left leg. Spalding felt a jolt this time but no pain. He reached down to grab his right thigh and blood spurted out between his fingers. He was both distressed and amazed. The way the light had shot through. He still felt no pain. He didn't want to look at it.

Then Maddox shouted, "I can't see! I can't see!"

The driver's helmet was askew and his glasses were knocked around sideways on his head.

"Put your glasses on, you dumb ass," Spalding said.

But Maddox had been hit in the back of the head. The round must have hit his helmet, which saved his life, but hit with such force that it had rendered him temporarily blind. The truck was rolling out of control and Spalding, with both legs shot, couldn't move over to grab the wheel.

They couldn't stop in the field of fire, so there was nothing to do but shout directions to Maddox, who still had his hands on the wheel.

"Turn left! Turn left! Now! Now!"

"Speed up!"

"Slow down!"

The truck was weaving and banging into the sides of buildings. It ran over a Somali man on crutches.

"What was that?" asked Maddox.

"Don't worry about it. We just ran over somebody."

And they laughed. They felt no pity and were beyond fear. They were both laughing as Maddox stopped the truck.

One of the D-boys, Sergeant Mike Foreman, jumped from the back of the truck, ran up, and opened the driver's side door to a cabin now splattered with blood.

"Holy shit!" he said.

Maddox slid over next to Spalding, who was now preoccupied with his wounds. There was a perfectly round hole in his left knee, but there was no exit wound. The bullet had evidently fragmented on impact with the door and glass and only the jacket had penetrated his knee. It had flattened on impact with his kneecap and just slid around under the skin to the side of the joint. The remainder of the bullet had peppered his lower leg, which was bleeding. Spalding propped both legs up on the dash and pressed a field dressing on one. He lay his rifle on the rim of the side window, changed the magazine, and, as Foreman got the truck moving again, resumed firing. He was shooting at everything that moved.

To make room for more wounded on the back of his Humvee, wounded Private Clay Othic, who had been shot in the arm at the beginning of the fight, jumped out the back and ran to the second truck. One of the men riding there proffered a hand to help him climb aboard, but with his broken arm Othic couldn't grab hold of anything. After several failed attempts he ran around to the cab, and Specialist Aaron Hand stepped out to let him squeeze in between himself and the driver, Private Richard Kowalewski, a skinny quiet kid from Texas whom they all called "Alphabet" because they didn't want to pronounce his name.

Kowalewski was new to the unit, and quiet. He had just met a girl he wanted to marry, and had been talking about leaving the regiment when his tour was up in a few months. His sergeant had been trying to convince him to stay. Minutes after Othic slid in next to him, Kowalewski was hit by a bullet in his shoulder, which knocked him back against the seat. He checked out the wound briefly and straightened back up behind the wheel.

"Alphabet, want me to drive?" asked Othic.

"No, I'm okay."

Othic was struggling in the confined space to apply a pressure dressing to the driver's bleeding shoulder when the RPG hit. It rocketed in from the left, severing Kowalewski's left arm and entering his chest. It didn't explode. The two-foot-long missile embedded itself in Kowalewski, the fins sticking out his left side under his missing arm, the point sticking out the right side. He was unconscious, but still alive.

Driverless, the truck crashed into the back end of the one before it, the one with the prisoners in back and with Foreman, Maddox, and Spalding in the cab. The impact threw Spalding against the side door and then his truck careened into a wall.

Othic had been knocked cold. He awakened to Specialist Hand shaking him, yelling that he had to get out.

"It's on fire!" Hand shouted.

The cab was black with smoke and Othic could see the rocket fuse glowing from what looked like inside Alphabet. The grenade lodged in his chest was unexploded, but something had caused a blast. It might have been a flashbang mounted on Kowalewski's vest or rocket propellant from the grenade. Hand jumped out his door. Othic reached over to grab Kowalewski and pull him out, but the driver's bloody clothes just lifted damply off of his pierced torso. Othic stumbled out to the street and noticed his and Hand's helmets had been blown off. Hand's rifle was shattered. They moved numbly and even a little giddily. Death had buzzed past close enough to kill Kowalewski and knock off their helmets but had left them virtually unscathed. Hand couldn't hear out of his left ear, but that was it. Both men found their helmets down the street—they had evidently blown right out the window.

Hand also found the lower portion of Kowalewski's arm. Just the left hand and a bit of wrist. He picked it up, ran back to the Humvee where the D-boys had placed Kowalewski, and put it in the mortally wounded man's pants pocket.

Still dazed, Othic crawled into a Humvee. As they set off again he began groping on the floor with his good left hand collecting rounds that guys had ejected from their weapons when they jammed. Othic passed them back to those still shooting.

Many of the vehicles were running out of ammo. They had expended thousands of rounds. Three of the twenty-four Somali prisoners were dead and one was wounded. The back ends of the remaining trucks and Humvees were slick with blood. There were chunks of viscera clinging to floors and inner walls. McKnight's lead Humvee had two flat tires, both on the right side. The vehicles were meant to run on flats, but at nowhere near normal speed. The second Humvee in line was almost totally disabled. It was dragging an axle and was being pushed by the five-ton behind it, the one that had been hit by the grenade that killed Kowalewski. The Humvee driven by the SEALs, the third in line, had three flat tires and was so pockmarked with bullet holes it looked like a sponge. SEAL Howard Wasdin, who had been shot in both legs, had them draped up over the dash and stretched out on the hood. Some of the Humvees were smoking. Carlson's had a gaping grenade hole in the side and four flat tires.

When the RPG hit Kowalewski in the cab of the first truck, it forced everything behind it to a halt. In the noise and confusion, no one in McKnight's lead Humvee noticed, so they proceeded alone up to Armed Forces Road, rolling now at about twenty miles per hour. The observation helicopters called for a right turn (the convoy had driven past the crash site a second time about seven blocks back, this time one block to the east of it, looking in vain for a street wide enough to make a left turn). When they reached Armed Forces Road, Schilling was surprised to find it deserted. They turned right and had gone only about forty yards, planning to turn right again and head back down toward the crash site, when Schilling saw out his right side window a Somali step out into an alley and level an RPG tube at them.

"RPG! RPG!" he shouted.

The Humvee's big turret gun was silent. Schilling turned to see why Pringle wasn't shooting, and saw the gunner down in back grabbing a fresh can of ammo. Pringle raised his hands to cover his head.

"GO!" Schilling screamed at the driver, Private Joe Harosky.

But instead of shooting out of the intersection, Harosky turned into it, and bore straight down on the man with the RPG tube. This happened in seconds. The grenade launched. Schilling saw a puff of smoke and heard the distinctive pop and the big ball of the grenade coming right for them. He froze. He didn't even raise his weapon. The grenade shot straight past the Humvee at door level on his side. He felt it *whoosh* past.

"Back up! Back up!" he shouted.

Schilling got off a few rounds, and Pringle was back up working the .50 cal before they'd cleared the alley. When Schilling turned around, worried they'd ram the Humvee behind them, he discovered they were all alone. Harosky backed out into Armed Forces Road, where they turned around and headed west. They spotted the rest of the column where they'd left it, still facing north just shy of the main road.

McKnight, who had been silent ever since the U-turn back by the Olympic Hotel, seemed to recover himself at this point. He got out of the Humvee and conferred with Sergeant Gallagher outside by the hood of the vehicle. Gallagher was furious about the confusion. But as he confronted McKnight, he was hit with a round that knocked him to the street. He fell right at Schilling's feet. Bright red blood pumped in spurts from his arm. Schilling had never seen such scarlet blood. It was obviously arterial. It shot out in powerful squirts. He pressed his fingers to it and fished for a field dressing in his medical pouch. He patched up Gallagher as best he could, shoving in Curlex (a highly absorbent gauze that is used to help stop bleeding) and bandaging it tightly. In their weeks in Somalia, the PJs had

given all of the men additional training with field dressings. They'd practiced with live goats, shooting the animals and then having the men work
on them, getting their hands in some real gore. The experience helped.
Gallagher walked back to his own vehicle, but Schilling kept his weapon.
He needed the ammo.

They had been wandering now for about forty-five minutes. McKnight
was ready to pack it in. There were now far more dead and wounded in
the convoy than there were at the first crash site. He called up to Harrell.

—*Romeo Six Four, this is Uniform Six Four. We've got a lot of vehicles that
will be almost impossible to move. Quite a few casualties. Getting to the crash site
will be awful tough. Are pinned down.*

Harrell was insistent.

—*Uniform Six Four, this is Romeo Six Four. Danny, I really need to get you
back to that crash site. I know you turned left on Armed Forces* [Road], *what's your
status?*

But McKnight and his men had had enough.

—*This is Uniform Six Four. I have numerous casualties, vehicles that are
halfway running. Gotta get these casualties out of here ASAP.*


They weren't home yet.

They began moving, and everyone heartened as word passed back
that they were finally pointed back to the base. Maybe some of them would
make it out alive after all.

They found Via Lenin, a four-lane road with a median up the center
that would lead them back down to the K-4 traffic circle and home.
Spalding began to lose feeling in his fingertips. For the first time in the
ordeal he felt panic. He thought he must be lapsing into shock. He saw a
little Somali boy who looked no more than five years old with an AK-47,
shooting it wildly from the hip, bright flashes from the muzzle of the gun.
Somebody shot the boy and his legs flew up into the air, as though he had
slipped on marbles, and he landed flat on his back. It happened like a slow-
motion sequence in a movie, or a dream. The D-boy driving, Foreman,
was a helluva shot. He had his weapon in one hand and the steering wheel
in the other. Spalding saw him gun down three Somalis without even slowing down. He was impressed.

He felt his hands curling up like someone with cerebral palsy. "Hey, man, let's get the hell back," he said. "I'm not doin' too good." "You're doin' cool," said Foreman.

SEAL John Gay's Humvee was now in the lead. It was riddled with bullets and smoking and slowing down, running on three rims. There were eight wounded Rangers and Joyce's body in back, with Wasdin's bloody legs splayed out on the hood (he'd been shot once more in the left foot). Wasdin was yelling, "Just get me out of here!" The Sammies had stretched two big underground gasoline tanks across the roadway with junk and furniture and other debris and had set it all on fire. Afraid to stop the Humvee for fear it would not start back up, they crashed over and through the flaming debris, nearly flipping, but the wide, sturdy vehicle righted itself and kept on going. The rest of the column followed.

It was 5:40 P.M. They had been battling through the streets now for more than an hour. Of the approximately seventy-five men in the convoy, soldiers and prisoners, nearly half had been hit by bullets or shrapnel. Eight were dead, or near death. As they approached K-4 circle, they braced themselves for another vicious ambush.

# OVERRUN

ABOVE: Delta snipers Gary Gordon (left) and Randy Shughart. Both men were awarded Medals of Honor for their efforts to save Durant and his crew. Courtesy: Paul Howe.

LEFT: Mohamed Shiek Ali, a veteran Aidid militiaman who fought against the Rangers on October 3 and was wounded in the right arm. Courtesy: Peter Tobia/*The Philadelphia Inquirer.*

(left to right) Winn G. Mahuron poses with Tommie Field, Bill Cleveland, Ray Frank, and Mike Durant, the crew of Black Hawk *Super Six Four.* Courtesy: U.S. Army Special Operations Command.

# 1

Too many things were happening at the same time, all of them bad. Task Force Ranger was two hours into a mission that was supposed to have taken an hour. For General Garrison and his staff in the airfield JOC, watching and listening on TV screens and radio, and to element commanders Harrell and Matthews in the C2 Black Hawk, circling over the fight, there came the awful recognition that events had slipped out of control.

Their force was now stretched beyond its limits. Durant's crash site was in imminent danger of being overrun. Most of the original assaulters—about 160 D-boys and Rangers—were now either cut to pieces on the limping ground convoy or strung out on foot between the target house and the first helicopter crash site. They belonged to the strongest military power on earth, but until some additional force could be brought to bear, they were stranded, fighting for their lives on city streets surrounded by thousands of furious well-armed Somalis. Forces from a full company of the 10th Mountain Division, another 150 men, had arrived at the task force's base and thrown itself into the effort to reach Durant's crash site, but they were running into the same problems as the other vehicles trying to move through the deadly ambushes and roadblocks that had been erected all over the city.

Two more 10th Mountain companies were en route, and the UN's Pakistani and Malaysian forces had agreed to add their tanks and armored personnel carriers to the fight, but the logistics of assembling this polyglot rescue convoy would be daunting, and would take hours. In two more hours it would be dark.

The men fighting for their lives out in the city knew nothing of the bigger picture. They could not see beyond the increasingly desperate struggle on their corner, and each still fought with the expectation that rescue was just minutes away.

Shortly before Durant's helicopter had been shot down, the one and only airborne rescue team had roped into the first crash site, the one just blocks away from the target building. They had flown in on Black Hawk

*Super Six Eight.* Air Force Technical Sergeant Tim Wilkinson had been seated between the two crew chiefs in the back of it when a white chalkboard was passed from man to man. Written on it in big black letters was "61 DOWN." The bad news produced a big jolt of adrenaline. It meant they were going in.

They had been practicing together for months, a mix of soldiers from different units and branches. Wilkinson was one of two air force PJs on board. With them was a five-man team of D-boys and seven Rangers. Ever since the mission had been drawn up earlier that summer, this team of fourteen men had been preparing to rope down to a crashed helicopter, first at Fort Bragg and then in Mogadishu. Everyone knew there was a chance a helicopter could be shot down on one of these missions, although it was considered so unlikely that the CSAR element had originally been cut from the deployment. Garrison had put his foot down and it had been reinstated, but the bird still had been considered something of a luxury and a nuisance, like the bulky boxes of emergency medical supplies and equipment Delta surgeon Major Rob Marsh had insisted on hauling all over the world for the last eight years. There was always a temptation to avoid taking such ominous precautions, like the way the D-boys went into battle with their blood types taped to their shoes. You didn't want to jinx yourself, but prudence dictated preparing for the worst. On the first six missions the CSAR team had flown in circles for an hour or so and then returned.

Wilkinson and the other air force guys practiced emergency medicine like an extreme sport. Their job was primarily rescuing downed pilots, and since there was no telling where or when a plane would crash, from midocean to mountaintop, from frozen tundra to the middle of a crowded city, their unit's motto, "Anytime, anywhere," was a point of pride. They were trained to climb cliffs, search deserts, and to dive out of airplanes at extremely high altitudes, if necessary, sometimes far behind enemy lines, to track lost and wounded flyers, patch them up, and bring them home. Their training was designed to push them beyond normal human constraints. Men sometimes died trying to pass the PJ course in the early 1980s when Wilkinson volunteered. He was twenty-five then, an avid outdoorsman. He decided to ditch a tamer career as an electrical engineer for something to make his heart pump faster. His personal nightmare had been the water drill at the army Special Forces SCUBA training facility. It was called "crossovers." Trainees were weighted down with water-filled tanks and dropped in a deep pool. Holding their breath, they had to *walk* twenty-five meters to the other end without coming up for air. For Wilkinson, it was hard enough just to go that distance without blacking out, but the instructors would deliberately detain him, push him backward, disorient him, pull off his mask and fins, rough him up, tangle him up with other trainees . . . simulating the helter-skelter, life-threatening stresses of a real-world rescue. To panic or black out meant failing the test. Those who made it across the pool had thirty seconds to catch their breath before setting out to recross the pool. This was done over and over again, until many of those who hadn't failed had decided to quit. And this was just one such sadistic exercise. Those who made it through tests like these, and who had years of experience performing difficult rescues, were gutsy, hardened risk takers. But in the Special Forces world, the "blueshirts" were still considered slightly effete. The D-boys called them "shake-and-bake" commandos because the PJ route was considered a shortcut into the special ops community. In most other instances, the air force was the least physically demanding of the branches. Some of the D-boys saw their presence and the four SEALs as a genuflection to intraservice rivalry. This was a "joint" operation. Everybody wanted a chance to play in this war. There were plenty of guys who rose above such pettiness, but there was enough of it in the hangar to color Wilkinson's weeks of deployment. It was something he and the other air force specialists had learned to live with.

When the chalkboard came around, Wilkinson was immediately hungry for more information. Where had *Six One* gone down? Was it burning? How many people were on board? For him, apart from the physical danger (in this case being shot at), rescues were a mental challenge. People's lives depended on how well he could think on his feet. He carried two heavy bags, one for medical supplies and the other containing tools for cutting open the helicopter and prying men loose. Training had taught him to cope with stress and how to handle the tools. The rest was all improvisation.

Specialist Rob Phipps, the "Phippster," was the youngest of the Rangers on board. He was twenty-two. To the more experienced men, battle was a grim necessity, part of their jobs. They had weighed the risks and for various reasons had accepted them. For Phipps, the prospect of going in was just thrilling. His pulse raced and his senses seemed twice as alert. The only thing he could compare it to was a drug. He could hardly sit still. He had been a hellion of a teenager growing up in Detroit, drinking and partying, breaking all the rules, running completely out of control. The Rangers had taken all that fearless exuberance and pointless bravado and channeled it. That was the secret core of all the *Hoo-ah* discipline and esprit. You would be given permission, in battle, to break the biggest social taboo of all. You killed people. You were *supposed* to kill people. It wasn't often talked about in just that way, but there it was. Phipps didn't consider himself bloodthirsty, but he'd been groomed and primed for a moment just like this, and he was eager. He had his CAR-15, which could fire upward of six hundred rounds per minute, and he'd been trained to hit what he aimed at. Part of him never believed he'd actually be asked to do it. Now he reminded himself: *This is for real!* He was frightened, excited, and nervous all at once. He had never felt this way.

As pilot Dan Jollata called back, "One minute," the men checked weapons, chambered rounds, and passed along whatever bits of information were offered by the crew chiefs and those at the doors, who could see below. They moved over Wolcott's downed Black Hawk exactly eight minutes after it crashed. Jollata flew in from the north, flared, and then hovered about thirty feet over the street. The Little Bird that had gone in to rescue the two wounded D-boys had landed right on Marehan Road, but the Black Hawk was much too big to go all the way down.

From his middle spot, Wilkinson couldn't see anything. He was taking his cues from Master Sergeant Scott Fales, his team leader. They made eye contact and nodded. *This is it.* Then Jollata said it was time, the ropes were kicked out, and men started sliding out. When it was his turn, Wilkinson noticed that the essential kit bags, which were supposed to be kicked out first, had been left behind. So he and Fales waited until the men before them had cleared the rope and then kicked out the bags themselves. They made one last check around inside the now-empty bird before they jumped.

The delay was costly. As Jollata held his hover these few extra seconds, an RPG exploded on the left side of his airframe. It rocked the Black Hawk like a roundhouse punch. Jollata instinctively began to pull up and away.

"Coming out. I think we have been hit," Jollata radioed. Confirmation was already coming from nearby Little Birds.

—*You have been hit.*

*—Behind your engines.*

*—Be advised you are smoking.*

"We still have people on the ropes!" one of his crew chiefs shouted. Jollata could hear his rotor blades whistling. Shrapnel from the blast had peppered them with holes. The aircraft sloshed from side to side. The blast had damaged the main rotor housing and had destroyed the engine cooling system. Instinct and training both dictated that he move out, fast, but Jollata eased the Black Hawk back down to a hover for the remaining seconds Wilkinson and Fales needed to finish sliding down the ropes.

Stretched out on the rope, Wilkinson heard the explosion above, but he was so intent on negotiating his descent through the brown dust cloud that he never felt the bird jerk forward and up, and didn't learn until much later how Jollata's cool had saved his life.

*—You had better set it down pretty quick somewhere,* came advice for Jollata from one of the helicopters above. *You have a big hole on top.*

"All systems are normal right now, just a little whine in the rotor system. I think I can make it back to the field," said Jollata.

*—Be advised you've got smoke coming out of the very top of the rotor. I suggest you go down to the new port. Put it down now.*

*—Let Six Eight make his call,* said Matthews from the C2 Black Hawk. *He looks all right.*

Once Wilkinson and Fales were on the ground, *Super Six Eight* limped low and slow across the city trailing a thin gray plume. Jollata struggled in the cockpit to fly it. It was like maneuvering a truck on a sheet of ice. The Black Hawk could survive without oil for a time, but losing the cooling system meant the gears would burn. He looked for an open field near the port.

"I've got the field in sight. All systems normal. I am losing transmission pressure right now."

The sturdy Black Hawk kept going. They flew past the open field and then slipped over the fencing to the airport base. Jollata still faced the challenge of putting it down. He knew the chopper couldn't hold a hover, so he warned the crew chiefs in back to brace themselves for a hard landing. He radioed for emergency crews on the ground to be ready, and then just slammed the bird down with a quick roll at sixty knots. He put it right on the wheels. They hit with a jolt, but the Black Hawk stayed upright and intact.

# 2

Wilkinson heard the snap of rounds passing nearby as soon as he hit the street. It was hot and in the cloud of dust he couldn't see. He ran to a wall on the right side of the street and waited for the dust to settle.

He was carrying a small medical pack and his CAR-15, sidearm, rounds, radio, canteen, and body armor. Instead of a K-pot (the standard U.S. Army Kevlar helmet), Wilkinson was wearing the lightweight plastic Pro-Tech hockey helmet preferred by most of the D-boys. Their specialized work called for them to move fast in and out of small places, so their primary concern was bumping their head, not taking a bullet or shrapnel. Wilkinson preferred the little helmet because he could glue a strip of Velcro to the top, where he could fasten a flashlight.

Wilkinson had one of the heavy ceramic plates in the front of his body armor, and with all the other gear must have weighed half again his 180 pounds, yet he didn't feel the extra weight. There had been some learned discussion in the CSAR bird about the pros and cons of wearing the armor plates. They were heavy, and in some cases were so oversized that the top of the breast plate jammed uncomfortably up under the chin of men seated in the choppers. Since so much of their time had been spent just sitting, there was ample sentiment in the bird for leaving the plates out altogether. The Kevlar itself could stop shrapnel and a 9 mm round. Wilkinson figured the standard Somali weapon to be the AK-47, which fires a faster round. So he endured the plate in front, but not in back. It was a reminder of the all-important rule: *Never turn your back on the enemy.*

Except, at this intersection of dirt roads and stone houses, the enemy seemed to be shooting from everywhere. He couldn't see anything. He took his heavy leather fast-roping gloves off and clipped them on his vest, waiting for the cloud to thin enough so he could see where he was.

They had put down on Marehan Road, a wide dirt road immediately east of the crash, though Wilkinson could not yet see *Super Six One.* As Mogadishu neighborhoods went, this one was upscale. This wide north-south street was intersected by narrow alleys running east-west. He knew *Super Six One* was in one of those. There were one- and two-story houses made of either rose-tinted, white, or gray-brown stone, roofed with tin, most arrayed around small inner courtyards. Some of the outer walls were smooth plaster and had been painted, although all were stained with the orange sand of the streets. Most of the walls were uneven. Even the ones made of modern cinder blocks were so sloppily mortared they resembled a hastily stacked pile of stones. It was clear that most of the construction, while in some cases ambitious, was strictly do-it-yourself. There were small trees inside the courtyards and some out on the street.

He saw some of his team across the road moving west, up a narrow alley. The kit bags and fast ropes were still in the middle of Marehan Road. Alongside was a long shard of *Super Six One*'s shattered rotors. At impact, pieces of the rotors had been hurled blocks away. Wilkinson ran across the road, still hearing the loud snap of bullets around him, and picked up both bags. As he rounded the corner to the alley, he saw the wreck. He was startled by its size. They were used to seeing Black Hawks in the air or out on spacious tarmacs. In this narrow alley it looked tragic, like a harpooned whale, beached on its left side. The T-shaped tail boom was twisted and bent down. On its side like that, the bird was about eight feet high. There were bits and pieces of rotor, engine, stone, and mortar scattered all over the top of it. Painted on the front end of the bird, under the right cockpit door facing upward, was a crude cartoon of a crooked-nosed Indian with a head feather, and the words, "Sitting Bull." He remembered that "Bull" Briley was *Six One*'s copilot.

Much had already happened. The rescue team's D-boys and Rangers, including the group from Chalk Two who had run over from the target building, had set up a small perimeter, basically guarding the alley to the front and rear of the downed aircraft. The crushed nose of the bird pointed east. There were a few dead Somalis scattered on the street. People would rush out, often women or children, to retrieve their weapons, and others would step out to pull bodies to cover.

Sergeant Fales was at the front end of the wreckage stretching up to peer inside when he felt a tug at his left pants leg. Then came the pain. It felt like a hot poker had been stabbed through his calf muscle. Fales, a big, broad-faced man who had fought in Panama and during the Gulf War, felt anger with the pain. Here he was after years of training for a moment like this, and after less than three minutes on the ground he'd been shot. How was he to do his job, direct this rescue, with a big bloody hole in his leg?

He hopped back from the front of the helicopter with a disappointed grimace. Wilkinson caught up as Fales hobbled back toward the tail of the bird. Delta Sergeant First Class Bob Mabry had him under one arm.

"What's up?" Wilkinson asked.

"I've been shot."

"What?"

"Been shot. Rat bastard shot me."

Fales and Mabry ducked into the hole the crashing helicopter had knocked in the south wall of the alley. Mabry cut open his pants with his scissors and saw that the bullet had passed through the calf muscle and out the front of his leg. It had apparently not broken the leg bones. By the look of it, with flaps of muscle tissue spilled out of the wound, they figured it ought to hurt badly, but other than that stabbing pain right after he'd been shot, Fales felt nothing. The anesthetic of fear and adrenaline. Mabry stuffed the muscle tissue back into the hole, packed some gauze into it, and then applied a pressure dressing. Both men then crawled back out into the alley, finding cover in a small cup-shaped space behind the main body of the helicopter created by the bent tail boom.

The injury to his partner heightened Wilkinson's sense of urgency. He had thought they'd have a few minutes to set up before the pressure came. In the past, it had usually taken ten to twenty minutes for a Somali crowd to gather around any action on the streets. Clearly this time was different. Speed was critical. Going in they had been told that the main body of the assault force would be moving from the target house in vehicles to this crash site, so he expected them at any minute. They had to have the wounded and dead out of the chopper, perform any emergency medicine necessary, and place them on litters by the time the convoy approached. Now he'd lost his team leader.

Wilkinson moved up to the front. A Delta sniper, Sergeant First Class James McMahon, who had been on *Super Six One* when it crashed, was already on top of the bird pulling out Bull Briley. McMahon's face was badly cut and swollen and had already turned black and blue. He looked like he was wearing a fright mask. Briley was obviously dead. On impact something had sliced cleanly through his head, angling up from just under his chin. He was relatively easy to get at because he was strapped in the right seat, which was now on the high side. Wilkinson helped McMahon pull

Briley up and out, and then handed his body down. McMahon climbed down into the cockpit and checked on Elvis.

"He's dead," he told Wilkinson.

The PJ felt the need to see for himself. He told McMahon to get some attention for his face, and then climbed up and into the bird.

It was eerily quiet inside. There had been no fire, and there was no smoke. Wilkinson was surprised at how intact it all was. Everything inside that hadn't been strapped down had come to rest on the left side, which was now the bottom. Most had been thrown to the front, and was now piled up against the back of the pilot's seat. There was a slight odor of fuel inside, and there were liquids draining from places. He ran a finger into some fluid dripping down the side, smelled and tasted it. It wasn't fuel. It was probably hydraulic fluid. Sunlight came through the wide right-side doors that now faced the sky.

He observed all this suspended upside down through the right side door. Reaching down, he checked Wolcott's neck for a pulse. He was dead. Both pilots had taken the brunt of the impact, and Wolcott, because his side had hit the ground, had gotten the worst of it. The whole front end of the helicopter had folded in on him from the waist down. He was still in his seat. His head and upper torso were intact, but the rest of him was wedged tightly under the instrument panel. Wilkinson tried to slide his hand between the panel and the pilot's legs, but there was no space above or below. He could not be lifted or pulled free. Wilkinson then slid completely into the helicopter and crawled behind the pilot's seat to see if it could be pulled back or reclined, so he could slide Wolcott out that way, but that vantage looked no better. He then climbed out and got down on the dirt by the smashed left underside of the cockpit, digging to see if there was a chance of creating an opening underneath the wreck out of which Elvis's body could be extracted. But all the tonnage of the Black Hawk had plowed hard into the soil. There was going to be no easy way to get him out.

# 3

Shortly before the other Rangers came down ropes to the crashed helicopter, Abdiaziz Ali Aden had darted out from under the green Volkswagen. The slender Somali teenager with the head of thick, bushy hair had seen the helicopter clip the roof of his house before falling into the alley. He had helped his family to safety and then returned to protect the house from looters, only to find himself in the middle of a gunfight.

He saw one of the Americans who roped down pick up an M-16 from a man he had just shot. As the soldier came toward him, Aden panicked. He slid out from under the car and ran back into his house, slamming the door shut. He ran to a small storage room in the front that had two windows, one that faced out over the alleyway where the helicopter lay, the other that looked out at Marehan Road where more Rangers were descending. The intersection and alley then swarmed with American soldiers, and the shooting was loud, constant, and accelerating. The walls of his house were built of heavy stone, so he had a safe, ringside seat.

Aden watched the American soldiers climb hurriedly in and out of the wrecked helicopter. They pulled a pilot out and carried him to the tail end of it. The pilot had a deep and terrible cut across his face and he looked eerily white and was clearly dead. Two of the Rangers placed a big gun on top of the Fiat across the street, which struck Aden as funny. It turned the little car into a kind of technical. Another of the soldiers crawled right into the trash hole. Aden's family and their neighbors disposed of trash by digging holes or ditches in the street outside their house, and filling it with their dumpings. When it was full, they burned it. This soldier just dug himself into the trash. Only his head and rifle stuck out from the debris. He was shooting steadily.

# 4

Sergeant First Class Al Lamb was grateful for the hole. He didn't care what was in it. They were taking fire from all directions, and there wasn't much to hide behind. Sammies were sticking their AK-47s down over the top of the walls. Lamb had gone to the end of the alley at the front of the chopper with a Delta operator, Ranger Sergeant Mark Belda, and eager young Specialist Rob Phipps.

Phipps had roped down to the street with Specialist John Belman, and the two had immediately knocked in a door to get off the street. They barged in on a woman in a turban and scarlet checkered robe who was missing a front tooth. She screamed. Phipps saw five or six small children hiding under a bed. The woman dropped to her knees and put her hands up, begging them with words they didn't understand. The Rangers backed out the door and then ran down to the alley, where they saw the tail of the helicopter. Standing there was Sergeant McMahon, who just shouted at them through his swollen, bruised face, "The twelve! The twelve!" meaning they needed more covering fire at the twelve o'clock position.

Phipps took a spot by the stone wall the chopper had fallen against. There was a small intersection about twenty feet ahead where another sandy alley crossed. On the opposite two corners were stone walls and behind them clumps of trees. Directly behind him, jutting up from under the wreck and growing halfway to the corner, was a big cactus bush. That and the downed chopper hid his position from anyone behind him. He stayed back from the corner so that he didn't present a target from the alley in front of him. At first he was there by himself. He got jumpy, so he called Sergeant Lamb on his handheld radio and asked for help. Then Staff Sergeant Steven Lycopolus moved up and crouched on the other side of the alley, just past the hole the Black Hawk had knocked in the south wall. His rear was protected by the heap of stone and mortar from the pulverized concrete. They were mainly looking to pick off gunmen to the east who were sending a steady flow of rounds up the alleyway, and to prevent any Sammies from approaching the crash from that direction. It didn't take long for one to try. A man in a loose white cotton shirt, baggy pants, and sandals came creeping up the alley right toward them with an AK, walking at a crouch with the weapon held forward. Phipps shot him and he fell sideways into the alley. Then another man ran out to retrieve the gun. Phipps shot him. Then another man ran out. Phipps shot him, too. Then Lamb, Belda, and Specialist Gregg Gould moved up to join Phipps and Lycopolus. Belda joined Phipps on his side of the alley, Gould went over by Lycopolus, and Lamb dug into the hole.

The Chalk Two Rangers who had been first to arrive had the six o'clock position covered. They'd fanned out to take all four corners of the big intersection west of the crash. The five men at the twelve o'clock spot dug in as best they could, covering the smaller intersection to the east. They stayed close to the helicopter. Lamb felt that moving his men across the intersection might break down the perimeter and risk getting them cut off.

It appeared as though many of the shots coming their way were from the clump of trees about twenty yards over, behind a high wall at the southeast corner across the intersection. Rounds were chipping stone and earth around Phipps and he could hear them puncturing the Black Hawk's thin metal hull.

Lycopolus and Gould were closest to the wall, and at Lamb's direction they began throwing their grenades over it. One by one they exploded, but the shooting continued. So Belda shot up the trees with his SAW while Phipps tossed his own grenades to Lycopolus. The staff sergeant threw them, and these, too, exploded, again without effect. So Belda tossed Lycopolus his grenades. The staff sergeant threw the first, which exploded, and then tossed the second. This time there was no blast. Instead, seconds later, what looked to be the same grenade came flying back over the high wall at them. Either Lycopolus had not removed the safety strap on the last grenade he threw, or that one had been a dud and the Somalis behind the wall had an American grenade of their own.

Phipps dove forward as several voices shouted, "Grenade!" The blast was like a gut punch. It just sucked all the air out of him. He felt like he was on fire and his ears rang from the blast and his nose and mouth were filled with a bitter stabbing metallic taste. When the initial ball of fire was gone he still felt terrible burning on both legs and on his back. The explosion had clobbered him. His face was blackened and beginning to swell and his eyes were puffing shut. As Phipps regained his senses, he lifted his head and looked back over his shoulder. Gould had also been hit and was bleeding from the buttocks. A Somali had run into the roadway and picked up the AK from the pile of dead and wounded where he had been shooting earlier. The man was taking aim when one of the D-boys back by the hole in the wall dropped him with a quick burst. The man's head just popped apart.

The operator waved at Phipps, shouting, "Come on! Come on!"

Phipps tried to stand but his left leg gave out. He tried again and fell again.

"Come on!" shouted the D-boy.

Phipps crawled. The burning sensation was fierce now and his left leg wasn't working right. When he got close enough the D-boy grabbed his face and pulled him the rest of the way in.

Phipps was panicked.

"Holy shit! I'm hit! I got shot! I got shot!"

"You're all right," the D-boy reassured him. "You'll be all right."

He tore open his pants and applied a field dressing.

The wind was out of young Phipps's sails. He was out of the fight.

# 5

Across the city about a mile southwest, Black Hawk pilots Mike Goffena and Jim Yacone circled over Durant's wrecked bird worriedly. The men in *Super Six Four* had been lucky. Most of this part of the city consisted of stone houses, hard structures, but the spot where Durant and his copilot Ray Frank had gone down was just rag shacks and tin huts, nothing hard enough to flip the chopper over. The bird was built with shock absorbers to withstand a terrifically hard impact so long as it landed in an upright position, which the Black Hawk had.

In other ways they were less lucky. The CSAR team had already fast-roped in at Wolcott's crash site. No one had anticipated two choppers going down. Durant and his copilot Ray Frank and their crew would have to be rescued by ground forces, which meant there was going to be a dangerous wait. Watching now from above, Goffena and Yacone could already see Somalis spilling into alleyways and footpaths, homing in on the downed helicopter.

A company of the QRF (2nd Battalion, 14th Infantry, 10th Mountain Division) had been summoned to help. Under the command of Lieutenant Colonel Bill David, 150 soldiers on nine deuce-and-a-half trucks and a dozen Humvees were making their way toward the Ranger base by a roundabout route that took them out of the city. Nobody was sure exactly how to find Durant's crash site. They could see it all too clearly on the screens in the JOC, but the picture couldn't tell them exactly where the downed chopper was. Instead of just waiting for the QRF to arrive, Garrison ordered up another emergency convoy with whatever force could be assembled at the base. Leading it out would be the Rangers and D-boys who had evacuated Private Blackburn, and joining them would be dozens of support personnel—armorers, cooks, ammo handlers, and communications specialists, including an air force air traffic controller—who volunteered to join the fight.

Even as this emergency convoy was leaving the base, it was apparent to the pilots over Durant's crash site that help would not come fast enough for the downed crew of *Super Six Four*. They were minutes from being overrun by a violent, angry Somali mob.

Trying to hold the crowds back were two Little Birds and Goffena's Black Hawk, *Super Six Two*. In addition to the two crew chiefs on *Six Two*, there were three D-boys, snipers Sergeant First Class Randy Shughart, Master Sergeant Gary Gordon, and Sergeant First Class Brad Hallings. With Sammy closing in, the Delta operators told the pilots they could be more effective on the ground. They might be able to hold off the mob until help arrived. Yacone requested permission to insert them.

"Hey, wait, we don't even know if anybody's alive yet," answered Colonel Matthews, the air commander sitting alongside Harrell in the C2 bird.

Hearing nothing from the crew on the radio, Goffena made a low pass and caught a glimpse of Durant sitting in the cockpit pushing at a piece of tin roof that had caved in around his legs. So he was alive. Yacone saw Ray Frank moving. Goffena flew low enough to catch the frustrated look on his friend's face. Frank had been in a tail-rotor crash just like this one several years before on a training mission. A number of men in that aircraft had been killed. Frank had broken his leg and crunched his vertebrae. He had been involved in a drawn-out legal battle over it ever since. To Goffena, the look on his friend's face said, *Shit, I can't believe this happened to me again!* In the back of the aircraft they discerned some movement, which meant either Bill Cleveland or Tommy Field had survived, perhaps both.

Yacone informed Matthews that there were survivors. The colonel told him to hold on.

So Shughart, Gordon, Hallings, and the crew chiefs of *Super Six Two* did what they could from the air. There were plenty of targets. The RPG gunners especially, it seemed, had been emboldened by success. When Goffena flared the Black Hawk in low, the wash from his rotors would literally blow thickening crowds back. As the crowd retreated, they exposed those with RPG tubes, who seemed determined to hold their ground. This made them easy targets for the snipers. Trouble was, once the snipers dropped them, others would dart out and pick up their weapons.

Goffena also noticed that every time he dropped low now he was drawing more fire himself. He and Yacone heard the tick of bullets puncturing the metal walls of the airframe. Now and then they saw a glowing arc out ahead, where rounds would clip their rotor blades and spark, tracing a bright line out in front of the cockpit. Goffena began flying faster and tried to keep to the south side of the crash site, where the fire didn't seem to be as heavy. But this was hazardous, too. He knew that immediately to the south was a neighborhood called Villa Somalia, which was known to have a sizable Aidid militia.

They worked the radio, urging immediate help.

—*Alpha Five One* [Matthews], *this is Super Six Two* [Yacone], *we're going to need more friendlies to secure crash site number two.*

They were repeatedly assured that rescue was imminent.

One of the Little Bird pilots reported:

—*We've got to get some ground folks down here or we're not going to be able to keep them off. There are not enough people left onboard the aircraft to do it.*

—*Roger, standby, we're working on it. . . . Okay, listen, this is Adam Six Four* [Garrison], *we've got a small Ranger element departing here in just a minute headed for the second crash site. Someone needs to vector him in.*

# 6

Dale Sizemore had been going nuts listening to the radio. These were his brothers, his Ranger buddies out there pinned down, and they were getting hammered. He heard screams of pain and fear in the voices of hardened men. This was the big fight they'd all been preparing for all these years, and here he was, pacing around the radio with a fucking cast on his arm!

Some days earlier, Sizemore had banged his elbow goofing off in the hangar. The task force officers had challenged all the NCOs to a volleyball match, but before the contest the lower ranks had ambushed their commanders and bound them to stretchers with flex cuffs and duct tape. They then carried them out to the volleyball court and poured water on them and humiliated them in various ways. Not all the brass had gone quietly. Ranger commander Steele put up the fight you'd expect from a former lineman on Georgia's national championship football team, and several of the Delta officers were even harder to take down. Sizemore was the first guy to hit Harrell, the Delta lieutenant colonel, and it had been like hitting a cliff. Sizemore was a thickly muscled kid, with legs like pilings, and he'd been a decent wrestler in high school, but Harrell just tossed him to the concrete like a flyweight. The fall dinged his elbow pretty good, but Sizemore hadn't given it a second thought. He and five other Rangers finally got Harrell tied down. The next day, in a chopper on a signature flight over the city, Sizemore had brushed the elbow on something again and noticed it was tender and had gotten pretty big.

He woke up on his cot under the bug net early Friday morning, two days before the raid, to find his elbow so swollen and painful he couldn't sleep. He swallowed four Motrins and dozed the rest of the night sitting up. At dawn he was flown up to the hospital at the old U.S. embassy, where they pronounced cellulitis and bursitis and made a four-inch incision to drain the joint. Then they stitched him back up, slapped a cast around it, put him on an IV antibiotic drip, and told him he would be flying home to Fort Benning on Monday.

Sizemore was crushed. He had sat alone on the hospital bed looking out the window at another bright African morning, amazed at how much he would miss this place. This was Sizemore's first real combat zone, and he loved it. The big blond SAW gunner from Illinois had both the Ranger tab and scroll tattooed on his bulging left deltoid. His buddies were his family.

And the hangar? Man, life in the hangar was a blast. They still had daily P.T. (physical training) and had to pull guard duty and other shit details, but ever since they hit Mog not even regular army mickey mouse could fill the available time. They played endless volleyball. An empty storage room with concrete walls and a high ceiling turned out to be a perfect Ping-Pong arena. The Romanians would come over and make the ball dipsy-doodle like it had an IQ. There was a running game of gin rummy (wily little Private Othic had accumulated a pile of winnings) and long sessions of board games like Risk, Scrabble, and Stratego. When they weren't training or on some other detail, guys passed time reading books, playing Gameboy, watching videotapes, writing home, or just hanging out. Sizemore liked to retreat to a hallway out behind the main hangar where there was a steady ocean breeze, clap on headphones, and just zone out for an hour now and then. Then there was the beach. Even though the ocean had sharks . . . a beach was a beach. With sand and dust everywhere and showers rationed every few days, beach mode more or less prevailed, at least compared to the usual Ranger standards.

To anybody but Rangers, the accommodations were austere. Each man had only about a four-by-eight-foot rectangle of space to call his own. An informal protocol had developed about that space; guys would ask permission before stepping in or walking across. Each cot had thin wooden poles sticking up from the corners from which, during the night, they could drape the netting to keep out Somalia's ferocious mosquitoes. The hangar itself was filthy. It had that musky Third World odor to it. The tarmac with all the choppers was right outside the big open front doors so the steady salt-air breeze that came through was scented sweetly with jet fuel and oil. Guys had to keep their weapons wrapped to ward off the fine dust and sand that accumulated on everything. The roof leaked in about a dozen spots. There were massive gaps here and there in the tin walls, so when it rained, water poured in from all directions. Some of the units sandbagged off their space to keep the floodwaters at bay, which broke up the cavernous space into warrens that had a more homey feel. The air force guys had built themselves a nifty clubhouselike enclosure toward the back. Before the rear wall was a big American flag draped from the rafters, alongside a homemade poster showing their 3rd Battalion, 75th Regiment crest. The chopper crews were just inside the front door, the D-boys had the corner of the hangar off to the left as you entered, and the rest were Rangers, Sizemore's buddies. His bunk was right in the middle toward the back. He could prop his boots on his rucksack and watch the rats scurry along the intricate interlace of rafters overhead, or watch the hawks who were raising chicks in a tree outside swoop in and nail pigeons in midflight.

And what could be cooler than living with the Delta operators, the "Dreaded D"? They were *the* pros, totally squared away. On the eighteen-hour flight aboard the giant C-141 Starlifter, when the air force blueshirts insisted that they all stay in their seats, the D-boys just blew them off. Right after takeoff they unrolled thermal pads (the shiny metal floor of the bird turns ice cold at altitude) and insulated ponchos, stuck earplugs in their ears, donned eye patches, swallowed "Blue Bombers" (Halcyon tablets), and racked out. They taught little tricks like wrapping tape around the pins of their grenades to make sure none accidentally snagged and pulled on a piece of equipment. They wore knee pads when they went into a fight, which made it easy to quickly drop and shoot, and stay there for hours if necessary. If it was hot, they didn't walk around in full battle gear. They wore T-shirts or no shirts at all, and shorts and flip-flops. They all had sunglasses. If they'd been up until all hours, they slept in a little in the morning. When they went out on a mission, they took the weapons they thought they'd need and left behind the stuff they didn't. With the D-boys, all of whom were ranked sergeant first class or higher, rank meant nothing. They all, officers and noncoms, called each other by their first names or nicknames. They were trained to think and act for themselves. Nothing was done by the book for its own sake; they were guided by their own experience. They knew their weapons and tactics and business better than anyone, and basically ran their own lives, which was an extraordinary thing in the U.S. Army.

Some of the operators, like blond Norm Hooten or short, stocky Earl Fillmore or the massively built Paul Howe, held training sessions with them, imparting the finer points of death-dealing and mayhem. Hooten showed Specialist Dave Diemer how to better shoot his modified SAW from the hip, and got one of the Delta armorers to fit out a custom grip for him. They supplied some of the guys custom-made black canvas bags to slip over a SAW, which kept the drum of the grenade launcher from getting knocked off when descending the rope (as often happened). Useful things. Fillmore, who was one of the youngest of the operators at twenty-eight, showed them how it was possible to knock a guy unconscious by delivering a hard kick to the thigh, shocking the femoral artery. Howe showed them techniques for using cover in urban terrain, and how to take down a room. It was great.

Delta operator Dan Busch had been a Ranger just a few years back before he'd vanished into the deeply covert. Some of the guys had known him before. Busch had changed a lot. He was *Dan* now, for one thing, not Sergeant Busch. A few of the guys in Bravo Company had known him as a hell-raiser. Busch had always been up to something fun. He'd surfaced here in Mog a changed man. The wild man was now quietly religious and real mellow, a totally different person. He spent a lot of time back on his cot just quietly cleaning his weapons, and whipping all comers at Scrabble.

Some were legendary soldiers, like the easygoing veteran Tim Martin, who had a quick dry wit, a big red blotch birthmark on his face, and a nickname, "Griz," that fit. Griz was over forty and had fought in nearly every conflict, open and secret, since Vietnam. He had been in the army for more than twenty years. Nothing fooled or fazed him. He had a wife and three daughters at home and talked about his plans of retiring the following year and starting up a business. But the coolest of all was "Mace," John Macejunas, a cheerful, unpretentious former Ranger with a bright blond flattop and a leathery tan that made him look like a surfer. Mace wasn't as burly as the other guys but his physique redefined the concept of being in shape. He had so little body fat and was so buff that he looked like a walking atlas of male musculature. In contrast to the easygoing Griz, Mace's engine throttle was stuck in high gear. He worked out so much, doing push-ups, sit-ups, leg lifts, chin-ups, and tormenting himself in ways of his own devising, that the Rangers regarded him as some sort of mutant strain. Even the other D-boys held Mace in awe. He was said to be absolutely fearless.

The Rangers had never had a chance to be around these guys before, even though they'd trained together once or twice. It was like an ongoing tutorial on soldiering from the best in the business.

The worst thing about hangar life, of course, was no women. There were women around, but they were all nurses who worked in a different part of the base or over at the UN compound and all were strictly off-limits. It was tough. There was plenty of porn around, of course, and many of the Rangers were humorously casual about masturbation. Most were discreet about it, but some had adopted a sort of crude defiance, standing up next to their cot to announce, "I'm going to the port-o-pot to fuckin' jack off." Specialist John Collett, a SAW gunner with absolutely no shame about such matters, would brag about his repertory, describing innovative new onanistic techniques—"Man, you shoulda seen me last night. I shit you not, I was gasping!" and coming up with new and unusual places to jack off. Collett claimed to have gotten a "harness-jack," that is, to have masturbated hanging from a parachute harness. It was pitiful. One of the air force PJs got a blow-up love doll in the mail and almost nobody laughed. All this horniness under pressure produced even more adolescent silliness than usual. Corporal Jim Cavaco walked around one night with a length of nylon cord tied around the end of his penis, holding the rope up delicately between two fingers, telling everybody, "Juss takin' the *dawg* out for a walk."

They played a lot of Risk, the board game where color-coded armies vied to conquer the world. It took hours, so it was great for killing time. Private First Class Jeff Young, a tall, fair-haired RTO (Radio Telephone Operator) from upstate New York with big glasses perched on a nose too

small for his long face, had grown up playing Risk with his five brothers
and was so good at it that the other guys formed coalitions to knock him
out first. Young and his sergeant, Mike Goodale, had borrowed the game
from the D-boys early on and monopolized it so much the Delta squadron had to have another game shipped over. Young and Goodale set it up
in front of their racks, and there was usually the same bunch of guys stooped
around it. Over the board, privates and sergeants and even officers all for-
got about rank. They'd be teasing each other, yelling at each other, just
like a regular bunch of guys.

Even the nightly mortar attack was kind of a joke. The Skinnies would
lob rounds into the fenced-off compound that landed with a loud *crump*,
like something very large falling on a big hollow stack of tin. It freaked
guys out at first. They'd drop or dive for cover. But the Skinnies had such
lousy aim that they rarely hit anything, and after a while guys would just
drop and cheer when one landed. Somebody, probably it was Dom Pilla,
discovered that by lifting the big door to the soda and water cooler and
then just letting it fall, it made a *crump* just like a mortar round. He sent
guys diving once or twice before everybody wised up. Pretty soon when
they heard the sound guys didn't even bother to drop. They'd cheer. One
night a mortar hit so close Sizemore could see sparks from the shrapnel
hitting the outer wall of the hangar. Everybody just clapped and hooted.
Across the road, spooked air force medical personnel, not exactly hardened battle types, were holding hands and singing prayer songs while the
crazy Hoo-ahs across the road were cheering like mad. The boys in the
hangar had even started a pool. For a buck you could pick a ten-minute
time slot, and if a mortar round fell in your slot, you took the pool. So after
everybody cheered, they would run to check the sheet to see who'd won.
Nobody had figured out what they'd do with the pot if the mortar happened to fall on the winner.

The movie room had three TVs and three VCRs. Guys always crowded
in to watch CNN. Sometimes their own missions were featured. In fact, when
the force got back from their first mission with their flex-cuffed Somali prisoners, before they had even finished stripping off their gear, they were astonished to see themselves on their top secret mission on CNN, with footage
shot from a distance by infrared cameras. Nobody ever answered the reporters' questions, and they would laugh and groan about how outrageously
wrong they got everything in the newspapers and on TV.

There were two armed forces radio stations, one that played almost all country music and one that divided its play time between "white" music, mostly classic rock, and "black" music, mostly rap. The Rangers, who unlike the 10th Mountain Division guys based across the city were nearly all white, would get a kick out of the dedications during "black" time: *Yo, my brothahs and sistahs, this is 2-G Smoothie 4-U flippin' out a disc fo' Regina at the 271st Supply from Dope Gangsta at the 33rd. Peace!* In the evening they practically wore out the collection of videotapes shipped over in boxes, mostly old heroic action-adventure-type stuff. One week they had a James Bond film festival, a different feature every night. One of the few new releases was *Last of the Mohicans,* which some of the guys had just finished watching twice in a row one night when Captain Steele came in, saw the final credits, and announced he hadn't seen that one yet. So they rewound it and watched it a third time.

Most days when there wasn't a mission they trained, which was totally cool. They got to go north of the city into the desert and blow things up, or practice lobbing grenades and rockets at targets or perfecting their marksmanship with various automatic weapons. In the dunes outside Mog there were lots of toys and more ammo than usual to go around, and they didn't have all the range restrictions that applied back home. Out there under the hot sun in their desert fatigues with their floppy camouflage sun hats on they were like a bunch of overgrown kids playing soldier . . . with real bullets and grenades. It was the sort of thing that made Rangering so cool. It was real soldiering. Hard core, heavy metal. It was way more fun than college. They were on an adventure, Sizemore and the rest of the guys bunked in that hangar. They were in *Africa,* not behind some desk or cash register or sitting in class staring out the window across a sleepy campus. They did things like jump out of airplanes, fast-rope out of helicopters, rappel down cliffs . . . stuff like what they were doing over here, doing *good,* chasing around an exotic Third World capital after a murderous warlord.

Sizemore had talked the doctor into letting him return to the hangar to spend his last day with his unit, and had just been packing his stuff up at the hospital for the chopper ride back when two men were brought in who had just been wounded in a Humvee in the city by a remote-controlled mine. There was a 10th Mountain Division guy who was all right, and a Somali-American interpreter who had been torn in half. From the waist down he was gone. His insides were laying next to him on the gurney.

Sizemore had never seen such a thing. One of the man's arms just twisted off the side of the stretcher, swinging, attached to the trunk by a hunk of meat. Who were these people? What made them think they could get away with this?

When he returned to the hangar, guys were suiting up for this mission. Sizemore had seethed with frustration and disappointment. All the guys were saying this might be a hot one. What if they were right? Had he come this far to miss out on it? In his place they were sending Specialist Stebbins, the company's training room clerk. Stebbins! Sizemore couldn't believe his luck.

The hangar had buzzed with jitters. Even Sergeant Lorenzo Ruiz, the boxer, was uneasy. Nothing usually bothered Lo.

"I got a bad feeling, Dale," he said.

Ruiz and Sizemore were tight. They had absolutely nothing in common, but for some reason they'd hit it off years back. Ruiz was a tough kid from El Paso, Texas, a former amateur boxer, who had joined the army after a judge had given him a choice between the military or prison. In the Ranger Regiment, Ruiz had pulled his life together and excelled. He was married and had a little girl. Sizemore was just a big suburban kid, something of a ladies' man—his buddies had nicknamed him, with his full lips and big blue eyes and broad shoulders, "Adonis." But Ruiz was the real romantic. Out drinking with the guys his temper would flash one minute and the next minute he'd be wiping away a tear, sniffling with his Mexican accent, "I *luff* you guys." Ruiz was superstitious, and had struggled with premonitions of his death in Somalia. Sizemore wasn't superstitious at all, but he'd made a pact with his buddy, to humor him. They would both write final letters to their families that were only to be mailed if they were killed. They had exchanged them for safekeeping. Sizemore's was addressed to his mom and stepfather and aunt, and mostly just told them how much he loved them. Ruiz's told his wife he loved her, and instructed his brother, Jorges, to care for their mother and grandmother. Both wrote that if they had been killed, they had died doing what they wanted to do. There was no need to say much more. That afternoon, as Ruiz kitted up for the mission to the Black Sea, he had reminded Sizemore about the letter.

"Shut up, Lo," he told him. "You'll be back in here in a few minutes."

But now Ruiz was out there with the rest of the guys catching hell—Sizemore didn't know it, but his buddy had already been mortally wounded.

Sizemore wondered where Ruiz was, and how Goodale and Nelson were making out. He worried about Stebbins. Jesus, Stebby was the guy who made coffee for them! Here he was, probably the best man with a SAW in the unit, and the company clerk was out there fighting his battle. Sizemore was glued to the radio outside the JOC with some other guys who had been left behind because they had gone out on a water run shortly before the mission came up. This group had their Humvees parked in a semicircle outside the big open front doors to the hangar, ready to roll if needed.

Listening to the sounds on the radio had a different effect on Specialist Steve Anderson. It scared him. Anderson had wanted to be a soldier so bad that he had lied about having severe asthma when he joined. He carried his inhaler with him everywhere. On the first day of basic training they were all warned sternly that *any* drugs were contraband and if caught with any they were in deep, dark shit. A box was passed around the barracks and they were told they had one last chance, an amnesty, to chuck anything they weren't supposed to have. Anderson panicked and threw in his inhaler, and then suffered such a terrible asthma attack three or four days later that he had to confess and was shipped out to a hospital. The next day the drill sergeant told Sizemore and the rest of the guys in the platoon that Anderson had died.

A month later, at airborne school, Sizemore spotted this tall, skinny ghost doing KP duty, walked over, and rubbed his eyes for a better look. Anderson had not only survived the asthma attack, somebody in the chain of command had admired his determination enough to let him stay in and keep his inhaler.

But now, faced with the prospect of such pitched battle, Anderson was infected by the panic on the radio. Everybody was talking twice as much as usual, as if they needed to stay in touch, as if the radio was a net to prevent their free fall. Anderson didn't show it but he was quaking. His stomach churned and he was in a cold sweat. *Do I have to go out there?* Until this mission, nobody had gotten seriously hurt. The missions were a gas. When the megaphone sounded "Get it on!" he had always felt, *cool, action.* Just like all the other guys. Not now.

The horror hit home when Sergeant Struecker's three-Humvee convoy had raced in, all shot up, and the docs lifted out the broken body of

Private Blackburn, the Ranger who had fallen from the helicopter to the street. Specialist Brad Thomas emerged from one of the Humvees with red eyes. He saw Anderson and choked out, "Pilla's dead." Thomas was crying and Anderson felt himself start to cry. The fear was palpable. Anderson was glad to be someplace safe. He was ashamed of himself, but that's how he felt.

He wasn't alone. Moments after they unloaded Pilla and Blackburn, they got orders to go back out. A second Black Hawk, Durant's, had crashed and was in danger of being overrun. Over the radio they learned that Casey Joyce, another of their buddies, was dead. Mace and the SEALs who had helped bring Blackburn back were already rearmed and ready. Anderson saw no hesitation whatsoever with these guys. But the younger Rangers, to a man, seemed shaken.

Brad Thomas couldn't believe it. He had been on the beach with Joyce and Pilla when they were called for this mission. Within the Ranger company, Thomas, Joyce, Pilla, Nelson, and a few other guys hung together. They were a few years older and had had a little more experience. Joyce and Thomas were both married. Thomas had gone to college for a few years, studying classical guitar, before enlisting. They were less boisterous and, when it came to taking risks, still willing but less eager.

Thomas had seen his friend Pilla killed, and had felt through the rest of that insane ride back to the base that he wasn't going to make it. When they arrived he had felt an enormous sense of relief. He figured the mission was over. Things had gone completely to shit and the rest of the guys would be rolling back in any minute. Emotionally, for him, the fight was done.

So when Struecker approached and instructed the men to start rearming, they were going back out, Thomas was incredulous.

How could they go back out into that? They'd barely escaped with their lives. The whole fucking city was trying to kill them!

Struecker felt his own heart sink. His vehicles were all shot up. The rear of his Humvee was splattered with Pilla's blood and brains. When the body was pulled out it didn't even look like Pilla anymore. The top of his head was gone and his face was grotesquely swollen and disfigured. Struecker's men were freaking out.

Mace, the grim Delta warrior, pulled Streucker aside.

"Look, Sergeant, you need to clean your vehicle up. If you don't, your guys are going to get more messed up."

So Struecker strode over to his squad.

"Listen, men. You don't have to do this if you don't want to. I'll do it myself if I have to. But we have to clean this thing up right now because we're fixin' to roll right back out. Everybody else go resupply. Go get yourselves some more ammunition."

Struecker asked his .50 gunner, "Will you help me clean up? You don't have to."

Together they set off for buckets of water, and working with sponges, they soaked up the blood and brain and scraped it from the interior.

Sizemore saw all this and it made him wild with anger.

"I'm going out there with you guys," he said.

"You can't, you're hurt," said Sergeant Raleigh Cash, who had been in charge of the squad that had gone on the water run.

Sizemore didn't argue. He was wearing gym shorts and a T-shirt and his own gear had been packed away for the flight home tomorrow, so he ran into the hangar, pulled on his pants and shirt, and grabbed any stray gear he could find. He found a flak vest that was three sizes too big for him and a helmet that lolled around on his head like a salad bowl. He grabbed his SAW and stuffed ammo in his pockets and pouches and came running back out to the convoy with his boots unlaced and his shirt un-buttoned and just climbed into Cash's Humvee.

"I'm going out," he told Cash.

"You can't go out there with that cast on your elbow."

"Then I'll lose it."

Sizemore ran back into the hangar and found a pair of scissors. He cut straight up the inside seam of the cast and then flung it away. Then he came back and resumed his place on the vehicle.

Cash just shook his head.

Anderson admired Sizemore's eagerness and felt all the more ashamed of himself. He had donned his own gear, as instructed, but he was morti-fied. He didn't know whether to feel more ashamed of his fear or his sheep-like acceptance of the orders. When it came time to climb in the vehicles he again followed orders, amazed at his own passivity. He would go out into Mogadishu and risk his life but it wasn't out of passion or solidarity or patriotism, it was because he didn't dare refuse. He showed none of this.

Not everyone was as passive. Brad Thomas pulled Struecker aside. "Man, you know, I *really* don't want to go back out."

The sergeant had been expecting this to happen, and dreading it. He knew how he felt about driving back into the city. It was a nightmare. Thomas's words expressed how everyone felt. How could he force those men back out into the fight, especially the men who had just come through hell to get back to base? The sergeant knew all the men were watching to see how he'd handle it. Struecker was a model Ranger, strong, unassuming, obedient, tough, and strictly by-the-book. He was like the prize pupil in class. The officers loved him, which meant at least some of the men regarded him with a slightly jaundiced eye. Challenged like this, they expected Struecker to explode.

Instead, he pulled Thomas aside and spoke to him quietly, man to man. He tried to calm him, but Thomas was calm. As Struecker saw it, the man had just decided he'd taken all he could take. Thomas had just been married a few months before. He had never been one of the chest-beaters in the regiment. It was a perfectly rational decision. He did not want to go back out there to die. The whole city was shooting at them. How far could they get? However steep a price the man would pay for backing down like that, and for a Ranger it would be a steep price indeed, to Struecker it looked like Thomas had made up his mind.

"Listen," Struecker said. "I understand how you feel. I'm married, too. Don't think of yourself as a coward. I know you're scared. I'm scared shitless. I've never been in a situation like this either. But we've got to go. It's our job. The difference between being a coward and hero is not whether you're scared, it's what you do *while* you're scared."

Thomas didn't seem to like the answer. He walked away. As they were about to pull out, though, Struecker noticed that he'd climbed on board with the rest of the men.

# 7

"You're going to go ahead and lead us out," Lieutenant Larry Moore had instructed Struecker. "We're going to take these three five-tons, your two vehicles in front, my two in the rear. The crash site is somewhere in this vicinity," he said, pointing to a location between the K-4 traffic circle and the target building. "We don't know for sure. You're going to flip to this channel," showing him the frequency on his radio, "and we have aircraft up in the sky, and the pilot is going to tell you where to go."

"Okay, whatever," said Struecker.

One of the company clerks, Sergeant Mark Warner, stepped up.

"Sergeant, can I go out?"

"You have a weapon and some ammo?"

"Yeah."

"Go ahead, get in the backseat."

Other volunteers were piling on vehicles down the convoy. Specialist Peter Squeglia, the company armorer, had pulled on fighting gear and climbed into a truck. He had injured his ankle playing rugby in the sand with some guys from New Zealand a few days before and had been relegated to guard duty at the hangar. There was no way he could use a sore ankle as an excuse to stay out of this. So now he sat with his M-16 pointed out the passenger-side window of a five-ton truck, wondering what he had had gotten himself into. You joined the army and volunteered for the Rangers ostensibly because you were willing to go into combat, but in this day and age you didn't really expect them to call your bluff. Squeglia considered himself more realistic about battle than most of his Ranger buddies, even though he had never gotten close to one. He had been put off by some of the bravado he'd seen in the previous weeks. He would caution his friends, "This is real stuff. One of us is probably going to get killed one of these times out." And they all laughed at him. Well, now at least one of them had definitely been killed—he'd seen them unload Pilla's body—and here he was in the thick of it. Here it was, a Sunday afternoon in early fall, the kind of day back home where he and his buddies would spend the afternoon watching football on TV and then head out to the bars of Newport, Rhode Island, trying to pick up girls, and here he was, smart-guy twenty-five-year-old Peter Squeglia, riding shotgun in a truck out into the streets of Mogadishu with what appeared to be the entire indigenous population trying to kill him. He felt the truck start to move.

As Struecker steered out the east gate he waited for guidance from the C2 Black Hawk above.

*—You need to turn left and then move to the first intersection and take another left.*

Struecker made the left turn on Tanzania Street, but as he approached the intersection gunfire erupted all around. They weren't more than eighty yards out the back gate.

In a Humvee behind Struecker's, Sergeant Raleigh Cash screamed, "Action left!"

His turret gunner swung around to face five Somalis with weapons, and Cash, who was in the front passenger seat, heard the explosion of gunfire and the zing and pop of rounds passing close. Cash had been taught that if you heard that crack it meant the bullet had passed near your head. A *zing*, which sounded to him like the sound made when you hit a telephone-pole guy wire with a stick, meant the bullet had missed you by a far margin. The shots were answered by a roaring fusillade.

In another of the rear Humvees, reluctant Steve Anderson heard the eruption of gunfire and felt his stomach turn. Then he realized most of what he heard were Ranger guns. Any Somali with a weapon faced a crushing wave of American lead, .50 cals on three of the Humvees, SAWs and all those M-16s massed on the trucks.

Anderson tried to shoot his SAW, too, but the weapon jammed. He pulled and pulled on the charging handle, trying to get it unjammed, but it wouldn't budge. So he picked up the driver's M-16 and took aim out the back of the moving vehicle. An instant before he took aim he saw a Somali with a rifle dart through a doorway, but it was too late for him to take a shot.

The lead vehicles were taking the brunt of it. An RPG skipped across the top of Struecker's Humvee with a *screech* of metal on metal and exploded across the street against a concrete wall with a concussion that lifted the wide-bodied vehicle up on two wheels. Then his .50 gunner returned fire to a massed burst of AK-47s. It occurred to the sergeant that Sammy was unschooled in the art of ambush. The idea was to let the lead vehicle pass and suck in the whole column, then open fire. The unarmored flatbed trucks in the middle loaded with cooks and clerks and other volunteers would have made fat, vulnerable targets. By opening up on the lead vehicles, it gave the convoy a chance to back out before things got worse.

Struecker shouted for his driver to throw the Humvee in reverse. Those following would just have to figure it out. They slammed into the front of the Humvee behind them, and then that driver threw his vehicle in reverse and backed into the first truck. Eventually they all got the message.

"You need to find a different route!" he told his eyes in the sky.

*—Go back where you came from and turn right instead of left. You can get there that way.*

Struecker got the whole column back up to the gate, and this time turned right. Looming ahead was a roadblock, a big one. While a lot of the people shooting at them were clearly amateurs, it was obvious there were some experienced military minds among them. This roadblock was nothing spontaneous. They had anticipated the routes a convoy might take from the Ranger base and had thrown up barriers of dirt, junk, furniture, vehicle hulks, chunks of concrete, wire, and whatever else was at hand. There were tires burning on it that threw churning clouds into the darkening sky. Struecker could taste the sting of the burning rubber. The convoy knew *Super Six Four* was down less than a mile away, directly ahead.

Durant would say later that he heard the sound of a .50 cal, which almost certainly was from Struecker's Humvee. The pilot believed deliverance was at hand. But the convoy could advance no closer. Beyond the roadblock, between where they sat and Durant's crippled Black Hawk, was a concrete wall surrounding the sprawling ghetto of huts and walking paths. Struecker knew his Humvees could roll over the roadblock, but there was no way the trucks behind him would make it. And even if they did, there wasn't going to be any way through the concrete wall.

*—See where those tires are burning? That's where the crash is. Go in one hundred meters past it.*

"You'll have to find us another route," Struecker responded.

*—There ain't another route.*

"Well, you need to find one. Figure out a way to get there."

*—The only other route is to go all the way around the city and come in through the back side.*

"Fine. We'll take it."

Struecker knew every minute mattered. Durant and his crew wouldn't last long. It seemed like it took forever for the five-tons to turn around on the narrow street. The trucks weren't delicate about it. They rammed into walls and ground gears. As the trucks fought their way around, most of the men moved out into the street to defend the convoy. On one knee in the dirt, Sergeant Cash took a whack on his chest that almost knocked him over. It felt like someone had punched him up near the shoulder. He ran his hand inside his shirt, looking for blood. There was none. The bullet had skimmed off the front of his chest plate, tearing the straps of his load-bearing harness so that it was now hanging by threads.

Squeglia saw a round clip off the side-view mirror of the truck on the driver's side, and reached his M-16 across the chest of the driver to return fire. Sizemore unloaded on everything he saw, venting his pent-up rage. Anderson kept his head down, looking for specific targets. He shot a few times, but didn't think he'd hit anyone.

When they all got pointed at last in the right direction, the convoy sped out along a road that skirted the city to the southwest, driving through an occasional hail of AK-47 fire. From the peak of one rise they could see Durant's crash site. It was down in a little valley, but there seemed no easy way to get there.

# 8

Up in their Black Hawk, Goffena and Yacone could see both convoys in trouble. Lieutenant Colonel McKnight's battered main convoy was steering back toward the K-4 circle, away from both crash sites, and the emergency convoy of cooks and volunteers wasn't getting close.

They again asked to insert their Delta snipers. They were down to just two now. Sergeant Brad Hallings had manned one of *Super Six Two*'s miniguns after one of the crew chiefs was injured. They would need him there.

Captain Yacone turned around in his seat to discuss the situation with the two Delta operators.

"Things are getting bad now, guys," Yacone told them, shouting over the chopper's engines and the sound of the guns. "The second convoy is taking intensive fire, and it doesn't sound like it's gonna make it to the crash site. Mike and I have ID'ed a field about twenty-five to fifty yards away from where they're down. There are lots of shacks and shanties in between. Once you get there, you could either hunker down and wait for the vehicles, or try to get the wounded to an open area, where we could come back in and get you."

Shughart and Gordon both indicated they were ready to go down.

Up in the command bird, Harrell pondered the request. It was terribly risky, maybe even hopeless. But one or two properly armed, well-trained soldiers could hold off an undisciplined mob indefinitely. Shughart and Gordon were experts at killing and staying alive. They were serious, career soldiers, trained to get hard, ugly things done. They saw opportunity where others could see only danger. Like the other operators, they prided themselves on staying cool and effective even in extreme danger. They lived and trained endlessly for moments like this. If there was a chance to succeed, these two believed they would.

In the C2 bird, seated side by side, Harrell and Matthews weighed the decision. Their entire air rescue team was on the ground already at the first crash site. The ground convoy wasn't going to get to Durant and his crew fast enough. But dropping in Shughart and Gordon would most likely be sending them to their deaths. Matthews turned down the volume on their radios momentarily.

"Look, they're your guys," he said to Harrell. "They're the only two guys we've got left. What do you want to do?"

"What are our choices?" Harrell asked.

"We can put them in or not put them in. Nobody else is going to get to that crash site that I can see."

"Put them in," said Harrell.

So long as there was even a tiny chance, they felt obliged to give it to the downed crew.

When Goffena's crew chief, Master Sergeant Mason Hall, passed word to the men that it was time to jump, Gordon grinned and gave an excited thumbs-up.

There was a small opening behind one of the huts. It was bordered by a fence and covered by some debris, but it might do. Goffena made a low pass at it, flaring up near the ground to blow over the fence and scatter the debris. He couldn't get rid of enough of it to land, so he held a hover at about five feet as Shughart and Gordon jumped.

Shughart got tangled momentarily on the safety line connecting him to the chopper and had to be cut free. Gordon took a spill as he ran for cover. Shughart stood motioning with his hands, indicating confusion. They'd gotten disoriented jumping down, and were crouched in a defensive posture in the open trying to get their bearings. Goffena dropped the chopper back down low, leaned out his door, and pointed the way. One of his crew chiefs flung a smoke grenade in the direction of the crash.

The operators both turned thumbs up and began moving that way.

# 9

More than a mile to the northeast, back at Chalk Two's original blocking position by the target building, the war had slowed down for Sergeant Ed Yurek. After stumbling into the small Somali schoolhouse and coaxing the teacher and children to the floor, Yurek had been left in charge of the remnants of his chalk when Lieutenant DiTomasso and eight other Rangers had sprinted down to help out at the first crash site. Yurek had seen the ground convoy drive off. As the fighting shifted to the Black Hawk crash site three blocks east, things grew so quiet on Yurek's corner he got spooked. With the lieutenant and his radioman gone, he had no contact with the command radio net. He was worried the whole force had forgotten them.

He used his personal radio to call DiTomasso.

"What's up, Lieutenant?"

—*You need to find your way to me.*

"Roger, sir. Where are you?"

—*Take that big alley three blocks east, then turn left. Go about two hundred meters. You can't miss us.*

"Roger."

It was and it wasn't good news. It felt like they'd finally gotten this small corner of Mogadishu tamed. They'd grown familiar with angles of fire and potential danger spots and had found what seemed to be adequate cover. The kids in the little tin schoolhouse had been quiet as mice. Yurek had been keeping an eye out for them. Out in this very dangerous city, with bullets and RPGs flying, he was loathe to give up what seemed to have become a safe and quiet corner. They could hear heavy shooting over by the crash site, and once they were up and moving down the road, they'd have no cover. DiTomasso and the first men down the road had at least had the element of surprise. Yurek's would be the second team to pass through the same gauntlet. He had no doubt Sammy would be waiting.

"Come on, guys. We gotta go!" he reluctantly informed the men.

They began moving east down the alley. They walked fast, weapons aimed and ready, in single file spread out down the south side of the alley. They stayed a few steps off the stone walls on that side of the street. The natural inclination was to get as close to the wall as possible. The wall suggested at least a margin of safety. But Sergeant Paul Howe, one of the

D-boys, had advised them against it. Bullets follow walls, he'd explained. The enemy can concentrate fire down an alleyway, and the walls on either side will act as funnels. Some rounds would actually ride the walls for hundreds of feet. Standing tight against a wall was actually more dangerous than being in the middle of the street.

At the intersections they would stop and cover each other. Yurek ran while his men laid suppressive fire north and south. Then he covered for the next man, and so on. They leapfrogged across.

It didn't take long for the shooting gallery to open. Sammies would pop up in windows or doorways or around corners and spray bursts of automatic fire. Most were clearly amateurs. The kick of the weapon and their own desire to stay behind cover meant they were unlikely to hit anyone. Yurek figured these were guys just trying not to lose face with their group. They would let a burst fly with their head turned away and eyes closed, fling the weapon, and run. Yurek didn't even bother returning fire for some of these. But some of the men who popped up in windows were different. They didn't shoot instantly. They took aim. They meant business. He figured these were Aidid's militia guys. There was usually one militia guy for every four or five who shot at them.

Yurek and his men invariably shot first. During the long boring weeks before this mission, they had trained almost daily. Captain Steele had insisted on it. They had unlimited ammo to work with, and out in the desert they had set up a variety of shooting ranges, including this very drill. In practice, targets would pop out unexpectedly. They had different shapes and colors. The rules were, shoot if you see the blue triangle, but hold your fire if it's a green square. Yurek felt the benefit of all that practice. He and his men engaged in a running series of gunfights. He shot one man in a doorway just ten feet away. The man stepped out and took aim, a bushy-haired, dusty man with baggy brown pants and a lightweight blue cotton shirt with an AK. He didn't shoot instantly, and that's what killed him. Yurek's eyes met his for a split second as he pulled the trigger. The Somali just fell forward out into the alley without getting off a shot. He was the second man Yurek had ever shot.

Specialist Lance Twombly blasted at one man with his SAW, shooting the big gun from his hip. The Sammy had stepped out from a corner with an AK and started shooting. Both he and the Ranger blasted away at each other not more than fifteen yards apart. Twombly saw his rounds—

there must have been forty of them—chipping the walls and spitting up
dirt all around his target, and he never hit the man. Nor did the Somali hit
Twombly. The Sammy ran off. Twombly just kept on moving, cursing himself for being such a bad shot.

Yurek could not believe it when they made it the entire three blocks
without any of his men being hit. But there was no respite. At the intersection of the main road he looked downhill and saw Waddell against the
wall on his side of the street. Across the street at the opposite corner, behind a big tree and car, were Nelson and Sergeant Alan Barton, who'd roped
in from the CSAR bird. Twombly moved down that side of the street and
crossed the road to add his SAW to Nelson's M-60. There were two dead
Somalis stretched out on the ground by the car. Across the street from them,
diagonally from Waddell, was a little green Volkswagen. DiTomasso and
some men from the CSAR bird were crouched there.

Yurek ran across the road to the car to link up with DiTomasso. He
passed the alley and saw the downed helicopter to his right. Just as he arrived, the Volkswagen began rocking from the impact of heavy rounds,
*thunk thunk thunk thunk*. Whatever this weapon was, its bullets were poking
right through the car. Yurek and the others all hit the ground. He couldn't
tell where the shooting was coming from.

"Nelson! Nelson, what is it?" he shouted across the street.

"It's a big gun!" Nelson shouted back.

Yurek and DiTomasso looked at each other and rolled their eyes.

"Where is it?" he shouted across to Nelson.

Nelson pointed up the street, and Yurek edged out to look around
the car. There were three dead Somalis on the street. Yurek stood and
pulled them together, stacking them, which enabled him to slide out to
his left a few feet behind cover. He saw two Somalis stretched out on the
ground up the street north behind a big gun mounted on a tripod. From
that position the gun controlled the street. Behind the tree across the street,
they couldn't see Nelson, and he'd have been a fool to expose his position.

Yurek had a LAW (Light Antitank Weapon) strapped to his back that
he'd been carrying around on every mission for weeks. It was a lightweight
disposable plastic launcher (it weighed only three pounds). He unstrapped
it, then climbed up and leaned forward on the car, taking aim with the
weapon's flip-up crosshairs. He guessed they were two hundred meters
away. The rocket launched with a punch of a back blast, and Yurek watched

it zoom straight in on his target and explode with a flash and a loud *woom!* The gun went flipping up in the air.

He was accepting congratulations on his shooting when the *thunk thunk thunk* resumed. The rocket had evidently landed just short, close enough to send the weapon flying and kick up a cloud of dirt, but evidently not close enough to destroy it or stop its shooters. He saw them up the street now kneeling behind the weapon, which they'd righted again on its bipod. Yurek picked up a LAW that someone had discarded nearby, but it looked bent and crushed. He couldn't get it to open up. So he loaded a 40 mm 203 round into the grenade launcher mounted under the barrel of his M-16. This time his aim was better. You could actually see the fat 203 round spiral into a target, and this one spun square into the center. The two Sammies just fell over sideways in opposite directions. He presumed the gun was destroyed. When the smoke cleared he could see it just lying there between the two men. No one else came out to get it. Yurek and the others kept a good eye on that gun until nightfall.

# 10

Barton and Nelson were behind a tree on the northeast corner of the big intersection directly west of the crash. A little Fiat was parked against the tree. It looked like the driver had left it with the gas cap wedged tightly against the tree to prevent Mogadishu's alert and enterprising thieves from siphoning the gas. Nelson had his M-60 machine gun propped on the roof of the car with belts of ammo draped over the side. From the two dead Somalis on the street alongside the car, blood formed red-brown pools in the sand.

"It can't get much worse than this," Barton said.

Just then an RPG exploded against the opposite wall with a brilliant flash and a chest-wrenching blast. This made them laugh. Laughter was a balm. It held panic at bay and it seemed to come easily. In these extreme circumstances it became unbearably funny just to act normal. If they could still laugh they were all right. This was definitely more fire than they'd ever expected to experience in Mogadishu. Nobody had anticipated a serious fight from these characters. Nelson wondered where his friends Casey Joyce and Dom Pilla and Kevin Snodgrass were and how they were faring.

It was raining RPGs. They would drop down from the north and hit the side of the stone buildings and splash along the walls, great streaking explosions, like someone throwing fireballs.

"Goddamn, Twombly, this is unreal," Nelson said.

He crouched down behind a two-foot concrete ramp between the tree and the wall and was fiddling with his M-60 when a Somali ducked out from behind a tin shed about ten feet up the street and fired at him and Twombly. Nelson knew he was dead. Rounds hit between his legs and he felt them passing next to his face. Twombly dropped the man.

Nelson saw Twombly mouth the words, "You okay?"

"I don't know."

Twombly had fired his SAW about two feet in front of Nelson's face, so close that his cheeks and nose had been singed by the muzzle heat. The blast had hammered his eardrums, blinded him, and his head was still ringing.

"That hurt," Nelson complained. "I can't hear and I can't see. Don't you ever fucking shoot your weapon off that close to me again!"

Just then another Somali took a shot at them and Twombly returned fire with his rifle directly over Nelson's head. After that, Nelson wouldn't hear a thing for many hours.

# 11

Sergeant Paul Howe and the three men of his Delta team had still been back on the target house roof when they saw the CSAR team roping down from a Black Hawk about a quarter mile northeast. They watched while the Black Hawk took the RPG hit with men still on its ropes, and were amazed at how the pilot held the bird steady after being hit until the last men were down. Howe knew something was going on over there, but since he had no radio link to the command net and had been too busy inside the target house to notice that a Black Hawk had been shot down, he didn't know why the CSAR team was roping in.

He got the full story when he was summoned downstairs by the Delta ground commander, Captain Scott Miller.

"We're going to move over there and secure it," Miller said. He explained that the ground convoy, which was loading the Somali prisoners out front, would drive over to the crash site. The rest of them were going to move there on foot. Ranger Chalk One, led by Captain Steele, would take the lead. The operators would follow, and Ranger Chalk Three on the south end of the target, led by Sergeant Sean Watson, would bring up the rear.

Howe knew the fight was bad and worsening out on the streets. The idea of moving on foot over to where he'd seen the CSAR bird rope its crew in was daunting. He thought, *This is going to be fun.*


Captain Steele saw the operators come spilling out of the courtyard, moving east toward him. This posed a novel situation for the Ranger commander. He and his men had trained to provide protection for Delta, but the two units didn't mix. Each had its own chain of command, its own separate radio links, and, most importantly, its own way of doing things. Now they were being thrown together for this move over to the downed Black Hawk. Steele and Miller conferred briefly about how to proceed, and agreed that the Rangers should take front and rear positions.

This column of about eighty men would set off on foot just minutes after Lieutenant Colonel McKnight's ill-fated convoy departed the target building. While that convoy wandered hopelessly lost through the city, getting hammered, and while Durant's Black Hawk was crashing about a mile southwest, this force of D-boys and Rangers were having their own tragic difficulties moving on foot to the first crash site.


They hadn't run more than a block when Sergeant Aaron Williamson got hit. He had been shot earlier, the round had taken off the tip of his index finger, but Williamson had kept fighting. Lieutenant Perino heard someone scream, and turned to see Williamson rolling on the street, writhing and screaming, holding his left leg.

"I've got a man down," Perino radioed up to Steele.

"Pick him up and keep on moving," Steele said.

As Howe and his team ran past Williamson, there were five Rangers stooped around the wounded man.

"Keep moving and let the medic handle it!" Howe shouted at them.

Williamson was carried back up the street to one of the Humvees in the ground convoy, which was about ready to roll.

Specialist Stebbins, the company clerk along for his first real mission, was out in front. His blocking position had been at the southeast corner, and they were moving east now. He trotted crouched and careful, staying away from the walls as the D-boys had advised. Every few feet down the road a doorway would open into a small courtyard. As Stebbins came upon one door, a Somali came running out of the building into the courtyard and Stebbins fired. It was instinctive. The man startled him. *Bang bang.* Two rounds. The man dropped to a sitting position, clutching his chest and looking amazed. Then he slumped over forward and began to rock and moan. He was a big man with short hair. He was wearing this disco-style bright blue shirt with long sleeves and a big collar. Most of the Sammies were dusty and wore shabby clothes but this man was dressed nicely, and he was clean. He had on corduroy bell-bottom pants and his belt had a big die-cast metal buckle. He seemed completely out of place. Stebbins had just shot him. He had never shot anyone before.

This all took place in seconds but it seemed much longer. Stebbins was readying to shoot the man again when his weapon was grabbed by Private Carlos Rodriguez.

"Don't waste your rounds on him, Stebby," he said. "Just keep moving."

Steele, who had a radio strapped to his broad back, fell further and further behind Lieutenant Perino and the rest of Chalk One. The idea was to stay spread out and provide covering fire for each other as they went through intersections. But right away, to Steele's dismay, the formation broke down. The D-boys ignored the marching orders and just kept moving forward. These were men trained to think for themselves and act independently in battle, and now they were doing it. Each of the operators had a radio earpiece under their little plastic hockey helmets—Steele called them "skateboard helmets"—and a microphone that wrapped around to their mouth. So they were usually in constant touch with each other. When the radios were not working or when the noise level was too high, as it was now, the D-boys communicated expertly with hand signals. Steele's Rangers relied on shouted orders from their officers and team leaders. They were younger, less experienced, and terrified. Some tended to just follow the operators instead of staying with their teams. Steele saw a complete breakdown of unit integrity before they'd moved two blocks.

It was typical of the problems he'd had with Delta from the start. For better or worse, the attitudes and practices of the elite commandos started to rub off on his Rangers when they began bunking together in the hangar. Before long, everywhere you looked was a teenage soldier in sunglasses with rolled-up shirtsleeves. Privates would pull guard duty in helmet, flak vest, gym shorts, and their regulation brown T-shirts. Younger soldiers began showing more and more impatience with what they saw as meaningless robot-Ranger formality.

When Steele cracked down, a lot of them thought it was because their captain felt threatened by the D-boys. In the year before this deployment, the broad-beamed former lineman moved through his men like muttering Jove through his hinds, the meanest, manliest man in the army. When Specialist Dave Diemer had defeated all comers in an arm wrestling contest, Steele took him on and beat him—leaving Diemer whining that the captain had cheated. Steele gave the unapologetic impression that he could break you with his bare hands if it weren't for his strict devotion to Jesus and army discipline. He was unbending even when his senior noncoms thought it was time to bend, like the time back at Fort Bragg when he'd ordered all the men awakened after midnight because they'd collapsed, with permission from their platoon sergeants, into bunks without cleaning their weapons after a days-long grueling training mission. But no matter how tough Steele was, of course, it was the D-boys who occupied the absolute pinnacle of the macho feeding chain. Most of them were NCOs, and not only did their very presence deflate any of the standard displays of gruff manhood, they were serenely and rather obviously unimpressed with Steele's captaincy.

The disdain was mutual. Steele accepted that these operators were good at their jobs, but he wasn't in awe of them. He found their civilian manner and contemptuous attitude toward Ranger discipline hard to take. Sure, it was a good idea to encourage individual initiative and creative thinking in combat, but some of these guys had strayed so far from traditional army norms it seemed unhealthy. They could be comically arrogant. When they'd gotten a list of potential target sites, for instance, the D-boys had divvied them up among different teams. Each was assigned to draw up an assault plan. Since his men were involved, Steele had sat in on the meeting when the various schemes were presented. The captain's experience with such a planning session was like this: You sat there and took notes and asked questions only to make sure you got things down correctly and then saluted on your way out. The D-boys' meeting was a free-for-all. One group would present its plan and somebody would pipe up, "Why, that's the stupidest thing I ever heard," which would provoke a sturdy "Fuck you," which quickly degenerated into guys screaming at each other. It looked to Steele like they were about to assume Kung Fu stances and have it out.

Steele could imagine what would happen if a company of Rangers operated that way. Some of his men were still boys. As far as the captain could tell, most had just emerged from a lifetime of lounging on sofas eating Fritos and watching MTV. Basic and Ranger training had shaped most of them up reasonably well, but the average private in Bravo company still had a long way to go before qualifying as a professional soldier. There were good, time-tested reasons for *Hoo-ah* discipline.

It was easy to see why Steele was destined for the losing end of a popularity contest with the D-boys. Most of his men didn't think through the causes. They saw it all as an ego conflict.

Like the time Steele was standing in line with his men at mess, and spotted Delta Sergeant Norm Hooten carrying a rifle with the safety off. Ranger rules required that any weapon, loaded or unloaded, have the safety on at all times when at the base. It was an eminently sensible rule, a basic principle of handling weapons safely.

He tapped the blond operator on the shoulder and pointed it out. Hooten had held up his index finger and said, "*This* is my safe."

Showed Steele up right in front of his men.

Now the very breakdowns the captain had feared were happening when it mattered most. There was nothing he could do about it. As his men passed by helter-skelter, Steele fell back near the middle of the pack. They'd sort things out at the crash site. If they could find it. Nobody was sure exactly where it was.


In short order, Howe and his Delta team were in front of the force. Howe saw bullets skipping off the dirt and skimming down the walls, chipping the concrete. He was way past worrying about staying in formation. The street was a kill zone. Survival meant moving like your hair was on fire. It was time to lead by example. The goal was to punch through to the downed helicopter, and every second mattered. If they failed to link up, then there would be two weak forces instead of a single strong one. Two perimeters to defend instead of one. So they moved quickly but also smartly. As Howe moved he thought about making every one of his shots count, and keeping his back to a wall at all times. They were in a 360-degree battlefield, so keeping a wall behind him meant one angle he couldn't be shot from. At each crossroads he and his team would pause, watch, and listen. Were bullets hitting walls? Bouncing off the streets? Were the shots going left to right or right to left? Every bit of experience and practical knowledge was useful now for staying alive. Were they machine-gun bullets or AKs? An AK only has twenty-five to thirty rounds in a magazine, so if you waited for the lull, Sammy would be reloading when you ran. The most important thing was to keep moving. One of the hardest things in the world to hit is a moving target.

He and his team had spent years training with each other, had fought together in Panama and other places, and moved with confidence and authority. Howe felt that they were the perfect soldiers for this situation. They'd learned to filter out the confusion, put up a mental curtain. The only information that came fully through was the most critical *at that moment*. Howe could ignore the pop of a rifle or the snap of a nearby round. It was usually just somebody shooting airballs. It would take chips flying from a wall near him to make him react. As they moved down the street it was one fluid process—scan for threats, find a safe place to go next, shoot, move, scan for threats. . . . The key was to keep moving. With the volume of fire on these streets, to stop meant to die. The greatest danger was in getting pinned down.

The Rangers followed as well as they could, leapfrogging across the intersections. Stebbins and 60-gunner Private Brain Heard kept up with them, reassured just to be close to the D-boys. These guys knew how to stay alive. Stebbins kept telling himself, *This is dangerous, but we'll make it. It's okay.* At the intersections he would take a knee and shoot while the man in front of him ran. Then the man behind him would tap his shoulder and he would take off, just closing his eyes and praying and running for all he was worth.

Sergeant Goodale, who had once bragged to his mother how eager he was for combat, felt terrified. He was waiting for his turn to sprint across a street when one of the D-boys tapped him on the shoulder. Goodale recognized him: it was the short stocky one, Earl, Sergeant First Class Earl Fillmore, a good guy. Fillmore must have seen how scared Goodale looked.

"You okay?" he asked.

"I'm okay."

Fillmore winked at him and said, "It's all right. We're coming out of this thing, man."

It calmed Goodale. He believed Fillmore.

By the time they were three blocks over, Howe's team was way out front. With them were Stebbins, Heard, Goodale, Perino, Corporal Jamie Smith, and a few other Rangers. They turned left onto Marehan Road, where the alley ended. The wide dirt road sloped uphill slightly and then downhill for several blocks, so when they made the turn they were just shy of the crest of a hill. Downhill to the south they could see Sammies running every which way. Over the crest of the hill to the north, Howe saw signal smoke from what must have been the crash. They were about two hundred yards away.

There was a blizzard of fire at that intersection. Automatic rifle fire and RPGs from all directions. Howe felt the force was in peril of getting stuck and cut to ribbons. He shouted back down the street to Captain Miller, "Follow me!" and plunged straight down the left side. Stebbins and several other Rangers followed. Perino, Goodale, Smith, and some others followed Hooten's Delta team across the street and started down the right wall. Immediately behind them was Sergeant First Class John Boswell's Delta team.

An RPG exploded on the wall near Howe and his men. Howe felt the wallop of pressure in his ears and chest and dropped to one knee. One of his men had been hit on the left side with a small piece of shrapnel. Howe abruptly kicked in the door to a one-room house on his left. He and his team had learned to move like they owned the world. Every house was their house. If they needed shelter, they kicked in a door. Anyone who threatened them would be killed. It was that simple. No one was inside. They caught their breath and reloaded their weapons. Running with all that gear was exhausting. The body armor was like wearing a wet suit. They were sweating profusely and breathing heavily. Howe drew his knife and cut away the back of his buddy's shirt to check the wound. There was a small hole in the man's back with about a two-inch swollen, bruised ring around it. There was almost no blood. The swelling had closed the hole.

"You're good to go," Howe told him, and they were out the door and moving again.

Moving up in front of Perino, Goodale saw the familiar desert uniforms down the street and inwardly rejoiced. *They'd made it!* Once they'd linked up, the convoy would arrive and they could all roll out of this hell. The sun was getting low in the sky. Goodale had promised his fiancée, Kira, that he'd call tonight. He *had* to get back in time to make that call.

Goodale ran up behind Sergeant Chuck Elliot, who was squatting at the corner of the first intersection on the slope, shooting east. Goodale pointed his gun down Marehan Road. He saw Howe and his team pushing on ahead across the street, in shadow. The low sun still lit Goodale's side of the street brightly. Because they were on a slope, he could shoot over the heads of the men down the street at Somalis moving three or four blocks north. It was a long shot, but he had no other targets. It occurred to him that no one was shooting to the left, the alley west. It blinded him to look that way. Goodale turned to squint into the light and pop off a few suppressive rounds when he felt a shooting pain. His right leg seized up and he fell over backward, right into Perino.

He said, "Ow!"

A bullet had entered his right thigh and passed through him, leaving a big exit wound on his right buttock. What immediately flashed into Goodale's mind was a story he'd heard about this 10th Mountain Division guy who had lost his hand the week before when a round detonated the grenade in the LAW he was carrying. He struggled to get the LAW off his shoulder.

Perino couldn't tell what Goodale was doing.

"Where are you hit?" he asked.

"Right in the ass."

Goodale dropped the LAW and yelled to Elliot, "There's a LAW right there!"

Elliot obligingly picked it up.

Perino got back on the radio to Steele, who was now trailing the column.

"Captain, I've got another man hit."

"Pick him up and keep moving," Steele insisted.

Instead, Perino moved on across the intersection with some of the other Rangers from Chalk One, and left Goodale with Sergeant Bart Bullock, the same Delta medic who had earlier in the fight helped patch up Ranger Todd Blackburn after his fall from the Black Hawk. Both Bullock and medic Kurt Schmid had rejoined their Delta units at the target house after sending Blackburn back to base in the three-Humvee convoy (the one on which Sergeant Pilla had been killed). Schmid was now moving a block north with Perino and several other Rangers. Goodale lay back on the dirt as Bullock looked him over.

"You got tagged," Bullock said. "You're all right though. No problem."

Goodale was disgusted. *Game over.* It was the same feeling he'd had getting injured in a football game. They carried you off the field and you were done. It was disappointing, but if the going had been particularly rough it could also be a relief. He took off his helmet, then saw an RPG fly past no more than six feet in front of him and explode with a stupendous wallop about twenty feet away. He put his helmet back on. This game was most definitely not over.

"We need to get off this street," Bullock said.

He dragged Goodale into a small courtyard, and the Delta team headed by Sergeant Hooten hopped in with them. Goodale asked Bullock for his canteen, which the medic had taken off when removing his gear. Bullock fished it out of Goodale's butt pack and discovered a bullet hole clean through it from the same round that had passed through his body. There was still water in the canteen.

"You'll want to keep this," Bullock said.


With the men at the rear of the column, Captain Steele's overriding goal was to consolidate his Ranger force and reestablish some order. Time was essential here. Steele had been told the convoy would probably reach the crash site before he and his men did. He had just heard on the radio that another Black Hawk had gone down (Durant's), which meant things were that much more urgent. From the C2 bird, Harrell explained:

— *We are going to try to get everyone consolidated at the northern site and exfil everyone off the northern site and move to the southern crash site, over.*

Steele had about sixty men to account for when those vehicles arrived, and right now he had only a vague idea where they all were.

As he arrived at the intersection at the top of the rise, he ran across to the right side of the street with Lieutenant James Lechner and several other Rangers. Sergeant Watson and the remainder of Chalk Three were the last to turn the corner.

Steele moved over the slight rise and started down the hill. He had gone only about ten yards when a burst of fire forced him and those with him to drop. He was on his belly, with his wide face nearly in the sand. Alongside to his left was Sergeant Chris Atwater, his radioman. Prone to Atwater's left was Lieutenant Lechner, Steele's second-in-command. Atwater and Steele, both big men, were trying to take cover behind a tree with a trunk only about one foot wide.

About three strides to their right, Delta team leader Hooten was in a steel doorway to the small courtyard where Bullock had dragged Goodale. Steele was watching another team of operators working their way up the street ahead of him. He intended to follow, but just then one of the D-boys, Fillmore, went limp. His little helmet jerked up and back and blood came spouting out of his head. It was obviously fatal. Fillmore just crumpled.

An operator grabbed Fillmore and began dragging him into a narrow alley. Then he was shot, in the neck.

Steele felt the gravity of their predicament hit fully home. *This is for keeps.*

# 12

Mohamed Sheik Ali moved swiftly around his neighborhood. Ali had been fighting in these streets already for a decade, since he was fourteen years old and had been drummed into Siad Barre's army. He moved mostly in crowds, darting from hiding place to hiding place, usually staying far enough away to make himself a hard target, but occasionally stealing close enough to fire off a few well-placed rounds from his AK. If the Americans spotted him, they saw a short, dusty little man with nappy hair whose teeth were brownish orange from chewing *khat* and whose eyes were wide with the effects of the drug and adrenaline.

Sheik Ali was a professional gunman, a killer, a man who had fought for and against the dictator, and then had put himself and his weathered weapon up for hire. Most Somalis had come to regard Sheik Ali and men like him as a plague. They were feared and despised. Now, with the Rangers to fight, men like him were valued again. To him, the Americans were just a new enemy to shoot at, and not a particularly brave one. Ali believed if the Rangers didn't have the helicopters helping them from above, he and his men would surround and kill them with ease, with their bare hands.

He relished the fight. There was no quarter given on either side. The black vests who came with the Rangers were especially ruthless killers. When they had come to Bakara Market they had come into his home uninvited and they would have to accept his punishment. Sheik Ali believed the radio broadcasts and flyers printed up by the Aidid's SNA. The Americans wanted to force all Somalis to be Christians, to give up Islam. They wanted to turn Somalis into slaves.

When the helicopter was shot down he rejoiced, and began running toward it. Unlike most of the crowd he did not run directly to the crash. He knew there would be armed men around it and that the Rangers would move to it. It would not be easy to get close.

Sheik Ali was part of a large number of irregular militia moving in the crowds that had begun to form a wide perimeter in the neighborhood around the crashed helicopter. He ran up a street parallel to the moving Rangers. He would run to a corner, wait by it, and shoot as the Rangers came across, then he would sprint to the next street and be waiting for them again. He was not weighted down with armor and gear, and he was not being shot at from all directions, so he could move faster and more freely than the Rangers. When he got to the perimeter around the crash site there were crowds, fighters like himself but mostly people who just came to see, women and children. The Americans were firing down the streets at everyone. Sheik Ali saw women and children fall.

He and several of the men in his band lay down behind a tree and shot at the Americans as they came down the slope toward the alley where the crashed helicopter was. There he saw a Ranger shot in the head, one of the black vests with the little helmets. His buddy tried to pull him to safety and he, too, was shot, in the neck.

Then Sheik Ali and his men moved on. They circled around the neighborhood where the helicopter was down, and crept back down toward it on Marehan Road. Sheik Ali found a tree and lay flat on his stomach behind it. There were Americans on his side of the street about two blocks south, hiding behind a car and a tree and a wall. There were more at the same intersection across the street. Between him and the Americans were more fighters, most of them crazy people with guns who didn't know how to fight. Sheik Ali waited behind his cover for a clean shot.

He was there for almost two hours, trading shots with the Americans, before his companion, Abdikadir Ali Nur, was shot. An American down the street behind an M-60 hit Nur with several shots that nearly tore off the left half of his body. Sheik Ali himself was hit by some shrapnel in the face when an M-203 round exploded nearby.

He then helped carry his friend to a hospital.

# 13

The odor of spent gunpowder had always been sweet for Private David Floyd. It reminded him of home. Out hunting with his father as a boy in South Carolina—which was not that long ago; he was just nineteen—he would pick up shotgun shells just to sniff them.

Now that odor, which was all around, meant something else. He ran with the others through the gunfire on the street, rounded the corner just behind a team of D-boys, and then jumped for whatever cover he could find on the left side of the street. He tucked himself into a corner by some roofing tin, facing south, disbelieving.

It had been an effort to keep moving. There was a big part of Floyd that just wanted to crawl into a little ball and hide somewhere. He knew it would be suicide to stop fighting, but he was that scared. He was scared enough to piss his pants. *I'm in it now.* It was like a movie only it was real and he was in the middle. He couldn't believe he was in actual combat and people were shooting at him, trying to kill him. *I'm gonna die on this dirty little street in Africa.* It was much too frantic a moment to be thinking about such things but it occurred to Floyd anyway, a sudden image in his mind's eye of a late summer Sunday morning at home with his parents sitting down to breakfast without the slightest notion that their precious son David was here, a million miles away, fighting for his life in this insane city they'd never even heard of, much less cared about. *What in the hell am I doing here?* The D-boys' presence helped keep those impulses under control. They encouraged the opposite impulse, that was there, too, which was to fight like hell, use every round and grenade and rocket at hand, use all the training he'd been given to inflict as much punishment as possible. Because it made him mad. To see one of his Ranger brothers shot down right beside him—he had seen Williamson go down, screaming—it just . . . well, it pissed Floyd off. So warring with the urge to crawl under a rock was this fury, this cornered-animal rage, like, *you motherfuckers asked for it now you're gonna get it.*

Then he saw Fillmore get hit. This was not supposed to happen. These guys knew how to stay alive. *Ho-oly shit.* If the D-boys were getting killed, what odds would you give Private First Class David Floyd for coming out of this alive?

He was against the west wall firing his weapon south pretty rapidly now down Marehan Road and realizing that the pile of tin around him was no real shelter at all. In the middle of the street, right in the middle, Specialist John Collett had crawled behind a hump in the road and was providing superb covering fire to the south with his SAW. Across the street was Sergeant Watson with a group of other Rangers.

Watson led the group with his own grim sense of humor. When a barrage of bullets slammed into a wall directly over his head, Watson turned to the men with his eyes open comically wide. "Oh, this sucks!" he said, in a way that made the others smile. His attitude was, *we're-in-the-shit-now-but-what-the-fuck!*


Sergeant Keni Thomas was closest to Fillmore when he got hit.

"Can you call for a medevac?" shouted Hooten.

Thomas ran back to Watson, who only heard the last part of what Thomas said. Watson knew there was no way they were going to be able to get Fillmore out, but he didn't have the heart to tell Thomas.

"Go ahead and ask the captain," he said.

So Thomas ran as far as he could in Steele's direction, then shouted, "We've got a head wound. We have to get him out!"

Steele gestured for Thomas to wait a second as he talked on the radio. Then he called back, "Is he one of ours?"

Weren't they all *one of ours?*

"A Delta guy," Thomas shouted.

Thomas was distressed. He'd never seen a man shot in the head.

"Just calm down," said Watson when Thomas returned. The sergeant said maybe they could get him on a vehicle. Where the hell were those vehicles anyway? When they left for the crash site, the convoy had been on the street right behind them.

Thomas ran back to Hooten.

"We can't land a bird in here," Thomas said, "but maybe we can get a Humvee."

"It's all right," said Hooten. "He's dead."

Thomas felt oddly emotionless about it. He felt angry at Captain Steele for asking, "Is he one of ours?" He also felt like a failure.


Collett was feeling good about his spot at the center of Marehan road. It didn't look like much. Guys on both sides of the street thought he was crazy. But Collett had deduced by the rounds cracking over his head that the hump was excellent cover. It looked to him as if it was the guys who were up and moving who were getting shot. He had good angles, but there was only room for one man. When Private George Siegler started crawling out toward him, Collett shouted, "Siegler, get back over there!" Siegler didn't argue. He just scooted around and crawled back to the wall.

Rounds poked through Floyd's tin shelter. Because the sun was low in the sky, when he heard the popping noise he saw shafts of light suddenly appear through the metal. It was like somebody was shooting at him with a laser. Then he saw Private Peter Neathery get hit across the street against the same wall where Fillmore had been shot. Neathery had been down on the ground working his M-60 machine gun when he screamed and rolled away clutching his right arm. Private Vince Errico took over the big gun, and seconds later let out a yelp. He, too, had been hit in the right arm. Both Neathery and Errico were now down, moaning. It was clear that the right side of the wall approaching the intersection, the place where Fillmore had been killed and where all these other men were being hit, was like a focal point for enemy fire. Walking through it was asking to be shot.

The bullet that hit Neathery had torn through his bicep. There was a lot of blood. Doc Richard Strous calmly examined it as Neathery looked up at Thomas.

"Damn, Sergeant, I hope they send me home for this."

"Does it hurt?" Thomas asked.

"Hell yeah! I'm all right, though. I do believe in God."

"That's okay," said Thomas. "He believes in you, too."

Thomas took over the M-60. He was squinting west, desperately looking for the shooter who had such a bead on them. Floyd and Specialist Melvin DeJesus were doing the same from their low vantage point in the shade. Floyd was feeling hopeless. *We're gonna buy it here.* Then a single brass cartridge plopped on the street right in front of them. It had to have rolled off the tin roof of the house they were up against. Whoever was up there would have a clear shot at the men along the sunny east wall. Floyd stood. He wasn't tall enough to see up on the roof, but he could reach it with his SAW. He placed the gun roughly parallel to the rooftop and squeezed a long burst. He heard a loud thumping and a shout. The shooting from that direction stopped.

Someone else was shooting from a courtyard to the south. Thomas had used up all the 60 ammo that was left, and he'd already tossed a grenade in that courtyard, and Floyd and DeJesus sprayed rounds toward it to no effect. They could see big muzzle flashes splash out from behind a low masonry wall backed with bushes.

"Use the LAW!" Floyd shouted.

Thomas had one of the disposable rocket launchers strapped to his back, but it was so lightweight and rarely used it was easy to forget about it.

He looked back at Floyd quizzically.

"The LAW! The LAW! On your back!" Floyd gestured to his shoulder.

Thomas's eyebrows went up theatrically, as if to say, *Oh yeah!*

He unstrapped the tube, extended it, and flipped up the sight. The rocket turned the courtyard into a ball of fire. Sergeant Watson saw Thomas exulting over the shot, the same man who had been so upset about Fillmore minutes before. *He solved his problem.* It was inspiring for Watson to see how determined and resilient men could be.

* * *

Specialist Mike Kurth was helping to bandage Errico when he saw a grenade drop and roll out past him. Its smoke trail first caught his eye, then he saw the pineapple shape on the ground, right next to the hump in the road hiding Collett.

"GRENADE!" sounded several voices together.

The men, Kurth, Errico, Neathery, and Doc Strous, all flopped to the sand and rolled as fast as they could. Private Jeff Young reached back to grab Strous and pull him away, and the explosion ripped the medic from his hands.

When it blew, Kurth felt himself driven hard into the ground and felt a flash of heat and light behind him. He was in just the right spot. The force of the explosion passed over him. He felt the shock and heat of it, and tasted its bitter chemical ignition, but in the frantic instants after the blast he moved his arms and legs and saw that he hadn't been hurt. The rest of the guys could not have been so lucky. Collett, for sure, was dead. Kurth sat up hesitantly, before the smoke had cleared.

"Doc, you good?" he asked.

"Yeah."

"Neathery?"

"Yeah."

"Errico?"

"Yeah."

"Young?"

"I'm okay."

He waited to name Collett last.

"Yeah, dude, I'm okay," his friend answered. The hump in the road had directed the blast up and away from him.

Strous got some shrapnel in one leg and Young caught a small piece in his boot, but otherwise everyone was intact.

Further down the slope on the sunny side of the street, just beyond a tin shack that jutted out from one of the houses, Captain Steele was still on the ground with his second in command, Lechner, and Atwater, his radioman. Sergeant Hooten was in the doorway to a courtyard about ten feet to Steele's right. It looked like he was trying to get the captain's attention.

Floyd saw the barrel of an M-16 protrude from behind the corner down his side of the street, pointing at the two Ranger officers.

# 14

What Hooten was trying to tell Steele was that he'd chosen a bad place to stop. Fillmore and one of the other operators had just been shot in that spot.

Steele motioned with his hand for Hooten to wait. He was talking on the radio. He wondered where in the hell the vehicles were. At the same time Steele's Rangers and the Delta operators had been running through the streets making their way to the first crash site, the ground convoy was wandering lost and taking terrible casualties. But Steele didn't know this. All he knew was that they had left the target house at the same time. Steele and some of his men had been pinned down now for about ten minutes. If those vehicles would show up they could all roll out of this mess.

Beside Steele, Lechner and Atwater were working out some fire support. They had trouble at first because the signal from Atwater's UHF radio was being overridden by the UHF emergency beacon from the downed Black Hawk a block away. Lechner was finally able to get through to one of the attack Little Birds on his FM radio. The pilot, Chief Warrant Officer Hal Wade, told Lechner to put out some big orange panels marking their positions. Lechner passed the word.

Once the panels were placed on the road, Wade came roaring down Marehan Road just above the low rooftops. Collett ducked his helmet into his chest. Gunfire erupted from all directions as the Little Bird flashed past, but the helicopter didn't fire. Wade was braving the fire to make sure he knew where his own forces were before shooting back. His chopper flew up and swept into a turn and came roaring back down the road again. There was another rattling explosion of gunfire, but once again Wade didn't shoot. He now had a pretty good fix on where his people were on the ground. Wade's Little Bird made another sweeping turn. This time when he came down his miniguns were blazing.

It was just after that first shooting run that a bullet sprayed sand into Steele's eye. Lechner turned left. He thought the shot came from across the road, but Steele rolled to his right and looked at the tin wall behind him. The shot had rung so loud he was certain it had come from there. His first thought was that one of the wounded Rangers behind him was shooting through the wall. He kept rolling away, which wasn't easy with the big radio strapped to his back.

Then two more holes poked through the tin with loud bangs and dirt flew and Lechner screamed.

He first felt a whipping sensation and then a crushing blow, as if an anvil had fallen on the lower half of his leg. The pain was unbearable. He gripped his upper leg and looked down at a gaping hole in his leg. The bullet had exploded his shinbone and traveled on down his leg and exited at his ankle, shredding the foot beneath the hole.

There had been three rounds. Steele and Atwater had reacted to the first by rolling away, but Lechner had not. Steele was rolling when he heard Lechner scream. There was more shooting. Hooten gesticulated wildly in the doorway, waving Steele in. Atwater was between Lechner and him and the doorway was close, so Steele got up and ran for it. There was a lip around the base of the entrance and he tripped over it. The big captain came sprawling into the courtyard. Atwater came flying in after him.

Steele saw Atwater and shouted, "We've got to get Lechner!"

He stood to run back out but saw the howling lieutenant, his leg a mess, being dragged toward the door by Bullock, who had run out to the street to help.

Steele took the radio mike from Atwater. Shouting, his words delivered in gasped phrases, his voice contrasted sharply with the even, cool voices of the pilots and airborne commanders, reflecting the drama on the ground.

—*Romeo Six Four, this is Juliet Six Four. We're taking heavy small arms fire. We need relief NOW and start extracting.*

Harrell responded evenly but with impatience.

—*This is Romeo Six Four. I UNDERSTAND you need to be extracted. I've done EVERYTHING I CAN to get those vehicles to you, over.*

Steele spoke wearily.

—*Roger, understand. Be advised command element* [Lechner] *was just hit. Have more casualties, over.*

Sergeant Goodale, who had been pulled into the same courtyard earlier after being shot through the thigh and buttock, had heard Lechner howl. It was a horrible sound, the worst sound he'd ever heard a man make.

His own wound, oddly, didn't hurt that bad. Lechner's looked horrific. He was still screaming when they got him inside. Goodale helped to pull the lieutenant's radio off. Minutes before, after his injury, Goodale had radioed Lechner to tell him he would be unable to continue calling in air support. That's why Lechner had been calling Wade. Now here the lieutenant was, screaming in agony, the upper part of his right leg normal, but the bottom half from just below the knee flopped grotesquely to one side. He was ghost white. Goodale sickened more as he saw a widening pool form under the leg. Blood flowed from Lechner's wound like it was pouring from a jug.

# 15

At roughly the same time, one and a half miles southwest, his helicopter pancaked into a squalid village of cloth and tin huts, Black Hawk *Super Six Four* pilot Mike Durant came to. There was something wrong with his right leg. He and his copilot, Ray Frank, had been knocked cold for at least several minutes, they weren't sure how long. Durant was upright, leaning slightly to the right. The windshield was shattered and there was something draped over him, a big sheet of tin. The Black Hawk seemed remarkably intact. The rotor blades had not flexed off. His seat, which was mounted on shock absorbers, had collapsed down to the floor. It had broken in the full down position and was cocked to the right. He figured that was because they had been spinning when they hit. The shocks had collapsed and the spin jerked the seat to the right. It must have been the combination of the jerk and the impact that had broken his femur. The big bone in his right leg had snapped on the edge of his seat.

The Black Hawk had flattened a flimsy hut. No one had been inside, but in the hut alongside a two-year-old girl, Howa Hassan, lay unconscious and bleeding. A hunk of flying metal from the helicopter had taken a deep gouge out of her forehead. Her mother, Bint Abraham Hassan, had been splashed with something hot, probably oil, and was severely burned on her face and legs.

The dazed pilots checked themselves over. Frank's left tibia was broken.

Durant did some things he later could not explain. He removed his helmet and his gloves. Then he took off his watch. Before flying he always took off his wedding ring because there was a danger it could catch on rivets or switches. He would pass the strap of his watch through the ring and keep it there during a flight. Now he removed the watch and took the ring off the strap and set both on the dashboard.

He picked up his weapon, an MP-5K, a little German 9 mm submachine gun. The pilots called them SPs, or Skinny-poppers.

Frank tried to explain what happened during the crash.

"I couldn't get them all the way off," he said, explaining his struggle to reach up and pull the power control levers back as they fell. Frank said he had reinjured his back. He had hurt it first in the crash years before. Durant's back hurt, too. They both figured they had crushed vertebrae. All this happened in the first moments after they came to.

Durant realized that with his leg and back broken, he would be unable to pull himself out of the chopper. He pushed the piece of tin roof away from him and resolved to defend his position through the broken windshield. They looked like they were in some little opening, a yard between huts. There was a hut facing him pieced together with irregularly shaped pieces of corrugated metal, and a small dirt alleyway alongside it. To his side was another flimsy wall pieced together like the house. Durant remembers seeing Frank sitting in the doorway opposite, about to push himself out. It was the last time he saw him.

That's when Shughart and Gordon showed up. Durant was startled. They were suddenly standing there. He'd either been out for a while or they'd come amazingly fast. He didn't know either of the Delta operators well, but he recognized their faces. Seeing them gave him an enormous sense of relief. It was over. He figured they were part of a rescue team. His next thought had been to get the radio up and operating, but now, with his rescuers already on the ground, there was no need. Shughart and Gordon were calm. There was gunfire, mostly from the choppers overhead. The D-boys reached in and lifted Durant out of the craft gently, one lifting his legs and the other grabbing his torso, as if they had all the time in the world, and set him down on his side by a tree. He was not in great pain. With the airframe and a wall joined behind him, and a wall to his left that ran all the way back behind the tail of the chopper, Durant was in a perfect position to cover the whole right side of the aircraft.

He could see that his crew chiefs had taken the brunt of the impact. There were no shock absorbers in back like the ones he and Frank had up front. He watched the operators lift Bill Cleveland from the fuselage. Cleveland had blood all over his pants and was talking but making no sense.

Then the D-boys moved to the other side of the helicopter to help Field. Durant couldn't see feet moving under the fuselage because the landing gear had been crushed on impact. The belly of the bird was on the dirt. He assumed they were setting up a perimeter over there, looking for a way to get them out, maybe looking for a place where another helicopter could set down and load them up. Skinnies were starting to poke their heads around the corner on Durant's side of the chopper. Just an occasional one or two. He'd squeeze off a round and they'd drop back behind cover. His gun kept jamming so he'd eject the round and the next time it would shoot okay. Then it would jam again. He could hear more and more shooting now from the other side of the airframe. It still hadn't occurred to him these two D-boys were it, and that there was no rescue team.

# 16

When Mo'alim got to the neighborhood where the second helicopter had crashed, the paths leading toward it were already littered with bodies. There were choppers shooting from above and, as Mo'alim had expected, there were still Americans around the crash capable of fighting.

There was only one direct approach, and Mo'alim could tell it was covered. He kept trying to hold the crowd back but they were angry and brazen. The slender, bearded militia leader squatted behind a wall and waited for more of his men to catch up so that they could mount a coordinated attack.

# 17

On each of his passes over the wreck, Mike Goffena in *Super Six Two* found the encircling mob larger. Shughart and Gordon had arrayed themselves and the chopper crew in a perimeter around the downed bird. Clearly, they had decided against trying to move the crew to open ground. They were dug in awaiting help. On the radio Goffena could hear the desperate problems the rescue convoys were having.

The ticking of bullets puncturing his airframe had accelerated, and he was flying through regular RPG airbursts. With two Black Hawks down already, his fellow pilots were warning him away.

—*Just had an airburst about two hundred meters behind ya.*

—*RPG passed right under, Super Six Two.*

But Goffena was absorbed with the drama unfolding below, and trying to get something done about it.

"This place is getting extremely hot," his copilot, Captain Yacone, pleaded on the radio. "We need to get those folks out of there!"

—*Roger, Six Two, can you tell what the situation is?*

"Taking fairly regular RPG fire and they're all close."

Yacone continued to direct support fire from the smaller attack helicopters, pointing them where the Somali mobs were thickest. Air commander Matthews didn't like what he was seeing from the C2 Black Hawk. RPG smoke trails were arcing up regularly now from the crowd pressing in around Durant's crash site. He had Little Bird pilots hovering over the scene, with copilots trying to pick off targets with M-16s.

—*Knock that shit off,* he said. *You're going to get yourselves shot down.*

The battle was at its most confusing point. There were now two crash sites. A rescue team had made it to the first, Cliff Wolcott's, and the entire assault force and original ground convoy had been directed to move there. A second hastily assembled rescue convoy had left the Ranger base and not gotten far. They were probing around the vicinity of this crash site, but not getting close. The first crash site had a fighting chance, but Durant's, even with the two D-boys they'd dropped in, wouldn't last long without more help.

Goffena flew a low orbit over Durant's downed Black Hawk. Every time he swung west he was blinded by the sun. He wished it would hurry and set. He and the other Night Stalkers felt most comfortable flying at night. In the darkness, with their technology, the chopper pilots and crew could see while the enemy could not. If Goffena's Black Hawk and the Little Birds could hold off the mob until nightfall, the men on the ground had a chance.

The mob below now filled all the footpaths back out to the main road. Every time Goffena made a low pass some of the crowd would scatter, but it would close back up behind him. It was like running his hand through water. He could see RPGs now flying past his helicopter very plainly. He saw one of the D-boys get shot.

"This is *Six Two*," copilot Yacone radioed. "Ground element crash site number two has no security right now. They have one guy on the ground."

Then, moments later, another plea.

"Are there any ground forces moving to crash site two at this time?" Yacone asked.

—*Negative, not at this time.*

On one of his turns back into the slowly setting sun Goffena's helicopter collided with what felt like a freight train. A resounding crash. It felt like the sky had caved. He had been banking in a steep turn to the right, about thirty feet off the rooftops, going about 110 knots, and the next thing he knew the airframe was perfectly level. He saw in front of him what looked like a big piece of a rotor blade, but when his eyes focused he saw it was a crack in his windshield. He wasn't sure for a moment if he was still flying or on the ground. All the screens in his cockpit were blank. There was a beat of silence. Then he heard all the shrieks and beeps of the chopper's alarm systems gradually sounding louder and louder, like somebody was slowly turning up the volume (he realized later that the initial RPG blast had deafened him, and that it wasn't the volume turning up, it was the gradual recovery of his hearing). The alarms were telling him that his engines were dead and that his rotors had stopped . . . but it felt like they were still flying.

Goffena realized he had been hit by an RPG on the right side. He couldn't tell if it had been in front or in back. He didn't know if he had anybody left in back (his crew chiefs, Sergeants Paul Shannon and Mason Hall, had not been hurt by this blast, but Sergeant Brad Hallings, the Delta sniper, had his leg almost completely shorn off and was riddled with shrapnel). Captain Yacone, Goffena's copilot, hung limp in his seat, head slumped straight down. He didn't know if Yacone was dead or just injured. They were definitely still flying, and Goffena was alert enough to realize that this was a crash sequence. He had practiced this in simulators. They were aloft but going down fast.

He saw a street below, an alley, really. If he could keep the bird heading toward that alley they might be able to slide down into it. It was so narrow it would shear off the rotors but they might impact upright, which was the key. Keep it upright. He saw hard buildings to the left and the street was fairly wide but there was a row of poles on the right and he wasn't going to clear the poles . . . maybe only the right rotor system would impact and maybe it would just shear the rotors. Goffena saw the poles out the right side window and he was just twenty feet over them when Yacone came back to life and shouted into the radio that they were going down and gave grid coordinates. As they cushioned themselves for impact, Goffena began instinctively pulling back on his control stick trying to keep the nose of the bird up, and he realized suddenly that the helicopter was responding! It wasn't dead! The controls weren't working properly but he did have some pitch control, enough to keep it in the air. They flew right on over and past the alley and the poles. Goffena held the nose of the bird up and it continued flying. He had no idea how long they would stay up. Were the engines unwinding? How long would his controls hold out? But the bird stayed fairly level, and the power stayed on. The road beneath them abruptly ended and what opened in front of him in the distance was what Goffena recognized as the new port facility, friendly ground! The helicopter was slowing and he was now in a gradual descent. He crossed low over the fence around the port and aimed the bird down. They touched ground at about fifteen knots and Goffena was about to congratulate himself on a perfect landing when the bird, instead of rolling to a stop, just keeled over to the right, crunching metal on sand. The right main landing wheels had been blown off. The chopper skidded and Goffena worried they would flip, but instead it just came to a stop and he shut everything down.

As he climbed out of the cockpit to check on the fate of the men in back he saw the familiar shape of a Humvee racing toward them.

# 18

Mike Durant still thought things were under control. His leg was broken but it didn't hurt. He was lying on his back, propped against a supply kit by a small tree, using his weapon to keep back the occasional Skinnie who poked his head into the clearing. There was just about a fifteen-foot space between the wall to his left and the tail of the chopper. Durant admired the way the Delta guy had positioned him.

He could hear firing over on the other side of the helicopter. He knew Ray Frank, his copilot, was hurt but alive. And there were the two D-boys and his crew chief, Tommy Fields. He wondered if Tommy was okay. He figured there were at least four men on the other side of the bird and probably more from the rescue team. It was only a matter of time before the vehicles showed up to take them out.

Then he heard one of the operators—it was Gary Gordon—cry out that he was hit. Just a quick shout of anger and pain. He didn't hear the voice again.

The other one—it was Randy Shughart—came back to Durant's side of the bird.

"Are there weapons on board?" he asked.

There were. The crew chiefs carried M-16s. Durant told him where they were kept, and Shughart stepped into the craft and rummaged around and returned with both. He handed Durant Gordon's weapon, a CAR-15 loaded and ready to fire.

"What's the support frequency on the survival radio?" Shughart asked.

It was then, for the first time, that it dawned on Durant that they were stranded. The pilot felt a twist of alarm in his gut. If Shughart was asking how to set up communications, it meant he and the other guy had come in on their own. *They* were the rescue team. And Gordon had just been shot!

He explained standard procedure on the survival radio to Shughart. There was a channel Bravo. He listened while Shughart called out.

"We need some help down here," Randy said.

He was told that a reaction force was en route. Then Shughart wished him luck, took the weapons, and moved back around to the other side of the helicopter.

Durant felt panicked now. He had to keep the Skinnies away. He could hear them talking behind the wall, so he fired his weapon into the tin. It startled him because he had been firing single shots, but this new weapon was set on burst. The voices behind the wall stopped. Then two Somalis tried to climb over the nose end of the chopper. He fired at them and they jumped back. He didn't know if he had hit them or not.

A man tried to climb over the wall and Durant shot him. Another came crawling from around the corner with a weapon and Durant shot him.

Then there came a mad fusillade on the other side of the helicopter that lasted for about two minutes. Over the din he heard Shughart cry out in pain. Then it stopped.

Overhead, worried commanders were watching.

—*Do you have video over crash site number two?*

*—Indigenous personnel moving around all over the crash site.*
*—Indigenous?*
*—That's affirmative, over.*

The radio fell silent.

Terror washed over Durant. He heard the sounds of an angry mob. The crash had left the clearing littered with debris and he heard a great shuffling sound as the mob pushed it away like some onrushing beast. There was no more shooting. The others must be dead. Durant knew what angry Somali mobs could do, gruesome, horrible things. That was now in store for him. His second weapon was empty. He still had a pistol strapped to his side but he never even thought to reach for it.

Why bother? It was over. He was done.

A man stepped around the nose of the plane. He seemed startled to find Durant. The man shouted and more Skinnies came racing around. It was time to die. Durant placed the empty weapon across his chest, folded his hands over it, and just turned his eyes to the sky.

# 19

Hassan Yassin Abokoi had been shot in the ankle by a helicopter as he stood with the crowd around the crashed helicopter. He now sat beneath a tree watching. His ankle stung at first and then had gone numb. It was bleeding badly. He hated the helicopters. His uncle that day had his head blown off by a cannon shot from a helicopter. It removed his head neatly from his shoulders, like it had never been there. Who were these Americans who rained fire and death on them, who came to feed them but then had started killing? He wanted to kill these men who had fallen from the sky, but he couldn't stand.

From where he sat, Abokoi could see the mob descend on the Americans. Only one was still alive. He was shouting and waving his arms as the mob grabbed him by the legs and began pulling him away from the helicopter, tearing at his clothes. He saw his neighbors hack at the bodies of the Americans with knives and begin to pull at their limbs. Then he saw people running and parading with parts of the Americans' bodies.

\* \* \*

When Mo'alim ran around the tail of the helicopter he was surprised to find another American, a pilot. The man did not shoot. He set his weapon on his chest and folded his hands over it. The crowd surged past Mo'alim toward him and began kicking and beating him, but the bearded fighter felt suddenly protective. He grabbed the pilot's arm and fired his weapon in the air and shouted for the crowd to stay back.

One of his men struck the pilot hard in the face with his rifle butt, and Mo'alim pushed him back. The pilot was injured and could not fight anymore. The Rangers had spent months capturing Somalis and holding them prisoner. They would be willing to trade them, perhaps all of them, for one of their own. The pilot was more valuable alive than dead. He directed his men to form a ring around the pilot to protect him from the mob, which was hungry for revenge. Several of Mo'alim's men stooped and began tearing Durant's clothing away. The pilot had a pistol strapped to his side, and a knife, and they were afraid he had other hidden weapons and they knew the American pilots wore beacons in their clothing so that the helicopters could track them, so they stripped the layers away.

# 20

Durant kept his eyes on the sky as the mob closed over him. They were screaming things he couldn't understand. When the man struck him in the face with a rifle butt it broke his nose and shattered the bone around his eye. People pulled at his arms and legs, and then others began tearing at his clothes. They were unfamiliar with the plastic snaps of his gear, so Durant reached down and squeezed them open. He gave himself over to them. His boots were yanked off, his survival vest, and his shirt. A man half unzipped his pants, but when he saw that Durant wore no underwear (for comfort in the equatorial heat) he zipped the trousers back up. They also left on his brown T-shirt. All the while he was being kicked and hit. A young man leaned down and grabbed at the green ID card Durant wore around his neck. He stuck it in Durant's face and shouted, "Ranger, Ranger, you die Somalia!"

Then someone threw a handful of dirt in his face, which went into his mouth. They tied a rag or towel over the top of his head and eyes, and the mob hoisted him up in the air, partly carrying and partly dragging him. He felt the broken end of his femur pierce the skin in the back of his leg and poke through. He was buffeted from all sides, kicked, hit with fists, rifle butts. He could not see where they were taking him. He was engulfed in a great wave of hate and anger. Someone, he thought a woman, reached out and grabbed his penis and testicles and yanked at them.

And in this agony of fright suddenly Durant left his body. He was no longer at the center of the crowd, he was in it, or above it, perhaps. He was observing the crowd attacking him. Apart somehow. And he felt no pain and the fear lessened and then he passed out.

# THE
# ALAMO

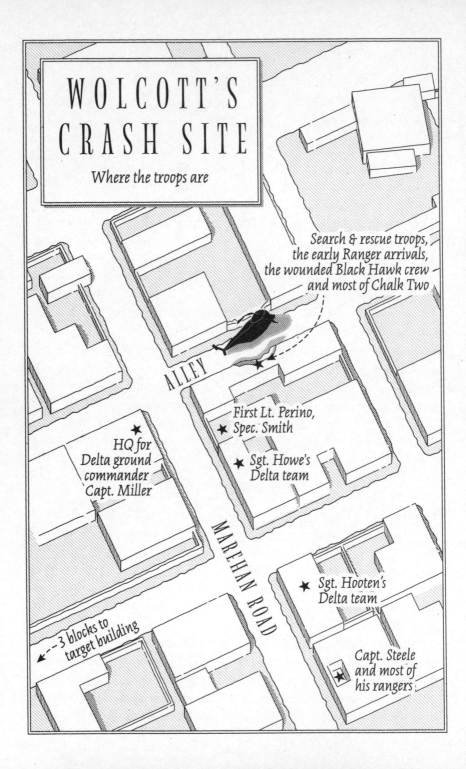

# WOLCOTT'S CRASH SITE

### Where the troops are

Search & rescue troops, the early Ranger arrivals, the wounded Black Hawk crew and most of Chalk Two

ALLEY

First Lt. Perino, Spec. Smith

Sgt. Howe's Delta team

HQ for Delta ground commander Capt. Miller

MAREHAN ROAD

Sgt. Hooten's Delta team

Capt. Steele and most of his rangers

3 blocks to target building

# 1

Air force parajumper Tim Wilkinson climbed back into the wrecked helicopter looking for a way to get more leverage to free pilot Cliff Wolcott's body. Maybe there was some way he hadn't seen at first to pull the seat back and get more room and a better angle. But it was hopeless.

He climbed back out. Kneeling on top of the wreck in the shattering din of automatic weapons fire, he peered down through the open right side doors into the rear of the aircraft. He thought they had accounted for everyone on board. He knew some of the men had been rescued earlier by the Little Bird that landed right after the crash. So Wilkinson was looking for sensitive equipment or weapons that would have to be removed or destroyed. PJs are trained to quickly erase the memory banks of any electronic equipment with sensitive data. All of the avionics equipment and every piece of gear that hadn't been strapped down had come to rest at the left side of the aircraft, which was now the bottom.

In the heap he noticed a scrap of desert fatigues.

"I think there's somebody else in there," he told Sergeant Bob Mabry, a Delta medic on the CSAR crew.

Wilkinson leaned in further and saw an arm and a flight glove. He called down into the wreck and a finger of the flight glove moved. Wilkinson climbed back into the wreckage and began pulling the debris and equipment off of the man buried there. It was the second crew chief, the left side gunner, Ray Dowdy. Part of his seat had gotten slammed and broken off the hinges but it was still basically intact and in place. When Wilkinson freed Dowdy's arm from under the pile, the crew chief began shoving things away. He still hadn't spoken and was only half conscious.

Mabry slithered down under the wreck and tried without success to crawl in through the bottom left side doorway. He gave up and climbed in through the upper doors just as Wilkinson freed Dowdy. The three men stood inside the wreck as a storm of bullets suddenly poked through the skin of the craft. Mabry and Wilkinson danced involuntarily at the sharp burst of snapping and crashing noises. Bits of metal, plastic, paper, and fabric flew around them like a sudden snow squall. Then it stopped. Wilkinson remembers noting, first, that he was still alive. Then he checked himself. He'd been hit in the face and arm. It felt like he'd been slapped or punched in the chin. Everyone had been hit. Mabry had been hit in the hand. Dowdy had lost the tips of two fingers.

The crew chief stared blankly at his bloody hand.

Wilkinson put his hand over the bleeding fingertips and said, "Okay, let's get out of here!"

Mabry tore up the Kevlar floor panels and propped them up over the side of the craft where the bullets had burst through. Instead of braving the fire above, they tunneled out, digging through the dry sand at the rear corner of the left side door. They slid Dowdy out that way.

Then the two rescuers climbed back inside, Wilkinson looking for equipment to destroy, Mabry handing out Kevlar panels to be placed around the tail of the aircraft where they had established a casualty collection point. Fire was coming mostly up and down the alley. They were still expecting the arrival of the ground convoy at any moment.

Wounded Sergeant Fales was too busy shooting to take notice of the Kevlar pads. He had a pressure dressing on his calf and an IV tube in his arm and he was lying out by the broken tail boom looking for targets.

Wilkinson poked his head out the top. "Scott, why don't you get behind the Kevlar?"

Fales looked startled. He had been so absorbed firing he hadn't seen the panels go up behind him.

"Good idea," he said.

Bullet hole after bullet hole poked through the broken tail boom.

Wilkinson was reminded of the Steve Martin movie *The Jerk*, where Martin's moronic character, unaware that villains are shooting at him, watches with surprise as bullet holes begin popping open a row of oil cans. He shouted Martin's line from the movie.

"They hate the cans! Stay away from the cans!"

Both men laughed.

After patching up a few more men, Wilkinson crawled back up into the cockpit from underneath, to see if there was some way of pulling Wolcott's body down and out. There wasn't.

# 2

A grenade came from somewhere. It was one of those Russian types that looked like a soup can on the end of a stick. It bounced off the car and then off Specialist Jason Coleman's helmet and radio and then it hit the ground.

Nelson, who was still deaf from Twombly's timely machine-gun blast, pulled his M-60 from the roof of the car and dove, as did the men on both sides of the intersection. They stayed down for almost a full minute, cushioning themselves from the blast. Nothing happened.

"I guess it's a dud," said Lieutenant DiTomasso.

Thirty seconds later another grenade rolled out into the open space between the car and the tree across the street. Nelson again grabbed the gun off the car and rolled with it away from the grenade. Everyone braced themselves once more, and this, too, failed to explode. Nelson thought they had spent all their luck. He and Barton were crawling back toward the car when a third grenade dropped between them. Nelson turned his helmet toward it and pushed his gun in front of him, shielding himself from the blast that this time was sure to come. He opened his mouth, closed his eyes, and breathed out hard in anticipation. The grenade sizzled. He stayed like that for a full twenty seconds before he looked up at Barton.

"Dud," Barton said.

Yurek grabbed it and threw it into the street.

Someone had bought themselves a batch of bad grenades. Wilkinson later found three or four more unexploded ones inside the body of the helicopter.

The American forces around Wolcott's downed Black Hawk were now scattered along an L-shaped perimeter stretching south. One group of about thirty men was massed around the wreck in the alleyway, at the northern base of the "L." When they learned that the ground convoy had gotten lost and delayed, they began moving the wounded through the hole made by the falling helicopter into the house of Abdiaziz Ali Aden (he was still hidden in a back room). Immediately west of the alley (at the bend of the "L") was Marehan Road, where Nelson, Yurek, Barton, and Twombly were dug in across the street at the northwest corner. On the east side of that intersection, nearest the chopper, were DiTomasso, Coleman, Belman,

and Delta Captain Bill Coultrop and his radio operator. The rest of the
ground force was stretched out south on Marehan Road, along the stem of
the "L," which sloped uphill. Steele and a dozen or so Rangers, along with
three Delta teams, about thirty men in all, were together in a courtyard
on the east side of Marehan Road midway up the next block south, separated from the bulk of the force by half a block, a wide alley, and a long
block. Sergeant Howe's Delta team, with a group of Rangers that included
Specialist Stebbins, followed by the Delta command group led by Captain Miller, had crossed the wide alley and was moving down the west wall
toward Nelson's position. Lieutenant Perino had also crossed the alley and
was moving downhill along the east wall with Corporal Smith, Sergeant
Chuck Elliot, and several other men.

As Howe approached Nelson's position, it looked to him as though
the Rangers were just hiding. Two of his men ran across the alley to tell
the Rangers to *start shooting.* Nelson and the others were still recovering
from the shock of the unexploded grenades. Rounds were taking chips off
the walls all around them, but it was hard to see where the shots were
coming from. Howe's team members helped arrange Nelson and the others
to set up effective fields of fire, and placed Stebbins and machine-gunner
Private Brian Heard at the southern corner of the same intersection, ori-
enting them to fire west.

Captain Miller caught up with Howe, trailing his radioman and some
other members of his element, along with Staff Sergeant Jeff Bray, an air
force combat controller. With all the shooting at that intersection, Howe
decided it was time to get off the street. There was a metal gate at the
entrance to a courtyard between two buildings on his side of the block.
He pushed against the gate, which had two doors that opened inward. Howe
considered putting a charge on the door, but given the number of soldiers
nearby and the lack of cover, the explosion would probably hurt people.
So the burly sergeant and Bray began hurling themselves against the gate.
Bray's side gave way.

"Follow me in case I get shot," Howe said.

He plunged into the courtyard and rapidly moved through the house
on either side, running from room to room. Howe was looking for people,
focusing his eyes at midtorso first, checking hands. The hands told you
the whole story. The only hands he found were empty. They belonged to
a man and woman and some children, a family of about seven, clearly ter-

rified. He stood in the doorway with his weapon in his right hand pointing at them, trying to coax them out of the room with his left hand. It took a while, but they came out slowly, clinging to each other. The family was flex-cuffed and herded into a small side room.

Howe then more carefully inspected the space. Each of the blocks in this neighborhood of Mogadishu consisted of mostly one-story stone houses grouped irregularly around open spaces, or courtyards. This block consisted of a short courtyard, about two car-lengths wide, where he now stood. There was a two-story house on the south side and a one-story house on the north. Howe figured this space was about the safest spot around. The taller building would shelter them from both bullets and lobbed RPGs. At the west end was some kind of storage shack. Howe began exploring systematically, making a more thorough sweep, moving from room to room, looking for windows that would give them a good vantage for shooting west down the alley. He found several but none that offered a particularly good angle. The alley to the north (the same one that the helicopter had crashed into one block west) was too narrow. He could only see about fifteen yards down in either direction, and all he saw was wall. When he returned to the courtyard, Captain Miller and the others had begun herding casualties into the space. It would serve as their command post and casualty collection point for the rest of the night.

As he reentered the courtyard, one of the master sergeants with Miller told Howe to go back out to the street and help his team. Howe resented the order. He felt he was, at this point, the de facto leader on the ground, the one doing all the real thinking and moving and fighting. They had reached a temporary safe point, a time for commanders to catch their breath and think. They were in a bad spot, but not critical. The next step would be to look for ways to strongpoint their position, expand their perimeter, identify other buildings to take down to give them better lines of fire. The troop sergeant's command was the order of a man who didn't know what to do next.

Howe was built like a pro wrestler, but he was a thinker. This sometimes troubled his relationship with authority—especially the army's maddeningly arbitrary manner of placing unseasoned, less-qualified men in charge. Howe was just a sergeant first class with supposedly narrower concerns, but he saw the big picture very clearly, better than most. After being selected for Delta he had met and married the daughter of Colonel

Charlie A. Beckwith, the founder and original commander of Delta. They had met in a lounge by Fort Bragg and when he told her that he was a civilian, Connie Beckwith, a former army officer then herself, nodded knowingly.

"Look," she said. "I know who you work for so let's stop pretending. My dad started that unit."

She had to pull out her driver's license to prove who she was.

Not that Howe had any ambition for formal army leadership. His preferred relationship with officers was for them to heed his advice and leave him alone. He was frequently aghast at the failings of those in charge.

Take this setup in Mogadishu, for instance. It was asinine. At the base, the huge hangar front doors wouldn't close, so the Sammies had a clear view inside at all hours of the day or night. The city sloped gradually up from the waterfront, so any Somali with patience and binoculars could keep an eye on their state of readiness. Every time they scrambled to gear up and go, word was out in the city before they were even on the helicopters. If that weren't bad enough, you had the Italians, some of them openly sympathetic to their former colonial subjects, who appeared to be flashing signals with their headlights out into the city whenever the helicopters took off. Nobody had the balls to do anything about it.

Then there were the mortars. General Garrison seemed to regard mortars as little more than an annoyance. He had walked around casually during the early mortar attacks, his cigar clenched in his teeth, amused by the way everyone dove for cover. "Piddly-assed mortars," he'd said. Which was all well and good, except, as Howe saw it, if the Sammies ever got their act together and managed to drop a few on the hangar, there'd be hell to pay. He wondered if the tin roof was thick enough to detonate the round— which would merely send shrapnel and shards of the metal roof slashing down through the ranks—or whether the round would just poke on through and detonate on the concrete floor in the middle of everybody. It was a question that lingered in his mind most nights as he went to sleep. Then there were the flimsy perimeter defenses. At mealtimes, all the men would be lined up outside the mess hall, which was separated from a busy outside road by nothing more than a thin metal wall. A car bomb along that wall at the right time of day could kill dozens of soldiers.

Howe did not hide his disgust over these things. Now, being ordered to do something pointless in the middle of the biggest fight of his life, he was furious. He began gathering up ammo, grenades, and LAWS off the wounded Rangers in the courtyard. It seemed to Howe that most of the men failed to grasp how desperate their situation had become. It was a form of denial. They could not stop thinking of themselves as the superior force, in command of the situation, yet the tables had clearly turned. They were surrounded and terribly outnumbered. The very idea of adhering to rules of engagement at this point was preposterous.

"You're throwing grenades?" the troop sergeant major asked him, surprised when he saw Howe stuffing all of them he could find into his vest pockets.

"We're not getting paid to bring them back," Howe told him.

This was war. The game now was kill or be killed. He stomped angrily out to the street and began looking for Somalis to shoot.

He found one of the Rangers, Nelson, firing a handgun at the window of the building Howe had just painstakingly cleared and occupied. Nelson had seen someone moving in the window, and they had been taking fire from just about every direction, so he was pumping a few rounds that way.

"What are you doing?" Howe shouted across the alley.

Nelson couldn't hear Howe. He shouted back, "I saw someone in there."

"No shit! There are friendlies in there!"

Nelson didn't find out until later what Howe had been waving his arms about. When he did he was mortified. No one had told him that Delta had moved into that space, but, then again, it was a cardinal sin to shoot before identifying a target.

Already furious, Howe began venting at the Rangers. He felt they were not fighting hard enough. When he saw Nelson, Yurek, and the others trying to selectively target armed Somalis in a crowd at the other end of a building on their side of the street, Howe threw a grenade over its roof. It was an amazing toss, but the grenade failed to explode. So Howe threw another, which exploded right where the crowd was gathered. He then watched the Rangers try to hit a gunman who kept darting out from behind a shed about one block north, shooting, and then retreating back behind it. The Delta sergeant flung one of his golf ball–sized minigrenades over the Rangers' position. It exploded behind the shed, and the gunman did not reappear. Howe then picked up a LAW and hurled it across the road. It landed on the arm of Specialist Lance Twombly, who was lying on his belly four or five feet from the corner wall. The LAW bruised his forearm. Twombly jumped to his knees, angry, and turned to hear Howe bellowing, "Shoot the motherfucker!"

Down on one knee, Howe swore bitterly as he fired. Everything about this situation was pissing him off, the goddamn Somalis, his leaders, the idiot Rangers . . . even his ammunition. He drew a bead on three Somalis who were running across the street two blocks to the north, taking a progressive lead on them the way he had learned through countless hours of training, squaring them in his sights and then aiming several feet in front of them. He would squeeze two or three rounds, rapidly increasing his lead with each shot. He was an expert marksman, and thought he had hit them, but he couldn't tell for sure because they kept running until they crossed the street and were out of view. It bugged him. His weapon was the most sophisticated infantry rifle in the world, a customized CAR-15, and he was shooting the army's new 5.56 mm green-tip round. The green tip had a tungsten carbide penetrator at the tip, and would punch holes in metal, but that very penetrating power meant his rounds were passing right through his targets. When the Sammies were close enough he could see when he hit them. Their shirts would lift up at the point of impact, as if someone had pinched and plucked up the fabric. But with the green-tip round it was like sticking somebody with an ice pick. The bullet made a small, clean hole, and unless it happened to hit the heart or spine, it wasn't enough to stop a man in his tracks. Howe felt like he had to hit a guy five or six times just to get his attention. They used to kid Randy Shughart because he shunned the modern rifle and ammunition and carried a Vietnam era M-14, which shot a 7.62 mm round without the penetrating qualities of the new green tip. It occurred to Howe as he saw those Sammies keep on running that Randy was the smartest soldier in the unit. His rifle may have been heavier and comparatively awkward and delivered a mean recoil, but it damn sure knocked a man down with one bullet, and in combat, one shot was often all you got. You shoot a guy, you want to see him go down; you don't want to be guessing for the next five hours whether you hit him, or whether he's still waiting for you in the weeds.

Howe was in a good spot. There was nothing in front or behind him that would stop a bullet, but there was a tree about twenty feet south against the west wall of the street that blocked any view of him from that direction. The bigger tree across the alley where Nelson, Twombly, and the others were positioned blocked any view of him from the north. So the broad-beamed Delta sergeant could kneel about five feet off the wall and pick off targets to the north with impunity. It was like that in battle. Some spots were safer than others. Up the hill, Hooten had watched Howe and his team move across the intersection while he was lying with his face pressed in the dirt, with rounds popping all around him. *How can they be doing that?* he'd thought. By an accident of visual angles, one person could stand and fight without difficulty, while just a few feet away fire could be so withering that there was nothing to do but dive for cover and stay hidden. Howe recognized he'd found such a safety zone. He shot methodically, saving his ammunition.

When he saw Perino, Smith, and Elliot creeping down to a similar position on the other side of the street, he figured they were trying to do what he was doing. Except, on that side of the street there were no trees to provide concealment.

He shouted across at them impatiently, but in the din he wasn't heard.

# 3

Perino and his men had moved down to a small tin shed, a porch really, that protruded from the irregular gray stone wall. They were only about ten yards from the alley where *Super Six One* lay. A West Point graduate, class of 1990, Perino at twenty-four wasn't much older than the Rangers he commanded. His group had gotten out ahead of Captain Steele and most of the Ranger force. They had pushed across the last intersection to the crash site after Goodale had been hit. They had cleared the first courtyard they passed on that block, and Perino had then led several of the men back out in the street to press on down Marehan Road. He knew they were close to linking up with Lieutenant DiTomasso and the CSAR team, which had been their destination when they started this move. The shed was just a few steps downhill from the courtyard doorway.

Sergeant Elliot was already on the other side of the shed. Corporal Smith was crouched behind it and Perino was just a few feet behind Smith. They were taking so much fire it was confusing. Rounds seemed to be coming from everywhere. Stone chips sprayed from the wall over Perino's head and rattled down on his helmet. He saw a Somali with a gun on the opposite side of the street, about twenty yards north of Nelson's position, blocked from those guys' view by the tree they were hiding behind. Perino saw the muzzle flash and could tell this was where some of the incoming rounds originated. It would be hard to hit the guy with a rifle shot, but Smith had a grenade launcher on his M-16 and might be able to drop a 203 round near enough to hurt the guy. He moved up to tap Smith on the shoulder—there was too much noise to communicate other than face-to-face—when bullets began popping loudly through the shed. The lieutenant was on one knee and a round spat up dirt between his legs.

Across the street, Nelson saw Smith get hit. The burly corporal had moved down the street fast and had taken a knee to begin shooting. Most of the men at that corner heard the round hit him, a hard, ugly slap. Smith seemed just startled at first. He rolled to his side and, like he was commenting about someone else, remarked with surprise, "I'm hit!"

From where Nelson was, it didn't look like Smith was hurt that badly. Perino helped move him against the wall. Now Smith was screaming, "I'm hit! I'm hit!"

The lieutenant could tell by the sound of Smith's voice that he was in pain. When Goodale had been hit he seemed to feel almost nothing, but the wound to Smith was different. He was writhing. He was in a very bad way. Perino pressed a field dressing into the wound but blood spurted out forcefully around it.

"I've got a bleeder here!" Perino shouted across the street.

Delta medic Sergeant Kurt Schmid dashed toward them across Marehan Road. Together, they dragged Smith back into the courtyard.

Schmid tore off Smith's pants leg. When he removed the battle dressing, bright red blood projected out of the wound in a long pulsing spurt. This was bad.

The young soldier told Perino, "Man, this *really* hurts."

The lieutenant went back out to the street and crept back up to Elliot.

"Where's Smith?" Elliot asked.

"He's down."

"Shit," said Elliot.

They saw Sergeant Ken Boorn get hit in the foot. Then Private Rodriguez rolled away from his machine gun, bleeding, screaming, and holding his crotch. He felt no pain, but when he had placed his hand on the wound his genitals felt like mush and blood spurted thickly between his fingers. He screamed in alarm. Eight of the eleven Rangers in Perino's Chalk One had now been hit.

At the north end of the same block there was a huge explosion and in it Stebbins went down. Nelson saw it from up close. An RPG had streaked into the wall of the house across the alley from him, over near where Stebbins and Heard were positioned. The grenade went off with a brilliant red flash and tore out a chunk of the wall about four feet long. The concussion in the narrow alley was huge. It hurt his ears. There was a big cloud of dust. He saw—and Perino and Elliot saw from across the street—both Stebbins and Heard flat on their backs. *They're fucked up,* Nelson thought. But Stebbins stirred and then slowly stood up, covered from head to foot in white dust, coughing, rubbing his eyes.

"Get down, Stebbins!" shouted Heard. So he was okay, too.

Bullets were hitting around Perino and Elliot with increasing frequency. Rounds would come in long bursts, snapping between them, over their heads, nicking the tin shed with a high-pitched ring and popping right through the metal. Rounds were kicking up dirt all over their side of the street. It was a bad position, just as Howe had foreseen.

"Uh, sir, I think that it would be a pretty good idea if we go into that courtyard," said Elliot.

"Do you really think so?" Perino asked.

Elliot grabbed his arm and they both dove for the courtyard where Schmid was working frantically to save Smith.

Corporal Smith was alert and terrified and in sharp pain. The medic had first tried applying direct pressure on the wound, which had proved excruciatingly painful and obviously ineffective. Bright red blood continued to gush from the hole in Smith's leg. The medic tried jamming Curlex into the hole. Then he checked Smith over.

"Are you hurt anywhere else?" he asked.

"I don't know."

Schmid checked for an exit wound, and found none.

The medic was thirty-one. He'd grown up an army brat, vowing never to join the military, and ended up enlisting a year after graduating from high school. He'd gone into Special Forces and elected to become a medic because he figured it would give him good employment opportunity when he left the army. He was good at it, and his training kept progressing. By now he'd been schooled as thoroughly as any physician's assistant, and better than some. As part of his training he'd worked in the emergency room of a hospital in San Diego, and had even done some minor surgery under a physician's guidance. He certainly had enough training to know that Jamie Smith was in trouble if he couldn't stop the bleeding.

He could deduce the path the bullet had taken. It had entered Smith's thigh and traveled up into his pelvis. A gunshot wound to the pelvis is one of the worst. The aorta splits low in the abdomen, forming the left and right iliac arteries. As the iliac artery emerges from the pelvis it branches into the exterior and deep femoral arteries, the primary avenues for blood to the lower half of the body. The bullet had clearly pierced one of the femoral vessels. Schmid applied direct pressure to Smith's abdomen, right above the pelvis where the artery splits. He explained what he was doing. He'd already run two IVs into Smith's arm, using 14-gauge, large bore needles, and was literally squeezing the plastic bag to push replacement fluid into him. Smith's blood formed an oily pool that shone dully on the dirt floor of the courtyard.

The medic took comfort in the assumption that help would arrive shortly. Another treatment tactic, a very risky one, would be to begin directly transfusing Smith. Blood transfusions were rarely done on the battlefield. It was a tricky business. The medics carried IV fluids with them but not blood. If he wanted to transfuse Smith, he'd have to find someone with the same blood type and attempt a direct transfusion. This was likely to create more problems. He could begin reacting badly to the transfusion. Schmid decided not to attempt it. The rescue convoy was supposed to be arriving shortly. What this Ranger needed was a doctor, pronto.

Perino radioed Captain Steele.

"We can't go any further, sir. We have more wounded than I can carry."

"You've got to push on," Steele told him.

"We CANNOT go further," Perino said. "Request permission to occupy a building."

Steele told Perino to keep trying. Actually, inside the courtyard they were only about fifty feet from Lieutenant DiTomasso and the CSAR force, but Perino had no way of knowing that. He tried to reach DiTomasso on his radio.

"Tom, where are you?"

DiTomasso tried to explain their position, pointing out landmarks. "I can't see," said Perino. "I'm in a courtyard."

DiTomasso popped a red smoke grenade, and Perino saw the red plume drifting up in the darkening sky. He guessed from the drift of the plume that they were about fifty yards apart, which in this killing zone was a great distance. On the radio, Steele kept pushing him to link up with DiTomasso.

"They need your help," he said.

"Look, sir, I've got three guys left, counting myself. How can I help him?"

Finally, Steele relented.

"Roger, strongpoint the building and defend it."

Schmid was still working frantically on Smith's wound. He'd asked Perino to help him by applying pressure just over the wound so he could use his hands. Perino pushed two fingers directly into the wound up to his knuckles. Smith screamed and blood shot out at the lieutenant, who swallowed hard and applied more pressure. He felt dizzy. The spurts of blood continued.

"Oh, shit! Oh, shit! I'm gonna die! I'm gonna die!" Smith shouted. He knew he had an arterial bleed.

The medic talked to him, tried to calm him down. The only way to stop the bleeding was to find the severed femoral artery and clamp it. Otherwise it was like trying to stanch a fire hose by pushing down on it through a mattress. He told Smith to lean back.

"This is going to be very painful," Schmid told the Ranger apologetically. "I'm going to have to cause you more pain, but I have to do this to help you."

"Give me some morphine for the pain!" Smith demanded. He was still very alert and engaged.

"I can't," Schmid told him. In this state, morphine could kill him. After losing so much blood, his pressure was precariously low. Morphine would further lower his heart rate and slow his respiration, exactly what he did not need.

The young Ranger bellowed as the medic reached with both hands and tore open the entrance wound. Schmid tried to shut out the fact that there were live nerve endings beneath his fingers. It was hard. He had formed an emotional bond with Smith. They were in this together. But to save the young Ranger, he had to treat him like an inanimate object, a machine that was broken and needed fixing. He continued to root for the artery. If he failed to find it, Smith would probably die. He picked through the open upper thigh, reaching up to his pelvis, parting layers of skin, fat, muscle, and vessel, probing through pools of bright red blood. He couldn't find it. Once severed, the upper end of the artery had evidently retracted up into Smith's abdomen. The medic stopped. Smith was lapsing into shock. The only recourse now would be to cut into the abdomen and hunt for the severed artery and clamp it. But that would mean still more pain and blood loss. Every time he reached into the wound Smith lost more blood. Schmid and Perino were covered with it. Blood was everywhere. It was hard to believe Smith had any more to lose.

"It hurts really bad," he kept saying. "It really hurts."

In time his words and movements came slowly, labored. He was in shock.

Schmid was beside himself. He had squeezed six liters of fluid into the young Ranger and was running out of bags. He had tried everything and was feeling desperate and frustrated and angry. He had to leave the room. He got one of the other men to continue applying pressure on the wound and walked out to confer with Perino. Both men were covered with Smith's blood.

"If I don't get him out of here right now, he's gonna die," Schmid pleaded.

The lieutenant radioed Steele again.

"Sir, we need a medevac. A Little Bird or something. For Corporal Smith. We need to extract him *now*."

Steele relayed this on the command net. It was tough to get through. It was nearly five o'clock and growing dark. All of the vehicles had turned back to the air base. Steele learned that there would be no relief for some time. Putting another bird down in their neighborhood was out of the question.

The captain radioed Perino back and told him, for the time being, that Smith would just have to hang on.

# 4

Stebbins shook with fear. Having his friends around him kept him going, but that was about all that did. You could be prepared for the sights and sounds and smells of war, but the horror of it, the blood and gore and heart-rending screams of pain, the sense of death perched right on your shoulder, breathing in your ear, there was no preparation for that. Things felt balanced on an edge, threatening at any moment to spin out of control. Was this what he had wanted so badly? An old platoon sergeant had told him once, "When war starts, a soldier wants like hell to be there, but once he's there, he wants like hell to come home."

Beside Stebbins, a burst of rounds hit Heard's M-60, disabling it permanently. Heard drew his 9 mm handgun and fired it. Squinting down the alley west into the setting sun, Stebbins could see the white shirts of Somali fighters. There were dozens of them. Groups would come running out and fire volleys up the alley, and then duck back behind cover. Over his right shoulder, across Marehan Road and down the alley, he could hear the rescue guys hammering at the wreck, still trying to free Wolcott's body. The sky overhead was getting darker, and there was still no sign of the ground convoy. They had actually seen the vehicles drive past just a few blocks west about an hour earlier. Where were they?

Everyone dreaded the approaching darkness. One distinct advantage U.S. soldiers had wherever they fought was their night-vision technology, their NODs (Night Observation Devices), but they had left them back at the hangar. The NODs were worn draped around the neck when not in use, and weighed probably less than a pound, but they were clumsy, annoying, and very fragile. It was an easy choice to leave them behind on a daylight mission. Now the force faced the night thirsty, tired, bleeding, running low on ammo, and without one of their biggest technological advantages. Stebbins, the company clerk, gazed out at the giant orange ball easing behind buildings to the west and had visions of a pot of fresh-brewed coffee out there somewhere waiting for him.

The Little Birds had the lay of the land well enough now to be making regular gun runs, and were doing a lot to keep at bay the Somalis crowded around the neighborhood. The tiny helicopters came swooping in at almost ground level, flying between buildings with their miniguns ablaze. It was an amazing sight. The rockets made a ripping sound and then shook the ground with their blasts. Twombly was admiring one such run when Sergeant Barton told him the pilots were still calling for more markers on the road to better outline the American positions.

"You're going to take this thing," said Barton, holding up a fluorescent orange plastic triangle, "and drop it right out there," pointing to the middle of the road.

Twombly didn't want to go. There was so much lead flying through that road that it felt like suicide to venture from cover, much less run out to the middle. It crossed his mind to refuse Barton's order, but just as quickly he rejected that. If he didn't do it, somebody else would have to. That wouldn't be fair. He had volunteered to be a Ranger, he couldn't back out now just because things had gotten rough. He grabbed the orange triangle angrily, ran out a few steps, and flung it toward the center of the road. He dove back to cover.

"That won't do it," Barton shouted at him. He explained that the rotor wash from the birds on their gun runs would blow the marker away.

"You have to secure it, put a rock on it."

Furious now, and terribly frightened, Twombly put his head down and ran out into the road again.

Nelson remembers feeling moved by his friend's courage. The second Twombly took off again there was shooting on the street and so much dust kicked up Nelson couldn't see him. *That's the last time I'll ever see Twombly.* But moments later the big man from New Hampshire came clomping back in, swearing fluently, unscathed.


An old man stumbled out from behind a wall wildly firing an AK. Rangers from all three corners were pointing guns at this man, who looked frail and had a shock of white hair and a long bushy white beard that was stained greenish on both sides of his mouth, presumably from *khat*. He was evidently drunk or stoned or so high that he didn't know what was happening. His rounds were so off target the Rangers watching him at first were just stunned, and then laughed. The old man made a stumbling turn and fired a round into the wall, far from any targets. Twombly flattened him with a burst from his SAW.

They saw strange sights as the fight wore on. In the midst of cascading gunfire, Private David Floyd watched a gray dove land in the middle of Marehan Road. The bird scratched at the dirt nonchalantly and strutted a few feet up the road seemingly oblivious to the fury around it. Then it flew away. Floyd wistfully watched it go. A donkey pulling a wagon wandered across the intersection up the hill, through one of the heaviest fields of fire (near where Fillmore had been killed), and crossed the road unscathed, then came trotting back out again minutes later, clearly confused and disoriented. It was comical. Nobody could believe the donkey hadn't been hit. Ed Yurek watched with pity, and amazement. *God loves that donkey.* Closer to the wrecked helicopter, a woman kept running out into the alley, screaming and pointing toward the house at the southeast corner of the intersection where many of the wounded had been moved. No one shot at her. She was unarmed. But every time she stepped back behind cover a wicked torrent of fire would be unleashed where she pointed. After she'd done this twice, one of the D-boys behind the tail of *Super Six One* said, "If that bitch comes back, I'm going to shoot her."

Captain Coultrop nodded his approval. She did, and the D-boy shot her down on the street.

Then there was the woman in a blue turban, a powerful woman with thick arms and legs who came sprinting across the road carrying a heavy basket in both arms. She was wearing a bright blue-and-white dress that billowed behind her as she ran. Every Ranger at the intersection blasted her. Twombly, Nelson, Yurek, and Stebbins all opened up. Howe fired on her from further up the hill. First she stumbled, but kept on going. Then, as more rounds hit her, she fell and RPGs spilled out of her basket onto the street. The shooting stopped. She had been hit by many rounds and lay in a heap in the dirt for a long moment, breathing heavily. Then the woman pulled herself up on all fours, grabbed an RPG round, and crawled. This time the massive Ranger volley literally tore her apart. A fat 203 round blew off one of her legs. She fell in a bloody lump for a few moments, then moved again. Another massive burst of rounds rained on her and her body came further apart. It was appalling, yet some of the Rangers laughed. To Nelson the woman no longer even looked like a human being; she'd been

transformed into a monstrous bleeding hulk, like something from a horror movie. Later, just before it got dark, he looked back over. There was a
large pool of blood on the street, blood and clothing and the basket, but
the RPG rounds and what remained of the woman were gone.

When the sun had slipped behind the buildings to the west, shadow
fell over the alley and it became easier for Stebbins and Heard to find the
Sammies who were shooting at them from windows and doorways. Their
muzzle flashes gave their positions away clearly. Stebbins squeezed off
rounds carefully, trying to conserve ammo. Heard was shooting now with
an M-16. Nearly deaf, he tapped Stebbins on the shoulder and shouted,
"Steb, I just want you to know in case we don't get out of this, I think you're
doing a great job."

Then the ground around them shook. Stebbins heard a shattering
*Kabang! Kabang! Kabang!* the sound of big rounds smashing into the stone
wall of the corner where they had taken cover. He was engulfed in smoke.
The wall that had been their shield for more than an hour began to come
apart. Somebody with a big gun down the alley had zeroed in on them,
and was just taking down their position. After the first shattering volley,
Stebbins stepped out into the alley and returned fire at the window where
he had seen the muzzle flash. Then he ducked back behind his corner, took
a knee, and kept placing rounds in the same place.

*Kabang! Kabang! Kabang!* Three more ear-shattering rounds hit the
corner again and Stebbins was knocked backward and flat on his ass. It was
as though someone had pulled him from behind with a rope. He felt no
pain, just a shortness of breath. The explosions or the way he had slammed
into the ground had sucked the air right out of him. He was dazed and
covered once again with white powder from the pulverized mortar of the
wall. He felt angry. *The son of a bitch almost killed me!*

"You okay, Stebby? You okay?" asked Heard.

"I'm fine, Brian. Good to go."

Stebbins stood up, infuriated, cursing at full throttle as he stepped
back out into the alley and resumed firing at the window.

Sergeant Howe, the Delta team leader, watched with amazement
from further up the street. He couldn't believe the Ranger didn't have the
good sense to find better cover. To Nelson, it looked like somebody had
flipped a switch inside Stebbins. For the second time that hour he thought
Stebbins had been killed. But the mild-mannered office clerk bounced back

up. He was a changed man, a wild animal, dancing around, shooting like a madman. Nelson, Twombly, Barton, and Yurek were all shooting now at the same window, when there came a *whooosh* and a cracking explosion and both Stebbins and Heard screamed and disappeared in a ball of flame.

*That's it for Brian and Stebby.*

Stebbins woke up flat on his back again. He had the same feeling as before, like he'd been punched in the solar plexus. He gasped for air and tasted dust and smoke. Up through the swirl he saw darkening blue sky and two clouds. Then Heard's face came swimming into view.

"Stebby, you okay? You okay, Stebby?"

"Yup, Brian. I'm okay," he said. "Just let me lay here for a couple of seconds."

"Okay."

This time, as he gathered his thoughts, common sense intruded. They needed help at this spot. More of the corner had been blown away. Stebbins figured he'd been hit in the chest by stones flying off the wall, enough to knock him over and out, but not enough to penetrate his body armor and seriously hurt him. The Sammies had set up some kind of crew-served weapon and it was going to take more than an M-16 to silence it. As he got back up, he heard Barton across the alley radioing for help. Then a voice came from ear level, right behind Stebbins. One of the D-boys was in the window of the corner building, the same window Nelson had fired at earlier. The voice sounded cool, like a surfer's.

"Where's this guy shooting from, dude?"

Stebbins pointed out the window.

"All right, we've got it covered. Keep your heads down."

From inside the building, the Delta marksman fired three 203 rounds, dropping them right into the targeted window. There was an enormous blast inside the building. Stebbins figured the round had detonated some kind of ammo cache, because there was a flash throughout the first floor of the building too bright and loud for a 203 round. After that it went dark. Black smoke poured from the window.

It got quiet. Stebbins and Heard and the guys across the alley shouted their congratulations to the D-boy for the impressive shot. Back on one knee a little further behind the chewed-up wall, Stebbins watched some lights flick on in the distance and was reminded that they were in the middle of a big city, and that in some parts of the city life was proceeding normally. There were fires burning somewhere back toward the Olympic Hotel, where they had roped in. It seemed like ages ago. He thought now that it was dark, maybe the Sammies would all put down their weapons and go home, and he and his buddies could walk back to the hangar and call it a night. Wouldn't that be nice?

A voice shouted across the intersection that everyone was to retreat back toward the bird. As darkness fell, the force was going to move indoors. One by one, the men on his corner sprinted across the intersection. Stebbins and Heard waited their turn. The volume of fire had died down. *Okay, the big part of the war is over.*

Stebbins then heard a whistling sound, and turned in time to see what looked like a rock hurtling straight at him. It was going to hit his head. He ducked and turned his helmet toward the missile, and then he vanished in fire and light.

# 5

Sergeant Fales, the wounded PJ, got a radio call for a medic. They needed somebody fast across the wide intersection west of the downed helicopter. Private Rodriguez was bleeding badly from the gunshot wound to his crotch. The men were all falling back into the various casualty collection points. The medic Kurt Schmid was in the courtyard up the road working on Corporal Smith. No one on the other side of Marehan Road had the skills to deal with an injury as severe as Rodriguez's. Fales was propped up behind the Kevlar plates near the tail boom of the helicopter, his hastily bandaged leg stretched out useless before him.

His buddy Tim Wilkinson, who was working on some of the wounded alongside him, had been making him laugh. The two air force medics had long commiserated over how unlikely they were to see real combat on this deployment. Wilkinson had just tapped Fales on the shoulder as the bullets flew overhead and said, "Be careful what you wish for."

Wilkinson was still working under the impression that the ground convoy (long since returned broken and bleeding to base) was going to arrive at any moment. He felt his job was to get all the wounded patched up and on litters, ready to be loaded up as soon as the trucks arrived. When he'd instructed Fales to get on a stretcher earlier that afternoon, the master sergeant had balked.

"Hey, you know the deal. Get on!" Wilkinson insisted.

Fales had climbed on reluctantly and had been strapped down, but as time wore on and the vehicles didn't show, Fales worked himself free of the straps, retrieved his weapon, and resumed firing. Now he heard the call from across the street.

"They need a medic, Wilky."

Bullets and RPG rounds formed a deadly barrier between their position and the men across Marehan Road. Wilkinson folded up his medical kit and moved toward the intersection. Then he stopped. If he was afraid, he had simply filed the emotion away. Ever since the rounds had peppered the inside of the helicopter, filling it with a little snowstorm of dust and debris, Wilkinson had just stopped worrying about bullets and focused on his job, which was demanding enough to block out everything else. He worked quickly and with purpose. There were more things to do than he could get done. It was as though he couldn't think about both things, about both the danger and the work. So he concentrated on the work. Now he turned to his friend and deadpanned an absurd and deliberately cinematic request.

"Cover me," he said.

And he ran, and ran, plowing across the wide road, head down as the volume of fire suddenly surged. Wilkinson's buddies would later joke that he wasn't shot because he was so slow the Sammies had all miscalculated his speed and aimed too far in front of him. To the medic, it just felt like he had willed himself safely across the street. Once inside the Delta command-post courtyard he began to assess the wounded, making quick triage decisions. It was obvious Rodriguez needed help first. He was bleeding heavily, and very frightened. Wilkinson tried to calm him.

The medic cut open Rodriguez's uniform to assess the damage. Rodriguez had been hit by a round that entered his buttock and bored straight through his pelvis, blowing off one testicle as it exited through his upper thigh. The first goal was to stop Rodriguez from bleeding out. If his femoral artery had been hit (as with Smith, across the street), he knew there wasn't much chance of stopping the bleeding. Wilkinson began applying field dressings, stuffing wads of Curlex into the gaping exit wound. He wrapped the area tightly with an Ace bandage. Wilkinson then slipped rubber, pneumatic pants over Rodriguez's legs and pelvis, and pumped them with air to apply still more pressure to the wound. The bleeding stopped. He dosed Rodriguez with morphine and started an IV to replenish fluids, which he quickly exhausted trying to get the private stabilized.

He radioed over to Fales, "You guys got any more fluids?"

They did. Wilkinson told them to just bag them up and toss them as far as they could in his direction. He watched across the street as one of the men there wound up for the heave, and realized that was a bad idea. He called back over and told them not to throw it. If the contents broke open, or were hit by a round, they'd waste precious fluids. If the bags spilled out, he'd be stuck in the middle of Marehan Road gathering it all up. He decided it would be better to brave the road twice at full speed than stop in the middle of it.

He ran across, again moving at what seemed tortoise pace, and again arriving unscathed. The men watching from their positions hunkered down around the intersection were amazed at Wilkinson's bravery. Wilkinson told Fales that he would have to go back for good this time. Rodriguez was in a critical state. He needed to be taken out immediately. Wilkinson would care for him until that happened. Then, with the fluids cradled in his arms, head down, he dashed across the road for the third and last time. Again, he arrived unhurt.

As he burst back into the courtyard, one of the D-boys told him, "Man, God really does love medics."

It was fast growing dark. Wilkinson got help moving Rodriguez and the others into a back room. He learned then that the convoy coming to rescue them had turned back, and that they were going to be spending the night.

Wilkinson sought out Captain Miller.

"Look, I've got a critical here," he said. "He needs to get out right now. The others can wait, but he needs to come out."

Miller gave him a look that said, *We're in a bad spot here, what can I say?*

# 6

Specialist Stebbins had his eyes closed but he still saw bright red when the grenade exploded. He felt searing flames and then he just felt numb.

He smelled burned hair and dust and hot cordite and he was tumbling, tumbling, mixed up with Heard, until they both came to rest sitting upright staring at each other.

"Are you okay?" Heard asked after a long moment.

"Yeah, but I don't have my weapon."

Stebbins crawled back to his position, looking for his weapon. He found it in pieces. There was a barrel but no hand grip. The dust was still thick in the air; he could feel it up his nose and in his eyes and could taste it. He could also taste blood. He figured he'd busted his lip.

He needed another weapon. He stood up and started for the door of the courtyard where the D-boys were holed up, figuring he'd grab one of the wounded's rifles, but he fell down. He got up and took a step and then fell down again. His left leg and foot felt like they were asleep. After falling the second time he walked, dragging his leg, toward the courtyard. He found his buddy Heard standing in the doorway telling one of the D-boys, "My buddy Steb is still out there."

Stebbins put his hand on Heard's shoulder.

"Brian, I'm okay."

Wilkinson grabbed hold of Stebbins, who looked a fright. He was covered with dirt and powder and dust, his pants were mostly burned off, and he was bleeding from wounds up and down his leg. He was groggy and seemed not to have noticed his injuries.

"Just let me sit down for a few minutes," Stebbins said. "I'll be okay."

The medic helped Stebbins limp into the back room where the other wounded were gathered. It was dark, and Stebbins smelled blood and sweat and urine. The RPG that had exploded outside had briefly set fire to the house, and there was a thick layer of black smoke now hanging from the ceiling about halfway to the floor. The window was open to air things out, and everyone was sitting low. There were three Somalis huddled on a couch. Rodriguez was in the corner moaning and taking short, loud sucking breaths. He had an IV tube in his arm and these weird inflated pants around his middle. *Fucking got his dick shot off.*

Heard was arguing with a medic, "Look, I've just got a little scratch on my wrist. I'm fine. Really. I should put a bandage on it and go back."

The Somalis moved to the floor and Wilkinson eased Stebbins down on the couch and began cutting off his left boot with a big pair of shears.

"Hey, not my boots!" he complained. "What are you doing that for?"

Wilkinson slid the boot off smoothly and slowly, removing the sock at the same time, and Stebbins was shocked to see a golf ball–sized chunk of metal lodged in his foot. He realized for the first time that he'd been hit. He had noticed that his trousers looked burned and singed, and now, illuminated by the medic's white light, he saw that the blackened flaking patches along his leg were skin! He felt no pain, just numbness. The fire from the explosion had instantly cauterized all his wounds. He could see the whole lower left side of his body was burned.

One of the D-boys poked his head in the door and gestured toward the white light.

"Hey, man, you've got to turn that white light out," he said. "It's dark out there now and we've got to be tactful."

Stebbins was amused by that word, "tactful," but then he thought about it—*tactful, tact, tactics*—and it made perfect sense.

Wilkinson turned off the white light and flicked on a red flashlight.

Stebbins thrust his hand back into his butt pack for a cigarette, and found the pack had been burned as well. Wilkinson wrapped Stebbins's foot.

"You're out of action," he said. "Listen, you're numb now but it's gonna go away. All I can give you is some Percocet." He handed Stebbins a tablet and some iodized water in a cup. Wilkinson also handed him a rifle. "Here's a gun. You can guard this window."

"Okay."

"But as your health care professional, I feel I should warn you that narcotics and firearms don't mix."

Stebbins just shook his head and smiled.

He kept hearing sounds out the window, coming up the alley. But there was no one there. His mind was playing tricks on him. Once or twice he shouted in panic and blasted a few rounds at the window, but it was just shadows.

Stebbins's outbursts and the blast of occasional RPG hits against the outside wall roused Rodriguez from his morphine reverie. He laughed and shouted out the window what bad shots the Somalis were. As bad as his wound was, he felt no pain, just discomfort. The rubber pants had the lower half of his body in a vise. He asked Wilkinson once or twice if he would release some of the pressure. The medic said no.

One of the D-boys came in and asked Stebbins where the RPG had come from that got him, which direction? Stebbins wasn't sure.

"From down the alley west," he said.

But that had been the direction he was facing, and his injuries were all on his back side. Then Stebbins remembered he had turned and looked back when he had seen it coming at him. It must have come from behind him.

"No, east. Not from over the bird though," he said. "From further up the street."

Finally he was left to sit there alone, his pants blown off, clutching his rifle, listening to Rodriguez breathing steadily and to the Somali woman complaining with words he didn't understand that her husband's flex cuffs were too tight. He realized he had to urinate badly. There was no place to go. So he just released the flow where he sat. It felt great. He looked up at the Somali family and gave them a weak smile.

"Sorry about the couch," he said.

# 7

Still out on the street one and a half blocks south, Private David Floyd was shooting at everything that moved. At first he had hesitated firing into crowds when they massed downhill to the south, but he had seen the Delta guy, Fillmore, get hit, and Lieutenant Lechner, and about three or four of his other buddies, and now he was just shooting at everybody. The world was erupting around him and shooting back seemed the only sensible response. But no matter how many rounds he and Specialist Melvin DeJesus poured down Marehan Road, the crowds kept on creeping in. Out in the street, still flat in his little dip in the middle of the road, Specialist John Collett was doing the same. They were the southernmost point on the perimeter and had no idea what was happening down around the crash site, or anywhere else for that matter. When Floyd hit someone with rounds from his SAW, he could see their bodies begin to twitch, like they were being zapped with electricity. They would usually make it only a step or two more before falling over.

A bullet or a casing or something hit him. Floyd jumped a foot. He felt down, afraid to take his eyes off the road ahead, and found that his pants had been ripped from his crotch to his boot, but the round hadn't even scratched him. It had evidently come through the tin wall.

"Whooo!" he said, looking over at DeJesus, grateful and frightened. His ears were ringing but for some reason he could still hear. DeJesus was starting to freak out. He was getting jumpier and jumpier, saying he couldn't stay there anymore. He had to move. He and Floyd had felt safe for a time pressed behind the tin shed wall on the west side of the road in shadow, but as it grew darker now, DeJesus wasn't staying low. He was up on his feet, hopping up and down. He said he had to do something. He had a bad feeling. He had to be somewhere else. Now!

Floyd felt like slapping him.

"Sit yer ass down!" he screamed at him.

As it happened, across Marehan Road men were waving them into the courtyard. Captain Steele had given up for the time being catching up to Lieutenants Perino and DiTomasso in the next block. He wanted all the men at this southern end of the perimeter to consolidate in the court-yard. Already there were three Delta teams and a number of wounded in the small space, including Neathery and Errico, who both had gunshot wounds to their biceps, and Lechner, who was still howling with the pain of his shattered right lower leg. Goodale was still working the radio while a medic stuffed Curlex into the exit wound in his buttock. The courtyard was a haven, but the wide road that separated Floyd, DeJesus, and the other members of Chalk Three from it loomed like an impassable gulf.

One by one, they ran for it. Private George Siegler went first. Then Collett jumped up from his spot in the middle of the road and sprinted for the door. Private Jeff Young, his big glasses bouncing on his nose and long legs pumping high, made it across next. As each man ran, Floyd and DeJesus, who had settled down again, blasted rounds to the south to pro-vide covering fire. Finally, only Floyd and DeJesus were left.

"You're gonna run across that road," Floyd told his buddy.

DeJesus nodded.

"But, listen here. When you get across, don't you go through that doorway, see? You turn around and start shooting, because as soon as you're across, I'm coming. Okay?"

DeJesus nodded. Floyd wasn't at all sure he'd gotten through.

He must have blasted fifty rounds as DeJesus ran. And his friend didn't forget. Before entering the courtyard, DeJesus turned, dropped to one knee, and started shooting. Floyd felt like he had lead in his boots as he ran. His torn pants were flapping around him like a skirt, and he wasn't wearing any underwear, so he felt naked in more ways than one as his legs churned up the road. It seemed like the doorway to the courtyard was actually receding while he ran.

But he made it.

# 8

Across the city, back at the Ranger's airfield base an hour or so earlier, the truckloads of injured and dead off the lost convoy had arrived. This was the kind of catastrophe Major Rob Marsh had long planned for, hoping he would never see. He had entered the army in 1976 as a Special Forces medic, and then had gone on to medical school at the University of Virginia. His father, John Marsh, was then Secretary of the Army. Marsh was working as a flight surgeon in Texas when he had met General Garrison. The two had hit it off. A few years later, as Delta commander, Garrison invited Marsh to be the unit's surgeon—no doubt mindful of the family connection. Marsh said no, fearing that the offer might have more to do with his father than his medical skills. But when the offer was renewed about a year later, he'd accepted. He'd been doctoring for the unit ever since, eight years now.

One of Marsh's proudest innovations were four large trauma chests, four-by-two-foot trunks, packed with IV fluid bags, gauze, Curlex, petroleum jelly, needles, chest tubes . . . all the things needed for initial treatment of wounds. Instead of just filling the chests with the equipment, Marsh and his staff had packaged fifteen separate Ziploc bags in each trunk, five serious-wound packets and ten for lesser wounds. The idea was to assess the seriousness of an injury, then grab the appropriate packet. Marsh had seen British forces do that during the Falkland Islands war. Delta had been lugging the trunks around with them now for years, not always happily. Officers had complained about how much space the trunks took up on pallets, and more than once had tried to have them removed. In Marsh's experience, it was always officers with actual combat experience like Garrison who would step in to save his chests. Now, for the first time, they needed them.

Marsh had been hovering around the JOC all afternoon as the mission deteriorated. At first, Garrison had been in the back of the room, chewing on his unlit cigar, listening and watching quietly. He was not one to interfere. Some top commanders insisted on calling most of the shots themselves, but Garrison wasn't like that. When they'd begun this deployment, the general had given a little speech explaining that, for the first time in his career, he'd been given command of men he felt he didn't need to lead. They knew how to lead themselves. Garrison told them his job was just to supply them with what they needed and stay out of their way. But as things began going wrong, the general had moved to the front of the room.

Marsh had to leave the JOC to tend to Private Blackburn—who had not, as the medic had feared, broken his neck when he fell from the Black Hawk. The young Ranger had suffered head and neck trauma, and had a few broken bones. Marsh was working on him when he got word that a Black Hawk was down in the city. When he returned to peek into the JOC, there was an anxious buzz about the place. Commanders seemed fixated on the TV screens. Garrison was fully engaged. Things had clearly gone amok.

The army field hospital at the U.S. embassy was alerted to be ready for casualties. There was some discussion about sending men directly there, but it was decided to do the primary care at Marsh's tent. He was ready. He had two surgeons, a nurse anesthetist, and two physician assistants. Nurses from the adjacent air force mobile surgical facility also volunteered to help. There would be a triage area just outside the tent. The most urgent cases would go directly inside. Those who could wait would go to a holding area out back. Those who were "expectant," near death and beyond help, would go to a separate spot near the ambulance, away from the other wounded. Marsh had designated his unit's ambulance for the dead. It was cool in there. The bodies would be out of the sun and out of view. Pilla's body was already there.

When the convoy pulled up it was like a scene out of some nightmarish medieval painting. The back of one of the five-tons opened on a mass of bleeding, wailing, moaning men. Griz Martin sat to one side holding his entrails in his hands, his legs shattered, awake but groggy. There hadn't even been time in most cases for the wounds to have been bandaged. Marsh had just seconds to make a judgment call on each as the litter bearers lifted them out. Private Adalberto Rodriguez, who had been blown up and run over, went into the tent. A Delta sergeant, whose left calf had been shot off, went out back to wait. Into the tent went Sergeant Ruiz, who had a sucking wound in his chest. Some of the wounded Rangers were dazed. They wandered around the triage area, sputtering angrily. Marsh noted they all were still carrying weapons. He asked the chaplain to start gathering those guys and talking to them.

Delta medic Sergeant First Class Don Hutchinson confronted Marsh about Griz. Hutch and Griz were close.

"He's hurt real bad, Doc."

Some of the other D-boys had come over to be with Griz, who was semiconscious with what Marsh recognized as a clearly nonsurvivable injury. His midsection was basically gone, and when Marsh tried to turn him over, he saw the whole back of his pelvis had been blown off. Griz was in shock level three going into four. His skin was pasty pale. He'd obviously lost a tremendous amount of blood. It was amazing that he was still alive, much less semiconscious, but when Marsh took his hand, Griz gripped it as hard as the doctor's hand had ever been gripped. He should have labeled him "expectant," or certain to die, and sent him back by the ambulance, but with all the guys from the unit pressing in, urging him to do something, Marsh felt compelled to act. He felt sure it was hopeless, but they'd give Griz a full-court press anyway.

Marsh sent into the tent Private Kowaleski, the Ranger driver whose torso had been penetrated by the unexploded RPG. Amazingly, he still had vital signs. Inside, Captain Bruce Adams, a general surgeon, examined the broken body of the soldier and recoiled at what he found. Kowaleski's left arm was gone—one of the air force nurses would find it, to her horror, in his pants pocket where Specialist Hand had placed it. Adams began working to restore Kowaleski's breathing while a nurse removed his clothing. They found the entrance wound of the RPG on one side of his chest, and, lifting a flap of skin under his right arm, Adams saw the tapered front end of the grenade.

Marsh came by for a quick second assessment and told Adams, "This guy's expectant. Don't waste any more time on him."

Assigned to help carry the nearly dead man back out was Sergeant First Class Randy Rymes, a munitions expert. It was Rymes who recognized that Kowalewski had a live bomb embedded in his chest. The detonator was on the tip, just under his right arm. Instead of taking him out by the ambulance, Rymes and another soldier built a sandbag bunker and placed Kowalewski's body inside it. Rymes then stretched out beside the bunker on his stomach and reached his hand around to delicately remove the tip of the grenade from under the man's skin.

While all this was going on, commanders inside the JOC had watched with horror as triumphant Somalis overran the site of the second Black Hawk crash, pilot Mike Durant's, and were now getting frantic calls for a chopper to medevac Smith and Carlos Rodriguez from the first crash site. They had ninety-nine men pinned down in the city, and no rescue force on its way. They knew it would be foolhardy to try to put another Black Hawk down there to evacuate the two badly injured Rangers. The volume of fire was much heavier there than anywhere else in Mogadishu, and the Somalis had already shot down four Black Hawks. Garrison had pilots who were willing to try, but there was no point in getting more men killed trying to save two.

It had been easy to believe, prior to this day, that the Somali warlord Aidid lacked broad popular support. But this fight had turned into something akin to a popular uprising. It seemed like everybody in the city wanted suddenly to help kill Americans. There were burning roadblocks everywhere. It was obvious Aidid and his clan had been waiting for the right moment, and this was it. At the second crash site, seen from high overhead, there was no sign of Shughart, Gordon, Durant, or the *Super Six Two* crew, only busy crowds of excited Skinnies still swarming over the wreckage. There was a brief flurry of hope when the observation birds picked up tracking beacons from Durant's and his copilot Ray Frank's flight suits, but it was quickly dashed when it became apparent that the beacons had been stripped from the pilots by canny Aidid militia and were being run all over the city to confuse the airborne search.

As for the men around the first crash site, they would be all right. Those ninety-nine were some of the toughest soldiers in the world. They were superbly trained, well-armed, and mean as hell. They owned that neighborhood and nobody was going to take it away from them, certainly no armed force in Mogadishu.

Unless they ran out of ammo, that is, or keeled over from dehydration. The C2 helicopter had begun calling for help shortly before dusk.

—*Need a resupply . . . IV bags, ammo, and water. . . . Obviously we need them to hurry as fast as they can. Our boys on the ground are running out of bullets.*

—*Romeo Six Four* [Harrell], *this is Adam Six Four* [Garrison]. *You want us to put resupply on a helo?*

—*If you can. Put resupply on a helo. Try to take it out to the northern crash site. They're running out of ammo, IV bottles, and water, over.*

Few of the Rangers had even bothered to take full canteens. They had been running and fighting now in sweltering heat for several hours. If they were going to make it through the night they would need more than skill and willpower. So even though it risked turning a bad situation worse, Garrison ordered a Black Hawk in. They could drop water and ammo and medical supplies, and, if possible, land and pull the two critical Rangers out. In the JOC, most of the officers believed the helicopter would be shot out of the sky. It would most likely crash-land right there on Marehan Road. Either way, the men on the ground would get their ammo and water.

Black Hawk *Super Six Six,* piloted by Chief Warrant Officers Stan Wood and Gary Fuller, moved down through the night just after seven o'clock, guided by infrared strobe lights set out on the wide street just south of the crash site. As the helicopter descended, machine-gun fire erupted again from points all around the Ranger perimeter, and RPGs flew. The men inside courtyards and houses were startled by how close the gunfire was to their positions, in some cases on the other side of the walls. The rotor wash from the Black Hawk kicked up a furious sandstorm.

It hovered for about thirty seconds, which was about twenty-eight seconds too long as far as Sergeant Howe was concerned. He held his breath as the deafening bird hung over the block, afraid that it was going to pancake in on them. Delta Sergeant First Class Alex Szigedi, who had survived the lost convoy earlier that afternoon, now hustled in the back of the helicopter with another operator to shove the kit bags filled with water, ammo, and IV bags overboard. The helicopter was getting riddled. Szigedi was hit in the face. Bullets poked holes in the rotor blades and the engine, which began sprouting fluids. One round passed through the transmission gearbox. *Super Six Six* kept flying. As it pulled up and away, men scurried out of the buildings to retrieve the new supplies.

Back in the JOC they heard Wood announce, calmly:

—*Resupply is complete.*

The stranded force had been tucked in for the night.

# 9

The fight now raged around three blocks of Mogadishu real estate. The block immediately south of the crash was occupied in two places. The CSAR team and Lieutenant DiTomasso's Chalk Two Rangers, about

thirty-three men in all, had moved in through the wall knocked over by
*Super Six One* on its way down. They had begun spreading out to adjacent
rooms and courtyards to the south. Abdiaziz Ali Aden was still hiding in
one of those back rooms. Lieutenant Perino had led his men into a courtyard on the same block through a door on the east side of Marehan Road.
He and about eight other soldiers were grouped where Sergeant Schmid
was still working on Corporal Smith, who was slowly fading away. Perino
still wasn't sure where the downed bird was or how close they were to
DiTomasso, although they were separated now by only a few feet. Captain Miller and his contingent of D-boys and wounded Rangers were in
the courtyard Howe had cleared on the west side of Marehan Road. Miller's
twenty-five men had spread out into that block, moving into rooms off the
courtyard. The third block was across a wide alley south on the same side
of the street as Perino. There, in the courtyard they'd sought shelter in
earlier, Captain Steele and three Delta teams were still stuck, unable to
push further down toward the wreck.

   This ungainly distribution of forces was problematic. The Little Bird
pilots, who were making frequent gun runs, were having a hard time clearly
delineating friendly force locations from targets. From the C2 Black Hawk
high above, Lieutenant Colonel Harrell radioed a request to Captain
Miller.

   —*Scotty, is it possible for you to get everybody in one small tight perimeter?
The problem we have is everyone is spread out. It's hard to get close accurate fire into
you. And mark your location. We need to know exactly where you are. Is there any
way you can accomplish that, over?*

   Miller explained that Steele seemed reluctant to move up, and that
the Delta teams with Steele were also pinned down by heavy fire.

   —*Roger, I know it's tough and you're doing the best you can but try to get
everyone at one site and have one guy talking down there if you can.*

   Miller conveyed the request to the team leaders cornered with Steele.
Then, just before dark, he ordered Sergeant Howe to move across Marehan
Road and into the courtyard opposite in order to improve their coverage
of the street. Howe thought it was a poor idea. It did nothing he could see
to improve their position. He'd been out on the street for long periods
earlier, and had a plan of his own. Steele and the others stranded at the
southernmost tip of this awkward perimeter should move up and consolidate with them. This would shorten the long leg of the "L," give them

a single strong position to hold, and give the Little Birds a clearly defined one-block area to work around. They could then establish strong
interlocking fire positions at each of the key intersections, both in front
of and behind the downed bird, and at the south end of the block. Looking around outside, Howe had seen three buildings that could be taken
down and occupied, which would have expanded their fire perimeter. A
two-story house at the northwest corner of the intersection off the bird's
tail would have provided a shooting platform that could push the Somali
gunmen to the north several blocks further out. Howe felt this was so
obviously the way to go it surprised him that the ground commanders
hadn't begun it already. Instead, as Howe saw it, they seemed overwhelmed. They had followed him into the courtyard and then squatted
there, just as Steele was now squatting in a worthless position off to the
south. Everything in Howe's training said that survival depended on
proactive soldiering. You constantly assessed your position and worked
to improve it.

Howe knew there was no point arguing. He and the three men on
his team ran across the road in groups of two. They barged through the
front door of a two-room house and cleared it. There was no one inside.
Through a barred window in back Howe saw Perino and his group. One
of Howe's team members knocked out the bars and just pushed down the
flimsy stone wall to open up a passage into their space. Perino and Schmid
strapped the dying Corporal Smith to a board and passed him through the
window into the room. There they would be sheltered from grenades
lobbed over the walls.

As far as Howe was concerned, his position sucked. From the doorway, he could see only the corners of the alleyways to the south and north.
Far from expanding their field of fire, he could see no more than twenty
yards out in each direction!

Just listening to the shouted questions and commands on the radio,
Howe sensed that some of those in charge were out of their depth. There
was just too much going on. He could see it in their faces. Sensory over-
load. When it happened you could almost see the fog pass over a man's
eyes. They just withdrew. They became strictly reactive.

Take the vaunted Rangers. Some of the Rangers were out there in
the fight, but nobody was telling them what to do, and they sure as hell
didn't know. Most of them were holed up in back rooms of the house

one block south with their commander, Steele, waiting to see what was going to happen next. Howe figured there were more than two dozen capable men and several heavy weapons back there in that house. What the hell were they doing? That was one thing he and Miller and even the commanders overhead seemed to agree on at least. Steele and his Rangers needed to pick up their wounded and move fifty fucking yards down the slope to consolidate the perimeter and join the fucking fight! But Steele wouldn't budge. It was as if the Rangers saw the D-boys as their big brothers, and since their big brothers were around, everything would be okay.

Shooting quieted down after the moon came up. It cast faint shadows out on the street. The Little Bird gun runs lit up the sky with tracers and rockets. Brass from their miniguns rained down on the tin rooftops like somebody banging on the side of an empty metal bucket. There were bodies of Somalis still stretched out on the road. Howe had noticed that the Sammies were good about hauling off their wounded and dead. Bodies tended not to stay put unless they were right in the middle of the street. Weapons, too. If there was a weapon down on the ground, it would be gone eventually unless it was broken. They were smart street fighters. Howe felt a grudging professional admiration. They were disciplined, and what they lacked in sophisticated weapons and tactics they made up for with determination. They used concealment very well. Usually all you saw of a shooter was the barrel of his weapon and his head. Once darkness fell and the amateurs went home, the firing became less frequent but more accurate.

Shortly after moonrise, Howe was startled by loud voices from around the corner north of his doorway, over where Stebbins and Heard had been hit. At first he thought it was Rangers. Who else would be dumb enough to be talking that loud out on the street? But the Rangers were all supposed to be off the street. He popped an earplug and listened harder. The voices were speaking Somali. They must have been half deaf like everybody else from all the explosions, and didn't realize how loud they were talking. Sometimes it took soldiers two or three days to regain full hearing after a fight. As three Somalis rounded the corner, one of the D-boys from across the street shone a white light on the first in line. His eyes looked as wide as a raccoon's startled in a garbage can. With his rifle resting on a doorjamb, Howe placed his tritium sight post on the second man and began shooting on full automatic, sweeping his fire in a smooth motion over the third man. All three Somalis went down hard. Two of the men struggled to their feet and dragged the third man up and around the corner.

Howe and the other operators let them go. They didn't want to expose their firing positions with more muzzle flashes. Howe was disgusted again with this 5.56 ammo. When he put people down he wanted them to stay down.

# 10

When Steele and his men had first moved into the courtyard it was bedlam. The noise was relentless: shooting, grenade blasts, helicopter rotors, radio calls, men shouting, crying, groaning, screaming back and forth, trying to be heard over the din, each one's need more urgent than the next man's. There was smoke and gunpowder and dust in the air. Poor Lieutenant Lechner was bleeding a river from his shattered right leg and bellowing with pain.

The courtyard itself was about fifteen feet wide and maybe eighteen feet long. There were two rooms to the right as you entered, two rooms to the left, and at the rear was a covered porch walled off from the open middle with ornate concrete latticework. The first room to the left was filled, floor to ceiling, with tires. The first room on the right held the Somali family who lived here. They had been searched, flex-cuffed, and placed in the corner. Steele had five wounded men back behind the concrete partition. Two of them, Goodale and Lechner, could no longer walk. Medics were still working on Lechner. Steele had three teams of D-boys mixed in with his force, none of whom answered to him, which further confused matters.

At one point the D-boys were talking about putting a heavy gun out on the street just outside the courtyard doorway. They all carried rifles. Specialist Collett nervously listened to them discussing it. He was a SAW gunner, and the only machine gunner who hadn't been injured. If anybody was going to be sent out there, it would be him. He'd spent more than an hour crouched behind a rock in the middle of Marehan Road, and now that he was finally safely indoors, going back out was the last thing he wanted. He'd do it, but he dreaded it.

"I'm not sending anyone back outside," Steele told them.

Collett heaved a quiet sigh of relief.

Steele shouted back to his ranking sergeant, Sean Watson, to see if there were any back doors to this house. With all the shooting going on out front he figured, when they left, it would be best to go out another way. Watson said there were no back doors.

He could talk on the radio to his lieutenants, Perino and DiTomasso, but he wasn't sure how far away either of them was. DiTomasso spent a few minutes on the radio trying to orient the captain, but they had come in from different directions and neither was familiar with the neighborhood so the discussion got nowhere. Steele felt like he was playing the childhood game where everyone is asked to turn their backs to the blackboard and draw a picture according to the teacher's instructions—the point of the game being how differently all the drawings turned out. In fact, Steele was no more than fifty yards away from Perino, who was separated from DiTomasso by nothing more than a eight-inch flimsy interior wall. They might as well have been miles apart.

Steele was desperate to get a fix on where all his men had gone, frightened that one or more had been left behind in the confusion. He'd lost track of Sergeant Eversmann and Chalk Four completely. The last he knew, he had ordered them to head to the crash site on foot. He did not know that they had been picked up by the ground convoy and then gone through hell before returning to base, where they were now. Perino and DiTomasso had given him a count on who was with them, and Perino had seen Rodriguez and Boren pulled into the casualty center across Marehan Road. But what of Stebbins and Heard? Steele had no direct radio link to Captain Miller, so he relayed his requests for information to the C2 bird, and they passed them along to Miller.

—*Kilo Six Four* [Miller], *this is Romeo Six Four* [Harrell]. *He* [Steele] *is requesting status on a Ranger Stebbins and a Ranger Heard. He thinks they are with you. Can you confirm, over?*

The C2 bird reported back to Steele:

—*Roger, Juliet, the answer is affirmative. They have those two Rangers with them, over.*

That was good news. But nobody seemed to know where Eversmann's chalk had gone. Steele had just begun to contemplate a next move when Perino radioed him again about Smith. The captain knew it was hopeless to keep asking for another helicopter to come down, but he also knew he wasn't the one covered with Smith's blood, watching the young man's life ebb away.

"I'm gonna ask for it, but it's going to be pretty hard to put a bird in," Steele said.

"I've got a big intersection right outside," said Perino. "They can put one down there."

Steele called up on the command net.

—*Romeo Six Four, this is Juliet Six Four. We need medevac NOW. We have a critical who is not going to make it.*

Word came back down minutes later.

—*Roger, understand. We are pressing the QRF to get there as quickly as they can. I doubt that we can get a Hawk in there to get anybody out, over.*

Medic Kurt Schmid had relayed a request for blood, getting Smith's type off his dog tags. After the resupply Black Hawk came and went, he approached Delta team leader Paul Howe.

"Was there any blood?"

"No," Howe told him.

Schmid figured the blood supply must be stretched thin dealing with all the casualties from the lost convoy. He had heard on the radio that the docs back at the base were drawing blood from donors to meet the sudden demand.

He kept working on Smith, even though it now felt helpless. He had Perino and others in their courtyard taking turns pressing into Smith's lower abdomen to keep pressure over the femoral artery. The medic had finally relented and given Smith a morphine drip. It had quieted the corporal. He was still conscious, but just barely. He looked pale and distant. He had begun to make peace with dying. Perino could tell that even though Smith was now quiet and weak he was still alert enough to be very scared. He talked about his family. His father had been a Ranger in Vietnam, and had lost a leg in combat. His younger brother, Mike, was planning to enlist and enter Ranger school. Mike's twin, Matt, also wanted to join. Jamie had grown up wanting to be nothing else. He had played football and lacrosse in high school in northern New Jersey, and done well enough in his classes to graduate, which was good enough. He hadn't been interested in books or school; he knew what he wanted to be. Nothing could deter him. Not even the scare his father, James Sr., had tried to put in him, speaking to him graphically about the horrors he had seen and experienced in Nam. Three years earlier, when he was still in basic training, Smith had written to his father, "Today while walking back from lunch I saw two Rangers walking through the company area. It's the dream of being one of those guys in faded fatigues and a black beret that keeps me going."

Smith was now asking the medic to tell his parents and family goodbye and to tell them that he had been thinking of them as he died, and that he loved them. They said prayers together.

"Hold tight," Schmid told the dying corporal. "We're working on getting you out of here. I'm doing everything I can."

Away from Smith, the medic kept telling Perino, "We need help. He's not going to make it."

But how to convey the urgency with so much else going on? The resupply had delivered more IV fluids, and Schmid pumped those into Smith, but the kid had lost too much blood. He needed a doctor and a hospital. Even that may not have been enough to save him. He was just barely alive.


When the moon came up, Steele kicked himself for letting the men leave behind their NODs. Here he was, the inflexible *by-the-book*-robot-Ranger tyrant, and he'd relaxed procedures this one time for what seemed like ample reason, and now they were in the fight of their lives, at night, lacking the most significant technological advantage they had over their enemy. If ever there was a more perfect illustration of why *not* to ignore procedure.

Still, it had seemed like such an obvious call that Sergeant Goodale had ridiculed Private Jeff Young back in the hangar for even asking about them as they had prepared to go out.

"Young, think about it. What time is it?"

"About three o'clock."

"How long have our missions been?"

"About two hours."

"Is it still light out at five?"

"Yeah."

"Then why would you want to bring your night vision?"

Steele was mortified by the stupidity of his call. In an hour or two it was going to be darker than four inches up a goat's butt. He made a quick check around the courtyard to see if anybody, maybe just accidentally, had brought NODs along. No one had. Out the half-opened metal doorway it now looked dark as a cavern. From where he stood in the second room at the north end of the courtyard—it appeared to be the kitchen—Steele could see moonlight reflecting blue off the barrels of his men's weapons sticking out of doorways. He called out to them one by one to make sure no one nodded off.

Miller wasn't sure what was going on down the block. After he'd re-layed the first request for Steele and his men to move up, Steele had declined an offer to speak directly to Miller via one of the D-boys' headsets. From the Delta command position, there was no telling what was wrong with Steele. There was some concern that the captain had been injured—the Ranger commander had broadcast that the "command element" had been hit, and nobody was sure if that meant him (Steele had been talking about Lechner). Miller had relayed a request for Steele to move at least some of his force down, if not across the intersection, then to the corner building on their block where they could help cover the southern inter-section. The Ranger commander had heard the urgings from the command helicopter, arguing that it would be easier for the Little Birds to do gun runs if the forces were in a tighter perimeter. The idea of stepping out of the relative safety of their fortified courtyard back into the street was hardly appealing; nevertheless, when the C2 bird made the initial request, Steele agreed.

He radioed Perino and asked him to throw a blue Chemlite out his courtyard door into the street.

"Roger, it's out," said the lieutenant.

Steele then stepped briefly out into the street. He was surprised how close the light was, only a short sprint up the road.

He radioed back to Harrell, "Okay. Hoo-ah."

Then he went back to tell Sergeant Watson to get ready for the move. Watson was blunt.

"Hey, sir, uh-uh," he said. "No way."

Watson said he thought the idea was crazy. They could expect a hail of bullets and grenades the second they stepped out the door. They had five wounded men, two of whom (Lechner and Goodale) would have to be carried. Fillmore's body would also have to be carried. To move quickly, that would mean four men for each litter, which would make convenient cluster targets for Somali gunmen. What was wrong with the position they had? The shooting had died down and it would take one hell of a lot to overrun that courtyard. If they stayed where they were, they had a bigger perimeter. Why move?

The Rangers listened nervously to the discussion. To a man, they sided with Watson. Private Floyd thought Steele was nuts to even suggest moving. Goodale certainly didn't relish the thought of making such a trip on a litter. Moving was unnecessary and dangerous. It was asking for more trouble when they already had plenty. Steele took a deep breath and reconsidered.

"I think you're right," he told Watson.

He conferred with the D-boys in the courtyard briefly, then radioed Harrell.

"Right now we're not going to be able to move, not with all these wounded."

This was frustrating news for Captain Miller. Nobody had clearly sorted out who was in charge on the ground. If some part of Steele's force moved just to the end of their block, they could better cover the wide alley that ran between them. Harrell refused to order Steele to make the move.

*—If you stay separated I cannot support you as well,* Harrell told Steele. *You're the guy on the ground and you have to make the call.*

Steele had made his call, and that was that. When one of the operators again offered Steele his headset so the captain could confer directly with Miller, Steele waved him away. So there were effectively two separate forces pinned down now, and their commanders were not talking to each other.

If Steele wouldn't budge, Miller would at least move his own men. As the D-boys prepared to leave, Steele was angry. If they moved out, it would more than halve the number of able-bodied men at his position. He felt it didn't make sense, and regarded Miller's move as a kind of "Fuck you," directed at him—and his men. But he did nothing to stop it.

The operators lined up in the courtyard. When the first group of four dashed out into the night, the whole neighborhood erupted. It sounded like the city of Mogadishu had sprung viciously back to life. Within seconds, all four of the D-boys came flying back into the courtyard, tripping over the same metal rim at the bottom of the door that had tripped Steele up early in the afternoon. They wound up in a heap on the ground, their gun barrels clinking together as they untangled.

Relieved that none had been injured, Steele watched them regroup with sober satisfaction.

—*Hey, Captain, we've got to get Smith out. He's getting worse,* came another radio call from Perino.

"Roger," Steele said.

He knew it was hopeless, but he felt he had a responsibility to Smith to at least try. He tried the command net once more. He called up to Harrell.

"Romeo Six Four, this is Juliet Six Four. Our guy is fading fast. There's a wide intersection suitable for LZ [landing zone] directly outside."

—*Can you mark it, Juliet? Is it big enough to bring in a Hawk?*

Steele said it was, and that they could mark it. He waited a few moments for a decision. He could hear the frustration in Harrell's voice when it returned.

—*We put a Hawk in there to resupply and it got shot so bad the bird is unusable. I think if we try to bring another MH* [MH-60, a Black Hawk], *we are just going to have another bird go down on the ground, over.*

"This is Juliet Six Four. Roger. What is the ETA on the armored vehicles?"

There was no answer for a few minutes. Steele called back, knowing he was pushing.

"Romeo, this is Juliet."

—*Go ahead, Juliet.*

"Roger. Do you have an ETA for me?"

—*I am working on it now, standby.*

Harrell's irritation showed.

Steele then heard Harrell pleading with the JOC.

—*We've got two critical pax* [Carlos Rodriguez was also in critical condition] *that are going to die if we do not get them out of that location. I don't think that it is secure enough to bring in a bird. Can you get an ETA for the ground reaction force, over?*

Then, minutes later.

—*If the QRF does not get there soon, there will be more KIAs* [Killed in Action] *from previously received WIAs* [Wounded in Action]. *Get the one-star*

[Brigadier General Greg Gile, commander of the 10th Mountain Division] *to get his people moving!*

From the commanders' perspective, other than the plight of Smith and Rodriguez, it made little sense to rush back out into the fray. Given the road-blocks and ambushes that had turned back the earlier convoys, the command-ers were not taking any chances with the next one. They were going back out in major force, with hundreds of men led by Pakistani tanks and Malay-sian armored personnel carriers. But it was taking time to assemble and organ-ize this force. Harrell was told it would be at least an hour (it would actually take three hours) before they were ready to move. Harrell reported back:

—*It is going to be an hour before they get in there. I don't think they will be able to get there within an hour.*

Steele told him that an hour was too long. Air commander Matthews explained:

—*Roger. I want to try to put a bird in but I'm afraid if I do that we are just going to lose another aircraft, over.*

Nobody wanted to write off the two young soldiers. Back at the JOC, the generals again considered landing a helicopter to take out Smith and Rodriguez. The pilots were ready to attempt it. Miller and Steele were asked again if they could adequately secure a landing zone to get a Black Hawk in and out. Perino walked out and consulted with Sergeant Howe, who told him a chopper could get in, but it damn sure wouldn't get back out.

Captain Miller's Delta command post was consulted. He answered:

—*We are willing to try and secure a site, but there are RPGs all over the place. It is going to be really hard to get a bird in there and get it out. I'm afraid that we are just going to lose another bird.*

Harrell delivered the reluctant verdict.

—*We are going to have to hold on the best we can with those casualties and hope the ground reaction force gets there on time.*

Steele sadly passed this word to Perino. "It's just too hot," Steele told him.

Not long afterward, Smith started hyperventilating, and then his heart stopped. Medic Schmid went into full emergency mode. He tried CPR for several rotations, compressions and ventilations, then he injected drugs straight into the Ranger's heart. It was no use. He was gone.

Harrell was still pushing hard for the ground rescue force.

*—We've got guys that are going to die if we don't get them out of there, and I can't get a bird in, over.*

It was at about eight o'clock when Steele got another radio call from Perino.

*—Don't worry about the medevac, sir. It's too late.*

Steele put out the news on the command net.

*—One of the critical WIAs has just been KIA.*

Medic Schmid was shattered by Smith's death. The corporal had gone from a fully alert, strong Ranger complaining, "I'm hurt," to a dead man in the medic's hands.

Schmid was the chief medic at his location, so he had other men to attend to and no time to brood, but Smith's prolonged agony and death would haunt him for years afterward. Still covered with Smith's blood, he went to work on the others. He felt drained, terribly frustrated, and defeated. Was it his fault? Should he have found someone and tried to set up a direct transfusion early on, back when he expected rescue was imminent? He went back over every step he had taken in treating Smith's wound, second-guessing himself, blaming himself for every decision that had turned out wrong and had wasted time.

Finally, he did his best to make peace with it. Schmid believed if he could have gotten Smith back to the base, his life would have been saved. He wasn't certain of it, but that was his gut feeling.

Steele, too, was shaken by news of Smith's death. He knew nothing yet of Pilla, nor of any of his men who had taken off with the lost convoy and been killed, Cavaco, Kowalewski, and Joyce. He'd seen Fillmore shot dead, but Smith was one of his own. He'd never lost a man before. Steele thought of them as *his* men, not the army's or the regiment's. His. They were his responsibility to train and lead and keep alive. Now he was going to be sending one of them home, somebody's precious young son, in a flag-draped coffin. He walked back to quietly tell Sergeant Watson. They decided not to tell the other guys yet.

\* \* \*

Goodale was in high spirits for somebody with a second hole through his ass. He showed off his canteen with a bullet hole through it. He felt no pain from the round that had passed through his thigh and left a nasty wound on his right buttock. It wasn't very dignified. When Floyd had come huffing in after all the men had been waved into the courtyard from the street, he took one look at the medic stuffing Curlex up Goodale's exit wound and said, "You like taking it up the ass, eh, Goodale?" In the same back room was Errico, a machine gunner who had been wounded in both biceps manning his gun, and Neathery, who'd been wounded in the upper arm when he took over for Errico. Neathery was distressed. The bullet had damaged both bicep and tricep and he couldn't make his right arm work at all.

One of the wounded men was crying, starting to freak out: "We're going to die here!" he kept repeating. "We're never going home!"

"Just shut the fuck up," said Sergeant Randy Ramaglia. The man fell silent.

Worst off was Lechner, who was now on a morphine drip. When Sergeant Ramaglia first came in the dark back room he flopped down into what felt like a warm puddle. Then he realized it was Lechner's blood. The room smelled of blood, a strong musky stink with a faint metallic tinge, like copper, an odor none of them would forget.

Watson came back at one point looking for more ammunition. They were down to about half of the supply they'd carried in.

"I have some flashbangs if you want them," said Goodale.

"No, Goodale, I don't want flashbangs," he said with gentle scorn. "We're not scaring them anymore. We're going to kill them now."

Like the rest of the guys, Goodale was frustrated with how long it was taking the rescue convoy to come. He'd ask Steele for an ETA, the captain would give him one, then that time would pass and Goodale would ask again. Steele would give him a new time, then that one would pass.

"Atwater," he shouted out to Steele's radioman. "Look, I promised my fiancée I'd call her back tonight and if I don't I'm really gonna be in some deep shit, so we've got to get out of here."

Atwater just gave him a pained grin.

"Hey, you motherfuckers better all quiet down in there," came the voice of the one of D-boys. "All it takes is one RPG through that back window and you're all fucked."

Word whispered around about Smith.

"Corporal Smith? What happened to Smith?" asked Goodale.

"He's dead."

The news hit Goodale hard. He and Smith were close. Both were smart-alecky, wiseass guys, always ready with a stinger, but Smith was the best. He always kept the guys laughing. Just before they got called up for this thing, Smith had confided in Goodale, "I've got this girl. I think I'm gonna marry her." They'd had a detailed discussion about ring buying, something Goodale had just gone through for Kira. Smith's decision to pop the question had brought them closer. It had moved them to a more serious level of manhood than the swaggering young cocksmen around them. They'd spent a lot of time together in the hangar playing Risk or just shooting the shit. *Smitty was dead?*


Private George Siegler guarded the Somalis whom they had found in the house. They had been herded into the back corner room, a bedroom. There was a bed and a night table. The baby-faced soldier, who looked no older than fifteen, trained his M-16 on the two women, a man, and four children. The adults were all on their knees. The youngest of them, a hugely pregnant woman, was crying. The others had been flex-cuffed, but not this woman, who couldn't hold the baby with her hands tied. She kept indicating with her hands that she was thirsty, so Siegler gave her his canteen. The children were all crying at first. The older ones looked to be between six and ten. One was an infant. In time the children stopped crying. So did the pregnant woman after he gave her water. They couldn't communicate, but Siegler hoped she understood they meant her no harm.

It got quieter and quieter as the night wore on. So long as they showed no light there was no shooting into the courtyard. Earlier, bullets had been coming through the open door and popping great divots in the concrete latticework in back, but now that had stopped. Specialist Kurth relieved Siegler of the prisoners after a few hours. He sat sweat-soaked and thirsty. Earlier, when they'd taken off on the mission, Kurth had felt like taking a leak but didn't, figuring they'd be back inside of an hour or so. He had ended up laying on his side out in the road behind the tin shack, urinating while gunfire snapped and popped around him, thinking, *This is what I get.*

This whole terrifying experience was having an effect on Kurth that he didn't fully understand. When he had been out on the street, crouched behind a rock that was nowhere near big enough to provide him cover, he'd thought about a lot of things. His first thought was to get the hell out of the army. Then, pondering it more as bullets snapped over his head and kicked up clods of dirt around him, he reconsidered. *I can't get out of the army. Where else am I going to get to do something like this?* And right there, in that moment, he decided to reenlist for another four years.

It grew quieter every hour as the night wore on. They kept getting situation reports, "sitreps," from the air force guy up the street monitoring the various radio nets. The convoy was just a half hour away. Then, forty-five minutes later, "the convoy's an hour away." You could hear ferocious shooting off in the distance as the rescue force finally moved out. Kurth was cotton-mouthed. They all were terribly thirsty. The taste of dust and gunpowder was in their mouths and their tongues were sticky and thick. Nothing in this world would taste as sweet as a cold bottle of water. Every once in a while a Little Bird would come roaring in low and there would be a frenzy of shooting and loud explosions, and the brass from the bird's gun would clatter off the tin roof and rain into the courtyard. Then it would get so quiet again Kurth could hear himself breathing and the steady, hurried beat of his heart.

# 11

Specialist Waddell never actually got to go indoors with the rest of the men. When darkness came and everyone moved inside, Lieutenant DiTomasso told him to pull security at the west side of the hole that had been made by the falling Black Hawk. From where he lay behind some rubble, Waddell was looking out beyond the chopper's bent tail boom. Sergeant Barton curled up at the other side of the hole, pointing his weapon east past the front of the bird.

Earlier in the afternoon, Waddell had been terrified they wouldn't get out before dark. But by dusk he was rooting for the sun to finish going down. It seemed to take forever. He figured once it was dark the shooting would die down and they could breathe easier. He watched the Little Birds scream in doing gun runs on the alley west, showering him with brass casings. Their rockets literally shook the ground. They made a sound like a giant piece of Velcro ripping open, and then there would be the flash and tremendous blast. The fact that it was so close felt good. That's where he wanted them. Close.

One of the D-boys stripped down and climbed back into the helicopter and fished out some extra SAW ammunition for Waddell and Barton and found a pair of NODs, which Waddell got. With the night vision on he could see all the way out past the big intersection west and use the laser-aiming device, which gave him a much better feeling. The little green Fiat that had so ably served as cover across the intersection for Nelson, Barton, Yurek, and Twombly was shot full of holes. Waddell could hear the radio keep promising to send out the rescue column. They were going to be there in twenty minutes. Then, an hour later, in forty minutes. After a while it got to be a joke. "They're on their way!" guys would say, and laugh. When the big column did start to move across the city about a half hour before midnight, with its tanks and armored personnel carriers, trucks and Humvees, he could hear them miles away. The convoy must have either been in terrific fighting or was basically lighting up everything in their path, because Waddell could track its movements by the sound of gunfire and by the way the sky lit up over it. He didn't think about the danger or the chances of being overrun and killed. He thought about stupid things. He was scheduled to take a physical fitness test the next day and wondered if, when they got back, they'd still make him take it. He asked Barton.

"Hey, Sergeant, am I going to have to take a P.T. test tomorrow?" Barton just shook his head.

Waddell thought about the Grisham novel he'd been reading before they left. He couldn't wait to finish that book. Wouldn't it be just his luck to get killed and never finish the last few pages?

Every thirty minutes or so during the night Barton would call over quietly, "You okay?" If Waddell hadn't heard from him in a while he'd call over to him, "Sergeant, you okay?" Like either of them was going to go to sleep. Toward the middle of the night the shooting stopped and during certain stretches the Little Birds weren't making runs and it got very still. That's when he could hear the relief column off in the distance. Waddell was one of the few Rangers who had actually brought a canteen full of water with him instead of stuffing his pouch with ammo, so he handed over his canteen and it was passed around greedily.

* * *

*When are we gonna get the fuck out of here?* That was what Specialist Phipps wanted to know. He was in a small, smoky, dusty back room with the rest of the wounded in the building adjacent to the crashed helicopter, his back and his right calf aching from shrapnel wounds, listening to the sounds of shooting and blasts outside, wondering when some wild-eyed Sammy was going to bust in and blow him away. He had no idea what was going on. Specialist Gregg Gould was in there with him. Gould has taken some shrapnel to his butt, so he looked pretty ridiculous with his bandaged ass stuck up in the air, talking on and on about his girlfriend and how much he missed her and how he couldn't wait to see her again when he got home . . . all of which further depressed Phipps, who had no girlfriend.

"Everything is gonna be cool. Man, when we get out of here I'm gonna drink me some beer," Phipps said, trying to move Gould off the topic. It didn't work.

Specialist Nick Struzik was in there. He'd been shot in the right shoulder. Phipps had seen him bleeding up against the stone wall outside earlier, not long before he'd been hit, and remembered being shocked by it, as though somebody had slapped him. Struzik was the first of his buddies he saw injured. Staff Sergeant Mike Collins was in really bad shape. He'd gotten tagged with a round in his right leg that had shattered both fibula and tibia. The bullet had entered just below the knee-cap and come out the back side of his leg, mangling it. Collins was in some serious pain and had bled a lot. Phipps figured sadly that ol' Sergeant Collins probably wouldn't make it. He couldn't believe they'd all left their NODs behind. The NODs had always given them that cocky we're-here-to-kick-ass feeling on previous night missions because it's one hell of an advantage when you can see the motherfuckers and they can't see you. Talk about an awesome lesson learned. They all took sips from the IV bags because they were so thirsty, just to wet their mouths. It tasted slimy but at least it was wet. Then, after the resupply bird came in, they all got a few sips of water.

When it was clear they would be staying longer, Sergeant Lamb took Sergeant Ron Galliette with him and explored all the doors around the inner courtyard. Behind one door they kicked open were two women, one very old, and three babies. The younger woman wanted to leave. She was just a teenager, maybe sixteen, and looked too tiny and thin to have borne the baby she clutched so tightly. She wore a brilliant blue robe with gold trim. The baby was wrapped in the same colors. She kept moving toward the door. Lamb told Sergeant Yurek to keep watch on her. Every time Yurek looked away she would move to the door again. He would hold up his rifle and she would sit back down. Yurek tried to talk to her.

"Look, if we were going to do anything to hurt you we would have done it by now, so just calm down," he said, but it was clear that she understood not a word.

Yurek talked to her anyway. He told her that she was far safer for the time being indoors than out. All she had to do was sit tight. As soon as they could leave, they'd be gone. When she made another move to the door he used his rifle to push her back into the corner.

"No, no, no! You *need* to stay here," he said, trying to frighten her into staying put. The woman argued back with him with words he didn't understand.

There was a spigot on the wall with the top broken off, and water was dripping steadily from it. Yurek collected some in his dry canteen and handed it to her. She turned her head and refused to take it from him.

"Be that way," he said.


Lamb counted fifteen wounded, along with the body of *Super Six One* co-pilot Donovan Briley. They needed more space, so they placed a small charge on a wall in the back. The stone and mortar were so flimsy that most walls you could just push down, so this charge blew a nice big hole about four feet high and two feet wide. It scared everyone when it went off, particularly the Somali woman Yurek was guarding. She went apoplectic. It even scared Twombly, who'd set the thing. He thought he had a thirty-second fuse on the charge and it was only twenty seconds, so he'd jumped a foot when it blew. The new hole opened into the room off the block's central courtyard, where Perino had originally been, so DiTomasso's unit and Perino's had finally, inadvertently, linked up. The shock of the explosion sent more of the outside wall tumbling down on Waddell and Barton out by the crashed helicopter.

Nelson was so deaf he didn't even hear the blast. His ears just rang constantly, ever since Twombly had fired his SAW right in his face. Nelson surveyed the carnage around him and felt wildly, implausibly, lucky. How could he not have been hit? It was hard to describe how he felt ... it was like an epiphany. Close to death, he had never felt so completely alive. There had been split seconds in his life when he'd felt death brush past, like when another fast-moving car veered from around a sharp curve and just missed hitting him head-on. On this day he had lived with that feeling, with death breathing right in his face like the hot wind from a grenade across the street, for moment after moment after moment, for three hours or more. The only thing he could compare it to was the feeling he found sometimes when he surfed, when he was inside the tube of a big wave and everything around him was energy and motion and he was being carried along by some terrific force and all he could do was focus intently on holding his balance, riding it out. Surfers called it The Green Room. Combat was another door to that room. A state of complete mental and physical awareness. In those hours on the street he had not been Shawn Nelson, he had no connection to the larger world, no bills to pay, no emotional ties, nothing. He had just been a human being staying alive from one nanosecond to the next, drawing one breath after another, fully aware that each one might be his last. He felt he would never be the same. He had always known he would die someday, the way anybody knows that they will die, but now its truth had branded him. And it wasn't a frightening or morbid thing. It felt more like a comfort. It made him feel more alive. He felt no remorse about the people he had shot and killed on the street. They had been trying to kill him. He was glad he was alive and they were dead.


When they moved the wounded into the bigger room cleared out by Twombly's charge, Sergeant Collins had to be passed through the hole on a stretcher. To get him through they had to strap him down and tilt the stretcher sideways. Collins protested as they readied him for this move.

"Guys, I've got a broken leg!"

"I'm sorry," Lamb told him. "We've got to get you through."

Collins screamed with pain as they passed him to the men on the other side.

They moved the body of Bull Briley back on a litter. Nelson had seen Briley playing cards and laughing in the hangar earlier that day. His head had been cut open in the crash, sliced from ear to ear just beneath his chin. His body was still warm and sweaty but it had turned a sickly gray. The slit through his head was an inch wide and had stopped bleeding. When they lifted his short, thick body on the litter the top of his head flopped back grotesquely. Lamb remembered seeing him running wearing Spandex shorts, a powerful man. *Jesus, this is a sad day.* When they'd worked him through the hole, Lamb climbed through and pulled Briley's body off the litter and put it up against the wall. The pilot's head hit the wall with a mushy thud that sickened Lamb. He flattened him out so that when rigor set in the body would not be folded at the waist.

Abdiaziz Ali Aden waited in darkness. The Rangers moved through his house. Through the small opening the helicopter had smashed in the roof he could see stars. The Rangers had hung red lamps out on the trees and on top of the houses. He had never seen lights like these. Gunfire was still loud out in the streets, coming from all directions. Helicopters swooped down low and rattled the rooftop with their falling shells. He could hear the Americans inside talking to the helicopters on their radios, directing their fire.

He wasn't sure which was more dangerous, to stay in the house with all of the Rangers on the other side of the wall, or to risk being shot running away through the night. He debated until the sound of the shooting died off, and decided to leave.

He pulled himself up to the top of an outer wall and jumped down to the alley. There were four people dead where he landed, two men, a woman, and a child. He ran and had only gone a short distance when a helicopter came roaring down behind him and bullets kicked up the dirt and bounced off the walls. He kept his head down and kept on running and was surprised he was not hit.

Tim Wilkinson, the PJ, watched over the wounded men off Captain Miller's courtyard across Marehan Road. Wilkinson sat in the doorway to the yard with a handgun. There were only occasional pops of gunfire. Now and then a Little Bird would come roaring down and light up the sky out the window.

Stebbins lit a match for a cigarette and Wilkinson, startled, wheeled around with his handgun.

"Just lighting a butt, Sergeant."

There was a moment of silence, then both men grinned, thinking the same thought.

"I know, I know," said Stebbins. "It could be hazardous to my health, right?"

# 12

Late in the night, Norm Hooten and the other D-boys, teams led by Sergeants First Class John Boswell and Jon Hale, along with a crew of Rangers headed by Sergeant Watson, left Captain Steele's southernmost courtyard and ducked into the narrow alley against its north wall, where Fillmore's body had been placed late in the afternoon. They had decided things were quiet enough for them to move as Captain Miller had wanted, into the corner building at the north end of their block. From there they could cover the wide east/west alleyway that separated the two pinned-down forces. The move left Steele in the courtyard with the wounded and only four or five able-bodied men, but the others weren't going far.

None of the Rangers was eager to go. One, a sergeant, flat out refused to leave the courtyard, even after Steele issued him a direct order. The man had just withdrawn. He protested something had scratched his eye. He was told to just get back and help with the wounded.

Sergeants Thomas and Watson followed the D-boys out into the night, trailed by Floyd, Kurth, Collett, and several other men. Floyd found a dead donkey on the side of the street just outside the door and crouched down behind it. The D-boys had gone up the alleyway and climbed into the corner building through a window that was only about three feet from the ground. By the time Floyd entered the alley, they had moved Fillmore's body in through the window.

Floyd tripped over something. He felt down and found Fillmore's CAR-15. The dried blood on it flaked off in his hands. He also found Fillmore's helmet with its headset radio and some of his other gear. He was gathering it up when Watson leaned out the window.

"What the fuck are you doing, Floyd? Quit playing. Get your ass through this window!"

Floyd had a hard time climbing through carrying all that gear. Watson gave him a pull and he landed in a space much larger than the one where Captain Steele and the others were. Fillmore's body was laid out in the middle in the moonlight. The D-boys had flex-cuffed the dead operator's arms down by his sides and his feet together to make him easier to carry. Across the alley from the window they had entered was another on the wall that divided them from the wounded next door. They smashed the shutters so they could more easily talk back and forth.

The D-boys set infrared strobes around the new space to mark it for the helicopters. Floyd searched the courtyard and found a full fifty-five-gallon drum under a dripping spigot. He sniffed at it first to see if it was gasoline, then he stuck his finger in and licked it. It was water. Kurth and the rest of the men had been sternly warned about drinking the local water. Nothing will make you sicker quicker, the docs had said. Well, Kurth decided, to hell with the docs. If he got sick, fine, he'd deal with that later. He filled his canteen and swallowed just enough to wet his throat.

Then he and Sergeant Ramaglia, who was in the room across the alley, began passing canteens back and forth on a broomstick. Ramaglia rounded up all the empties he could find, passing the stick through the holder on the plastic cap that screwed on the top of the canteen. One by one, Floyd filled the canteens from the big drum.

Then he and Collett sat for a long time and talked in whispers. The D-boys had all the windows and doorways covered, so there was nothing for them to do. The moon was up, casting soft light over Fillmore's body in the middle of the courtyard. Collett kept checking his watch. Floyd poked around the courtyard, his pants flapping open around his bare middle. On the ground next to his boot he found a brand-new dustcase for an M-16.

"Hey, Collett, look at this 'ere."

They'd been told all the Sammies had were beat-up old weapons. This one still had the packing grease on it.

Collett was feeling bored. He couldn't believe it, bored in a combat zone? How could that happen? The whole scene was weird, too weird for belief. Nobody would ever believe this shit back home. They listened to the gun runs overhead and to the approaching roar of weaponry as the giant rescue convoy fought its way in.

"Hey, Floyd."

"Yeah."

"I've got an idea."

"What?"

"Wanna get a Combat Jack?"

Floyd couldn't believe his ears. Collett was suggesting they both beat off. This was a running joke with the Rangers, getting a "jack" in exotic places. Guys would brag about getting a Thailand Jack, or an Egypt Jack, or a C-5 Jack.

They both laughed.

"Collett, you're fuckin' high, man. Yer crazier 'n hell," Floyd said.

"No, man. Think about it. You would definitely be the first kid on your block. How many people can say they got one of those, huh?"

# 13

From overhead, the commanders watched the contested neighborhood through infrared and heat-sensitive cameras that sketched the blocks in monochrome. They could see crowds of Somalis moving around the perimeter in groups of a dozen or more, and kept hitting at them with helicopters. Aidid's militia was trucking in fighters from other parts of the city. The Little Birds made wall-rattling gun runs throughout the night. One of the birds shot at a Somali carrying an RPG who must have been toting extra rounds on his back. They placed a seventeen-pound rocket on him, which killed him and must have blown the extra rounds, because he went up like a Roman candle. When the chopper went back to refuel they found pieces of the man's body pancaked on their windshield.

Sergeant Goodale, lying with his wounded butt cheek off the ground, had resumed the job of coordinating gun runs from inside Captain Steele's courtyard. He couldn't see anything from where he sat, but he acted as a clearinghouse for all the other radio operators calling in fire. He decided which location needed the help most and relayed it up to the command bird.

Late in the evening he got word that two very large forces of Somalis were moving from south to north.

For the first time, Steele felt a stab of panic. *Maybe we're not going to make it out of here.* If a determined Somali force stormed the entrance to the courtyard, he and his men would kill a lot of them but probably couldn't stop them. He moved around making sure all of his men were awake and ready. He was kicking himself now for having let his men rope in without carrying bayonets, another item called for in the tactical standing procedures but which they had jettisoned to save weight. Who would have thought they'd need bayonets? Steele poked his head in the back room where Goodale was with the rest of the wounded, and informed him with grim humor:

"If you see somebody coming through this doorway and they're not yelling 'Ranger! Ranger!' you go ahead and shoot 'im because we're all out here dead."

Goodale was shocked. The quiet had lulled him into a false sense of safety. He reasoned with himself. *Okay, I might die here. I'd rather not but if I do, then that's what's supposed to happen and there's not a damn thing I can do about it.* And he thought about what a terrible thing it was to have turned over responsibility for his life, his very existence, to the U.S. government, and that because of it he might be breathing his last breaths in this shithole back room, on this back street dirt floor in Mogadishu-fucking-Somalia. He thought about how much he'd wanted to go to war, to see combat, and then he thought about all those great war movies and documentaries he'd seen about battles. He knew he'd never see another of those films and feel the same way about it. *People really get killed.* He found the best way to accept his predicament was to just assume he was dead already. He was dead already. He just kept on doing his job.

One block up, Sergeant Yurek was now positioned at a window peering east down the crash alley. It was sketched in soft shades of blue, the pale earth of the alley, the thickets of cactus and a wall about eight feet high with a fence just beyond it, no more than two car-lengths away. Yurek tried to sit as quietly as he could, figuring he'd hear somebody coming in before he'd see them. Then he saw the fence shake. He brought his M-16 up to his shoulder and drew a bead on the top of the fence as first one, and then another Sammy lightly pulled themselves up and then squatted on the adjacent wall, evidently looking for a place to jump down. *This is getting too easy.* One of the men spotted Yurek just before the sergeant squeezed the trigger. He had just enough time to begin a shout and reach for his weapon before Yurek's rounds blew him and the other backward off the wall. One of the men's weapons dropped on Yurek's side. He heard a commotion on the other side and then it was quiet again.

Looking out on the main road, Sergeant Howe still felt boxed in. He'd been stuck in a bad position, and for the first time he began to feel like he might not make it out of here alive.

The Somalis had been sending three- to six-man teams down the alleys, probing their positions, trying to figure out exactly where they were. Howe could see these men and knew exactly what they were doing. One put his weapon around the corner and fired toward Miller's position across the street, then waited, hoping to see muzzle flashes to guide his shooting. When he saw none he edged around the corner. Howe decided to let him move well down the street in front of his position before shooting him, because if he shot the man and didn't kill him, he could return to point out Howe's position. Then they'd be a fat target for an RPG. Just as he prepared to fire two D-boys across the road did and dropped the man. He did not get back up. At the same time they lit up a group of five Somalis preparing to move around the corner. Wounded, these men dragged themselves back up the street.

The quiet was in some ways more unnerving than the early din of battle. It was hard not to imagine large groups of Sammies forming up just around the corners. If there was a sudden rush from a large enough group, Howe felt, they could all be overrun. He began preparing a checklist for himself, the steps he would take in his final fight. He was going to take as many of them with him as was humanly possible. He still had six or seven magazines left for his CAR-15, along with his .45 and some shotgun ammo. He would shoot his rifle until it ran out of ammo, then the shotgun, then his pistol, and finally he would use his knife. Hopefully he'd find an enemy weapon to pick up.

Howe called together his team and told them to hold their fire on any Somalis until they were fully committed down the street, as he had been doing. They were all to conserve ammo, pick their shots with care. All of the other operators would radio whenever they used their weapons, telling each other what they shot at and where, and whether they hit where they aimed. It helped keep track of emerging trouble spots. The night had reached a critical juncture.

The Little Birds took care of the two large elements of approaching Somalis. Goodale heard one of the helicopters come screaming down Marehan Road and after the rattle of its guns and the satisfying *boom!* of a rocket, he shouted, "Make that one large element!"

Another gun run eliminated the second threat.

Sergeant Bray, the air force combat controller at Miller's position, asked for a gun run on the two-story house adjacent to their courtyard. The building overlooked them and had a separate entrance around the corner. If there were Somalis inside that house, they'd be able to shoot right down at them. The building was adjacent to the Delta command post courtyard and no more than twenty yards in front of Howe's position, which meant hitting it from the air without hurting any of the Americans on the ground would take one hell of a shot. Howe's men marked the building with lasers for the Little Bird pilot, who radioed down to ask if they were sure they wanted his miniguns firing that close. From the air, it was like trying to paint a thin line between two friendly positions.

"Keep your heads down," the pilot warned.

His fire was right on the mark. Watching the miniguns tear the house apart, Howe turned to one of his teammates and said, "Don't try this at home!"

Some time later, two Somalis came walking down the middle of the street as though out for a stroll. The moon was high now and lit the scene about half as bright as a cloudy afternoon. The men were spaced about forty yards apart. Howe watched the first walk down past his position. He tried to put his infrared cover on his gun light, and for a moment accidentally shone the white light out the door. He watched the first man double back, looking for where the flash had originated. Howe pulled out his .45. He didn't want to shoot the man with his rifle, because there were D-boys in the building directly across the street, and the bullets would likely pass right through him and on toward them. He also knew the muzzle flash from either rifle or handgun would be clearly visible to the second man. Howe radioed for one of his men to shoot the guy as soon as he passed out of the perimeter. As the man moved on, one of the men across the street shot him in the right lower back. The man spun around with a startled look and was immediately hit by four more bullets that knocked him flat. Howe was disgusted that it had taken so many rounds to drop the man. The second Somali walked down the same way minutes later and was also shot dead.

By midnight the rescue convoy was getting close. The men pinned down listened to the low rumble of nearly one hundred vehicles, tanks, APCs (armored personnel carriers), and Humvees. The thunderclap of its guns edged ever closer. After a while, the rhythm of its shooting sounded like an extended drum solo in a rock song, very heavy metal. It was the wrathful approach of the United States of America, footsteps of the great god of red, white, and blue.

It was the best fucking sound in the world.

# N. S. D. Q.

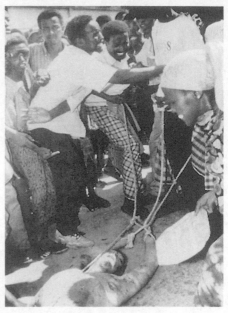

Mike Durant as he appeared on the videotape shot by his Somali captors the day after he was shot down and taken captive. Courtesy: Cable News Network. Copyright © 1998 Cable News Network, Inc. All Rights Reserved.

Enraged Somalis drag the body of Black Hawk crew chief Bill Cleveland through the streets of Mogadishu the morning after the battle. Courtesy: Paul Watson/*The Toronto Star.*

View from a Black Hawk doorway over one corner of Mogadishu's Bakara Market. Courtesy: Lance Twombly.

# 1

Michael Durant heard the guns of the giant rescue convoy roaring into the city. The injured Black Hawk pilot was flat on his back bound with a dog chain on a cool tile floor in a small octagonal room with no windows. Air, moonlight, and sounds filtered in through a pattern of crosses cut high in the upper third of the concrete walls. He tasted dust in the air and he smelled of blood and gunpowder and sweat. The room had no furniture and only one door, which was closed.

When the angry mob had closed over him, he thought he was going to die. He still did not know the fate of the three other men on his crew, copilot Ray Frank and crew chiefs Tommy Field and Bill Cleveland, or of the two D-boys who had tried to protect them. Durant did not know those men's names.

He had passed out when the mob carried him off. He'd felt himself leaving his body, watching the scene from outside himself, and at the worst of the chaos and terror it had calmed him. But the feeling hadn't lasted. He'd come to when he was thrown into the back of a flatbed truck with a rag tied around his head, surprised to still be alive and expecting at any moment to die. He was driven around. The truck would go and then stop, go and then stop. He guessed it was about three hours after the crash when they'd brought him to this place, removed the rag, and wrapped his hands with the chain.

What Durant didn't know was that he had been taken from the first group of Somalis who seized him. Yousef Dahir Mo'alim, the neighborhood militia leader who had spared him from the attacking crowd after it had overwhelmed and killed the others, had intended to carry Durant back to his village and turn him over to leaders of the Habr Gidr. As they'd left the crash site, however, they were stopped by a better-armed band of maverick *mooryan*, who had a technical with a big gun in back. This group considered the injured pilot not a war prisoner to be swapped for captured clan leaders, but a hostage. They knew somebody would pay money to get him back. Mo'alim's men were outnumbered and outgunned, so they'd reluctantly given Durant up. This was the way things were in Mogadishu. If Aidid wanted the pilot back, he would have to fight for him, or pay.

Durant's right leg ached where the femur was broken and he could feel the ooze of blood inside his pants where one end of the broken bone had pushed through his skin in the manhandling. It did not hurt that badly. He didn't know if that was good or bad. He was still alive, so the bone had not punctured an artery. His back was what really bothered him. He figured he'd crushed a vertebrae in the crash.

He managed to work one hand free of the chain. He was sweating so his hand slid out easily when he relaxed it. It gave him his first sense of triumph. He had fought back in some small way. He could wipe the dirt from his nose and eyes and straighten his broken leg somewhat and get a little more comfortable. Then he wrapped his hand back into the chain so that he still appeared to be bound.

At one point he heard several armored vehicles roll right past outside. He heard shooting and thought he was about to be rescued, or killed. There was a furious firefight. He heard the low pounding of a Mark 19 automatic grenade launcher and the explosion of what sounded like TOW missiles. He had never been at the receiving end of a barrage and he was shaken by how powerful and frightening it was. The explosions came closer and closer. The Skinnies holding him grew more and more agitated. They were all young men with weapons that looked rusty and poorly maintained. He listened to them shouting at each other, arguing. Several times one or more barged into the room to threaten him. One of the men spoke some English. He said, "You kill Somalis. You die Somalia, Ranger."

Durant couldn't understand the rest of their words but he gathered they would shoot him before letting the approaching Americans take him back.

He listened to the pitched battle with hope and fear. Then the sounds marched off and faded. He felt disappointed, despite the danger. They had been so close!

Then a gun barrel poked around the door. Just the black barrel. Durant caught the motion in the corner of his eye and turned his head just as it flamed and the room rang with a shot. He felt the impact in his left shoulder and his left leg. Eyeing his shoulder, he saw blood and the back end of a bullet protruding from his skin. It evidently had hit the floor first and had ricocheted into him without enough force to fully penetrate. A bit of shrapnel had punctured his leg.

He slid his hand from the chain and tried to wrench the bullet from his shoulder. It was an automatic move, a reflex, but when his fingers touched it they sizzled and he winced with pain. It was still hot. It had burned his fingertips.

He thought: *Lesson learned; wait until it cools down.*

# 2

Word of the big fight in Mogadishu reached Washington early Sunday. General Garrison had received a call several hours into the battle from General Wayne Downing, an old friend who was commander in chief of U.S. Special Operations Command. Downing had come to his office at MacDill Air Force Base in Tampa after a morning jog, and had decided to ring up his friend in Mogadishu to see how things were going. This was about two hours into the fight. Garrison quickly summarized what had happened so far: There had been a successful mission, two of Aidid's lieutenants and a slew of lesser lights had been captured, but two helicopters were down, lots of lead was flying, and the boys were still in the thick of it. Downing asked Garrison if there was anything he could do right away, and then got off the phone. The last thing his friend needed at that moment was some desk jockey thirteen thousand miles away looking over his shoulder.

Downing spread the word. National Security Adviser Tony Lake was given the bare outline at the White House that morning, two Aidid lieutenants captured, two helicopters down, rescue operation underway. Lake was more preoccupied just then with events in Moscow, where Russian President Boris Yeltsin was fending off a right-wing coup d'état. President Clinton did not mention Mogadishu at a press conference that morning, which took place at the same time Task Force Ranger was pinned down around the first crash site. Clinton and the rest of America remained ignorant of the drama in faraway Mogadishu. After the press conference, the president flew to San Francisco for a planned two-day speaking tour.

Garrison's move back into the city came with crushing force. If Aidid wanted to play, the U.S. Army would play. Centered around twenty-eight

Malaysian APCs and four Pakistani tanks, the convoy numbered almost a hundred vehicles and was nearly two miles long, with enough firepower to blaze their own roads if necessary. Lieutenant Colonel Bill David was given responsibility for quickly assembling this force at the New Port, about two miles up the coast from the Ranger base.

David's reaction, upon being handed this assignment, was, *You've got to be kidding me.* His own men, two 10th Mountain Division rifle companies, three hundred men strong, had amassed at the airport. David's Charlie Company, the "Tigers," had taken some light casualties at the K-4 circle ambush trying to get to Durant's crash site, but they were otherwise fresh and eager to join the fight. They'd been joined by Alpha Company, under the command of Captain Drew Meyerowich. The armor would be nice, but what was David going to do with Malaysians and Pakistanis? He huddled with General Gile, second in command of the 10th. They agreed that once their men linked up with the foreign troops at the New Port, they would ask the Malaysians to take their own infantry out of the APCs and fill them with American troops. It would be, *Thank you very much, we'll take your vehicles and drivers, but we don't need your men.* David could sense how that was going to go over.

"Do these guys speak English?" he asked.

Most of the officers spoke some, Gile said, and there would be liaison officers to help smooth the process.

David had walked out of the JOC with his head spinning. The forty-year-old career army officer (West Point, Class of '75) from St. Louis, Missouri, had just been handed the assignment of a lifetime. He had been in Mogadishu for two months, commanding a battalion of peacekeepers there to back up the UN forces. He'd never been particularly happy about the presence of Garrison's Task Force Ranger, which had flown in and begun its own secret missions independent of the force structure already in place. Regular army units both admire and resent the elite special forces. The conventional divisions don't get nearly as much money to train, or the choice assignments. Watching Task Force Ranger move into Mogadishu and steal their thunder was not easy for the proud officers and men of the 10th, which has its own distinguished battle history. Since the daring mission had gone bad, it was easy to regard it as foolhardy—What were they doing in Aidid's notorious Black Sea neighborhood in broad daylight? Where was the reserve force? Now David and his men, sometimes scorned by the elite forces, were charged with pulling Delta's and the Rangers' asses out of the fire.

He had to move his men, along with what was now called the "Cook Platoon," volunteers combined with the remnants of the original assault forces, north to the New Port, negotiate with the Malaysians and Pakistanis, develop a plan, and then allow for his subordinates to disseminate it up and down the giant convoy. Then he had to steer them out into the city and keep it all together in the dark as they battled their way to the two crash sites.

While the commanders were working up this plan, the Rangers assigned to the rescue column fretted and paced. Their buddies were still trapped out there! Those who had already been in the fight knew how terrible the battle had become. The uninjured had helped move their wounded and dead buddies from the lost convoy's Humvees and trucks to the field hospital, where Dr. Marsh and his team of doctors and nurses were furiously working to save their lives. The Rangers known to be dead were Pilla, Cavaco, and Joyce. In bad shape were Blackburn, Ruiz, Adalberto Rodriguez, and the Delta operator Griz Martin. There were dozens more injured. It was a ghastly scene. Even those soldiers who had not been hurt were so blood-splattered they *looked* injured.

Some of the medical aides approached Sergeant Eversmann, who had commanded Chalk Four and come out with his men on the lost convoy. Eversmann was unhurt, but most of the men on his chalk had been hit. On the ride out, he had been sandwiched on the back of a Humvee with the wounded, so his uniform was caked with blood. As he stood by now, helping to unload them, two medics grabbed him and began cutting off his pants.

"Leave me alone!" he said. "I'm okay!"

They paid him no mind. Some of the men who were really wounded protested in the same way.

"Look, I'm fine. Work on them!" he shouted, pointing to men who were waiting for attention.

Eversmann was losing it. He'd been through a lot this day, and just the sight of all this blood, and all those mangled men—his men!—dismayed him. It was hard to stay even. He was venting on the nurses and medics when one, an older man, pulled him aside.

"Sergeant, what's your name?"

"Matt Eversmann."

"Well, Matt, listen. You need to calm down."

"Roger."

"We are going to take care of these guys. They're going to be fine. You just need to calm down."

"I *am* calm," shouted Eversmann, who clearly was not. "I just want you to take care of them!"

"What these guys need right now from you is to see you being a stand-up guy. Don't let them see you being nervous because that just makes them nervous."

Eversmann realized he was making a fool of himself.

"Okay," he said.

He stood helplessly for a few moments, turned, and walked slowly back to the hangar. It was hard to remove himself from the emotions of the fight. He felt himself in a kind of aftershock. Having to identify the dead was chilling. Casey Joyce was one of his men. He'd last seen Joyce when he ran off with the litter carrying Blackburn back to the convoy. He'd lost track of him after that. Now he saw his face pale and stretched with the life drained out. During the fight there hadn't been time to react to the terror or even to recoil at what was grotesque. Now it all sank in.

It helped when Lieutenant Colonel McKnight asked him to reinforce perimeter security at the airport. There were fears that with all the fighting, Aidid might try storming the base. So Eversmann packed his brooding away and went to work. He still had six men from his chalk who were able.


The stitches on Specialist Sizemore's elbow, where he had earlier cut off his cast to join the fight, were open and bleeding, but he waved the nurses away. He didn't want to be sidelined again. He was haunted by images of his buddies out there in the city under siege, waiting for him. He was angry, and like many of his Ranger buddies, he wanted revenge. He thought about Stebbins, who had taken his place on the bird, and was infuriated that the company clerk was out there in his place. He had to get out there. *What was holding things up?* Sizemore was pacing around the waiting Humvees when a D-boy approached and asked, "Anybody here know Alphabet?"

Sizemore said he did. They walked together through the gate and past the hospital tent to the fire station. Behind it the minibunker of sand-bags built by Sergeant Rymes was now covered by a white sheet. The sergeant lifted the sheet. Inside was Kowalewski's body with the RPG still embedded in his torso.

"Is this Kowalewski?" the D-boy asked.

Sizemore nodded, or he thought he did. He was stunned. The D-boy asked him again.

"Is this Kowalewski?"

"Yes, that's him."


Lanky Steve Anderson tried to motivate himself for going back out. He had gone out the first time reluctantly. The events of the day so far had stirred up a mess of strong feelings, but anger predominated. Until today Anderson had been as gung ho as the rest of the guys, but now, seeing all the dead and wounded, he just felt used and stupid. His life was being put at risk and he was being thrust into a situation where he had to shoot and kill people in order to survive... and it was hard to see why. How could some politicians in Washington take men like him and put them in such a position, guys who are young, naive, patriotic, and eager to do the right thing, and take advantage of all that for no good reason?

He listened to one of his buddies, Private Kevin Matthews, who had been in the small Humvee column when Pilla was killed and had gone back out with the first rescue convoy. Matthews was going on about this guy he had killed out on the street a few hours before, about how the man shook as five, ten, fifteen rounds slammed into him, and it sounded to Anderson like Matthews was bragging. Except, as he listened more, he saw that the young private was actually upset and was going on because he just needed to talk about what had happened. Matthews was trembling. He wanted to be reassured that he had done the right thing.

"What else could you do?" Anderson said.

Anderson had just talked to his parents the night before back in Illinois, and he'd told them everything was okay, nothing was happening, and probably nothing would. And now, this.

* * *

An effort was launched to identify men who could drive the five-ton trucks wearing NODs. The night vision goggles blocked all peripheral vision and sharply foreshortened the view. It took time to get used to driving with them. Specialist Peter Squeglia, the company armorer, had some experience riding a motorcycle wearing NODs, so one of the lieutenants asked him to take a truck.

"Sir, if you're telling me to drive it, I'll drive it. But I've never driven a truck before."

The idea of grinding gears and stalling out in the middle of a gunfight, where one stalled vehicle can hold up an entire column, or, worse, *get left behind*, terrified Squeglia. The lieutenant made a face, and walked off to find someone else. Squeglia went back to collecting weapons off the dead and wounded. Later he would clean and repair them. For now he just piled them next to his cot, a heap of blood-smeared steel. The lieutenant's expression left Squeglia feeling deflated and guilty. Everybody was scared. Some guys were frantic to join the fight while others were looking for a way to avoid going out. Squeglia was somewhere in the middle. After what he had seen of the lost convoy, part of him felt like going out into that city was like committing suicide. It was crazy, but they had to do it. They were going to load Rangers on the back of flatbed trucks lined with sandbags that weren't going to stop a damn thing, and roll them out into the streets where every one of these skinny Somali motherfuckers was trying to kill them, and for what? At least the Malaysians had armored vehicles. Squeglia was going to go. He was going to do his part, but he wasn't going to do anything foolish, like decide to learn how to drive a big truck in the middle of a firefight.

When it came time to climb aboard, Squeglia picked up his pistol and his CAR-15, which he had rigged with an M-203 grenade launcher. He made sure he got in the truck after most of the others. He figured the safest spot in the flatbed, if anyplace was safe, was toward the rear where the spare tire and muffler came up. He crouched down behind that. Maybe it would stop something. The sandbags certainly wouldn't.

Just before the convoy left the base, Specialist Chris Schleif dashed back into the hangar, rooted through Squeglia's pile of weapons, and fished out Dominic Pilla's M-60 and ammo. The gun and ammo can were still slick with Pilla's blood and brain matter. Schleif ditched his own weapon and boarded the Humvee with Pilla's.

"He didn't get a chance to kill anybody with it," Schleif explained to Specialist Brad Thomas, who like Schleif was heading back out into the city for the third time. "I'm going to do it for him."


It was 9:30 P.M. when the rescue force left the airport and drove north to the New Port to link up with the Malaysians and Pakistanis. Most of the Rangers, all of the D-boys, SEALs, and air force combat controllers who hadn't been killed or injured, and both companies of the 10th Mountain Division made up a force of nearly five hundred men. Waiting for them there were the Malaysian APCs, German-made "Condors," rolling steel Dumpsters painted snow white with a driver in front and a porthole in the back for a gunner. Each was built to hold about six men. The Paki tanks were American-made M-48s. The armor was lined up and ready to go when the long convoy of trucks and Humvees arrived, but coordinating movement of this strange collection of vehicles—Lieutenant Colonel David called it a "gagglefuck"—was going to take more time.

He plunged right into it. With a map spread out on the hood of his Humvee, and with soldiers gathered around holding up flashlights to illuminate it, he began improvising a plan. To David's relief, most of the Malaysian and Pakistani officers spoke English. There was little argument or discussion. The Malaysian officers at first balked at removing their infantry from the APCs, but relented when David agreed to let each vehicle retain a Malaysian driver and gunner. The various units did not have radios that were compatible, so American radios had to be placed with all the vehicles. They worked out fire control procedures, steps to prevent friendly fire incidents, call signs, the route, and a host of other critical issues.

David felt a sense of urgency, but not an overriding one. He knew there were critically injured soldiers at the first crash site for whom every minute was important. On the other hand, this convoy was it. If they screwed up, failed to reach the crash site, and got broken up or bogged down, who was going to come in and rescue them? If one or two soldiers died waiting it would be tragic, but rescuing the other ninety-seven men, and getting his own in and out safely, had to be the priority.

To the Rangers and the 10th Mountain Division soldiers eyeing the Condors for the first time, they looked like caskets on wheels. Choosing between the APCs and the sandbagged five-ton trucks was like choosing your poison: You could get riddled with bullets in the back of a flatbed or toasted by a grenade dropped into the turret or poked through the skin of an APC. The men reluctantly began to board the Condors an hour or so after they'd arrived at the New Port. There were only little peepholes in the sides, so most of the force would be riding blind. The idea of being driven out by Malaysians didn't make them feel any better.

As the hours crept by without action, the Rangers stewed with impatience. As they saw it, they were being held back by this slow-moving, by-the-book regular army unit that didn't fully appreciate the urgency of the situation. Further back in the column it looked like nothing was being done. Some of the 10th Mountain guys were dozing in the back of vehicles. Sleeping! Ranger Sergeant Raleigh Cash couldn't contain himself. His buddies were dying out in the city and these guys were taking naps? *Why the hell weren't they moving?* He had made peace with himself riding out with the cook convoy in that aborted effort to rescue Durant and his crew. If he was going to die today, so be it. The pull of loyalty felt stronger in him than the will to survive. He had thought it through methodically. He was wearing body armor, so if he got shot, it would probably be to the arms or legs and there were medics who would take care of him. It would hurt, but he had been hurt before. If he was shot in the head, then he would die. He wouldn't feel any pain. His life would just be over. Just like that. The end. His friends would take care of his family for him. If he died then that was what was meant to happen.

When word came that Smith was dead, that he had bled out waiting for rescue, Cash lost it. He vented his anger and impatience on a 10th Mountain Division officer. He told the officer that before the Rangers had gotten saddled with his unit they'd had no trouble finding the fight.

"Look, we're not holding things up," the officer protested. "We're ready to go just as much as you are. You have to have a little faith in your leaders."

"It's taking too long," Cash said, his voice rising with anger. "*My friends are dying out there!* We need to get going now!"

Cash's platoon leader came over and quieted him.

"Look, we all want to get going."

By about 11 P.M., David had the "gagglefuck" set to go, and was feeling pretty good about it. He regarded the organizational effort as one of his major life accomplishments. The Paki tanks would lead the convoy out into the city. Behind them, each platoon would have four APCs interspersed with trucks and Humvees. The QRF's Cobra gunships would provide air support. They'd roll out to a staging point on National Street, then one half of the force would steer south toward Durant's *Super Six Four* crash site and the other would push north to Wolcott's *Super Six One,* where the bulk of the task force was pinned down. They had commo links established, liaison officers dispersed throughout the convoy . . . they were good to go.

Then one of the Pakistani officers ran up. His commander objected to the tanks leading the convoy. This was a problem because tanks were needed to plow through the formidable barricades (ditches, abandoned shells of cars and trucks, heaps of stone, burning tires and debris) the Somalis had erected to block most of the main roads leading out of the UN facilities. Since the New Port was home base for the Pakis, and they were the ones who had proposed the route to the holding point, a compromise was reached. The tanks would lead the way out to the K-4 circle, then fall back to the midfront of the column.

Then new problems surfaced. It was easy to see how, with enough commanders, a battle could be debated into defeat. After conferring with their superiors, the Malaysians said they had been ordered to keep their APCs on the main roads, for the same reason that Garrison had earlier judged Mogadishu the wrong place to fight with armor. It was hard for tanks and APCs to maneuver in the city's complex web of narrow streets and alleys. The big vehicles were vulnerable when they moved slowly through streets where the enemy could creep up close or drop grenades down from rooftops and trees, or fire armor-piercing rounds at close range.

David got back out of his Humvee and huddled with the officers again. He told Captain Meyerowich, "Look, Drew, here's the situation. I need for your company to lead us out."

The Pakistanis agreed to lead the convoy as far as the K-4 circle, which was the borderline of Aidid's turf. At that point Meyerowich's company, most of them riding in the Condors, would pull through and take the lead.

It was now 11:23 P.M.

# 3

As he heard the guns of the giant convoy approaching, Captain Steele knew this was the most dangerous time of the night. The moon was high and shooting in the neighborhood around the first crash site had all but stopped. There were a few pops every once in a while. The air had cleared of smoke and gunpowder. Now there was just that musky stink of Somalia, the trace of desert dust in the air, and the slight aftertaste of the iodine pills in their canteens. Sammies would still inexplicably wander right into the middle of their perimeter up the street. The D-boys would let them walk until they reached a cross-fire zone and then drop them with a few quick shots. Every once in a while the Little Birds would rumble in and unleash a rocket and spray of minigun fire. But now the only noise that concerned Steele was the intensifying thunder of guns as the rescue column moved closer to their position. With that much shooting, with two jumpy elements of soldiers about to link up in a confusing city in darkness, the biggest threat to his pinned-down men were their rescuers.

—*Romeo Six Four* [Harrell], *this is Juliet Six Four* [Steele]. *How we gonna keep from running out of the building and getting smoked?*

—*They're looking for your position to be marked with an IR strobe. If there's any doubt in your mind, flash a red desert flashlight at them.*

Up the street, Captain Miller had his own concerns.

—*Okay, this task force is made up of Malaysians and who, over?*

—*Malaysians and Americans. They have Rangers with them, over.*

Miller added hopefully:

—*Okay, so every vehicle should have some type of NODs so they can ID the strobe, over?*

—*That was the instruction sent back, over.*

Then, a few minutes later, the command helicopter reassured Miller.

—*Yeah, they're moving. The lead element has night vision devices so they should be able to pick up your IR strobe, Scotty, over.*

Miller was also informed that members of the Delta unit, including Major James Nixon, John Macejunas, Matt Rierson, and Chuck Esswein, would be leading the column in, which to him and the other Delta team leaders was an enormous relief.

The rescue convoy was coming from the south. By the sound of it, they were moving along the same route the Rangers and D-boys had taken that afternoon, east from the Olympic Hotel, which meant they would reach Steele's position first. They were coming steadily but slowly, and from the sound of it they were just shooting at everything. It was about ten minutes before two in the morning. Without the NODs nobody could see that far down the street. They just had to hunker down and wait and hope the convoy did not come blasting its way down the middle of their street.

—*Romeo Six Four, this is Juliet Six Four. We're going to put IR strobes out in front of the buildings here. We plan on throwing a red Chemlite as well to mark for casualties. If we can have the APCs pull in as close to those red chems as possible that will facilitate the loading of the casualties, over.*

—*Roger, but you better be real careful with those red Chemlites or the bad guys will start shooting at them, over.*

—*Okay, but you're saying all the guys will have NODs, right?*

—*They've got people in the lead element with NODs and they should be homing in on your IR strobes, over.*

It was tense. Nearly an hour had gone by since Steele had been told the convoy would reach him in twenty minutes.

—*Romeo, this is Juliet. I understand now they may have turned north. The ground reaction force turned north. Do they have an ETA at this location?*

—*No, they are moving slowly, taking their time. It is going to take them a while, Mike. Probably fifteen to twenty minutes based on where I think they are, over.*

—*Okay. We are fairly secure here. I think the Little Bird runs dampened the rebels' spirits.*

Word came from the command helicopter at about two o'clock.

—*Okay, start getting ready to get out of there, but keep your heads down. Now is a bad time.*

—*Roger, copy. Positions are marked at this time. We are ready to move,* said Steele.

—*Roger, they are going to be coming in with heavy contact so be real careful.*

—*You better believe it, over.*

"We're about to link up," Steele radioed Perino. "I want everybody to back up out of the courtyards, and to stay away from the doors and windows."

So the Rangers drew back like hermit crabs into their shells, and listened. They were all terrified of the 10th Mountain Division, whom they regarded as poorly trained regular army schmoes, just a small step removed from utterly incompetent civilianhood.

Five minutes passed. Ten minutes passed. Twenty minutes passed. Then another radio call from the command bird.

*—Just to give you an update. They are still at that U-turn off. They had a little bit of a direction problem amongst themselves. They should be moving now. Will let you know as soon as they start rolling northbound.*

Perino called Captain Steele. "Where are they?" he asked.

Steele said, "Any minute now."

Both men laughed.

# 4

Captain Drew Meyerowich was with the Delta operators who were leading his portion of the rescue convoy toward Steele and Miller's position. It had been a pitched battle much of the way in. Two of the Malaysian drivers had taken a wrong turn and driven about thirty of Meyerowich's men off in the wrong direction. They'd been ambushed and caught up in a severe firefight, and one of their men, Sergeant Cornell Houston, had been mortally wounded.

For all his careful planning, Specialist Squeglia ended up in a Humvee. The banging of gunfire was constant, most if it coming from the convoy, which stretched so far in both directions Squeglia could not see the front or rear. No one had lights on, but muzzle flashes and explosions lit up the whole line. In the reflected light he saw two dead donkeys by the side of the road, still strapped to carts. The air was filled with diesel fumes, and through the open side window of the Humvee Squeglia smelled the gunpowder from his weapon mingled with the burning tires and trash and the general pungent, rotten smell of Somalia itself. He was out in it now.

In a sudden volley of gunfire an RPG bounced off the hood. The explosion a few feet away sounded like somebody had dropped an empty Dumpster off a roof. Squeglia felt the concussion like a blow to the inside of his chest, and then smelled smoke. Everybody had ducked at the blast.

"Holy shit, what was that?" shouted Specialist David Eastabrooks, who was driving.

"Jesus," said Sergeant Richard Lamb, who was in the front passenger seat. "I think I've been hit."

"Where you hit?" Squeglia asked.

"In the head."

"Oh, Jesus."

One of the men in the Humvee fished out a red light flashlight, and they shined it on Lamb. He had a trickle of blood running down his face and a neat hole, a small one, right in the middle of his forehead.

"I think I'm okay," Lamb said. "I'm still talking to you."

He wrapped a bandage around his head. Doctors would later determine that a piece of shrapnel had lodged between the frontal lobes of his brain, missing vital tissues by fractions of an inch in either direction. He was all right. It felt like he had just banged his head. It hurt lots worse minutes later when he took a bullet to his right pinkie, which left the tip of it hanging by a piece of skin. Squeglia could see the bone of his finger jutting from the mangled flesh. Lamb just swore and stuck the fingertip back on, wrapped it with a piece of duct tape, and continued working his radio.

All the way out from the base, Specialist Dale Sizemore was shooting. He'd cut the cast off his arm to join the fight, and at last he was in it. Night vision gave him and the other men on this massive column a tremendous advantage over the Somalis. Sizemore spread out on his stomach in the back of the Humvee just looking for people to shoot. When there weren't people he shot at windows and doorways. Most of the time he couldn't see whether he'd hit anybody or not. The NODs severely restricted peripheral vision. He didn't want to know, really. He didn't want to start thinking about it.

At one point a spray of sparks flew up in his face. He turned his head to discover a fist-sized hole in the Humvee wall just inches from his head. He hadn't felt a thing. When an RPG hit one of the trucks ahead, men came running down the street looking for space on the Humvees as tracers flew. One, Specialist Erik James, a medic, approached Sizemore's open back hatch carrying a Kevlar blanket.

"You got room?" he asked. He looked dazed and scared.

Sizemore and Private Brian Conner moved over to make a space for him.

"Just get in here and keep that blanket over your head and you'll be all right," said Sizemore. He figured it was always a good idea to have a medic close by. James felt Sizemore had just saved his life.


Specialist Steve Anderson was in a Humvee near Sizemore's in the column. He was in the back on the driver's side with his eyes pressed to the night-vision viewfinder on his SAW. Whenever the column stopped, which was often, everyone was expected to pile out and pull security. The first time they stopped Anderson hesitated. He didn't want to stick his legs out of the car. He had just started skydiving lessons at home before this deployment, and now, suddenly, he felt immobilized by the particular fear of being shot in the legs—he'd received a minor injury to his legs on an earlier mission. Back home he had just made his first freefall jump. It had been such a thrill. What if he got his foot shot off and could never jump again? Anderson reluctantly forced himself out on the street.

At one stop he and Sizemore stood for a long time, it seemed like hours, watching the windows of a three-story building for some sign of a shooter. They had been there for a time when Anderson noticed a dent and scrape on the roof of the Humvee right next to them. A round had ricocheted off it.

"Did you notice that before?" he asked Sizemore.

Sizemore hadn't. It hadn't been there when they got out either. Which meant a bullet had passed between them, missing them both by inches, without their even knowing it.

That was the way Anderson felt most of the time. Totally in the dark. He saw tracers and there were times the gunfire was so loud the night seemed ready to split at the seams, but he could never seem to tell where it was coming from, or find anyone to shoot. Sizemore, on the other hand, was going through ammunition as fast as he could load his weapon. Anderson was in awe of his friend's confidence and selflessness, and felt both inspired and diminished by it.

Sizemore unloaded what must have been a full drum of ammo at the front of a building about fifty feet away. When he was done, Anderson could see rounds glowing and smoldering from the ground where he had been shooting, which meant he must have hit something. When rounds hit the ground or street or a building, they deflected off in other directions. But when they hit flesh, they would glow for a few moments.

"Didn't you see them?" Sizemore asked Anderson. "There was a whole bunch of them there, shooting at us."

Anderson hadn't noticed. He felt completely out of his element. Minutes later he noticed another dent and scrape on the top of the Humvee, right alongside the first one. He hoped his buddy had silenced the gun that put it there.

At one stop on a wide street, when Anderson and the men in his Humvee were positioned near a two-story building, a Malaysian APC pulled up about twenty feet behind them and its machine gunner opened fire. He was shooting at the roof of the building alongside Anderson. The rounds traced red lines through the darkness, so Anderson could follow their trajectory, and they were all bouncing off the building next to him. The wall was made of irregular stone. Any one of those rounds could easily come his way. There was nothing he could do but watch. One of the rounds hit the building and then traced a wicked arc across the street like a curveball.


Private Ed Kallman was somewhere else along the giant convoy, driving again, equally amazed by the light show. Kallman's left arm and shoulder were massively bruised from the unexploded RPG that had hit the door of his Humvee the previous afternoon and knocked him cold. He felt fine, excited again, and reasonably safe in such a massive force. There would be long periods of relative quiet, then suddenly the night would explode with light and noise. One or two shots from the dark houses or alleys on both sides of the street would trigger a violent explosion of return fire from the column. Up and down the line tracers splashed out from the long line, literally thousands of rounds in seconds, just hosing down whole blocks of homes. His NODs framed the scene in a circle and offered little depth perception. It also gave off heat just a half inch from his face that after a while started to bother his eyes. Then he would take a break and just look straight down or off to the side.

They eventually stopped and waited in the same spot for several hours. Kallman was asked to pull his Humvee back down the road, about a half block, which he did, and no sooner had he moved than an RPG exploded on what looked like the spot he had just left. He and others in his vehicle laughed. An explosion on the wall above sent a shower of debris down on them. No one was hurt. Kallman moved the Humvee forward a few feet just to make sure it wasn't stuck.

Through the remainder of the night he just listened to the radio, trying to make sense out of the constant chatter, trying to figure out what was going on.

Ahead of them in the long column, Sergeant Jeff Struecker was shocked by all the shooting. He had heard a sergeant major from the 10th Mountain Division telling his men before they left, "This is for real. You shoot at anything," and clearly these guys had taken him seriously.

Streucker had warned his own gunner to pick targets carefully. "When you shoot that fifty cal, that round goes on forever," the sergeant explained. It was clear the rest of the convoy was not taking such precautions. They were throwing lead all over that part of Mogadishu.

# 5

Earlier in the day, the American helicopters had attacked the garage of Kassim Sheik Mohamed, a tall, beefy businessman with a round face, a swaggering walk, and a troublemaker's smile. Kassim's garage was bombed because he had, being a wealthy man, a fairly large number of armed men guarding it. At the height of the battle, any large number of well-armed Somalis in the vicinity of the fight was a target. The attack was not too misdirected. Kassim was a well-to-do member of the Habr Gidr and a supporter of Mohamed Farah Aidid.

When the bombing started, Kassim ran to a nearby hospital, figuring it was a place the Americans would not attack. He stayed there for two hours. When he returned to his garage, much of it was a smoldering ruin. An explosion had flipped a white UN Land Rover Kassim had purchased about twelve feet into the air and deposited it upright atop a stack of steel shipment boxes, as though someone had parked it up there. Some of his most valuable earthmoving equipment was destroyed. Dead was his friend and accountant, forty-two-year-old Ahmad Sheik, and one of his mechanics, thirty-two-year-old Ismael Ahmed.

It was late in the day, and the dead, according to Islamic law, needed to be buried before sundown, so Kassim and his men took the bodies to Trabuna Cemetery. On their way there, a helicopter swooped down low over them and fired rounds that hit all around the car but missed them.

The cemetery was crowded with wailing people. In the darkness, as the guns of the fight still pounded in the distance, every open space was crowded with people digging graves. Kassim and his men drove to one of the only quiet corners. They took shovels and the two bodies from the back of their cars and began carrying them. Then another American helicopter came down, frightening them, so they dropped the bodies and shovels and ran.

They hid behind a wall until the helicopter was gone, and then went back out and picked up the bodies, which were wrapped in sheets, and continued carrying them. Another helicopter zoomed in low over them. Again they dropped the bodies and shovels and ran to the wall. This time they left the bodies of Ahmad Sheik and Ismael Ahmed and drove away, agreeing to come back later in the night to bury them.

Four of Kassim's men came back at about midnight. The guns still pounded out in the city. They carried the bodies up to a small rise and began digging. But another American helicopter appeared, hovering low and shining a floodlight down. Kassim's men ran, leaving the bodies on the ground.

They returned at three in the morning and were finally able to bury Ahmad Sheik and Ismael Ahmed.

# 6

Half of the rescue convoy had steered south to Durant's crash site, but had gotten stalled on the outskirts of the ghettolike village of rag and tin huts where *Super Six Four* had gone down. In darkness, the unmapped maze of footpaths leading into the village looked potentially deadly—it was like probing directly into the heart of the hornet's nest. Sergeant John "Mace" Macejunas, the fearless blond Delta operator, on his third trip out into the city, slipped off a Humvee and personally led a small force on foot, wearing NODS and feeling his way into the village toward the wrecked heli-copter, where hours before Mace's buddies Randy Shughart and Gary Gordon had made their last stand.

Around the wreckage they found pools and trails of blood, torn bits of clothing, and many spent bullet shells, but no weapons and no sign of their buddies Shughart and Gordon, nor of Durant and the three other crew members. The soldiers searched the huts around the crash site, demand-ing information about the downed Americans through a translator, but no one offered any. Risking drawing fire, they bellowed into the night the names of all six of the missing men: "Michael Durant!" "Ray Frank!" "Bill Cleveland!" "Tommie Field!" "Randy Shughart!" "Gary Gordon!" There was only silence.

Macejunas then supervised the setting of thermite grenades on the helicopter. They stayed until *Super Six Four* was a ball of white flame, and then returned to the convoy.

Meyerowich's northern half of the convoy had been delayed by a big road-block on Hawlwadig Road up near the Olympic Hotel, which the Malay-sian drivers refused to roll through. In the past, such roadblocks had been heavily mined.

Meyerowich pleaded with the liaison officer. "Tell them small arms fire is ineffective against them!" he said.

Once or twice he got out of his Humvee and walked up to the lead APC and shouted, waving his arms, urging the vehicle forward. But the Condor drivers refused to proceed. So the convoy was stalled while sol-diers climbed off the vehicles and dismantled the roadblock by hand.

Meyerowich and the D-boys decided not to wait for the roadblock situation to be sorted out. They ran up and down the line of vehicles bang-ing on the doors, shouting for all the men to pile out of the vehicles. They knew they were only blocks from the pinned-down force.

"Get out! Get out! Get out! Americans, get out!"

One of those who emerged warily was Specialist Phil Lepre. Earlier in the ride out, when the shooting got heavy and rounds were pinging off the sides of the APC, Lepre had removed a snapshot of his baby daughter he carried in his helmet and kissed it good-bye. "Babe," he said, "I hope you have a wonderful life." He stepped out now into the Mogadishu night, ran to a wall with two other soldiers, and pointed his M-16 down an alley. When his eyes adjusted to the darkness he saw a group of Somalis a few blocks down, edging their way toward him.

"I've got Somalians coming down this way!" he said.

One of the D-boys told him to shoot, so Lepre fired down toward the crowd. First he shot over their heads, but when they didn't disperse he fired straight into them. He saw several fall. The others dragged them off the alley.

Out in the intersection, soldiers were pulling apart the barricade by hand under heavy fire. Lepre moved once or twice up the road with the rest of the men. They were spread out now on both sides of an alley a few blocks ahead of the APCs. They would move, stop, and wait, then move again, like parts of a human accordion slinking its way east. At one of the places where they stopped they began taking heavy fire from a nearby building. Men moved to take better cover and find an improved vantage to return fire.

"Hey, take my position," he called back to twenty-three-year-old rifleman Private James Martin.

Martin hustled up and crouched behind the wall. Lepre had moved only two steps to his right when Martin was hit in the head by a round that sent him sprawling backward. Lepre saw a small hole in his forehead.

Lepre's voice joined others shouting, "Medic! We need a medic up here!"

A medic swooped over the downed man and began loosening his clothes to help prevent shock. He worked on Martin a few minutes, then turned to Lepre and the others and said, "He's dead."

The medic and another soldier tried to drag Martin's body to cover but were scattered by more gunfire. One of them ran back out and braved the gunfire, firing his weapon with one hand and dragging Martin to cover with the other. When he got close, others ran out to help, pulling the body into the alley.

Lepre was behind cover just a few feet away, gazing at Martin's body. He felt terrible. He had asked the private to take his position, and then the man had been shot dead. All the dragging had pulled Martin's pants down to his knees. Few of the guys wore underwear in the tropical heat. Lepre couldn't bear seeing Martin sprawled there like that, half naked. So despite the gunfire, he stepped out into the alley and tried to pull up the dead soldier's pants, to give the man some dignity. Two bullets struck the pavement near where he stooped, and Lepre scrambled reluctantly back to cover.

"Sorry, man," he said.

# 7

The command bird continued to coax the force linkup at the first crash site.

*—They are leading the mounted troops by dismounted troops. The dismounted troops and the mounted troops are holding south of the Olympic Hotel....*

Then, talking to the convoy, as they approached the left turn:

*—Thirty meters south of the friendlies. They are one minor block to the north of you right now. If your lead APC continues moving he can make the next left and go one block, over.*

Steele heard the vehicles making the turn. Out the door his men saw the dim outline of soldiers. Steele and his men called out, "Ranger! Ranger!"

"Tenth Mountain Division," came the response.

*—Roger, we've got a linkup with the Kilo and Juliet element, over.*

Steele stuck his head out the door.

"This is Captain Steele. I'm the Ranger commander."

"Roger, sir, we're from the 10th Mountain Division," a soldier answered.

"Where's your commander?" Steele asked.

# 8

It took hours to pry Elvis out of the wreck. It was ugly work. The rescue column had brought along a quickie saw to cut the chopper's metal frame away from his body, but the cockpit was lined with a layer of Kevlar that just ate up the saw blade. Next they tried to pull the Black Hawk apart, attaching chains to the front and back ends of it. A few of the Rangers, watching this from a distance, thought the D-boys were using the vehicles to tear the pilot's body out of the wreckage. Some turned away in disgust.

The dead were placed on top of the APCs, and the wounded were loaded inside them. Goodale hobbled painfully out to the one that had stopped before their courtyard, and was helped through the doors. He rolled to his side.

"We need you to sit," he was told.

"Look, I got shot in the ass. It hurts to sit."

"Then lean or something."

At Miller's courtyard they carried Carlos Rodriguez out first in his inflated rubber pants. Then they moved the other wounded. Stebbins was feeling pretty good. Out the window he could see 10th Mountain Division guys lounging up and down the street, a lot of them. He protested when they came back for him with a stretcher.

"I'm okay," he told them. "I can stand on one leg. Just help me over to the vehicle. I've still got my weapon."

He hopped on his good foot and was helped up into the armored car.

Wilkinson climbed into the back of the same vehicle. They all expected to be moving shortly, but instead they sat. The closed steel container was like a sauna and it reeked of sweat and urine and blood. What a nightmare this mission had become. Every time they thought it was over, that they'd made it, something worse happened. The injured in the vehicles couldn't see what was going on outside, and they didn't understand the delay. They'd all figured the convoy would arrive and they'd scoot home. It was only a five-minute drive to the airport. It was now after three o'clock in the morning. The sun would be coming back up soon. Bullets occasionally pinged off the walls. What would happen if an RPG hit them?

There was a brief mutiny under way in Goodale's Condor.

"Shouldn't we be moving?" Goodale asked.

"Yeah, I would think so," said one of the other men crammed in with him.

Goodale was closest to the front, so he leaned up to the Malay driver.

"Hey, man, let's go," he said.

"No. No," the driver protested. "We stay."

"God damnit, we're not staying! Let's get the fuck out of here!"

"No. No. We stay."

"No, you don't understand this. We're getting shot at. We're gonna get fucked up in this thing!"

The commanders were also growing impatient.

—*Scotty* [Miller], *give me an update please,* asked Lieutenant Colonel Harrell.

Other than brief stops back at the base to refuel, Harrell and air commander Tom Matthews were up over the city in their C2 Black Hawk throughout the night.

Miller responded:

—*Roger. They're trying to pull it apart. So far no luck.*

—*Roger. You've only got about an hour's worth of darkness left.*

There were more than three hundred Americans now in and around these two blocks of Mogadishu, the vanguard of a convoy that stretched a half mile back toward National Street, which created a sense of security among the recently arrived 10th Mountain troops that was not shared by the Rangers or the D-boys who had been fighting all night. The weary assault force watched with amazement as the regular army guys leaned against walls and lit cigarettes and chatted out on the same street where they had just experienced blizzards of enemy fire. To Howe, the Delta team leader who had been so disappointed by the Rangers, these men seemed completely out of place. The wait for them to extract Elvis's body was beginning to worry everybody.

When an explosion rocked Stebbins's APC, men shouted with anger inside. "Get us the fuck out of here!" one screamed. Rodriguez was moaning. Stebbins and Heard were taking turns holding up the machine gunner's IV bag. They were wedged into the small space like pieces of a puzzle. Soon after the explosion the carrier's big metal door swung open and a soldier from the 10th who had been hit in the elbow was lifted in on a litter. He screamed with pain as he hit the floor.

"I can't believe it!" he shouted.

The Malaysian driver kept turning back, trying to keep things calm. "Any minute now, hospital," he would say.

After patching up the new arrival, Wilkinson sat back against the inner wall and saw through a peephole that darkness had begun to drain from the eastern sky. The volume of fire was starting to pick up. There were more pings off the side of the carrier.

The wounded who had been so eager to board the big armored vehicles now prayed to get off. They felt like targets in a turkey shoot. Goodale had only a small peephole to see outside. It was so warm he began to feel woozy. He removed his helmet and loosened his body armor, but it didn't help much. They all sat in the small dark space just staring silently at each other, waiting.

"You know what we should do," suggested one of the wounded D-boys. "We should kind of crack one of these doors a little bit so that when the RPG comes in here, we'll all have someplace to explode out of."

About an hour before sunrise, there was an update from the C2 bird to the JOC:

*—They are essentially pulling the aircraft instrument panel apart around the body. Still do not have any idea when they will be done.*

*—Okay, are they going to be able to get the body out of there?* Garrison demanded. *I need an honest, no shit, for-real assessment from the platoon leader or the senior man present. Over.*

Miller answered:

*—Roger. Understand we are looking at twenty more minutes before we can get the body out.*

Garrison said:

*—Roger. I know they are doing the best they can. We will stay the course until they are finished. Over.*

As the sky to the east brightened, Sergeant Yurek was startled by the carnage back in the room where they had spent the night. Sunlight illuminated the pools and smears of blood everywhere. As he poked his head out the courtyard door he could see Somali bodies scattered up and down the road in the distance. One of the bodies, a young Somali man, appeared to have been run over several times by one of the vehicles being used to pull apart the helicopter. Yurek was especially saddened to see, at a corner of Marehan Road, the carcass of the donkey he had watched miraculously crossing the street back and forth through all the gunfire the day before. It was still hooked to its cart.

Howe noticed among the bodies stacked on top of the APCs the soles of two small assault boots. There was only one guy in the unit with boots that small. It had to be Earl Fillmore.

Everybody knew the respite here was about to end. Daylight would bring Sammy back outdoors. Captain Steele stood outside the courtyard door checking his watch compulsively. He must have looked at it hundreds of times. He couldn't believe they weren't moving yet. The horizon was starting to get pink. Placing three hundred men at jeopardy in order to retrieve the body of one man was a noble gesture, but hardly a sensible one. Finally, at sunup, the grim work was done.

—*Adam Six Four* [Garrison], *this is Romeo Six Four* [Harrell]. *They are starting to move at this time, over. . . . Placing the charges and getting ready to move.*

Then came the next shock for the Rangers and D-boys who had been fighting now for fourteen hours. There wasn't enough room on the vehicles for them. After the 10th Mountain Division soldiers reboarded, the anxious Malaysian drivers just took off, leaving the rest of the force behind. They were going to have to run right back out through the same streets they'd fought through on their way in.

It was 5:45 A.M., Monday, October 4. The sun was now over the rooftops.

# 9

So they ran. The original idea was for them to run with the vehicles in order to have some cover, but the Malay drivers had sped out.

Still hauling the radio on his back, Steele ran alongside Perino. Eight Rangers were strung out behind them. Behind them were the rest of Delta Force, the CSAR team, everybody. It happened so fast, men at the far end of the line were surprised when they made the right turn at the top of the hill to find that the others had moved out already.

Yurek ran with Jamie Smith's gear. Nobody had wanted to touch it. It was like acknowledging he was gone. The whole force ran the same route the main force had used coming in, stopping at each intersection to spray covering fire as they one by one sprinted across. As soon as they began moving the shooting resumed, almost as bad as it had been the afternoon before. The Rangers shot at every window and door, and down every cross street. Steele felt like his legs were lead weights and that he was moving at a fraction of his normal speed, yet he was running as fast as he could.

When they got up to their original blocking position there was withering fire across the wide intersection before the Olympic Hotel. Sergeant Randy Ramaglia saw the rounds hitting the sides of the armored vehicles blocks ahead. *We're going to run through that?* It was the same shit as yesterday. He had made it up to the intersection when he felt a sharp blow to his shoulder, like someone had hit him with a sledgehammer. It didn't knock him down. He just froze. It took a few seconds for him to regain his senses. At first he thought something had fallen on him. He looked up.

"Sergeant, you've been shot!" shouted Specialist Collett, who had been running beside him.

Ramaglia turned to him. Collett's eyes were wide.

"I know it," he said.

He took several deep breaths and tried to move his arm. He could move it. He felt no pain.

The round had hit Ramaglia's left back, taking out a golf ball–sized scoop of it. The round had then skimmed off his shoulder blade and nicked Collett's sleeve, tearing off the American flag he had stitched there.

"Are you okay?" a Delta medic shouted at him from across the street.

"Yeah," said Ramaglia, and he started running again. He was furious. The whole scene seemed surreal to him. He couldn't believe some pissant fucking Sammy had shot him, Sergeant Randal J. Ramaglia of the U.S. Army Rangers. He was going to get out of that city alive or take half of it with him. He shot at anyone or anything he saw. He was running, bleeding, swearing, and shooting. Windows, doorways, alleyways . . . especially people. They were all going down. It was a free-for-all now. All semblance of an ordered retreat was gone. Everybody was just scrambling.

\* \* \*

Sergeant Nelson, still stone deaf, ran alongside Private Neathery, who had been shot in the right arm the afternoon before. Nelson had his M-60 and carried Neathery's M-16 slung across his back. They ran as hard as they could and Nelson shot at everything he saw. He had never felt so frightened, not even at the height of things the previous day. He and Neathery were toward the rear and were terrified that in this wild footrace they would be left behind or picked off. Neathery was having a hard time running, which slowed them down. When they caught up to a group providing covering fire at the wide intersection they were supposed to stop and take their turn, cover for that group to advance, but instead they just ran straight through.

Howe kicked in a door of a house on the street and the team piled in to reload and catch their breath. Captain Miller stepped in, breathing hard, and told them to keep moving. Howe went around the room double-checking everybody's status and ammo and then they pushed back out to the street. He was shooting his CAR-15 and his shotgun. Up ahead the APC gunners were shooting up everything.

Private Floyd ran with his torn pants flapping, all but naked from the waist down, feeling especially vulnerable and ridiculous. Alongside him, Doc Strous disappeared suddenly in a loud flash and explosion that knocked Floyd down. When he regained his senses and looked over for Strous, all he saw was a thinning ball of smoke. No Doc.

Sergeant Watson grabbed Floyd's shoulder. The private's helmet was cockeyed and his eyes felt that way.

"Where the hell is Strous?"

"He blew up, Sergeant."

"He blew up? What the hell do you mean he blew up?"

"He blew up."

Floyd pointed to where the medic had been running. Strous stepped from a tangle of weeds, brushing himself off, his helmet askew. He looked down at Floyd and just took off running. A round had hit a flashbang grenade on Strous's vest and exploded, knocking him off his feet and into the weeds. He was unhurt.

"Move out, Floyd," Watson screamed.

They all kept running, running and shooting through the brightening dawn, through the crackle of gunfire, the spray of loose mortar off a

wall where a round hit, the sudden gust of hot wind from a blast that sometimes knocked them down and sucked the air out of their lungs, the sound
of the helicopters rumbling overhead, and the crisp rasp of their guns like
the tearing of heavy cloth. They ran through the oily smell of the city and
of their own bodies, the taste of dust in their dry mouths, with the crisp
brown bloodstains on their fatigues and the fresh memory of friends dead
or unspeakably mangled, with the whole nightmare now grown unbearably long, with disbelief that the mighty and terrible army of the United
States of America had plunged them into this mess and stranded them there
and now left them to run through the same deadly gauntlet to get out. *How
could this happen?*

Ramaglia ran on some desperate last reserve of adrenaline. He ran and shot
and swore until he began to smell his own blood and feel dizzy. For the
first time he felt some stabs of pain. He kept running. As he approached
the intersection of Hawlwadig Road and National Street, about five
blocks south of the Olympic Hotel, he saw a tank and the line of APCs
and Humvees and a mass of men in desert battle dress. He ran until he
collapsed, with joy.

# 10

At Mogadishu's Volunteer Hospital, surgeon Abdi Mohamed Elmi was
covered with blood and exhausted. His wounded and dead countrymen
had started coming early the evening before. Just a trickle at first, despite
the great volume of shooting going on. Vehicles couldn't move on the
streets so the patients were carried in or rolled in on handcarts. There were
burning roadblocks throughout the city and the American helicopters were
buzzing low and shooting and most people were afraid to venture out.

Before the fight began, the Volunteer Hospital was virtually empty.
It was located down near the Americans' base by the airport. After the
trouble had started with the Americans most Somalis were afraid to come
there. By the end of this day, Monday, October 4, all five hundred beds in
the hospital would be full. One hundred more wounded would be lined in
the hallways. And Volunteer wasn't the biggest hospital in the city. The

numbers were even greater at Digfer. Most of those with gut wounds would die. The delay in getting them to the hospital—many more would come today than came yesterday—allowed infections to set in that could no longer be successfully treated with what antibiotics the hospital could spare.

The three-bed operating theater at Volunteer had been full and busy all through the night. Elmi was part of a team of seven surgeons who worked straight through without a break. He had assisted in eighteen major surgeries by sunrise, and the hallways outside were rapidly filling with more, dozens, hundreds more. It was a tidal wave of gore.

He finally walked out of the operating room at eight in the morning, and sat down to rest. The hospital was filled with the chilling screams and moans of broken people, dismembered, bleeding, dying in horrible pain. Doctors and nurses ran from bed to bed, trying to keep up. Elmi sat on a bench smoking a cigarette quietly. A French woman who saw him sitting down approached him angrily.

"Why don't you help these people?" she shouted at him.

"I can't," he said.

She stormed away. He sat until his cigarette was finished. Then he stood and went back to work. He would not sleep for another twenty-four hours.

# 11

Abdi Karim Mohamud left his friend's house in the morning after the Americans had gone. The day before he'd been sent home early from his job at the U.S. embassy compound and had run to witness the fighting around the Bakara Market. It was so fierce he'd spent a long sleepless night on the floor at his friend's house, listening to the gunfire and watching the explosions light up the sky.

The shooting flared up again violently after sunrise as the Rangers fought their way out. Then it stopped.

He ventured out an hour or so later. He saw a woman dead in the middle of the street. She had been hit by bullets from a helicopter. You could tell because the helicopter guns tore people apart. Her stomach and insides were spilled outside her body on the street. He saw three children, tiny ones, stiff and gray with death. There was an old man facedown in the street, his blood in a wide pool dried around him, and beside him was his donkey, also dead. Abdi counted the bullets in the old man. There were three, two in the torso and one in the leg.

Bashir Haji Yusuf, the lawyer, heard the big fight resume at dawn. He had managed to fall asleep for a few hours and it awakened him. When that shooting stopped he told his wife he was going to see. He took his camera with him. He wanted to make a record of what had happened.

He saw dead donkeys on the road, and severe damage to the buildings around the Olympic Hotel and further east. There were bloodstains all over the buildings and streets, as if some great thrashing beast had been through, but most of the dead had been carried off. He snapped pictures as he walked down one of the streets where the soldiers had run, and he saw the husk of the first Black Hawk that had crashed, still smoldering from the fire the Rangers had set on it. As he walked he saw the charred remains of Humvees, one that was still burning, and several Malaysian APCs.

Then Bashir heard a great stir of excitement, people chanting and cheering and shouting. He ran to see.

They had a dead American soldier draped over a wheelbarrow. He was stripped to black undershorts and lay draped backward with his hands dragging on the dirt. The body was caked with dry blood and the man's face looked peaceful, distant. There were bullet holes in his chest and arm. Ropes were tied around his body, and it was half wrapped in a sheet of corrugated tin. The crowd grew larger as the wheelbarrow was pushed through the street. People spat and poked and kicked at the body.

"Why did you come here?" screamed one woman.

Bashir followed, appalled. *This is terrible.* Islam called for reverential treatment and immediate burial of the dead, not this grotesque display. Bashir wanted to stop them, but the crowd was wild. These were wild people, ghetto people, and they were celebrating. To step forward and ask, "What are you doing?" to try to shame them, as Bashir wanted to do, would risk having them turn on him. He snapped several pictures and followed the mob. So many people had been killed and hurt the night before. The streets filled with even angrier, more vicious people. A festival of blood.

\* \* \*

Hassan Adan Hassan was in a crowd that was dragging another dead American. Hassan sometimes worked as a translator for American and British journalists, and wanted to be a journalist himself. He followed the crowd down to the K-4 circle, where the numbers swelled to a sizable mob. They were dragging the body on the street when an outnumbered and outgunned squad of Saudi Arabian soldiers drove up on vehicles. Even though they were with the UN, the Saudis were not considered enemies of the Somalis, and even on this day their vehicles were not attacked. What the Saudis saw made them angry.

"What are you doing?" one of the soldiers asked.

"We have Animal Howe," answered an armed young Somali man, one of the ringleaders.

"This is an American soldier," said another.

"If he is dead, why are you doing this? Aren't you a human being?" the Saudi soldier asked the ringleader, insulting him.

One of the Somalis pointed his gun at the Saudi soldier. "We will kill you, too," the gunman said.

People in the back of the crowd shouted at the Saudis, "Leave it. Leave it alone! These people are angry. They might kill you."

"But why do you do this?" the Saudi persisted. "You can fight and they can fight, but this man is dead. Why do you drag him?"

More guns were pointed at the Saudis. The disgusted soldiers drove off.


Abdi Karim was with the crowd dragging the dead American. He followed them until he grew afraid that an American helicopter would come down and shoot at them all. Then he drifted away from the mob and went home. His parents were greatly relieved to see him alive.

# 12

The Malaysians led everyone to a soccer stadium at the north end of the city, a Pakistani base of operations. The scene there was surreal. The exhausted Rangers drove in through the big gate out front, passed through the concrete shadows under the stands, like going to a football or baseball game at home, and then burst out blinking into a wide sunlit arena, rows of benches reaching up all around to the sky. In the lower stands lounged rows and rows of 10th Mountain Division soldiers, smoking, talking, eating, laughing, while on the field doctors were tending the scores of wounded.

Dr. Marsh had flown to the stadium with two other docs to supervise the emergency care. Unlike the first load of casualties that had come in with the lost convoy, these had mostly been patched up by medics in the field. Still, Dr. Bruce Adams found it a hellish scene. He was used to treating one or maybe two injuries at a time. Here was a soccer pitch covered with bleeding, broken bodies. The wounded *Super Six One* crew chief Ray Dowdy walked up to Adams and held up his hand, which was missing the top digits of two fingers. The doctor just put his arm around him and said, "I'm sorry."

For the Rangers, even the ride from the rendezvous point on National Street to the stadium had been traumatic. There was still a lot of shooting going on and barely enough room on the Humvees to take all the men who had run out, so guys were piled in two and three layers deep. Private Jeff Young, who had badly twisted his ankle on the run out, was picked up by one of the D-boys, who dropped him into the backseat of a Humvee and then unceremoniously sat on his lap. Private George Siegler had hopefully sprinted up to the hatch of an APC just as a voice yelled from inside, "We can only take one more!" Lieutenant Perino already had one leg in the hatch. Out of the corner of his eye Perino saw the younger man's desperation. He withdrew his leg from the hatch and said, cloaking his kindness with officerly impatience, "Come on, Private, come on." It would have been easy for the lieutenant to say he hadn't seen him. Siegler was so moved by the gesture he decided then and there to reenlist.

Nelson found himself in a Humvee that had four full cans of 60 ammo, so he worked his pig the whole way out of the city, shooting at anybody he saw. If they were on the street and he saw them he shot at them. He was close to coming out of this mess alive, and he was doing everything he could to make sure he did.

On his way out, Dan Schilling, the air force combat controller who had ridden out the bloody wandering of the lost convoy and then come back out into the city with the rescue convoy, saw an old Somali man with a white beard walking up the road with a small boy in his arms. The boy appeared to be about five years old and was bloody and looked dead. The old man walked seemingly oblivious to the firefight going on around him. He turned a corner north and disappeared up the street.

For Steele, the worst moment in the whole fight had come as they pulled away from National Street. The captain was looking down the line of APCs, watching men climb on board, and he saw Perino down at the end of the line step back and let Siegler in the hatch, and then, *boom!* the vehicles took off. There were still guys back there, Perino and others! He beat frantically on the shoulders of the APC driver, screaming at him, "I've got guys still out there!" but the Malay driver had a tanker helmet on and acted like he didn't hear Steele and just kept on driving. The captain got on the command net. Reception was so bad inside the carrier that he could barely hear a response, but he broadcast his alarm in disjointed phrases:

—*We got left back on National. . . . The Paki vehicles were gonna follow us home, the foot soldier. . . . But we loaded up but we had probably fifteen or twenty still had to walk. They took off and left us. We need to get somebody back down there to pick them up.*

—*Roger. I understand,* Harrell had answered. *I thought everybody was loaded. I got about three calls. They were telling me they were loaded. Where are they on National?*

—*Romeo, this is Juliet. I'm sending this blind. I need those soldiers picked up on National ASAP!*

In fact, Perino and the others had been picked up, but not without some trouble. The lieutenant and about six other men, Rangers and some D-boys, were the last ones on the street when what looked like the last of the vehicles approached. The exhausted soldiers shouted and waved but the Malaysian driver paid them no mind until one of the D-boys stepped out and leveled a CAR-15 at him. He stopped. They just piled in on top of the other men already jammed inside.

Steele didn't find out until he got to the stadium. Some of the Humvees had gone straight back to the hangar, so it took a last stressful half hour to account for them. Finally someone back at the JOC read him a list of all the Rangers who had come back there. It was only then that the captain took a long look around him and the magnitude of what had happened began to register.

* * *

Lieutenant Colonel Matthews, who had been aloft in the command bird with Harrell for the last fifteen hours except for short refueling breaks, stepped out of the bird and stretched his legs. He'd become so used to the sound of the rotors by now that he perceived the scene before him in silence. The wounded were on litters filling half of the field, tethered to IV bags, bandaged and bloody. Doctors and nurses huddled over the worst of them, working furiously. He saw Captain Steele sitting by himself on the sandbags of a mortar pit with his head in his hands. Behind Steele were rows of the dead, neatly arrayed in zippered body bags. Out on the field, moving from wounded man to wounded man, was a Pakistani soldier holding a tray with glasses of fresh water. The man had a white towel draped over his arm.

Those who were not wounded walked among the litters on the soccer pitch with tears in their eyes or looking drained and emotionless— thousand-mile stares. Helicopters, Vietnam-era Hueys emblazoned with the Red Cross, were coming and going, shuttling those who were ready back to the hospital by the hangar. Private Ed Kallman, who earlier had thrilled at the chance to be in combat, now watched as a medic efficiently sorted the litters as they came off vehicles like a foreman on a warehouse loading dock—"What have you got there? Okay. Dead in that group there. Live in this group here." Sergeant Watson wandered slowly through the wounded, taking account. Once the medics and doctors had cut off their bloody, dirty clothes and exposed the wounds, the full horror of it was much greater. There were guys with gaping bruised holes in their bodies, limbs mangled, poor Carlos Rodriguez with a bullet through his scrotum, Goodale and Gould with their bare wounded asses up in the air, Stebbins riddled with shrapnel, Lechner with his leg mashed, Ramaglia, Phipps, Boorn, Neathery . . . the list went on.

Specialist Anderson, despite his deep misgivings about coming out with the main convoy, had come through it unhurt. He was thrilled to find his skydiving buddy Sergeant Keni Thomas still alive and unhurt, but other than that he just felt emotionally spent. He recoiled at the ugliness of the scene, the wounds, the bodies. When the APC with *Super Six One* copilot Bull Briley's body on top arrived, Anderson had to turn away. The body was discolored. It looked yellow-orange, and through the deep gash in his head he could see brain matter spilled down the side of the carrier. When the medics came over looking for help getting the body down, Anderson just ducked away. He couldn't deal with it.

Goodale was laid out in the middle of the big stadium with his pants cut off looking up at a clear blue sky. A medic leaned over him dropping ash from his cigarette as he tried to stick an IV needle in his arm. And even though it was sunny and probably close to ninety degrees again, Goodale's teeth chattered. He was chilled to the bone. One of the doctors gave him some hot tea.

That's how Sergeant Cash found him. Cash had just arrived on the tail end of the rescue convoy and was wandering wild-eyed across the field looking for his friends. At first sight he thought Goodale, who was pale and shivering violently, was a goner.

"Are you all right?" Cash asked.

"I'll be all right. I'm just cold."

Cash helped flag a nurse, who covered Goodale with a blanket and tucked it in around him. Then they compared notes. Goodale told Cash about Smith, and went down the list of wounded. Cash told Goodale what he had seen back at the hangar when the lost convoy came in. He told him about Ruiz and Cavaco and Joyce and Kowalewski.

"Mac's hit," said Cash, referring to Sergeant Jeff McLaughlin. "I don't know where Carlson is. I heard he's dead."


Rob Phipps fell out of the hatch of his APC when it stopped in the stadium. After hours locked in that stinking container with all the other wounded, there was a sudden scramble for the fresh air as soon as the hatch was pushed open. Phipps landed with a thud, but the fresh air was so sweet he didn't mind the fall. He found he couldn't stand, so a soldier he didn't know picked him up and carried him to the doctors. Phipps had been fixed with an IV in his arm when one of the guys from his unit walked up and told him about Cavaco and Alphabet.

Floyd climbed up over the railing and mounted the benches to a group of 10th Mountain Division guys and bummed a cigarette. On his way down, Sergeant Watson waved him over to join the rest of his squad who were still standing. Watson somberly went down the list of those killed. Floyd was especially shocked to hear about Pilla. Smith and Pilla were his best friends in the world.

Stebbins sucked in large lungfuls of fresh air when the hatch of his APC finally swung open. He helped get some of the others off and then a litter was lifted on for him. He was dragging himself toward it when a 10th Mountain sergeant shouted, "Don't make him crawl, boys," and suddenly hands came in from all sides and Stebbins was lifted gently.

He was set down among a group of his buddies, naked from the waist down. Sergeant Aaron Weaver brought him a hot cup of coffee.

"Bless you, my son," said Stebbins. "Got any cigarettes?"

Weaver had none. Stebbins asked everyone who walked past, without luck. He finally grabbed one soldier from the 10th by the arm and pleaded, "Listen, man, you got to find me a fucking cigarette." One of the Malaysian drivers, a guy everybody in the APC (including Stebbins) had been screaming at an hour earlier, walked up and handed him a cigarette. The driver bent down to light it and then handed him the rest of the pack. When Stebbins tried to hand it back, the Malaysian took it and stuffed it in Stebbins's shirt pocket.

Watson approached.

"Stebby, I hear you did your job. Good work," he said, then he reached down and took a two-inch flap of cloth from Stebbins's shredded trousers and tried to place it over his genitals. They both laughed.


Dale Sizemore couldn't wait to find the guys on his chalk. He desperately wanted them to know that he hadn't sat out the fight back at the hangar, but had fought in after them, twice. It was important that they know he had come after them.

The first person he found was Sergeant Chuck Elliot. When they saw each other they both cried, happy to be alive, to see each other again. Then Sizemore started telling Elliot about the dead and wounded Rangers who had been on the lost convoy. They wept and talked and watched the dead being loaded on helicopters.

"There's Smitty," said Elliot.

"What?"

"That's Smith."

Sizemore saw two feet hanging out from under a sheet. One was booted, the other bare. Elliot told him how he and Perino and the medic had taken turns for hours putting their fingers up inside Smith's pelvic wound trying to pinch off the femoral artery. They had cut off the one pants leg and boot, that's how he knew it was Smith. He choked up and cried.

Then Sizemore found Goodale, with his butt in the air.

"I got shot in the ass," Goodale announced.

"Serves you right, Goodale, you shouldn't have been running away," Sizemore told him.

Steele was shocked when he learned that more of his men were dead. The sergeant who told him didn't have an accurate count yet, but he thought it might be three or four Rangers. *Four?* Up until he reached the stadium, Smith was the only one Steele had known about for sure. He strode off to be by himself. He grabbed a bottle of water and just sat drinking it, alone with his thoughts. He felt this overwhelming sadness, but dared not break down in front of his men. There was no one else of his rank around him, no one he could confide in. Some of his men were in tears; others were chattering away like they couldn't talk fast enough to get all their stories out. The captain felt odd, hyperalert. It was the first time in almost a full day when he felt he could let down for a minute, just relax. Every sight and sound of the busy scene before him registered fully, as though his senses had been finely tuned for so long that he couldn't pull back. He found himself a place to sit at the edge of a mortar pit and laid his rifle across his lap and just breathed deeply and swished the cool water in his mouth and tried to review all that had happened. Had he made the right decisions? Had he done everything he could?

Sergeant Atwater, the captain's radio operator, wanted to go over and say something to him, comfort him somehow. But he felt it wouldn't have been appropriate.

One by one the wounded were loaded on helicopters and flown either to the army hospital at the U.S. embassy or back to the hangar.

The chopper ride back was calming for Sizemore, the sensations so reminiscent of all those days in Mog before this fight, the profile flights, the heady first six missions where everything had gone so well. Feeling the wind through the open doors and looking out over the now-familiar squalor below, the ocean stretching off to the east, things felt normal again. It was a reminder of how they had been just a day before, full of fun and so spoiling for a fight. That was just twenty-four hours ago. Nothing would be like that for them again. There was no chatter now in the Black Hawk on the way back to the base. The men all rode silently.

Nelson looked out over the deep blue waters at a U.S. Navy ship in the distance. It was like he was seeing things through someone else's eyes. Colors seemed brighter to him, smells more vivid. He felt the experience had changed him in some fundamental way. He wondered if other guys were feeling this, but it was so strange, he didn't know how to explain it or how to ask them.

As his chopper lifted off, Steele watched the tight network of streets that had closed in on them the previous afternoon open up once again to a broader panorama, and he was struck by how small the space was they had fought over, and it reminded him just how remote and small a place Mogadishu was in the larger world.

As Sergeant Ramaglia was loaded on a bird, a medic leaned over him and said, "Man, I feel sorry for you all."

"You should feel sorry for *them*," the sergeant said, "'cause we whipped ass."

# 13

After depositing their dead and wounded, the D-boys quickly boarded helicopters and were flown back to the hangar. Sergeant Howe and his men went solemnly back to work, readying themselves to go right back out. They had trained to function without sleep for days at a time, so they were in a familiar place, one they called the "drone zone," a point at which the body transcends minor aches and pains and grows impervious to hot and cold. In the drone zone they motored on with a heightened level of perception, nonreflective, as if on autopilot. Howe didn't like the feeling, but he was used to it.

Some of the Rangers and even some of his friends in the unit were acting like they had been beaten, which pissed off the big sergeant. He knew he and his men had inflicted a lot more damage than they'd absorbed. They had been put in a terrible spot and had not only survived, they'd mauled the enemy. He didn't know the estimated body counts, but whatever the numbers he knew they'd just fought one of the most one-sided battles in American history.

He pulled off his sweat-soaked Kevlar and gear and spread it all out on his bunk. He restuffed all of the pouches and pockets with ammo. Then he methodically stripped down each of his weapons, cleaned and relubricated each, concluding each procedure with a function check. When he had everything ready and packed again he stood over it with a strong sense of satisfaction. His kit, and the precise way that he'd packed it, had served him well, and he wanted to remember exactly how everything was, for the next time. The only thing he would have done differently is take along those NODs. He stuffed them in his backpack. He would never again go on a mission without them, night or day.

Howe was surprised to still be alive. The thought of heading straight back out into the fight scared him, but the fear was nothing next to the loyalty he felt to the men stranded in the city. Some of their own were still out there—Gary Gordon, Randy Shughart, Michael Durant, and the crew of *Super Six Four*. Alive or dead, they were coming home. This fight wasn't over until every one of them was back. *Fuck it, let's go out there and kill some folks.* That was how he set his mind.

And if they were going back out, there was going to be hell to pay.

# 14

Sizemore didn't find out that his buddy Lorenzo Ruiz was dead until after he got back to the hangar.

"You heard about Ruiz, right?" asked Specialist Kevin Snodgrass.

Sizemore knew right away what had happened and he couldn't stop crying. When they had flown Ruiz out earlier in the afternoon for the hospital in Germany he was still alive. Not long after he left, word came back that he had died. Ruiz had tried to hand Sizemore the packet of letters for his parents and loved ones before the mission and Sizemore had refused it. Now Ruiz was dead. Sizemore couldn't believe it was Ruiz and not him who had been killed. Ruiz had a wife and a baby. Why would Ruiz be taken and not him? It seemed deeply unfair to Sizemore. Sergeant Watson sat with him for hours, consoling him, talking things through with him. But what could you say?

Sergeant Cash had seen Ruiz not long before he had been flown out. "You're going to be fine," he told him.

"No. No I'm not," Ruiz said. He had barely enough strength to form the words. "I know it's over for me. Don't worry about me."

Captain Steele got the accurate casualty list when he returned to the hangar. First Sergeant Glenn Harris was waiting for him at the door. He saluted.

"Rangers lead the way, sir."

"All the way," Steele said, returning the salute.

"Sir, here's what it looks like," Harris said, handing over a green sheet of paper.

Steele was aghast. One list of names ran the entire length of the page. There weren't just four men killed. On this list the death toll was thirteen. Six others were missing from the second crash site and presumed dead. Of the three critically injured men already flown out to a hospital in Germany—Griz Martin, Lorenzo Ruiz, and Adalberto Rodriguez—Ruiz had already been reported dead. Seventy-three men had been injured. Among the dead, six were Steele's men—Smith, Cavaco, Pilla, Joyce, Kowalewski, and Ruiz. Thirty of the injured were Rangers. Harris had started a second column at the top that ran almost to the bottom of the page. One third of Steele's company had either been killed or injured.

"Where are they?" Steele asked.

"Most are at the hospital, sir."

Steele stripped off his gear and walked across to the field hospital. The captain put a great store on maintaining at least a facade of emotional resilience, but the scene in the hospital undid him. It was a mess. Guys were lying everywhere, on cots, on the floor. Some were still bandaged in the haphazard wraps given them during the fight. He choked out a few words of encouragement to each, fighting back the well of grief in his craw. The last soldier he saw was Phipps, the youngest of the Rangers on the CSAR bird. Phipps looked to Steele like he'd been beaten with a baseball bat. His face was swollen twice normal size and was black-and-blue. His back and leg were heavily bandaged and there were stains from his oozing wounds. Steele laid his hand on him.

"Phipps?"

The soldier stirred. When he opened his eyes there was red where the whites normally were.

"You're gonna be okay," Steele said.

Phipps reached up and grabbed hold of the captain's arm.

"Sir, I'll be okay in a couple of days. Don't go back out without me."
Steele nodded and fled the room.

Private David Floyd was struck by how empty the hangar looked. He
dragged himself back to his cot and stripped off his gear. But instead of
feeling relieved, he felt this great weight and soreness descend. Around
him, guys were talking and talking and talking. It was like they were trying to work the whole thing out. They accounted for all of their number.
For every one of the killed or scores of injured there was a story to be told
about how and when and where and why. Sometimes the stories differed.
One thought Joyce was still alive for a time in the back of the truck while
another insisted he was killed almost instantly. Somebody thought it was
Diemer who had pulled Joyce from the line of fire, but another was sure it
was Telscher. Stebbins had gone down four times. No, somebody argued,
it was only three. They told of the long futile struggle to keep Jamie Smith
alive. They wept openly.

Nelson, one of the last to return to the hangar, found Sergeant
Eversmann in tears.

"What's wrong?" Nelson asked. Then, knowing his friend Casey Joyce
had been on Eversmann's chalk, he asked, "Where's Joyce?"

Eversmann looked at him with surprise, and then got too choked up
to speak. Nelson ran into the hangar and sought out Lieutenant Perino,
who gave him the bad news. He also told him Pilla, his partner in the hangar skits, was dead. Nelson broke down.

Joyce's death particularly grieved him. He owed the man an apology. Fed up with the order to stand guard duty in full battle dress a few
days earlier, Nelson had told the men on his team it was okay to ignore it.
He told them to wear their body armor and helmet over shorts and T-shirts.
If it caused trouble, he said, he'd take the heat. He hadn't really thought
that through, however, because when the trouble came it landed not on
him but on Joyce, who was nominally his superior. Joyce had been sternly
upbraided for not being able to control his men.

Nelson had pulled guard duty early Sunday morning, between three
and seven, and Joyce had roused himself to come out to talk. They had been
together ever since basic training, and they had a special, almost family connection. They had actually met each other years before joining the army. It

was just a wild coincidence. Nelson's stepbrother had roomed with Joyce's older brother in an apartment in Atlanta, and they had met each other there once or twice as kids. Nelson admired Joyce. He had never seen the man say or do anything unseemly. Just about everybody had tied one on at a local bar or secretly smoked dope or bad-mouthed somebody or tried to get away with something against the rules. Not Casey Joyce. As far as Nelson was concerned, Joyce was the most thoroughly decent guy he'd ever met, genuine to the core. Joyce had gotten his sergeant stripes first, but they both knew Nelson would be getting his soon. It was awkward for Joyce to be Nelson's superior. They were friends. They had made plans with Pilla and a few of the other guys to drive out to Austin and stay with Joyce's sister for a few days when they got back. Nelson felt bad about getting his friend in trouble. Just over twenty-four hours ago they had sat together behind a machine gun surrounded by sandbags under a nearly full moon. The guard post was up on a Conex that had been stacked on another to create a nice high vantage point. It was quiet. The low rooflines of Mogadishu spread before them rolling uphill to the north. In the distance they could hear the steady banging of small generators that kept, here and there, a lightbulb or two burning. Otherwise the city was draped in pale blue moonlight.

"Look, I'm as tired of this chain-of-command shit as you are," Joyce had told Nelson. "Just do me a favor. Whatever happens, don't do anything that gets First Sergeant Harris and Staff Sergeant Eversmann on my back. Let's do what we need to do so we can get out of here. Don't let this come between you and me."

Joyce hadn't bitched at him, which he had every right to do and which most guys would have. He was making a plea, man to man, friend to friend. The right thing for Nelson to do was to apologize, and the words were right there on the tip of his tongue, but Nelson didn't say them. He was still angry about the rule, which he thought was pointless and stupid, and he wouldn't swallow his pride. Not even for his friend. The apology had still been there on the tip of his tongue the previous afternoon when he'd helped Joyce pull on his gear. Joyce was squad leader and had to be the first one out to the helicopter, so Nelson always helped him. He'd been close to saying the apology, but instead just watched his friend walk off. Now he would never have the chance.

Nelson was asked to inventory his friend's gear. He found Joyce's Kevlar vest, the one he had helped him put on the day before. It had a hole

in the upper back right at the center. He rooted through the vest pockets—
a lot of guys stuffed pictures, love letters, and things in the pockets. In the
front of Joyce's vest he found the bullet. It must have passed right through
his friend's body and been caught up in the Kevlar in front. He put it in a
tin can. In Pilla's belongings he found a bag of the little explosives his friend
used to insert in people's cigarettes.

Sergeant Watson walked over to the morgue to see Smith one last time.
He unzipped the body bag and gazed at his friend's pinched, pale lifeless
face. Then he leaned over and kissed his forehead.

# 15

America awakened Monday morning (it was already late afternoon in
Mogadishu) to news reports of an ugly fight in Somalia, a place most people
had to consult an atlas to find. It wasn't the biggest news. Russian president Boris Yeltsin was fending off a coup d'état. Washington was preoccupied with developments in Moscow.

Sandwiched in between the dramatic reports from Russia, however,
came increasingly distressing news from Somalia. At least five soldiers had
been killed and "several" wounded, the early reports said. Even those numbers indicated the worst single day in Mogadishu since the United States
had committed troops ten months before. Then, later in the day, came the
grotesque images of dead American soldiers being dragged through the city's
dusty streets by angry crowds.

President Clinton was in a hotel room in San Francisco when he saw
the pictures. He had been informed earlier in the day that there had been
a successful raid in Mogadishu, but that the Rangers had gotten in a scrape.
The TV images horrified and angered him, according to an account in
Elizabeth Drew's book *On the Edge*.

"How could this happen?" he demanded.

The trickle of news was a peculiarly modern form of torture at the homes
of the men serving in Somalia. Stephanie Shughart, the wife of Delta Ser-

geant Randy Shughart, had gotten a phone call at ten o'clock Sunday night. She was home alone. She and Randy had no children. One of the other Fort Bragg wives left her with a chillingly imprecise bit of bad news.

"One of the guys has been killed," she said.

*One of the guys.*

Stephanie had talked on the phone with Randy on Friday night. As usual, he'd said nothing about what was going on, just that it was hot, he was getting enough to eat, and he was getting a great tan. He told her he loved her. He was such a gentle man. It had always seemed so incongruous to her how he made a living. He didn't say anything about his work when they first met. Some of Stephanie's better-connected friends had whispered to her that Randy was "an operator." She'd figured he worked on the phones.

*One of the guys.*

In a bedroom in Tennessee, just across the state line from the Night Stalkers' base at Fort Campbell, Kentucky, Becky Yacone sat with Willi Frank. Both their husbands, Jim Yacone and Ray Frank, were Black Hawk pilots, and they knew two helicopters had gone down over Mogadishu. Willi had been awakened at six A.M. by a chaplain and commander from the base. She knew right away why the men were at her door. She'd been through exactly the same thing three years before, when Ray's chopper had crashed on the training mission. She'd met Ray on her birthday twenty-two years earlier, when she was managing a bar in Newport News. Her employees had surprised her with a cake, and everybody ate it except Ray. When she'd asked him why, he'd told her, like it was something everybody in the world with any sense would know, "You don't eat cake when you're drinking beer." They'd gotten married in Las Vegas that same year.

"Ray is missing in action," the men said.

"How long will it be before we know?" she asked.

They were startled by the question.

"Last time it only took two hours," Willi explained.

This time it would take longer. Her support unit showed up, wives of two other men in the unit, and then Becky came over. Becky was a Black Hawk pilot herself. She'd met her husband when they were classmates at

West Point. She had no news about Jim yet. They all agreed that if anybody could get out of a mess like this alive, downed in the streets of a hostile
African city, it was their husbands.

Then the pictures came on the TV. The first of them came on just
after noon. They were images of dead Americans. The pictures were distant and shot from such odd angles it was impossible to tell who the dead
men were.

"That one has dirty fingernails," said one of the women. "He must
be a crew chief."

There was some discussion about that. The bodies were in the dirt.
"They're all dirty," said another woman.

Nobody at Willi's thought to tape the show and rerun it. Maybe it
was too ghoulish. Besides, they didn't need to tape it. CNN kept showing
the same pictures every half hour. At these short intervals conversation
would cease and the women would all crowd anxiously around the screen.

"That's Ray," said Willi. Something about the way the body was lying,
the turn of the shoulders and arms . . .

"No, he's too small," said Becky. They knew Randy Shughart and
Gary Gordon were missing, and they were both much shorter than Ray.

"No," said Willi. "I just know that's Ray."

She said she was, but she wasn't sure. She had a bad feeling, but she
wasn't giving up hope.


At the hangar in Mogadishu, the men watched like everybody else the
images of their dead comrades being put on display by the jeering Somali crowds. The men who filled the TV room at the hangar saw it replayed again and again. No one said a word. Some of the men turned and
left the room. Captains Jim Yacone and Scott Miller sat together before
the screen trying to figure out if the body they were looking at was Randy
Shughart's or Ray Frank's. Both men had the same build and gray hair.
Ray's had turned gray almost overnight. He had contracted a rare disor-
der in his early thirties and had become allergic to the pigment of his
own hair. It had all fallen out and grown back snowy white. Ray also had
scars on his torso from the extensive surgery he'd undergone after the
Black Hawk crash in training. The D-boys were convinced
the body was Randy's. It was galling to watch the Skinnies strutting

around the bodies, poking at them with rifles, dragging them. What kind of animals . . . ?

The pilots wanted to get up over those crowds and mow them down, just mow them all down. Fuck the whole lot of them. Then land and recover the bodies. These were American soldiers. Their brothers.

Garrison and Montgomery said no. There were big crowds around those bodies. It would be a massacre.

Mace, Sergeant Macejunas, went back out into the city. The blond operator had gone out into the fight three times the day and night before. Leading the force on foot to Durant's crash site when the vehicles could go no further was enough to make his courage legendary. Now he was going out alone, dressed as a civilian, a journalist. The D-boys had arranged with one of the sympathetic local NGOs for help finding the six men still missing from the second crash site, Durant, Frank, Field, Cleveland, Shughart, and Gordon. Mace was going along.

To a man, the task force dreaded the prospect of going back into the city, but they were prepared to do it, with as much weaponry, armor, and ammo as they could carry. Here was Mace heading back out without any of that. He was going to find his brothers, alive or dead. The Rangers who saw him were in awe of the man's courage and cool.

# 16

Mike Durant's captors asked if he would make a videotape.

"No," said Durant.

He was surprised they'd asked. If they wanted to make a video, they were going to anyway. But, since they'd asked . . . .

Durant had been trained how to handle himself in captivity. How to avoid being helpful without being confrontational. The pilot knew if he got out of this alive, his actions would be scrutinized. It was safer not to be in that position, speaking to the world from captivity.

They showed up with a camera crew that night anyway. It had been more than twenty-four hours since he crashed and was carried off in an angry swarm of Somalis. He was hungry, thirsty, and still terrified. He had a compound fracture of his right leg, a crushed vertebra, and bullet and shrapnel wounds in his shoulder and thigh. His face was bloody and swollen from where he had been clubbed in the face with the butt of a rifle. His dark hair, caked with sweat and dirt and blood, stuck straight up on end like some cartoon depiction of fright.

There were about ten young men in the crew. They set up lights. Only one of the crew spoke to him, a young man with good English. Durant knew the key to getting through something like this was to offer as little pertinent information as possible, to be cagey, not confrontational. There was a code of conduct spelling out what he could say and what he couldn't say, and Durant was determined to abide by it. His interrogators were not skillful. Men had been questioning him on and off all day, trying to get him to tell them more about who he was and what his unit was trying to do in Somalia. When the camera was turned on, the interviewer began pressing him on the same points. The Somalis considered all the Americans with the task force to be Rangers.

"No, I'm not a Ranger," Durant told him. He explained he was a pilot.

"You kill people innocent," the interviewer insisted.

"Innocent people being killed is not good," Durant said.

That was the best they got out of him. Those were the words people all over the world would be seeing on their TV the next day. Somalia had been a back-burner news item in the weeks before this battle. None of the major American newspapers or networks even had a correspondent in Mogadishu. Now this east African coastal city was front and center. The coup d'état fizzled in Moscow and the images of the Somali crowds humiliating American bodies had drawn the attention of the world, and the outrage of America. Durant's swollen, bloody face, with that wild, frightened look in his eye, lifted off the videotape, would soon be in newspapers and on the covers of newsmagazines worldwide. It was an image of American helplessness. More than one American asked the same question President Clinton had asked, *How could this have happened? Didn't we go to Somalia to feed starving people?*

Willi Frank got down on her hands and knees and peered closely at the TV. She was trying to see around the corners of the screen. She was sure, if they had Durant, they must have other members of the crew. They probably had Ray, too. He was probably sitting right next to Mike, just off the frame!

Durant felt okay about the interview. After the camera crew left, a doctor came. He was kind, and he spoke English well. He told Durant he had been trained at the University of Southern California. He apologized for the limited supplies he had with him, just some aspirin, some antiseptic solution, and some gauze. He used forceps and gauze and the solution to gently probe Durant's leg wound, where the broken femur poked through the skin, and he cleaned off the end of the bone and the tissue around it.

It was sharply painful, but the pilot was grateful. He knew enough about wounds to know that a femur infection was relatively common and deadly, even with simple fractures. His was compound, and he had been lying on a dirty floor all night and day. Durant asked about his crew and the D-boys, but the doctor said he knew nothing.

When the doctor left, the pilot was moved from the room where he had awakened that morning to the sounds of birds and children. He was pushed to the floor in the back of a car, and a blanket was placed over him. It was terribly painful. Then two men got in the car and sat on him. His leg was moving all over the place. It had swelled badly, and the slightest move was torture.

They brought him to a little apartment and left him in the care of a gangly, nearsighted man he would come to know well over the next ten days. It was Abdullahi Hassan, a man they called "Firimbi," the propaganda minister for clan leader Mohamed Farrah Aidid.

The pilot didn't know it, but the warlord had paid his ransom.

Now, to get Durant back, America would have to negotiate with Aidid.

# 17

Garrison and the task force were willing, but Washington had lost its stomach for the fight.

Former U.S. Ambassador to Somalia Robert Oakley had been attending a party at the Syrian embassy in Washington on Tuesday, October 5, when he got a phone call from the White House. It was Anthony Lake, national security adviser to President Clinton.

"I need to talk to you first thing in the morning," Lake said.

"Why, Tony?" Oakley said. "I've been home for six months."

Oakley, a gaunt, plainspoken intellectual with a distinguished career in diplomacy, had been President George Bush's top civilian in Mogadishu during the humanitarian mission that had begun the previous December. With the famine over and a new administration in Washington, Oakley had departed the city in March 1993, at about the same time his old friend Admiral Jonathan Howe had taken over the top UN job in Somalia.

Since his return, Oakley had watched with dismay the course of events in Somalia. He had frequent conversations with former colleagues in the State Department, but despite his long experience there, no top officials in the administration had consulted with him. He wasn't offended, but he was concerned about prospects for the government-building process he'd help set in motion. He'd watched with growing concern as events and UN resolutions pushed Aidid out of the peace process, and felt the idea of tracking the clan leader down like an outlaw was bound to fail. But no one had asked his opinion.

"Can you come to breakfast tomorrow at seven-thirty?" Lake asked.

Now they were in trouble. The day after the October 3 battle, Secretary of Defense Les Aspin and Secretary of State Warren Christopher had been grilled by angry members of Congress. How had this happened? Why were American soldiers dying in far-off Somalia when the humanitarian mission there had supposedly ended months before? As many as five hundred Somalis had been killed and over a thousand injured. Durant was still a captive. The public was outraged, and Congress was demanding withdrawal.

Senator Robert C. Byrd, Democratic chairman of the Appropriations Committee, called for an immediate end "to these cops-and-robbers operations."

"Clinton's got to bring them home," said Senator John McCain, a Republican member of the Armed Services Committee and former prisoner of war in Vietnam.

There were perceived intelligence failures up and down the line. In Mogadishu, the escalating violence between the Habr Gidr and UN forces had been perceived as individual incidents, not the probing actions of a determined enemy force. In Washington, officials at the Pentagon, White House, and Congress were stunned by the size, scope, and ferocity of Aidid's counterattack on October 3. In retrospect, Aspin's inaction on General Montgomery's September request for tanks and Bradley armored vehicles seemed indicative of an administration that had fallen asleep on its watch—something Republican legislators could use to batter the Clinton administration.

The battle was also a blow to an administration already unpopular with the military establishment. It made Clinton look uninterested in the welfare of America's soldiers. The president had been getting briefed on Task Force Ranger's missions in advance. This one had been mounted so quickly he had not been informed. Clinton complained bitterly to Lake. He felt he had been blindsided, and he was angry. He wanted answers to a broad range of questions from policy issues to military tactics.

At the breakfast table in the East Wing on Wednesday were Lake and his deputy, Samuel R. Berger, and U.S. Ambassador to the UN Madeleine K. Albright. They talked about what had happened informally, and then walked Oakley into the Oval Office, where they joined the president, the vice president, Christopher, Aspin, the chairman of the Joint Chiefs of Staff, and several other advisers.

The meeting lasted six hours. The thrust of the discussion was: What do we do now? Staying in Mogadishu to pursue Aidid was out of the question, even though Admiral Howe and General Garrison were eager to do so. They believed Aidid had been struck a mortal blow and that it wouldn't take much more to finish the job. If the reports from local spies were correct, some of Aidid's strongest clan allies had fled the city fearing the inevitable American counterattack. The clan's arsenals of RPGs were severely depleted. Others were sending peace feelers, offering to dump Aidid to ward off more bloodshed. But it was clear listening to the discussion that morning in the White House that America had no intention of initiating any further military action in Somalia.

America was pulling out. The meeting ended with a decision to reinforce Task Force Ranger, make a show of military resolve, but call off any further efforts to apprehend Aidid or his top aides. After enough tanks, men, planes, and ships poured into Mogadishu to level the city, the forces were to simply stay put for a while. Renewed efforts would be made to negotiate a stable Somali government that would *include* Aidid, but the United States would make a dignified withdrawal, by March 1994. The Somali warlord didn't know it yet, but his clan had scored a major victory. Without U.S. muscle, there was no way the UN could impose a government on Somalia without Aidid's cooperation.

Oakley was dispatched to Mogadishu to deliver this message and to try to secure the release of Durant.

There would be no negotiating with Aidid over Durant. Oakley was instructed to deliver a stern message: The president of the United States wanted the pilot released. Now.

# 18

Firimbi was a big man for a Somali, tall with long arms and big hands. He had a potbelly, and squinted through thick, cloudy black-framed glasses. He was extremely proud of his position in the SNA. Once Aidid had purchased Durant back from the bandits who had kidnapped him, Firimbi was told, "Anything bad that happens to the pilot will also happen to you."

When Durant arrived that night, Firimbi found him angry, frightened, and in pain. He met the pilot's sullen demeanor with his own earnest hostility. America had just caused a bloodbath in Firimbi's clan, and he held men like this pilot accountable. It was hard not to be angry.

Durant had no idea where he'd been taken. In the drive through the city he had been under a blanket in the backseat. They might have been taking him out to kill him. The men who brought him carried him up steps and along a walkway and set him down in a room.

Firimbi greeted him, but the pilot at first didn't answer. Durant could speak a little Spanish, and Firimbi, like most educated Somalis, could speak Italian. The languages were similar enough for them to communicate somewhat. After they had been alone together for a time they spoke enough to establish this basis for limited conversation. Durant complained about his wounds. Despite the efforts of the doctor who visited him at the other place, they had become swollen, tender, and infected. Firimbi sullenly helped wash him again and rebandaged them. He passed word along that Durant needed a doctor.

That night, Monday, October 4, Durant and Firimbi heard American helicopters flying overhead, broadcasting haunting calls:

"Mike Durant, we will not leave you."

"Mike Durant, we are with you always."

"Do not think we have left you, Mike."

"What are they saying?" Firimbi asked.

Durant told him that his friends were worried about him, and would be looking for him.

"And we treat you so nicely," said his captor. "It is a Somali tradition never to hurt a prisoner."

Durant smiled at him through his battered, swollen face.

# 19

For Jim Smith, the father of Corporal Jamie Smith, the nightmare had begun during a Monday afternoon meeting in the conference room of the bank where he worked in Long Valley, New Jersey. The meeting was interrupted when his boss's wife opened the door and stepped in.

She said she was sorry to interrupt, then turned to Smith.

"I just got a call from Carol," she said. "Call home."

Obviously, Smith's wife, Carol, had felt this was urgent. They'd been ignoring the office phones during the meeting, so Carol had called the boss's home number, looking for a way to track him down.

Smith called his wife from an adjoining office.

"What's the matter?" he asked.

He will always remember her next words.

"There are two officers here. Jamie has been killed. You have to come home."

When he opened the door at home, Carol said, "Maybe they're wrong, Jim. Maybe Jamie is just missing."

But Smith knew. He had been a Ranger captain in Vietnam, and lost a leg in combat. He knew that in a tight unit like the Rangers, death notification wouldn't go out unless they had the body.

"No," he told his wife quietly, trying to make the words sink in. "If they say he's dead, they know."

Camera crews began to arrive within hours. When everyone in his immediate family had been given the news, Smith walked out to the front yard to answer questions.

He was repulsed by the attitude of the reporters and the kinds of questions they asked. How did he feel? *How did they think he felt?* He told them he was proud of his son and deeply saddened. Did he think his son had been properly trained and led? Yes, his son was superbly trained and led. Whom did he blame? *What was he supposed to say: The U.S. Army? Somalia? Himself, for encouraging his son's interest in the Rangers? God?*

Smith told them that he didn't know enough about what had happened yet to blame anybody, that his son was a soldier, and that he died serving his country.

A Mailgram arrived two days later with a stark message signed by a colonel he didn't know. It resonated powerfully with Smith, even though he knew its contents before reading the words. It joined him in a sad ritual as old as war itself, with every person who had ever lost someone beloved in battle:

"THIS CONFIRMS PERSONAL NOTIFICATION MADE TO YOU BY A REPRESENTATIVE OF THE SECRETARY OF THE ARMY, THAT YOUR SON, SPC JAMES E. SMITH, DIED AT MOGADISHU, SOMALIA, ON OCTOBER 3, 1993. ANY QUESTIONS YOU MAY HAVE SHOULD BE DIRECTED TO YOUR CASUALTY ASSISTANCE OFFICER. PLEASE ACCEPT MY DEEPEST SYMPATHY IN YOUR BEREAVEMENT."

# 20

Stephanie Shughart got word about her husband, Randy, that same Monday morning. She had been up all night after getting the word that "one of the guys" had been killed. Anticipating further news, she had called her boss to say she wouldn't be in for work—a family emergency. The families at Bragg braced themselves. At least one family was going to take a hit.

Stephanie's boss knew that Randy was in the army, and he sometimes did dangerous work. She also knew how uncharacteristic it was for Stephanie to stay home from work. She drove straight over to the Shugharts' house.

The two women drank coffee and watched CNN. Stephanie was in a perfect agony of suspense as the first TV reports aired about what had happened in Mogadishu. She and her boss were talking when two silhouettes appeared outside the door.

Stephanie opened it to two men from her husband's unit. One was a close friend. *This is it. He's dead.*

"Randy is missing in action," he said.

So it was better news than she expected. Stephanie was determined not to despair. Randy would be okay. He was the most competent man alive.

Her mental image of Somalia was of a jungle. She pictured her husband in some clearing, signaling for a chopper. When her friend told her that Randy had gone in with Gary Gordon, she felt even better. *They're hiding somewhere.* If anybody could come through it alive, it was those two.

News came rapid-fire over the next few days, all of it bad. Families learned of the deaths of Earl Fillmore and Griz Martin. Then there were the horrible images of a dead soldier being dragged through the streets. Then word came that Gary's body had been recovered. Stephanie despaired. When proof came that Durant was alive and being held captive, her hopes soared. Surely they had Randy, too. They just weren't showing him on camera. She prayed and prayed. First she prayed for Randy to be alive, but as the days went by and her hopes dimmed, she began to pray that he not be someplace suffering, and that if he were dead, that he died quickly. Over the next week she went to several funerals. She sat and grieved with the other wives. Eventually all the missing men except Shughart had been accounted for. All were dead, their bodies horribly mutilated.

Stephanie asked her father to stay with her. Her friends took turns keeping her company. This went on for days. It was hell.

When she saw a car pull into her driveway with several officers and a priest inside, she knew.

"They're here, Dad," she said.

"The Somalis have returned a body, and it's been identified as Randy," one of officers said.

"Are you sure?" she asked.

"Yes," he said. "We're sure."

She was discouraged from viewing Randy's body—and, being a nurse, Stephanie could imagine why better than most. She sent a friend to Dover, Delaware, where the body had been flown. When he came back, she asked, "Could you tell it was him?"

He shook his head sadly. He hadn't been able to tell.

# 21

DeAnna Joyce had been feeling lucky. On Friday night, two nights back, they'd held a lottery over at the lieutenant's house on post at Fort Benning to see when the wives would get to talk to their husbands. They hadn't seen the men for months, ever since they'd left to train at Fort Bliss earlier that summer. Eighteen of the women would get to take phone calls Saturday night, eighteen more Sunday night, and two on Monday. DeAnna had gotten stuck with one of the Mondays, but as she was leaving another of the wives had wanted to switch, so she'd gotten to speak to Casey Saturday night. Then all the calls for Sunday and Monday were canceled.

There had always been that good fortune in Casey's smile. She'd met him at a mall in Texas. DeAnna was working as a saleswoman for a clothing store chain, The Limited, and this guy she knew stopped in to ask her a question about a girl. He'd introduced her to Casey. They must have said all of two words to each other.

"Hey."

"Howyadoin'?"

Like that. Only, she learned later, on his way out of the store Casey had informed his friend, "I'm going to marry that girl."

They started dating, and then Casey transferred from the University of Texas to North Texas University in order to attend the same school as DeAnna. He was studying journalism. But he didn't like going to class and wasn't doing that well and told her one day in 1990 that he was going to leave school and join the army. Or, he asked her. She'd said, "Do what you want." So he'd gone through basic, then airborne school, where he'd gotten this horrible fist-sized tattoo on the back of his right shoulder. It was supposed to be a Rottweiler, but it looked more like a wildcat. It sported an airborne unit maroon beret. Then he decided to push on through the Ranger Indoctrination Program.

Casey's father, a retired lieutenant colonel, had never won a Ranger tab, so it was something Casey was bound and determined to do. It wasn't easy. He and his buddy Dom Pilla had both just about decided to quit— Casey called and asked DeAnna if she'd think less of him, and she'd said no—but then Casey and Dom had talked each other into staying. They'd both made it. He returned home a Ranger, making plans to get the maroon beret on his tattoo recolored with the black beret of the Rangers. They were married on May 25, 1991.

DeAnna started crying when she got on the phone with him Saturday night, and couldn't stop. It upset Casey, too. They both just sobbed back and forth how much they loved each other. She was desperate for him to come home.

All the wives were invited over to the lieutenant's house that Sunday, where they learned that the company had been involved in a firefight. All of them, even the cooks. All the women were panicky, but DeAnna was feeling lucky. The more experienced wives explained that for guys who got injured, there would be a phone call. For those who were dead, there would be a knock at the door. DeAnna lay awake that night thinking about that.

There was a knock on the door at 6:30 A.M. DeAnna threw on her robe, and ran down to the door. *He's dead. Casey is dead.* She opened the door, but instead of finding soldiers there were two neighbor children.

"Our mother's father died last night and we have to leave, and we wanted to know if you'd take care of our dog."

As DeAnna dressed to go next door, she kicked herself for having even had such a morbid, terrible thought about Casey. *How could you even think that?* She was next door, getting instructions for minding the dog and consoling her friend, whose father had died in another state, when one of the other neighbors present mentioned that she'd heard eleven Rangers had been killed in Somalia.

When DeAnna got home there was a message on the machine from Larry Joyce, Casey's dad, asking her to call. Larry knew DeAnna would get word first if anything had happened, and he'd phoned her when he'd seen the TV report. She called him.

"President Clinton has already been on TV expressing condolences to the families," her father-in-law said. The president had used the expression "unfortunate losses," and voiced continued, determined support for the mission.

DeAnna said she'd heard nothing. They agreed that this was probably good news. She was about to make another call when there was a new knock on the door.

She started down the stairs again, figuring it was the next-door kids with more dog instructions, only this time it was three men in uniform.

"Are you Dina?" one asked.

"No, I'm not," she said, and shut the door.

The men pushed the door open gently.

"Are you Mrs. Joyce?"

Sometime in the first week of shock and grief, DeAnna received Casey's affects. With them was a letter he had been writing her just before leaving on the fatal mission. DeAnna knew that the experience in Somalia had shaken Casey, and that in the months he was away he had brooded over minor problems in their relationship.

"I miss you so much," the letter said, speaking now from beyond the grave. "I've said it probably a thousand times, but I want things to be different, and I know they will be. I love you so much! I can't say it stronger. I want you to love me with all your heart. I think you already do, but just in case I want to prove to you that I'm worth it. I'm not going to come home and be a total nerd slush, if you know what I mean, but I'm going to be myself. I'm going to make you into the most important person in my life. I'm not going to lose sight of this ever again. I want you to know that I want to grow old with you. I want you to realize this because I can't do it all by myself. I know most of the problems are me and I want to change. I want to go to church. I want us to be happy. Anyways, I can't say it enough, but I want to start doing things about it. I can't do anything until I get home. . . . By the time you get this letter I might be on my way home, or real close to it."

# 22

Durant's fear of being executed or tortured eased after several days in captivity. After being at the center of that enraged mob on the day he crashed, he mostly feared being discovered by the Somali public. It was a fear shared by Firimbi.

The propaganda minister had grown fond of him. It was something Durant worked at, part of his survival training. He made an effort to be polite. He learned the Somali words for "please," *pil les an,* and "thank you," *ma hat san-e.* The two men were together day and night for a week. They shared what appeared to be a small apartment. There was a small balcony out the front door, which reminded Durant of an American motel.

The woman who owned the house where Durant was staying insisted on fixing the pilot a special meal, as is the custom for guests in Somalia. She slaughtered a goat and made a meal of goat meat and pasta. The meal was delicious, and huge. Durant thought the chunk of meat and bone in his bowl could feed five people. But the next day both the pilot and his captor had diarrhea. Firimbi helped keep the bedridden pilot clean, which was uncomfortable and embarrassing for both men.

Firimbi kept trying to cheer up the pilot.

"What do you want?" he kept asking.

"I want a plane ticket to the United States."

"Do you want a radio?"

"Sure," Durant said, and he was given a small black plastic radio with a volume so low he had to hold it up to his ear. That radio became his lifeline. He could hear the BBC World Service, and reports about his captivity. It was wonderful to hear those English voices coming from his own world.

In subsequent days, they laughed and teased each other about the flatulence that followed the worst of the ailment. The mood of his captivity lightened. Durant's leg had been splinted, but was still swollen and painful. Day and night he lay on the small bed. Sometimes it would be silent for hours. Sometimes he and Firimbi would talk. Their pidgin "Italish" got better.

Durant asked Firimbi how many wives he had.

"Four wives."

"How many children?"

Firimbi lied.

"Twenty-seven," he said.

"How do you provide for so many?" the pilot asked.

"I'm a businessman," Firimbi said. "I used to have a flour and pasta factory," which was true. He also had grown sons who had left Somalia and sent money, he said. (Firimbi actually had nine children.)

Durant told him he had a wife and a son.

Firimbi tried to explain to the pilot why Somalis were so angry at him and the other Rangers. He talked about the Abdi House attack, how the helicopters had killed scores of his friends and clansmen. Firimbi complained about all the innocent people the Americans had killed, women and children. There were hundreds, perhaps thousands, he said. He explained that Aidid was an important and brilliant leader in his country, not someone the UN or the Americans could just label an outlaw and carry off. Not without a fight anyway. Firimbi considered Durant a prisoner of war. He believed that by treating the pilot humanely, he would improve the image of Somalis in America upon his release. Durant humored his jailer, asking him questions, indulging his whims. For instance, Firimbi loved his *khat*. One day he handed cash to a guard and sent him to purchase more. When the man returned he began dividing the plant into three equal portions, one for himself, Firimbi, and another guard.

"No," Firimbi said. "Four."

The guard looked at him quizzically. Firimbi gestured toward Durant. Durant quickly figured out what his jailer was up to. He nodded at the guard, indicating a cut for himself.

When the guard left, Firimbi scooped up the two piles for himself, winking at Durant and flashing an enormous grin.

Firimbi identified so strongly with the pilot that when Durant refused food, he refused food. When Durant couldn't sleep because of his pain, Firimbi couldn't sleep, either. He made Durant promise that when he was released he would tell how well treated he had been. Durant promised he would tell the truth.

After five miserable days in captivity, Durant got visitors. Suddenly the room was cleaned and the bedsheets were changed. Firimbi helped the pilot wash, redressed his wounds, gave him a clean shirt, and wrapped his midsection and legs in a *ma-awis,* the loose skirt worn by Somali men. Perfume was sprayed around the room.

Durant thought he was about to be released. Instead, Firimbi ushered in a visitor. She was Suzanne Hofstadter, a Norwegian who worked for the International Red Cross. Durant took her hand and held on tight. All she had been allowed to bring along were forms with which he could write a letter. In the letter Durant described his injuries and noted that he had received some medical treatment. He told his family he was doing okay, and asked them to pray for him and the others. He still didn't know the fate of his crew or D-boys Shughart and Gordon.

He wrote that he was craving a pizza. Then he asked Firimbi if he could write another letter to his buddies at the hangar, and his jailer said yes. He wrote that he was doing okay, and told them not to touch the bottle of Jack Daniels in his rucksack. Durant didn't have much time to think. He was trying to convey in a lighthearted way that he was okay, to lessen their worry for him. At the bottom of this note he wrote, "NSDQ."

Later, Red Cross officials, concerned about violating their strict neutrality by passing along what might be a coded message, scratched out the initials.

After Hofstadter left, two reporters were ushered in: Briton Mark Huband of the *Guardian* and Stephen Smith from the French newspaper *Liberation.* Huband found the pilot lying flat on his back, bare-chested, obviously injured and in pain. Durant was still choked up from the session with Hofstadter. He had held her hand until the last moment, unwilling to see her leave.

Huband and Smith had brought a recorder. They told him he didn't have to say anything. The reporters pitied Durant, and tried to reassure him. Huband said he'd done a lot of reporting in Somalia, and had developed a sense for when things were bad and when they weren't. He said his sense was that these people meant Durant no harm.

Durant weighed talking to them and decided it was better to communicate with the outside world than not. He agreed to discuss only the things that had happened to him since the crash. So with the tape recorder rolling, he briefly described the crash and his capture. Then Huband asked why the battle had happened, and why so many people had died. Durant said something he would later regret:

"Too many innocent people are getting killed. People are angry because they see civilians getting killed. I don't think anyone who doesn't live here can understand what is going wrong here. Americans mean well. We did try to help. Things have gone wrong."

It was that "things have gone wrong" line that haunted him after the reporters left. Who was he to pronounce a verdict on the American mission? He should have just said, "I'm a soldier and I do what I'm told."

He grew depressed. He really did believe things had gone wrong, but he felt he had stepped over a line by saying it.

Durant stayed down until the next day when he heard his wife Lorrie's voice on the BBC. She had made a statement to the press. He listened intently to her voice. At the end of her statement, Lorrie said four words that brought tears to his eyes. What she said were the four words whose initials the pilot had penned at the bottom of his note—still visible despite the Red Cross scratches. It was the motto of his unit, the 160th Special Operations Aviation Regiment.

Lorrie said, "Like you always say, Mike, *Night Stalkers Don't Quit.*"
His message of defiance had gotten through.

# 23

In the week following the battle, the men of Task Force Ranger worked through a broad range of emotions as they girded themselves for another fight. They were furious at the Somalis and filled with grief for their dead comrades. They felt disgust for the press that kept showing the horrible images of the dead soldiers being humiliated in the city, less than a mile or two from where they sat. They watched with frustration as a fresh Delta squadron and Ranger company arrived, and grudgingly accepted a backseat, although every man was prepared and expected to be sent back out into the city. They observed the swagger and casual boasting of the new arrivals with the weary eyes of experience. They all knew that if intel located Durant, they'd be going in with more force than Mogadishu had yet seen. The idea of making this fight was both terrifying and grimly necessary. It was a prospect they both dreaded and welcomed. It was odd that the two emotions could stand side by side. So the men who'd come through the battle unhurt worked to get their weapons, vehicles, minds, and hearts ready.

Then, two days after the fight, a Somali mortar round fell just outside the hangar and killed Sergeant Matt Rierson, leader of the Delta team that had first stormed the target house and taken the Somali targets captive, and whose resolve and experience had helped shore up the lost convoy during the worst of the fight. It seemed bitterly unfair to have come through the storm unhurt only to be felled while standing outside the hangar in idle conversation two days later. Severely injured with Rierson was Dr. Rob Marsh, the Delta surgeon. Alert though in great pain and bleeding profusely, Marsh helped direct the medics who gave him emergency care.

Rangers struggled to accept their profound losses. There was no doubt that they had more than held their own in the battle. What other ninety-nine men would have survived a long afternoon and night besieged by the well-armed angry citizenry of a city of more than a million? Still, each death mocked their former cockiness and appetite for battle. A whole generation of American soldiers had served careers without experiencing a horror of an all-out firefight. Now another had. There was a recognition in the faces of the survivors, a hard-won wisdom.

Sergeant Eversmann mentally replayed his every move during the battle, as he would still be doing years later, from the moment he accidentally tore the headphones out of the hovering Black Hawk to finding Private Blackburn broken and unconscious on the street, to watching his men get hit, one after the other, to that long and bloody ride on the lost convoy. Why had he kept them out on the street when the fire grew so bad? Shouldn't he have directed them to break down a door and move indoors? How did they get so lost on the ride back? He'd lost Casey Joyce on that ride. There was nothing he could have done about that. Word was that doctors might be able to save Scotty Galentine's thumb. They had sewed Galentine's hand with the thumb into his stomach, hoping to foster regeneration of the blood vessels they'd need to reconnect it. And word was that Blackburn was going to make it, too. He was conscious again, although he had no memory of his fall or anything else that happened on the street. He would recover, but never be the same guy his buddies remembered before the fall. The rest of the injuries were minor. But Eversmann had only about six of his guys left.

From Chalk One, the one led in by Captain Steele and Lieutenant Perino, they'd lost Jamie Smith, whose agonizing death at the first crash site would continue to haunt Perino and Sergeant Schmid, the Delta medic who'd torn open Smith's wound trying to save him. Smith's death would become the most controversial of the battle, since his was the one life that might have been saved if the force around Wolcott's crash site had been rescued sooner. Carlos Rodriguez, the Ranger shot in the crotch at crash site one, was going to recover as well. Dale Sizemore had fended off the doctors who still wanted him sent home because of his elbow. He paced the hangar hoping for another chance to avenge his friends. Steve Anderson wrestled with feelings of guilt. So many others had died or been hurt. Why had he escaped injury? He wasn't sure what made him angrier, the reluctance he'd felt about joining the fight or the politicians in Washington who'd gotten so many of his friends killed and hurt chasing a stupid warlord in Mogadishu. He would grow angrier and angrier brooding over it, and as time went by he was filled with distrust for the system he had enlisted to defend. Mike Goodale, his wounded thigh and rear end bandaged and healing, would be back home in Illinois with his girlfriend Kira before the week was out. Goodale asked Kira to marry him the first time he talked to her on the phone from Germany. He'd seen how short life could be and was determined not to put an important thing off ever again. Lieutenant Lechner faced a long recovery, as doctors at Walter Reed Army Hospital painstakingly stimulated bone growth to heal the hole an AK-47 round had driven through his shin. Undergoing virtually the same procedure in the bed next to his was Sergeant John Burns, whose lower leg had been shattered by a bullet on the lost convoy. Stebbins was home with his wife within the week. The garrulous company clerk would receive a Silver Star for his part in the fight, and was on his way to becoming a legend in the company, an example of how even those in the unit's least glamorous jobs were Rangers, too.

The ground convoy had been decimated. Only about half of the fifty-two men who had ridden out on October 3 were still at the hangar. Their vehicles were wrecked. Nearly all of the convoy's leaders had been injured and had been flown home, including Lieutenant Colonel Danny McKnight. Clay Othic and his buddy Eric Spalding were back home from Germany before the week was out. On the long transport flight home, his right arm still bandaged and disabled, Othic had scribbled a final entry in his Mogadishu diary with his unsteady left hand: "Sometimes you get the bear; sometimes the bear gets you." Within days, he and Spalding, their wounds bandaged and healing, made the drive home to Missouri they'd promised themselves to catch the end of deer-hunting season. Cruising the interstate in Spalding's pickup they listened to occasional radio reports about the unfinished business in Mogadishu, a million miles away.

Worst hit was the Delta squadron, which had lost the devout Dan Busch, little Earl Fillmore, Randy Shughart, Gary Gordon, Griz, and then Rierson. Brad Hallings, the Delta sniper whose leg was sheared off inside *Super Six Two*, would learn to get around so well on an artificial limb that he was able to rejoin the unit. Paul Leonard, who had the calf of his left leg blown away manning a Mark-19 on the lost convoy, would end up doing a long recuperation and rehab at Walter Reed with Burns, Lechner, Galentine, and some of the other more seriously injured guys. President Clinton visited them there one day about two weeks after the battle. He came without fanfare, and seemed shocked and uncharacteristically speechless when confronted with the flesh-and-blood consequences of the fight.

The men had been given curt instructions to keep their opinions of Clinton, if negative, to themselves. Galentine posed for a snapshot with the president, a T-shirt pulled over the hand sewed to his abdomen. In the snapshot both men looked equally startled to be in each other's company.

The war wasn't over yet in Mogadishu, however. The soldiers who had come through the fight unscathed expected things to get worse before they got better. They did what they could to salute their fallen brothers and move on. In the days following the battle the Night Stalkers erected a makeshift memorial before the JOC in memory of the men they'd lost. General Garrison assembled all of the men for a memorial service, and captured their feelings of sadness, fear, and resolve with the famous martial speech from Shakespeare's Henry V:

*Whoever does not have the stomach for this fight, let him depart. Give him money to speed his departure since we wish not to die in that man's company. Whoever lives past today and comes home safely will rouse himself every year on this day, show his neighbor his scars, and tell embellished stories of all their great feats of battle. These stories he will teach his son and from this day until the end of the world we shall be remembered. We few, we happy few, we band of brothers; for whoever has shed his blood with me shall be my brother. And those men afraid to go will think themselves lesser men as they hear of how we fought and died together.*

# 24

Willi Frank got the word about her husband exactly a week after he was reported missing. It had been a terrible week. Those who hadn't gotten final word on the fate of their men had continued to scrutinize the news photos and videotapes of the dead.

One of the most widely circulated shots of a body being dragged through the streets, the one with the left leg bent up awkwardly, was Tommie Field. The other of the dragged bodies, the one most often seen on TV, was Randy Shughart. The still photo of a body draped backward over a handcart was Bill Cleveland. There was no official confirmation from the army, but the families knew.

Willi was attending the funeral service for Cliff Wolcott when she heard beepers go off in several places around the church. Two of the beepers that sounded were held by members of her support unit.

They took her aside after the service. Willi thought they were escorting her to spend a few minutes with Chris Wolcott. Instead, they told her Ray's body had been identified.

"How do you know it was Ray?" she asked them. "Was his hair gray?"

The hair was gone on the body, they said, but they described his remains. The body had been clothed, they told her. She asked them to describe the pants, the underpants. Ray had left on such short notice that Willi hadn't had time to dry out his military skivvies. Instead she'd packed his civilian underwear. When they told her what kind of shorts he was wearing, she knew.

# 25

In his second week of captivity, Durant was moved again, this time to what appeared to be a private residence with a perimeter fence. He was given a box of gifts from the Red Cross. One of the items in the box was a pocket Bible.

Keeping track of time was one of the skills Durant had been taught in survival training. Prisoners of war in Vietnam had found that having some sense of time elapsed and ordering the events of each day, no matter how mundane, helped to keep them sane. Keeping a record was an act of faith. It implied you would eventually be released and have a story to tell.

He was not an especially religious man, but Durant found his own use for the Bible. He began reconstructing the events of his captivity in the margins of it, using code words, beginning with his crash. He wrote:

"Bump," recalling the sensation of being hit by the RPG.

"Spin."

"Horizon," for the blurring of earth and sky as the chopper spun down.

And so forth. He pressed on, eventually reconstructing the entire term of his captivity almost hour by hour. The margins of the Bible were beginning to fill with his jottings.

Firimbi watched the pilot studying and making notes in his Bible and assumed Durant was a very religious man.

"If you convert to Islam, you will be freed," the captor said.

"You pray to your God, and I'll pray to mine, and maybe we'll both be released," Durant joked.

On the radio they played selections of music that Durant liked.

During one of his nights in captivity, Durant had a dream. He dreamed he was one of the Rangers, and that he was supposed to get on a chopper with Chalk Four. Instead he stumbled blindly, asking, "Where's Chalk Four? Where's Chalk Four?" He didn't recognize the faces of the people he was questioning. Suddenly, everyone else in the dream was gone. Overhead a chopper rose into the sky and flew off, leaving him alone on the ground.

# 26

When Robert Oakley arrived in Mogadishu on October 8, Aidid was still in hiding. It took several days to arrange, but he eventually met with the warlord's clan. He told the Habr Gidr leaders that the U.S. military operation against Aidid was over and that Task Force Ranger's original mission had ended. The Somalis were skeptical.

"You'll see for yourself over time that it's true," Oakley said. Then he told them that President Clinton wanted Durant released immediately, without conditions. The Somalis were incredulous. The Rangers had rounded up sixty or seventy men from their leadership. The top men, including the two most important men taken on October 3, Omar Salad and Mohamed Hassan Awale, were being held in a makeshift prison camp on an island off the coast of Kismayo. Any release of Durant would at least involve a trade. That was the Somali way.

"I'll do my best to see that these people are released, but I can't promise anything," Oakley said, pointing out that the Somalis were, technically, in the custody of the UN. "I'll talk to the president about it, but only after you've released Durant."

Then the former ambassador delivered a chilling message. He was careful to say, "This is not a threat," but the meaning was plain.

"I have no plan for this, and I'll do everything I can to prevent it, but what will happen if a few weeks go by and Mr. Durant is not released? Not only will you lose any credit you may get now, but we will decide that we have to rescue him. I guarantee you we are not going to pay or trade for him in any way, shape, or form. . . . So what we'll decide is we have to rescue him, and whether we have the right place or the wrong place, there's going to be a fight with your people. The minute the guns start again, all restraint on the U.S. side goes. Just look at the stuff coming in here now. An aircraft carrier, tanks, gunships . . . the works. Once the fighting starts, all this pent-up anger is going to be released. This whole part of the city will be destroyed, men, women, children, camels, cats, dogs, goats, donkeys, everything. . . . That would really be tragic for all of us, but that's what will happen."

The Somalis delivered this message to Aidid in hiding, and the warlord saw the wisdom of Oakley's advice. He offered to hand the pilot over immediately.

Mindful of not upstaging his old friend Admiral Howe, Oakley asked them to delay for a few hours to give him time to leave the country. He asked them to turn Durant over to Howe, and he flew back to Washington.

# 27

Firimbi told Durant he was going to be released the next day. The propaganda minister was very happy to deliver this news, but also very nervous. He was happy for his friend and for himself. He joked that both of them were going to be released. Firimbi would be free to go back to his normal life. He thought releasing Durant without any conditions was a stunning demonstration of Aidid and Habr Gidr munificence. He got choked up just talking about it. This gesture, he said, would undo at a stroke the awful images of the mob mutilating dead American soldiers, a scene that embarrassed Firimbi and other educated men of his clan. He repeatedly urged Durant to reassure him that he would tell the world how well he had been treated in captivity.

The decision was such a good one, Firimbi grew afraid something would spoil it. What if an angry faction of Somalis got wind of the deal and came looking for Durant to kill him? What if the Americans were setting them up? The Americans could send someone to kill Durant, and the world would believe Aidid and the Habr Gidr had done it. Firimbi requested more protection, and the clan ringed the residence where Durant was held with armed men.

That morning, Firimbi helped Durant wash. This time, instead of being thrown in the back of a car and sat on, men arrived with a litter to carry him out gently and placed him in the back of a flatbed truck. Durant knew this was it. He would be nervous until he was back in American hands, but Firimbi was so happy and excited he knew that it was true.

They drove him to a walled compound and waited. When Red Cross officials arrived, an army doctor came in with the team and examined him. He wanted to give the pilot a shot for the pain, but Firimbi said no. He was afraid the doctor would poison Durant.

The pilot was handed over without ceremony. Red Cross officials gave him a letter from Lorrie and from his parents that they had been unable to deliver. The doctor who examined him emerged from the compound to tell reporters that the pilot had a broken leg, a shattered cheekbone, a fractured back, and relatively minor bullet wounds to his leg and shoulder, but had been treated well by his captors.

"The leg was in a splint, but it hasn't been set and is quite painful," the doctor said.

Then he was carried out by Red Cross officials. Durant clutched the letter and tears rolled from his eyes as he was carried past reporters and driven back to the airport Ranger base where he had taken off eleven days earlier.

Every American who survived the Battle of Mogadishu would be home within the month. Most would stay bitter about the decision to call off their mission. If it had been important enough to get eighteen men killed, and seventy-three injured, not to mention all the Somalis dead or hurt, how could it just be called off the day after the fight? Within weeks of Durant's release, American Marines (at Oakley's direction) would escort Aidid to renewed peace negotiations. President Clinton would accept Oakley's plea on behalf of the Somali leaders. Several months later Omar Salad, Mohamed Hassan Awale, and every man captured by Task Force Ranger was released.

The reinforced task force was waiting for Durant when the Red Cross convoy arrived at the airport. They had turned out, a force now of more than a thousand, dressed in khaki fatigues and floppy desert hats, glad to at last have something to celebrate. They formed a corridor leading from the base driveway to the platform of the transport plane that would carry Durant to Germany, where Lorrie had flown and was waiting for him. The men all had paper cups with a swallow of bourbon, ostensibly from the fifth of Jack Daniels the pilot had stashed in his rucksack and warned his buddies, in his note from captivity, to keep their hands off.

It was a day of joy and enormous relief, but also a day of sadness. Durant had just learned that he would be the only man from the crew of *Super Six Four* and its two brave Delta defenders to come back alive. He smiled and fought back tears as he was carried through the corridor on a litter, an IV in his arm, clutching his unit's red beret.

The men around him cheered and then, as the stretcher approached the ramp to the plane, they began to sing. The song started in one or two places at first, boldly, then spread to every voice.

They sang "God Bless America."

# EPILOGUE

The Battle of the Black Sea, or as the Somalis call it, *Ma-alinti Rangers* (The Day of the Rangers), is one that America has preferred to forget. The images it produced of dead soldiers dragged by jeering mobs through the streets of Mogadishu are among the most horrible and disturbing in our history, made all the worse by the good intentions that prompted our intervention. There were no American reporters in Mogadishu on October 3–4, 1993, and after a week or so of frenzied attention, world events quickly summoned journalists elsewhere. President Clinton's decision just days after the fight to end Task Force Ranger's mission to Somalia accomplished what he intended; it slammed the door on the episode. In Washington a whiff of failure is enough to induce widespread amnesia. There was a Senate investigation and two days of congressional hearings that produced a partisan report blaming the president and Secretary of Defense Les Aspin, who resigned two months later, but that was it.

Even inside the military, where one might expect to find strong professional interest in the biggest firefight involving American soldiers since Vietnam, there appears to have been little in the way of a detailed postmortem. Proper respects were paid to the dead, and the heroism of many soldiers formally honored, but beyond that, if the battle's decorated veterans are to be believed, the battle is a lost chapter.

When I began working on this project in 1996, my goal was simply to write a dramatic account of the battle. I had been struck by the intensity of the fight, and by the notion of ninety-nine American soldiers surrounded and trapped in an ancient African city fighting for their lives. My contribution would be to capture in words the experience of combat through the eyes and emotions of the soldiers involved, blending their urgent, human perspective with a military and political overview of their predicament. With the exception of great fiction and several extremely well written memoirs, the nonfiction accounts of modern war I'd read were primarily written by historians. I wanted to combine the authority of a historical narrative with the emotion of the memoir, and write a story that read like fiction but was true. Since I was starting my work three years after the battle, I expected the historical portion of the work had already been done. Surely somewhere in the Pentagon or White House there was a thick volume of after-action reports and exhibits detailing the fight and critiquing our military performance. The challenge, I thought, would be fighting to get as much of it as possible declassified. I was wrong.

No such thick volume exists. While the Battle of the Black Sea may well be the most thoroughly documented incident in American military history, to my surprise no one had even begun to collect all that raw information into a definitive account. So instead of just writing a more vivid version of the story, I found myself in the lucky and exciting position of breaking new ground.

In the months since portions of this book premiered as a newspaper series in *The Philadelphia Inquirer,* I have spoken to hundreds of active U.S. military officers whom I met at conferences or seminars, or who contacted me seeking copies of the newspaper series or more detailed information about certain aspects of the fight. Among that number have been teachers at the military academies and the Army War College in Carlisle, Pennsylvania, the National Defense Analysis Institute, the Military Operations Research Society, officers at the U.S. Marine Corps' training base at Parris Island, the Security Studies Program at MIT, and even the U.S. Central Command, where the commander, General Anthony Zinni, invited me to take part in a seminar before his staff at MacDill Air Force Base in Tampa, Florida. I was flattered in every instance, but uneasy with the idea that our armed forces would rely on a journalist with no military background to inform them about a battle fought by many men who are still on active duty. As one of the former Delta team leaders remarked after hearing of yet another invitation I'd received, "Why aren't they talking to us?"

One reason why the battle had not been seriously studied is that the units involved, primarily Delta Force and the Rangers, operate in secrecy, and so much official information about the battle remains classified. It seems the military is best at keeping secrets from itself. But the bigger reason, I suspect, is the same one that sent politicians diving for cover. The Battle of the Black Sea was perceived outside the special operations community as a failure.

It was not, at least in strictly military terms. Task Force Ranger dropped into a teeming market in the heart of Mogadishu in the middle of a busy Sunday afternoon to surprise and arrest two lieutenants of warlord Mohamed Farrah Aidid. It was a complex, difficult, and dangerous assignment, and despite terrible setbacks and losses, and against overwhelming odds, the mission was accomplished.

It was, of course, a Pyrrhic victory. The mission was supposed to take about an hour. Instead, a large portion of the assault force was stranded through a long night in a hostile city, surrounded and fighting for their lives. Two of their high-tech MH-60 Black Hawk helicopters went down in the city, and two more crash-landed back at the base. When the force was extricated the following morning by a huge multinational rescue convoy, eighteen Americans were dead and dozens more were badly injured. One, Black Hawk pilot Michael Durant, had been carried off by an angry Somali mob and would be held captive for eleven days. News of the casualties and images of gleeful Somalis abusing American corpses prompted revulsion and outrage at home, embarrassment at the White House, and such vehement objections in Congress that the mission against Aidid was immediately called off. Major General William F. Garrison's men may have won the battle, but, as he'd predicted, they lost the war.

The victory was even more hollow for Somalia, although it's not clear even five years later how many people there understand that. The fight itself was a terrible mismatch. The Somali death toll was catastrophic. Conservative counts numbered five hundred dead among more than a thousand casualties. Aidid could and did claim that his clan had driven off the world's mightiest military machine. The Habr Gidr had successfully resisted UN efforts to force him to share power. The clan now celebrates October 3 as a national holiday—if such a thing is possible where there is no nation. The pullout of American forces, months after the battle, aborted the UN's effort to establish a stable coalition government there. Aidid died in 1996 without uniting Somalia under his rule, a victim of the factional fighting the UN had tried to resolve. His clan still struggles with rivals in Mogadishu, trapped in the same bloody, anarchic standoff. Clan leaders I spoke with in that destroyed city in the summer of 1997 seemed to think that the world was still watching their progress anxiously. Photographer Peter Tobia and I were the only guests at the Hotel Sahafi during most of our stay there. We were the first and only Americans who have returned to Mogadishu trying to piece together exactly what happened. I told the Habr Gidr leaders who were hostile to our project that this would likely be their only chance to tell their side of the story, because there weren't journalists and scholars lined up at the border. The larger world has forgotten Somalia. The great ship of international goodwill has sailed. The bloody twists and turns of Somali clan politics no longer concern us. Without natural resources, strategic advantage, or even potentially lucrative markets for world goods, Somalia is unlikely soon to recapture the opportunity for peace and rebuilding afforded by UNOSOM. Rightly or wrongly, they stand as an enduring symbol of Third World ingratitude and intractability, of the futility of trying to resolve local animosity with international muscle. They've effectively written themselves off the map.

Nobody won the Battle of the Black Sea, but like all important battles, it changed the world. The awful price of the arrests of two obscure clan functionaries named Omar Salad and Mohamed Hassan Awale rightly shocked President Clinton, who reportedly felt betrayed by his military advisers and staff, much as an equally inexperienced President Kennedy had felt in 1961 after the Bay of Pigs. It led to the resignation of Defense Secretary Les Aspin and destroyed the promising career of General Garrison, who commanded Task Force Ranger. It aborted a hopeful and unprecedented UN effort to salvage a nation so lost in anarchy and civil war that millions of its people were starving. It ended a brief heady period of post–Cold War innocence, a time when America and its allies felt they could sweep venal dictators and vicious tribal violence from the planet as easily and relatively bloodlessly as Saddam Hussein had been swept from Kuwait. Mogadishu has had a profound cautionary influence on U.S. military policy ever since.

"It was a watershed," says one State Department official, who asked not to be named because his insight runs so counter to our current foreign policy agenda. "The idea used to be that terrible countries were terrible because good, decent, innocent people were being oppressed by evil, thuggish leaders. Somalia changed that. Here you have a country where just about everybody is caught up in hatred and fighting. You stop an old lady on the street and ask her if she wants peace, and she'll say, yes, of course, I pray for it daily. All the things you'd expect her to say. Then ask her if she would be willing for her clan to share power with another in order to have that peace, and she'll say, 'With those murderers and thieves? I'd die first.' People in these countries—Bosnia is a more recent example—don't want peace. They want victory. They want power. Men, women, old and young. Somalia was the experience that taught us that people in these places bear much of the responsibility for things being the way they are. The hatred and the killing continues because they want it to. Or because they don't want peace enough to stop it."

So, for better or worse, the USS *Harlan County* was turned away from the dock at Port-au-Prince one week after the Mogadishu fight by an orchestrated "riot" of fewer than two hundred Haitians. The U.S. government (and the UN) looked on as genocidal spasms killed a million people in Rwanda and Zaire, and as atrocity was piled on atrocity in Bosnia. There was some cynical posturing in the White House and Congress after the Battle of the Black Sea about never again placing U.S. troops under UN command, when everyone involved understood perfectly well that Task Force Ranger and even the QRF were under direct U.S. command at all times. Even the decision to target Aidid and his clansmen was driven by the U.S. State Department. The single most forceful advocate for Task Force Ranger's mission in Mogadishu was U.S. Admiral Jonathan Howe, a former deputy on the National Security Council during the Bush administration, who was the top UN official on site in Mogadishu. Task Force Ranger was wholly an American production.

Congress moved quickly to apportion blame. Hadn't Aspin turned down an initial Task Force Ranger request for the AC-130 gunship, and again, just weeks before the fateful raid, rejected a request for Abrams tanks and Bradley armored vehicles from General Thomas Montgomery, QRF commander? It seems fairly obvious that a light infantry force trapped in a hostile city would be better off with armored vehicles to pull them out, and few aerial firing platforms are as deadly effective as the AC-130 Spectre. Many of the men who fought in Mogadishu believe that at least some, if not all, of their friends would have survived the mission if the Clinton administration had been more concerned about force protection than maintaining the correct political posture. Aspin himself, before he stepped down, acknowledged that his decision on the force request had been an error. The 1994 Senate Armed Services Committee investigation of the battle reached the same conclusions. The initial postmortem on the battle was summed up in a powerful statement to the committee by Lieutenant Colonel Larry Joyce, U.S. Army retired, the father of Sergeant Casey Joyce, one of the Rangers killed.

"Why were they denied armor, these forces? Had there been armor, had there been Bradleys there, I contend that my son would probably be alive today, because he, like the other casualties that were sustained in the early phases of the battle, were killed en route from the target to the downed helicopter site, the first crash site. I believe there was an inadequate force structure from the very beginning."

This is the line picked up by David Hackworth, the retired U.S. Army colonel who has made a second career writing about the military. Hackworth devotes a chapter of his 1996 book, *Hazardous Duty*, to the battle. Pausing to vent his disappointment with not having been invited to observe the action with the Rangers, he calls Garrison "inept" and accuses the White House and military brass of "striking heroic poses," by not putting "their weapons systems where their mouths were." Hackworth calculated that tanks would have spared six killed and thirty wounded. There are telling inaccuracies in Hackworth's account, and it lacks even the pretense of fairness, but the colonel's critique has nevertheless shaped understanding of the fight both in and out of the military. Garrison is the butt of his assault. He incorrectly suggests that the general was directing the battle from a helicopter overhead, and even quotes one of the platoon sergeants on the ground wishing that he'd had a "Stinger," to shoot the general down (anyone who fought in Mogadishu that day would have known Garrison was not in the command helicopter). Hackworth concludes that Garrison should have refused to conduct the operation when the initial force package was trimmed. He quotes Joyce as follows: "Initially, I gave Garrison the benefit of the doubt, but the more Rangers I've talked to, the clearer it became that he had no good reason to launch the raid the way he did. The tactics were completely flawed. Garrison was a cowboy going for his third star at the expense of his guys."

From a man who lost his son in the fight, this is a terrible accusation.

I lack the standing to critique the military decisions made by Garrison and his men that day, but the work I have done on *Black Hawk Down* does qualify me to report authoritatively on the memories, feelings, and opinions of the men who fought. I have interviewed more Rangers, Delta soldiers, and helicopter pilots who were involved in the battle than anyone, and I have yet to meet one who expressed the opinions of the mission or of Garrison reported by Hackworth. The men who undertook the raid on October 3 were confident of their tactics and training and committed to their goals. While many offered incisive criticism of decisions large and small made before and during the fight, and differed substantially with their commanders on some points, they remain proud of successfully completing their mission. I was struck by how little bitterness there is among the men who underwent this ordeal. What anger exists relates more to the decision to call off the mission the day after the battle than anything that happened during it. The record shows that in the weeks prior to this raid, Garrison took more heat for being too careful about launching missions than doing so recklessly. The general, who retired in 1996 after a stint heading the JFK School of Special Warfare at Fort Bragg, is held in universally high regard by the men who served under him.

Garrison took full responsibility for the outcome of the battle in a handwritten letter to President Clinton the day after the fight. This letter has been called a ploy by the general's critics, although one strains to see what advantage he gained by writing it. It is a document that speaks plainly for itself, the honorable act of an honorable man—and one who clearly feels no shame for the way he or his men conducted themselves in the fight:

I. *The authority, responsibility and accountability for the Op rests here in MOG with the TF Ranger commander, not in Washington.*

II. *Excellent intelligence was available on the target.*

III. *Forces were experienced in area as a result of six previous operations.*

IV. *Enemy situation was well known: Proximity to Bakara Market (SNA strongpoint); previous reaction times of bad guys.*

V. *Planning for the Op was bottom up not top down. Assaulters were confident it was a doable operation. Approval of plan was retained by TF Ranger commander.*

VI. *Techniques, tactics and procedures were appropriate for mission/ target.*

VII. *Reaction forces were planned for contingencies: A.) CSAR on immediate standby (UH60 with medics and security).*

VIII. *Loss of 1st Helo was supportable. Pilot pinned in wreckage presented problem.*

IX. *2nd Helo crash required response from the 10th Mtn. QRF. The area of the crash was such that SNA were there nearly immediately so we were unsuccessful in reaching the crash site in time.*

X.   *Rangers on 1st crash site were not pinned down. They could have fought their way out. Our creed would not allow us to leave the body of the pilot pinned in the wreckage.*

XI.   *Armor reaction force would have helped but casualty figures may or may not have been different. The type of men in the task force simply would not be denied in their mission of getting to their fallen comrades.*

XII.   *The mission was a success. Targeted individuals were captured and extracted from the target.*

XIII.   *For this particular target, President Clinton and Sec. Aspin need to be taken off the blame line.*

*William F. Garrison*
*MG*
*Commanding*

While the facts support Garrison's accounting overall, I believe he is wrong in this letter on several counts. Only part of points IV and VII are supported by the evidence. Aidid's tactics were well-known, and the task force's planning was effective, but only to a point. The Black Hawk helicopter proved more vulnerable to RPG fire than anticipated. Once two of them crashed (three others were crippled but made it back to friendly ground), the task force's "techniques, tactics and procedures" were stretched beyond their limits. There was clearly insufficient reaction force standing by to rescue the pilots and crew of *Super Six Two*, Michael Durant's helicopter. The CSAR bird was the primary contingency for a helicopter crash. It was a well-stocked, superbly trained chopper full of expert rescuers and ground fighters. They were deployed minutes after the crash of Cliff Wolcott's *Super Six One*, and were instrumental in rescuing a portion of the crew and recovering the bodies of Wolcott and copilot Donovan Briley. But when Durant's Black Hawk crashed twenty minutes later, there was no such rescue force at hand. Durant and his crew had to await (tragically, as it turned out) the arrival of a ground rescue force.

Prior to launching the mission, Garrison had alerted the 10th Mountain Division, the QRF, but had decided to let them stay at the UN compound north of the city instead of moving them down to the task force's airport base. They were promptly summoned after Wolcott's Black Hawk crashed, but moved to the Ranger base by such a roundabout route (avoiding crossing through the city) that they didn't arrive until fifty minutes after the first helicopter crash (almost a half hour after Durant's helicopter went down). So for the first thirty minutes Durant and his crew were on the ground, the only rescue force Garrison could muster was a hastily assembled convoy comprised mostly of support personnel, well-trained soldiers all, but men whom no one anticipated throwing into the fight. Ultimately neither this convoy nor the QRF could fight their way in. They were barred by blockades and ambushes that Aidid's militias had plenty of time to prepare. The task force knew that it would encounter trouble if it took longer than thirty minutes to get in and out of the target, but few anticipated how many RPGs Aidid's fighters would bring to the fight. The price was paid in downed Black Hawks.

Garrison's point X is also debatable. The men I interviewed who spent the night around the first crashed Black Hawk say they were pinned down. In strictly military terms, being pinned down means a force can do nothing. Arguably, if Task Force Ranger's commanders had wanted to move the force out of the city they could have. More intensive air support was available in the form of Cobra attack helicopters attached to the QRF. But no such decision was made, and from the perspective of the men on the ground, they were pinned down. This is the opinion of everyone I interviewed, from the ranking officers to the lowliest privates. While it may have been possible to fight their way back to the base on foot, the men believe they would have sustained terrible losses. The men on the lost convoy took better than 50 percent casualties moving through the streets in vehicles. The force at crash site one would have had to carry their dead and wounded. The men holed up with Captain Steele at the southern end of the perimeter on Marehan Road balked at having to move one block on foot at the height of the battle. There is no doubt Garrison's men, if so ordered, would have tried to fight their way out, but they stayed put for reasons that went beyond loyalty to the pinned body of Chief Warrant Officer Cliff Wolcott. Arguing otherwise puts a noble cast to the predicament, but falls short of the facts.

The rest of Garrison's statement squares well with the facts. The president and Secretary of Defense of course bear ultimate responsibility for any actions of the U.S. military, but without the advantage of hindsight, their decisions regarding the deployment of Task Force Ranger are defensible. Trimming the AC-130 gunship from the initial force request, in light of growing congressional pressure to bring the troops home from Somalia, seems particularly so. Garrison himself felt the gunship was not only unnecessary, but likely to be a less effective firing platform over a densely populated urban neighborhood than the AH-6 Little Birds. If both the Little Birds and the gunship had been in the air, one or the other would have been severely restricted. The small helicopters, flying below the gunship, would have had to clear out to avoid crossing the gunship's fire. As it was, the Little Birds provided extremely effective air support throughout the battle. To a man, the soldiers pinned down around the first crash site credit brave and skillful Little Birds' pilots with keeping the Somali crowds at bay. The Somali fighters we interviewed in Mogadishu agreed. They believe the helicopters were the only thing that prevented a total rout of the pinned-down force. Soldiers trapped around the wrecked chopper understandably found themselves longing for the devastating firepower of the AC-130, which could have carved out a corridor of fire for their escape. But command concerns about limiting collateral damage were legitimate. The corridor of fire envisioned by the men on the ground would have pulverized a wide swath of Mogadishu, likely killing many more noncombatants than Aidid's fighters. Support for the gunship was lukewarm on up the ranks, all the way to General Colin Powell, who in his final weeks as chairman of the Joint Chiefs of Staff acquiesced without complaint to the decision. Interviewed for this book, Powell said that while he formally endorsed the entire force request, even in retrospect he could not fault Aspin's decision to trim the gunship.

Garrison's task force never requested or envisioned armor as part of its force package. Its tactics were to strike with surprise and speed, and up until October 3, those tactics worked. It is fair for military experts to criticize Garrison's judgment in this, but hardly fair to accuse Aspin of turning down a request the task force never made. General Montgomery asked for Abrams tanks and Bradley vehicles in late September for his QRFs, and these were turned down, again because of pressure in Washington to lower, not raise, the American military presence in Mogadishu. It is easy to dismiss these pressures as effete concerns, but strong congressional support is vital to sustain any military venture. In our system of government, everything requires a balancing act. At that point, any move that appeared to be deepening America's commitment to the military option in Mogadishu weakened support for it. Even if Montgomery had gotten his Bradleys, it's questionable what impact they would have had in the battle. It is doubtful they would have been in place by October 3. Since they would have been assigned to the 10th Mountain Division, they would not have been part of the Ranger ground reaction force. Lieutenant Colonel Joyce has argued that Bradleys might have saved his son's life, but since the armor would have been assigned to a unit across the city that was not thrown into the fight until after Sergeant Joyce was killed, it's hard to see how. The rescue force that finally did extricate the men pinned down at crash site one came in with armor, Pakistani tanks and Malaysian APCs. It may have arrived faster if the QRF had been equipped with the superior Bradleys, but the one soldier who died awaiting rescue, Corporal Jamie Smith, bled to death early in the evening. The rescue column would have had to have left four or five hours before it did to save his life, assuming surgeons could have saved him—by no means a definite thing. Again, the quarrel is over Garrison's call, not with weak-kneed Washington politicians undercutting forces in the field. Maybe Garrison, General Wayne Downing, General Joseph Hoar, General Powell, and the rest of the military command should have insisted on armor and the AC-130 from the start. They didn't. I believe these are issues over which well-meaning military experts differ. But it was, as the general noted in his letter, his call.

The suggestion that Garrison and his men should have refused to fight without getting their full force request puts me in mind of General George McClellan, whose battle-shy Union army stayed safely encamped for years demanding more and more resources. President Lincoln finally fired him for suffering a terminal case of "the slows." The men of Task Force Ranger were daring, ambitious soldiers. They were more inclined to think in terms of working with what they had than refusing to work until they got everything they wanted.

As battles go, Mogadishu was a minor engagement. General Powell has pointed out that the deaths of eighteen American soldiers in Vietnam would not have even warranted a press conference. Old soldiers may snort over the fuss generated by this gunfight, but it speaks well of America that our threshold for death and injury to our soldiers has been so significantly lowered. This does not mean that military action is never worth the danger, or the price. Our armed forces will be called upon again to intervene in obscure parts of the world—as they already have in Bosnia. To prepare for these twenty-first-century missions, there are probably few more important case studies than this one.

The mistakes made in Mog weren't because people in charge didn't care enough, or weren't smart enough. It's too easy to dismiss errors by blaming the commanders. It assumes there exists a cadre of brilliant officers who know all the answers before the questions are even asked. How many airborne rescue teams should there have been? One for every Black Hawk and Little Bird in the sky? Some of the failures deserve further study. During the battle, efforts to steer the lost convoy from the air turned into a black comedy. At risk of a cliché, how is it that a nation that could land an unmanned little go-cart on the surface of Mars couldn't steer a convoy five blocks through the streets of Mogadishu? Why did it take the QRF fifty minutes to arrive at the task force's base when things started to go bad? Shouldn't they have been better positioned at the outset? But these are all questions that are only obvious in retrospect. The truth is, Task Force Ranger came within several minutes of pulling off its mission on October 3 without a hitch. If Black Hawk *Super Six One* had not been hit, the "bad" choices made by Garrison would have been called bold. We will never know if Admiral Jonathan Howe was right to believe a lasting peace might have been achieved in Somalia if Aidid had been captured or his clan dismantled as a military force. It seems unlikely. In the years since the warlord's death, little in Mogadishu has changed. The Habr Gidr is a large and powerful clan planted deep in Somalia's past and present political culture. To think that 450 superb American soldiers could uproot it violently, thereby clearing the way for, as General Powell puts it, "an outbreak of Jeffersonian democracy," seems far-fetched. In the end, the Battle of the Black Sea is another lesson in the limits of what force can accomplish.

I began working on this story about two-and-a-half years after the battle was fought. I had been intrigued by the early accounts of the fight, both as a citizen and as a writer. It was clearly an important and fascinating episode, one with tragic consequences for many and lasting implications for American foreign policy. Given the fierce but limited nature of the gunfight—a small force of Americans pinned down overnight in an African city—I realized that it might be possible to tell the whole story. But the undertaking intimidated me. I had no military background or

Black Hawk Down 343

sources, and assumed that someone with both would tell the story far better than I could.

Nevertheless I remained curious enough to read whatever stories I saw about the incident. I was especially intrigued by President Clinton's subsequent struggles to deal with it. Particularly poignant were newspaper accounts I read of Clinton's meetings with the parents of the men killed in the battle. Larry Joyce and Jim Smith, the father of Corporal Jamie Smith, had reportedly questioned the president sharply in one of those meetings. I wondered about the informal visit the president paid to soldiers wounded in Mogadishu as they recuperated at Walter Reed Army Hospital. How did those men feel about meeting with the man who had sent them on the mission, and then abruptly called it off? At the Medal of Honor ceremony for the two Delta soldiers, I read that the father of posthumous honoree Sergeant Randy Shughart insulted the president, telling him he was not fit to be commander in chief.

When I was asked by *The Philadelphia Inquirer* to profile President Clinton in its magazine as he ran for reelection, I tried to answer some of these questions. Interviewing some of the families for an account of their session at the White House, I drove up to Long Valley, New Jersey, one spring afternoon to meet with Jim Smith, a retired U.S. Army captain and former Ranger who had lost a leg in Vietnam. Jim and I sat in his den for several hours. He described the meeting with Clinton, and then talked at length about his son Jamie, how it had felt to lose him, and what little he knew about the battle and how his son had died. I left his house that day determined to find out more.

My initial requests to the Pentagon media office were naive and went nowhere. I filed Freedom of Information requests for documents that, two years later, I have not received. I was told the men I wanted to interview were in units off-limits to the press. My only hope of finding the foot soldiers I wanted was to ask for them by name, and I knew only a handful of names. I combed through what little had been written about the battle, and submitted the names I found there, but I did not receive a response. Then Jim Smith sent me an invitation. The army was dedicating a building at the Pixatinny Arsenal near his home in memory of Jamie. I debated whether to drive up. It would take the whole day and, with my lack of success, the story had receded in priority. Still, I had been moved by my conversation with Jim. I have sons just a few years younger than his Jamie.

I couldn't imagine losing one of them, much less in a gunfight someplace like Mogadishu. I made the drive.

And there, at this dedication ceremony, were about a dozen Rangers who had fought with Jamie in Mogadishu. Jim's introduction helped break down the normal suspicion soldiers have for reporters. The men gave me their names and told me how to arrange interviews with them. Over three days at Fort Benning that fall I conducted my first twelve interviews. Each of the men I talked to had names and phone numbers for others who had fought there that day, many of them no longer in the army. My network grew from there. Nearly everyone I contacted was eager to talk. In the summer of 1997, the *Inquirer* sent Peter Tobia and me to Mogadishu. We flew to Nairobi, paid our weight in *khat*, climbed in the back of a small plane with sacks of the drug, and flew to a dirt airstrip outside Mogadishu. Accompanied by Ibrahim Roble Farah, a Nairobi businessman and member of the clan, we spent just seven days in the city, long enough to walk the streets where the battle had taken place and to interview some of the men who had fought against American soldiers that day. We learned how Somalis had perceived the sometimes brutal tactics in the summer of 1993, as UN troops led a clumsy manhunt for Aidid, and how widespread appreciation for the humanitarian intervention had turned to hatred. Peter and I left with a feel for the place, for the futility of its local politics, and some insight into why Somalis fought so bitterly against American soldiers that day.

In the months after I returned, I found military officers who were eager to hear what I could tell them about the Somali perspective, and about the battle. My work from the ground up eventually led me to a treasure of official information. The fifteen-hour battle had been videotaped from a variety of platforms, so the action I had painstakingly pieced together in my mind through interviews could be checked against images of the actual fight. The hours of radio traffic during the battle had been recorded and transcribed. This would provide actual dialogue from the midst of the action and was invaluable in helping to sort out the precise sequence of events. It also conveyed, with frightening immediacy, the horror of it, the feel of men struggling to stave off panic and stay alive. Other documents fleshed out the intelligence background of the assault, exactly what Task Force Ranger knew and was trying to accomplish. None of the men on the ground, caught up completely in their own small corner of the fight, had a complete vision of the battle. But their memories, combined with this documentary material, including a precise chronology and the written accounts of Delta operators and SEALs, made it possible for me to reconstruct the whole picture. This material gave me, I believe, the best chance any writer has ever had to tell the story of a battle completely, accurately, and well.

Every battle is a drama played out apart from broader issues. Soldiers cannot concern themselves with the forces that bring them to a fight, or its aftermath. They trust their leaders not to risk their lives for too little. Once the battle is joined, they fight to survive as much as to win, to kill before they are killed. The story of combat is timeless. It is about the same things whether in Troy or Gettysburg, Normandy or the Ia Drang. It is about soldiers, most of them young, trapped in a fight to the death. The extreme and terrible nature of war touches something essential about being human, and soldiers do not always like what they learn. For those who survive, the victors and the defeated, the battle lives on in their memories and nightmares and in the dull ache of old wounds. It survives as hundreds of searing private memories, memories of loss and triumph, shame and pride, struggles each veteran must refight every day of his life.

No matter how critically history records the policy decisions that led up to this fight, nothing can diminish the professionalism and dedication of the Rangers and Special Forces units who fought there that day. The Special Forces units showed in Mogadishu why it is important for the military to keep and train highly motivated, talented, and experienced soldiers. When things went to hell in the streets, it was in large part the men of Delta and the SEALs who held things together and got most of the force out alive.

Many of the young Americans who fought in the Battle of Mogadishu are civilians again. They are beginning families and careers, no different outwardly than the millions of other twenty-something members of their generation. They are creatures of pop culture who grew up singing along with *Sesame Street*, shuttling to day care, and navigating today's hyperadolescence through the pitfalls of drugs and unsafe sex. Their experience of battle, unlike that of any other generation of American soldiers, was colored by a lifetime of watching the vivid gore of Hollywood action movies. In my interviews with those who were in the thick of the battle, they remarked again and again how much they felt like they were *in a movie*, and had to remind themselves that this horror, the blood, the deaths, was real.

They describe feeling weirdly out of place, as though *they did not belong here*, fighting feelings of disbelief, anger, and ill-defined betrayal. *This cannot be real.* Many wear black metal bracelets inscribed with the names of their friends who died, as if to remind themselves daily that it was real. To look at them today, few show any outward sign that one day not too long ago they risked their lives in an ancient African city, killed for their country, took a bullet, or saw their best friend shot dead. They returned to a country that didn't care or remember. Their fight was neither triumph nor defeat; it just didn't matter. It's as though their firefight was a bizarre two-day adventure, like some extreme Outward Bound experience where things got out of hand and some of the guys got killed.

I wrote this book for them.

Group shot of Task Force Ranger without Delta Force. Humvees are in rear.
Courtesy: David Diemer.

Black Hawk *Super Six Four,* piloted by CWO Mike Durant, moves in from the ocean over Mogadishu. Courtesy: Shawn Nelson.

Rangers Alan Barton, Ron Galliette, and Rob Phipps pose after returning from a night mission. Courtesy: Shawn Nelson.

Rangers Jamie Smith and Aaron Williamson in the Mogadishu hangar. Courtesy: James Smith, Sr.

Ranger Keni Thomas aboard a Black Hawk heading out on a mission. Courtesy: Jeff Young.

(left to right) Ranger Joe Harsoky, Air Force Combat Controller Dan Schilling, and Ranger Mike Pringle posing before their Humvee, which led the Lost Convoy through the city. Courtesy: Dan Schilling.

A Black Hawk flares before landing on one of the many practice missions in Mogadishu's dunes. Courtesy: Dale Sizemore.

The only photograph taken from the ground during the battle on October 3. It was snapped looking west from Chalk One's position at the southeast corner of the target block. Target building looms in the background to the right. Courtesy: Jim Lechner.

Rangers pose in a Humvee topped with a Mark-19. Courtesy: Clay Othic.

Rangers Brian Heard (left) and David Floyd pose in the hangar prior to a mission. Courtesy: Dale Sizemore.

Maj. Gen. William F. Garrison, commander of Task Force Ranger, as he testified before the U.S. Senate committee in 1994. Courtesy: Associated Press.

Ranger Clay Othic posing behind the .50 caliber machine gun in the turret of a Humvee. Courtesy: Dan Schilling.

President Clinton with Ranger Scott Galentine at Walter Reed Army Hospital. Galentine had his severed thumb sewn back onto his hand. Courtesy: Shawn Nelson.

Ranger Lorenzo Ruiz, who was killed after taking the wounded Othic's place in the Humvee turret. Courtesy: Dale Sizemore.

# SOURCES

So many of the men who fought in this battle agreed to tell me their stories that most of the incidents related in this book were described to me by several different soldiers. Where there were discrepancies, one man's memory generally worked to improve the others'. In some cases, comparing stories was a useful check on embellishment. I found most of the men I interviewed to be extraordinarily candid. Having had this experience, they seemed to feel entrusted with it. Most were forthright to the point of revealing things about themselves they found deeply troubling or embarrassing. Once or twice, having been unable to corroborate a story, when I pressed the soldier who originally related it to me, he backed down and apologized for having repeated something he himself did not witness. I have stayed away from anecdotes told secondhand.

With very few exceptions, the dialogue in the book is either from the radio tapes or from one or more of the men actually speaking. My goal throughout has been to re-create the experience of combat through the eyes of those involved; to attempt that without reporting dialogue would be impossible. Of course, no one's recollection of what they said is ever perfect. My standard is the best memory of those involved. Where there were discrepancies in dialogue they were usually minor, and I was able to work out the differences by going back and forth between the men involved. In several cases I have reported dialogue or statements heard by others present, even though I was unable to locate the actual speakers. In these cases the words spoken were heard by more than one witness, or recorded in written accounts within days after the battle.

For understandable reasons, very few of the Delta operators who played such an important role in this battle agreed to talk to me about it. Their policy and tradition is silent professionalism. Master Sergeant Paul Howe, who has left the unit, obtained official permission, but risked the opprobrium of his former colleagues for speaking so candidly with me. Several current members of the unit also found ways to communicate with me. I am grateful to them. I also obtained the written accounts of several key members of the Delta assault force. It enabled me to provide a rare picture of these consummate soldiers in action, from their own perspective. All told, this input represents a small fraction of the unit, so the Delta portion of this story is weighted more heavily from Howe's and the others' perspectives than I would have liked.

## INTERVIEWS

Hassan Yassin Abokoi; Abdiaziz Ali Aden; Aaron Ahlfinger, a state trooper now in Colorado; Abdikadir Dahir Ali; Steve Anderson; Chris Atwater, W. F. "Jack" Atwater, Abdi "Qeybdid" Hassan Awale; Mohamed Hassan Awale; Abdullahi

Ossoble Barre; Alan Barton, who received the Bronze Star with Valor Device and now works for the Phoenix *City Post* office; DeAnna Joyce Beck; Maj. Gen. E. R. "Buck" Bedard, U.S. Marine Corps; John Belman, who received the Bronze Star for Valor and now works for a newspaper publishing company in Cincinnati; Anton Berendsen, who received the Bronze Star for Valor and is now attending college in Georgia; Matthew Bryden; John Burns, who received the Bronze Star for Valor Device and is attending college in Georgia; Lt. Col. L. H. "Bucky" Burruss, U.S. Army, ret.; Tory Carlson, who received the Purple Heart and now works as a highline electrician in Florida; SSGT Raleigh Cash, U.S. Army, who is still serving with the Ranger Regiment; John Collett; Col. Bill David, U.S. Army, who is now garrison commander at Fort Bragg; David Diemer, who received the Bronze Star for Valor and now does construction work with his father in Newburgh, New York; CPT Tom DiTomasso, U.S. Army, who received the Silver Star and still serves with the Ranger Regiment; Col. Peter Dotto, U.S. Marine Corps; GEN Wayne Downing, U.S. Army, ret.; CWO Michael Durant, U.S. Army, still with the 160th SOAR, who received the Distinguished Flying Cross and the Bronze Star; Abdullahi Haji Elia; Abdi Mohamed Elmi; Mohamed Mahamud Elmi; SSGT Matt Eversmann, who received the Bronze Star for Valor and still serves with the Ranger Regiment; Abdi Farah; Halima Farah; Hussein Siad Farah; Ibrahim Roble Farah; Mohamed Hassan Farah; David Floyd, who is attending college in South Carolina; Willi Frank; Scott Galentine, who received a Purple Heart and is now attending a community college in Auburn, Georgia (surgeons reattached Galentine's thumb and he has partial use of it); Hobdurahman Yusef Galle; Chief John Gay, U.S. Navy, who is still a SEAL; CWO Mike Goffena, U.S. Army, who received a Silver Star and was killed in February 1998 in a helicopter crash; Kira Goodale; Mike Goodale, who received the Purple Heart and Bronze Star for Valor and now lives with his wife Kira in Illinois and is completing studies to become a high school social studies teacher (he still serves in the National Guard); Gregg Gould, who now works as a police officer in Charleston, South Carolina; Jim Guelzow; Ali Gulaid; SFC Aaron Hand, U.S. Army; Abdullahi "Firimbi" Hassan; Bint Abraham Hassan; Hassan Adan Hassan; Mohamed Ali Herse; Adm. Jonathan Howe, U.S. Navy, ret.; MSG Paul Howe, U.S. Army, who received the Bronze Star for Valor; Mark Huband; Abdullahi Mohamed Hussein; Ali Hussein; Mark Jackson; Omar Jess; CWO Keith Jones, U.S. Army, who received the Silver Star, and is still flying with the 160th SOAR; LTC Larry Joyce, U.S. Army, ret.; SGT Ed Kallman, U.S. Army; Jim Keller; Michael Kurth, who is working as a waiter in Houston, Texas; Abdizirak Hassan Kutun; SFC Al Lamb, U.S. Army, who received the Silver Star and is still with Special Forces based in Tampa, Florida; Anthony Lake, who teaches at Georgetown University; CPT James Lechner, U.S. Army, who received the Purple Heart (doctors were able to stimulate enough bone growth to save Lechner's leg and he is now based in Hawaii); Phil Lepre, who works for an advertising firm near Philadelphia; SFC Steven Lycopolus, who works as a senior instructor at Fort Lewis, Washington; SFC Bob Mabry, U.S. Army; MAJ Rob Marsh, M.D., U.S. Army, ret.; COL Thomas Matthews, U.S. Army; LTC Dave McKnight, dec.; SGT Jeffrey McLaughlin, U.S. Army; Lt. James McMahon, U.S. Navy, ret.; CPT Drew Meyerowich, U.S. Army, who received the Silver Star; Yousuf Dahir Mo'alim; Elmi Aden Mohamed; Kassim Sheik Mohamed; Nur Sheik Mohamed; Sharif Ali Mohamed; Abdi Karim Mohamud; Jason Moore, who works for an investment company in New Jersey; Gunnery Sgt. Chad D. Moyer, U.S. Marine Corps; Shawn Nelson, who was working as a trail guide in the Grand Tetons before getting married and moving to Atlanta; Ambassador Robert Oakley; Clay Othic, who received the Bronze Star with Valor Device and the Purple Heart and now works as a special agent for the Immigration and Naturalization Service in Wichita, Kansas; Capt. Larry Perino, U.S. Army, who received the Bronze Star with Valor Device and still serves with the Ranger Regiment; Rob Phipps, who received the Purple Heart and now lives in Augusta, Georgia; Benjamin Pilla; Gen. Colin Powell, U.S. Army, ret.; Randy Ramaglia, who received the Bronze Star for Valor and now helps manage a rock band in Columbus, Georgia; S. Sgt. Carlos Rodriguez, U.S. Army, based at Fort Lewis, Washington; Omar Salad; Daniel Schilling, who works as an administrator at the University of Phoenix in Provo, Utah, and is finishing his master's degree; SFC Kurt Schmid, U.S. Army, based in Japan; LTC Mike Sheehan, U.S. Army, ret.; Stephanie Shughart; SSG George Siegler, who is still with the Ranger Regiment; Dale Sizemore; CPT Jim Smith, U.S. Army, ret.; Eric Spalding, who serves as a special agent for the Immigration and Naturalization Service in Arizona; LT Scott Spellmeyer, U.S. Army; Peter Squeglia, who works for an investment company in Boston, Massachusetts; SGT John Stebbins, U.S. Army, who received the Silver Star; MAJ Mike Steele, U.S. Army, who received the Bronze Star for Valor and now serves with the 82nd Airborne; MAJ David Stockwell, U.S. Army; SGT Jeff Struecker, U.S. Army, who received the Bronze Star for Valor and still serves with the Ranger Regiment (in 1997, Struecker won the coveted "Best Ranger" award); Osman Mohamud Sudi; Abdi Tahalil; Jim Telscher; SSG Brad Thomas, who still serves with the Ranger Regiment; Keni Thomas, who received the Bronze Star for Valor and now works with delinquent children and plays in a rock band in Columbus, Georgia; Lance Twombly; SPC John Waddell, who is in training to become a Special Forces medic and is bound for medical school; SFC Sean Watson, U.S. Army, who received the Bronze Star for Valor; T. Sgt. Tim Wilkinson, who received the Air Force Cross and still serves as a pararescueman based at Hurlburt Field, Florida; Jason Wind; LT Damon Wright, U.S. Army; CPT Becky Yacone, U.S. Army, ret.; CPT Jim Yacone, U.S. Army, ret., who received the Silver Star, who now works for the FBI; Jeff Young, SSG Ed Yurek, U.S. Army, who still serves with the Ranger Regiment at Fort Benning; Bashir Haji Yusuf; Brig. Gen. Anthony Zinni, USMC, who is now commanding general of USCENTCOM.

# BOOKS

*Hazardous Duty,* COL David H. Hackworth, U.S. Army, Avon Books, 1997. Hackworth herein continues his war against the status quo in the U.S. Army, and offers a brief but fairly accurate account of the battle in Chapter Six, "Unfortunate Casualties." There are inaccuracies (as noted below and in the Epilogue) and some slippery reasoning, but Hackworth's highly opinionated account is basically correct and makes for spirited reading.

*Losing Mogadishu,* Jonathan Stevenson, Naval Institute Press, 1995. This is a critique of the overall UN/U.S. effort in Somalia and is a classic exercise in summing up policy mistakes in retrospect, rife with "flagrant misreadings" and "precisely wrong" approaches, which is the easiest of all academic sports. The battle itself gets very short shrift.

    *Mogadishu, Heroism and Tragedy!* Kent Delong and Steven Tuckey, Bergin & Garvey, 1994. A hasty, sincere effort at a re-creation of the battle based on interviews with a few of the participants, most of them pilots. It is full of mistakes, everything from misspelled soldiers' names to screwed-up time sequences, but it is well-meaning and right out of the old rah-rah school of military reporting.

    *On the Edge,* Elizabeth Drew, Simon & Schuster, 1994. Drew's book is an account of President Clinton's first two years in office, and affords the best insights into the decision making (or lack of same) that led to the battle, and the administration's reaction in its aftermath.

    *Out of America,* Keith Richburg, A New Republic Book, Basic Books, 1997. Richburg is a *Washington Post* reporter who wrote about the events in Somalia as they happened. His book records his mounting disillusion, as an African-American, with Africa after traveling and reporting there for several years. Some of his insights into Aidid and the situation that led up to the battle are excellent, although understandably much colored by his anger over the brutal deaths of Dan Eldon and Hos Maina on July 12 at the hands of a Somali mob.

    *The Road to Hell,* Michael Maren, The Free Press, 1997. This is a well-written book about the international policies that led to the complete collapse of Somalia, and ultimately to the UN intervention and this battle. Maren offers fresh insights into the sometimes destructive role played by international goodwill.

    *Savage Peace: Americans at War in the 1990s,* Daniel P. Bolger, Presidio, 1995. I found this to be a very impressive and accurate book. Chapter Seven on Somalia, "Down Among the Dead Men," is the best thing I had read about the battle and the entire intervention from a military point of view. Bolger is fair, thorough, and accurate.

    *Somalia and Operation Restore Hope,* John L. Hirsch and Robert B. Oakley, United States Institute of Peace Press, 1995. This is the definitive narrative account of the UN and U.S. intervention in Somalia, much of it through Oakley's eyes (he is a former U.S. ambassador to Somalia and served as President Clinton's envoy to Somalia after the battle).

    *The United Nations and Somalia, 1992–1996,* The United Nations Blue Books Series, Volume III, Department of Public Information, UN, 1996. This is the definitive reference book for the UN interventions in Somalia.

## ARTICLES

"Experiences of Executive Officer from Bravo Company, 3rd Battalion, 75th Ranger Regiment and Task Force Ranger during the Battle of the Black Sea on 3–4 October, 1993 in Mogadishu, Somalia," Capt. Lee A. Rysewyk (published in-house by the Combined Arms and Tactics Division, U.S. Army Infantry School, Fort Benning, Georgia). A good overview of the battle that includes the official operational time line.

    "Fast Rope into Hell," Dale B. Cooper, *Soldier of Fortune,* July 1994. A spirited account of part of the fight, in true guts-and-glory style, primarily based on interviews with air force PJs Fales and Wilkinson.

"Heroes at Mogadishu," Frank Oliveri, *Air Force Magazine,* June 1994. An account of the actions of air force personnel Wilkinson, Fales, and Bray.

"Mission to Somalia," Patrick J. Sloyan, *Newsday,* December 5–9, 1993. A superb analysis of how and why the battle took place, with some good bits from the fight itself.

"Mogadishu, October 1993: A Personal Account of a Rifle Company XO," Capt. Charles P. Ferry, *Infantry,* October 1994. A rather dry account of the actions of the 10th Mountain Division.

"The Raid That Went Wrong," Rick Atkinson, *The Washington Post,* January 30, 1994. An excellent and amazingly accurate account of the battle from both the American and Somali points of view.

"Rescue of the Rangers," Ed Perkins, *Waterdown Daily Times,* October 2, 1994. A very ambitious, readable, and accurate account of the actions of the 10th Mountain Division.

"A Soldier's Nightmare," Philip F. Rhodes, *Night Flyer,* 1st Quarter 1994. Another account of Fales's experiences, also packaged as "Courage Under Fire" in *Airman,* May 1994.

"Task Force Ranger Operations in Somalia 3–4 October 1993," U.S. Special Operations Command and U.S. Army Special Operations Command History Office, June 1, 1994 (unpublished). The official twelve-page summary of the battle with fifty-six pages of brief accounts of individual heroism.

# NOTES

## The Assault

1    **"At liftoff . . . usually amounted to nothing,"** Eversmann, Diemer, Sizemore, Nelson, McLaughlin, Galentine. In the early days of air mobile assaults, aircraft loads were noted with a numeral chalked on the side of the fuselage. Hence the term, *chalk.* One of the unique things about today's army, especially elite units like the Rangers, is that the men assigned to it live and train together, often for years. Mission statement and overall design is from "Task Force Ranger Operations in Somalia 3–4 October 1993," prepared by the U.S. Special Operations Command (USSOC) and the USSOC History Office, dated June 1, 1994 (hereafter called USSOC report). **"Waiting for the code word . . . on a taut rope,"** Details of the armada are from the USSOC report and Matthews, McMahon, Durant, P. Howe, and Jones. **"There were signs . . . 'Be careful.'"** Dave McKnight, Struecker, Eversmann, Schilling. Description of Garrison also from Ranger snapshots. **"The swell . . . festering urban rot,"** Eversmann, Nelson, Diemer, Lechner, M. Goodale, Stebbins, etc. Description of the city is from my trip to Mogadishu and from videotape and photographs taken by Rangers and by army observation helicopters and the spy plane. (I have seen a total of about an hour and a half of highlights from the approximately fifteen hours of battle video shot from the plane and observation helicopters, extremely high-quality color videotape for the most part.) **"In his bird . . . was among them,"** Eversmann et al. and the USSOC report. The acceptance rate for those soldiers invited to try out for Delta varies from class to class, but 10 percent is a fair average according to Howe and Burruss, who served

as Garrison's second in command when he commanded the unit. Some of the more general insights into Ranger mentality came from conversations with M. Goodale, Nelson, Sizemore, Squeglia, Floyd, Anderson, Waddell, Perino, Othic, and Spalding, who gave me the "all-star football team analogy." I interviewed the P-3 pilot, Jim McMahon, who was airborne over the city until about dusk, at which point the OH-58Ds took over surveillance and taping.

2     **"It was only a three-minute flight . . . alerted Eversmann,"** Eversmann, Matthews, P. Howe, USSOC report. Quotes in italics set off by the long dash are of radio transmissions and in the text are meant to indicate a voice being heard on the radio. Most are taken directly from transcripts of command-net radio traffic during the fight, which was recorded. Some from the Ranger company net or Delta assault net are based on interviews. References to time here and throughout come from the operational time line constructed by Task Force Ranger's operations cell, which notes every significant event in the fight from "Oct. 3, 1993, 1350—CISE reports possible Salad/Qeydid mtg at house near VIC olympic Hotel," to "Oct. 4, 1993, 0916—Ground commanders report all pers accounted for except for the 4 crewmembers and 2 snipers inserted into crash site 2." **"The Little Birds moved . . . fired a shot,"** radio transcripts, USSOC report, and battle video. **"Delta rode in on benches . . . assault's outer perimeter,"** P. Howe, USSOC report, battle video, Jones, and various written accounts of the battle prepared in the days after the fight by members of the Delta teams. Descriptions of the actions of Howe and Rierson come from my interviews with Howe, who spoke with Rierson at length about the gunfight immediately afterward. Rierson was killed on October 6 in a mortar attack on the airfield. Hooten's memories are from his written account of the battle. **"As ropes dropped . . . one going in,"** Thomas. **"Hovering high . . . something overripe,"** Eversmann, Diemer. **"Blackburn was bleeding . . . behind two parked cars,"** Eversmann and an account of Good's actions prepared by USSOC historians who interviewed dozens of participants in the days after the fight. Eversmann recalls the chopper jerking suddenly just as Blackburn leapt for the rope, but no such movement is visible on the videotape, which clearly shows the young Ranger tumble out the door. Blackburn, who I did not interview, has reportedly made a full physical recovery, but has no memory of his fall or of subsequent events on October 3. **"Eversmann shouted . . . weren't being heard,"** Eversmann, Moore. **"Eversmann tried . . . *sharpshooting me*,"** Eversmann, Perino. **"The radio call brought . . . an IV,"** Schmid and an account of Bullock's actions by a USSOC historian. **"Fire was growing . . . *roll out of here*,"** Eversmann, Diemer, McLaughlin. Rick Atkinson's excellent reconstruction of the battle in *The Washington Post* (January 30, 1994) quotes Somali militia leaders who described efforts to bus fighters to the market area primarily from the north, which would help explain why Chalk Four was so embattled. **"Schmid, the Delta medic . . . 'he's gonna die,'"** Schmid, Eversmann. **"Eversmann called Perino . . . on his own,"** Eversmann, Perino, McLaughlin, Schmid.

3     **"On the screens . . . near that part of town,"** Dave McKnight, Marsh. The description of how events in Mogadishu had deteriorated after the Marines withdrew is from J. Howe. **"It was the one place . . . lose the war,"** Garrison's prescient memo was quoted in Samuel Bolger's book, *Savage Peace*, and also in news accounts subsequent to the battle. **"The timing was also . . . that much more deadly,"**

Matthews, Goffena, Durant, Jones,Yacone. **"Night afforded . . . worst possible time,"** Dave McKnight, Burruss, Bryden, and my observations in Mogadishu. **"Still, the chance . . . pressure for success was mounting,"** Matthews, Dave McKnight, State Department and Task Force Ranger memos. The line from Smith is from a September 17 letter to his parents. **"Just that morning . . . go and be stupid,"** description of Garrison is from Dave McKnight, Marsh, Burruss, and Rangers. Details of the general's frustration come from his three-page October 3 memo to General Hoar, entitled "To Keep You Informed." Gosende's memo was written September 15. **"And just that morning . . . rockets on the Little Birds,"** USSOC report, Steele, Matthews, Rangers. **"Lieutenant Jim Lechner . . . 'Roger,'"** Lechner.

**4**     This section is primarily based on my interview in Mogadishu of Ali Hassan Mohamed. A number of the Somalis I interviewed were clearly making up stories about where they were and what they saw on October 3, but thanks to the detailed accounts I'd gotten from American soldiers it was pretty easy to sort fact from fiction. The "Rangers" Ali saw were most likely men from the Delta command Black Hawk who roped in about a block off target, and initially cleared out a courtyard about a block west of the target building, where they consolidated before moving back out on the street. The shot that killed Ali's brother probably came from a minigun providing covering fire for their movement.

**5**     This section is based largely on my interviews with P. Howe, although the overall impressions of Delta were also influenced by interviews with other present and former members of that unit, and with the Rangers who fought with them in Somalia. Friction between Steele and the D-boys started on the first day they trained together at Fort Bragg. Steele's company had been involved in manuevers at Fort Bliss when they were summoned quickly to Bragg. When they arrived, according to Steele, Delta wanted to throw his men right into a training exercise. Steele said he demanded more time to get his unit organized, and wanted a more precise plan of action for his men than the operators were inclined to present. I have seen a videotape purporting to show the friendly fire incident on top of the target building. It shows Howe and his team crouched defensively behind a low concrete wall as chunks of it fly around them. There is no way from the videotape to tell exactly where the shots were coming from, but several sources in Delta and the Rangers confirmed the shooter was a Ranger with Chalk Two. Sergeant First Class Steven Lycopolus, then a staff sergeant, took the blame for the shooting, which he said was actually done by a junior member of his chalk. According to Lycopolus, he refused to turn over the culprit when Captain Steele demanded to know who the shooter was, so Steele told him, "Then you will have to accept the responsibility." Other Rangers discount this story and point the finger at Lycopolus, who was unpopular anyway because of another alleged fratricide incident described in Part III. The source of the earlier shooting was not identified.

**6**     **"Specialist John Stebbins . . . as they zipped past,"** Stebbins, Galentine. **"Up the street . . . not seen again,"** Steele. **"Across the alley . . . *Was this the right thing?*"** M. Goodale, K. Goodale. Kira Goodale choked up reading the passage from Mike's letter over the phone. The only photograph I know to have been taken from the ground during the early part of this fight was snapped by Lechner looking west from Chalk One's southeast blocking position. Through the dusty haze it shows Goodale and Williamson crouched behind the car hulk, and Stebbins prone covering an alley south. In the distance you can see the members of Chalk Three spaced out along the south wall of the target. The target house itself rises above the wall in the background. One of the fast ropes is stretched out across the alley. **"At his corner . . . woman fell dead,"** Perino. Somalis I interviewed vehemently denied that women and children were used as human shields, although they did say women and children helped as spotters. Nearly all the Rangers who roped into the fight told me independently of witnessing women and children spotting for and shielding gunmen, especially early in the fight.

7      **"As he roped in . . . most of the fire,"** Waddell. **"Nelson had been . . . the top of the wall,"** Nelson, Waddell, Yurek. DiTomasso's concerns and actions were recorded in detail in his extensive written account. **"The fire was not . . . and enter blasting,"** Yurek. **"From his position . . . *Goddamn!*"** Nelson, Waddell, Yurek, Twombly.

8      Bray's written account, Hooten's written account, P. Howe, Dave McKnight.

9      **"After the helicopter force . . . an assistant gunner,"** Streucker, Burns, Othic, Spalding, and Schilling. **"Dom Pilla was . . . their next skit,"** Nelson. Diemer was the soldier Steele questioned about going to church. **"Streucker and the rest . . . convoy at the hotel,"** Struecker, B. Thomas. **"Before the convoy . . . returning fire,"** Gay, who told me of this in an interview and who also wrote a detailed, colorful account of his actions and observations during the battle, entitled "Post-Op Report/Strong Point Assault/10-3-93." It is also recorded in SEAL Homer Nearpass's written account. When he returned to the States, Gay hoped to make some money endorsing the Randall knife for the manufacturer. Not many people could say their knife blade stopped a bullet. The manufacturer expressed no interest. **"Struecker was assigned . . . silence followed,"** Struecker, B. Thomas, and the written account of SEAL Richard Kaiser.

10     Ali Hussein.

11     Struecker, B. Thomas.

12     **"Private Clay Othic . . . 'tough go cyclic,'"** Othic, Spalding, P. Howe. **"Othic's Missouri buddy . . . fast and accelerated,"** Spalding. **"For Sergeant John Burns . . . with amazement,"** Burns. **"One Humvee back . . . moving again,"** Kallman. **"From his turret . . . took the gun,"** Othic.

13     Galentine, Eversmann, Diemer, Berendsen.

## Black Hawk Down

1      **"Mohamed Hassan Farah heard . . . was too much,"** details of the July 12 attack on the Abdi House are drawn from my interview of Mohamed Hassan Farah in Mogadishu and an interview there with Abdullahi Ossoble Barre. Both

men were injured inside the house. The surprise missile attack was also witnessed by former Canadian military officer Matthew Bryden, who was working for an international aid organization in Mogadishu at the time. I interviewed Bryden in Nairobi, where he was working for an organization called the Wartorn Societies Project. He heard Cobra helicopters move in low over the city and, stepping outside, watched as they formed a semicircle around the target house and began shooting. An experienced hand in Somalia, Bryden left the city, warned by a Somali friend that there would be trouble. Four Western journalists, Dan Eldon, Hos Maina, and Anthony Macharia of Rueters and Hansi Kraus, a German photographer working for the Associated Press, rushed to the scene after the attack and were set upon and killed by an angry mob. The incident was widely reported around the world after it happened, but the emphasis in the stories was on the deaths of the four journalists. In fact, the Abdi House attack represented an unprecedented step by the UN, what *Washington Post* reporter Keith Richburg, in his book *Out of America*, called "the UN's first-ever officially-authorized assassination" (p. 79). The incident was provoked by Aidid's escalating violence. The warlord had taken to assassinating Somalis employed by the UN. The July 12th attack did more than any single act to stir up local support for Aidid and the Habr Gidr, and turned many moderate Somalis who had supported the intervention against the international mission. In my interviews with J. Howe, he told me that he believes there was a separate meeting of Habr Gidr elders going on in the neighborhood at the same time, and that propagandists have deliberately confused that with the one under way in the Abdi House. I think he is mistaken. The eyewitness accounts of Farah and Barre agree in every particular, and correspond to the official version of the attack in the UN Blue Book, Volume VIII, *The United Nations and Somalia 1992–1996* (The UN Blue Book Series, p. 404). The initial casualty counts differed. UNOSOM acknowledged 20 deaths, all men—while videotape taken at the scene showed women among the dead (Richburg, pp. 79–80). The International Committee of the Red Cross said there were 215 Somali casualties, including 54 dead. Aidid's supporters distributed a list of 73 dead, including women and children. According to Richburg, American officials in Somalia at the time conceded the Red Cross estimate was probably correct (p. 80), and every eyewitness I interviewed placed the number of dead at 70 or more. Oakley accepts the higher figure. Bryden, Farah, and Barre all said many of the Somalis killed were well-respected moderates opposed to Aidid's murderous acts against the UN. The attack still stirs up deep anger and bitterness among the Somalis from all walks of life I interviewed in Mogadishu. The deaths of the four journalists prompted most Western news organizations to pull reporters out of Mogadishu. The AP hung on until September, when Aidid started threatening to kidnap American journalists. When the battle happened on October 3, there were no American journalists in Mogadishu. The videotape and most of the still photos seen on TV and in the world press were shot by Somali stringers, with the exception of still photos by *Toronto Star* photographer Paul Watson. **"Bashir Haji Yusuf heard the helicopters . . . and harrassed,"** Yusuf. I was skeptical of the story about the baby, but Burns confirmed it. He said that on one mission after fast-roping down, he and his men went looking for an infant that had been swept from its mother's arms as they descended. The flex-cuffed woman screamed hysterically until a translator arrived to explain. Burns said he found the baby unhurt. It had been blown through the wall of a nearby rag hut. The diary of a member of the 160th who asked not to be identified also notes the phenomenon—"the Black Hawk blew the baby right out of her arms and [it] rolled down the street." **"Yusuf was disappointed . . . the shooting start,"** Yusuf. The September 9 incident is noted in the UN Blue Book (p. 407), which officially notes one Pakistani soldier killed, two Paki soldiers injured, and three U.S. soldiers injured. The official account notes the use of TOW missiles and cannon by QRF Cobra helicopters, but does not estimate the number of Somali dead. It notes, "This incident was followed by media accusations of indiscriminate fire by UNOSOM, on Somali crowds. UNOSOM, admitting 'numerous' casualties on the Somali side among the combatants, denied the allegations, which remain unconfirmed." The diary of the 160th member records the skirmish and the Paki death and injuries, and goes on to say, obviously secondhand: "Well, it did not take long for the place to [be] considered a free fire zone, and in came the Cobras. They put two TOW missiles into the dozer so the locals could not get it, and the 20 mm cannon took out 30 to 40 of the bad guys." The next day's entry notes, "Well, as it turned out the skinnies are real pissed off, the Cobras killed as many as 100, they were shooting into crowds where they were taking fire. Remember, it was a free fire zone, for some reason, these people are strange, or maybe smart depending on how you look at it. They will use women as cover and concealment for when they shoot at us to make it harder to see who is doing the shooting, if we can see them at all. Then they call us killers of women and children when we shoot the very same people who are shooting at us and we kill some of the people that they are using for cover."

2      Waddell, Nelson, DiTomasso.

3      Dowdy, Frank, J. Yacone, B. Yacone, radio tapes.

4      Nelson, DiTomasso, Diemer, Eversmann, Twombly, and radio tapes.

5      Aden. His account of *Super Six One*'s downing and subsequent events checked out perfectly with battle video and accounts of men who survived the crash. Few unpaved streets in Mogadishu have official names. I have relied on Aden and on Bushir Sudi, a Mogadishu native who now lives in St. Louis Park, Minnesota, who assured me the streets around the first crash site were widely known as Marehan Road and, one block west of the crash, Wadigley.

6      Battle video. Insights into Garrison's predicament came from interviews with Dave McKnight, P. Howe, Marsh, and others.

7      Nelson, DiTomasso, Waddell, Steele, Yurek.

8      **"Piloting the Little Bird . . . up the alley."** Jones, battle video, Goffena, J. Yacone. **"Lieutenant DiTomasso . . . round the corner,"** DiTomasso, Nelson. **"As the rest . . .** *coming out*," Jones, radio tapes. The quote from Busch is reported in the May 30, 1994, commemorative issue of *The Army Times*.

9      Durant, Goffena, Jones, Frank, and B. Yacone. Some of the background on Durant came from reporting at the time of his capture by *The Philadelphia Inquirer* and *The New York Times*.

10    **"Admiral Jonathan Howe's first inkling . . . slipped away,"** J. Howe, Oakley, Lake, Powell. Additional insights into Aidid are from Richburg's *Out of Africa*, and from Michael Maren's *The Road to Hell*, which argues that the UN and U.S. manhunt for Aidid significantly strengthened the warlord's standing in Mogadishu. **"Legend on the streets . . . into a folk hero,"** The story of Aidid's escape from the UN cordon, which may be apocryphal, reflects the warlord's growing local stature through this ordeal. It was told to me by Mohamed Hassan Farah. **"The decision to attack . . . Howe relented,"** J. Howe, who still believes only about twenty Somalis were killed, and only key military planners for Aidid's militia. **"Howe kept pushing . . . America's white whale,"** J. Howe, Lake, Powell, and Elizabeth Drew's *On the Edge*, an account of Clinton's first years in the White House. Drew's is the best account I've read of the Somalia episode from the White House's perspective. My requests to interview President Clinton were denied. **"Task Force Ranger . . . out of business,"** January 5, 1994, memo from Garrison to Chairman, Joint Chiefs of Staff, summarizing the entire Task Force Rangers mission (hereafter "January 5 Garrison memo"). **"Howe had initially . . . razor wire,"** J. Howe, January 5 Garrison memo. **"Aidid was feeling . . . very tense,"** transcript of a September 26 interrogation of a clan "colonel." This was the day after the 10th Mountain Division Black Hawk was shot down. The colonel told his interrogators, "As a result [of the downing] Aidid has received increased support and encouragement. Up until now the people did not believe he could destroy a helicopter, now they do. They are not as afraid of the helicopters as they were before." The colonel also warned that Aidid was trying to assemble five hundred men to assault the airport Task Force Ranger base. **"In late August . . . Garrison's pressure,"** J. Howe, Oakley, Lake, *On the Edge*. **"Peace had been the reason . . . once and for all,"** J. Howe.

11    Abdi Karim Mohamud, who on several occasions acted as a guide for Peter Tobia and myself in Mogadishu. Abdi Karim and his friend Abdi Tahalil visited us several times and sat up late discussing the story. They brought us eyewitnesses to the fighting. Abdi Tahalil's wife was shot on one of the earlier Ranger missions. She recovered, but will be unable to bear children. His brother was killed in the fighting around the target house on October 3. According to Abdi Tahalil, his brother was driving a taxi and got caught up in the assault. They found his charred remains inside the burned vehicle. A number of the American soldiers I interviewed expressed surprise at the employment of Somalis to perform work in and around U.S. compounds. Abdi Karim was employed at the old U.S. embassy, but there were Somalis who were contracted to do electrical work at the Task Force Ranger hangar and to service the portable toilets outside. Given that the Ranger base was considered secret enough to confiscate film from those who just snapped pictures of it from the outside, it seems odd that Somali workers were allowed inside. The workers all got a pretty good eyeful of the task force's numbers, weapons, and locations inside the fences, information that would have been helpful to know—even just for the mortar crews who nightly lobbed rounds into the airport base.

12    Schilling, USSOC report, battle video, radio tapes.

13    Durant, Matthews, radio tapes, battle video, Goffena, J. Yacone.

**14**    **"After they had . . . right rear window,"** McLaughlin, Carlson. **"About a hundred yards . . . 'We're driving over,'"** Eversmann, Steele. In his book *To Fight with Intrepidity,* Major John D. Lock notes Eversmann's actions here as a significant lapse: "Eversmann informed his company commander that he was moving out when, in reality, he had no intention of doing so. Only by luck and accident were he and his men discovered by LTC McKnight when he drove by the squad's position with his convoy. If it weren't for this fortuitous moment, there would have been an additional twelve Rangers added to the KIA total." Perhaps. I think Major Lock overstates the point. Eversmann did intend to follow Steele's order to move his men out on foot, even though he didn't convey to the captain how difficult this was going to be. Had Chalk Four not been picked up by the convoy and been stranded, it certainly is possible that they would all have been killed. It's also possible they would have been spotted from the air, or been able to move to the crash site on foot. **"Schilling provided . . . still, unscathed,"** Schilling, Eversmann, Gay. **"Nobody in the rear . . . fret over it,"** Spalding, Gay, Burns, Othic, P. Howe, Schilling, McLaughlin, etc.

**15**    Goffena, J. Yacone, radio tapes, Durant.

**16**    **"Yousuf Dahir Mo'alim . . . ran on ahead."** Mo'alim. The description of the nature of Aidid's militia comes from Mo'alim and also my interview with militia leader Sharif Ali Mohamed and with Oakley and Bryden. In the September 26 interrogation of the cooperative Habr Gidr "colonel," he explained, "First you must understand you are dealing with essentially two different groups of people here. The first group are Aidid's 'Revengers' who are given money and *khat* prior to an operation. If they complete an operation successfully, they receive the remainder of their pay. These people will not lay down their weapons as long as Aidid continues to pay them. The second group are the innocents, the ones who live in the neighborhoods the revengers launch their attacks from. Once the U.S./UNOSOM launch a reactionary or counterattack, innocent people have their homes damaged, and are sometimes killed and/or wounded. These events Aidid follows up with such propaganda as, 'First they will kill your family, then enslave you, then force you to change your religion.' Most families don't understand what is going on, and know if they speak up the revengers will kill them. Aidid has no solid, organized force. His tendency is to use small groups like revengers, of which there are no more than 50 or 60. They hide within the people—because he knows your response will hurt the people, turning them against you." Radio warnings of approaching Aidid militia conform in time, description, and direction of approach to the movement of Mo'alim and his men. There were other groups moving at the same time and in the same manner and direction. **"Ali Hussein . . . the running crowd,"** Ali Hussein.

**17**    **"In ordinary circumstances . . . from those places,"** Matthews, battle video, Burns, Schilling, Gay, P. Howe. **"There was an added . . . situation really was,"** McMahon. **"Eversmann, still lying . . . the hornet's nest,"** Eversmann, Schilling. Schilling went to great lengths to help me with this chapter. His friend and former colleague, Technical Sergeant Tim Wilkinson, had strongly urged me to phone Dan months earlier, but I didn't get around to contacting him until after the first version of this chapter had already appeared in *The Philadelphia Inquirer.* My mistake. Dan clarified the meandering course taken by the convoy, and helped me understand how and why the confusion took place (although that's an issue that deserves even more scrutiny than I've been able to give it here). We did several phone interviews, and Dan wrote a compelling sixteen-page narrative that has vastly improved my account, and now forms the backbone of this chapter. He was able to place the events that occurred on this terrible drive in chronological order, and even drew a detailed map of the convoy's convoluted course. Critics of the battle have focused primarily on the political decisions that dictated what equipment the troops had, and on General Garrison's decision to commit the force in daylight (although three of the previous six successful missions had been done in daytime). To me, the communications mix-up that left five soldiers dead and dozens badly injured was the single biggest snafu of the battle. **"The convoy was bearing south . . . pushed on,"** radio tapes, Schilling. **"Heavy fire . . . to shape things up,"** Eversmann, P. Howe. Howe spoke at length to Rierson in the days after the fight and recorded his buddy's angry recollections of the lost convoy in his diary. I walked the streets around crash site one, and found them particularly deceptive because, while they appear to form a neat grid, they in fact often do not. Just when you think you have the pattern fixed in your head, you find a road that strays off at one angle or another. To the eye of a foreigner, every block looks the same. **"As they passed . . . right over him,"** McLaughlin, Carlson, Spalding, and an account of A. Rodriguez's experience recorded by an army historian. **"The convoy stopped . . . 'he's gonna die!'"** Spalding, Hand, Carlson, Gay. **"The convoy lurched forward . . . shrieked with pain,"** Schilling, Burns, Spalding. **"The volume of fire . . . own pouches,"** Schilling.

18     Radio tapes.

19     **"In the convoy's . . . Humvee,"** Burns. **"They were still pointed . . . lying down again,"** Schilling, Moore. **"Not long after . . . needed him,"** Carlson. **"In the second . . . he was fine,"** Kallman. **"Dan Schilling felt . . . 'all fucking dead,'"** Schilling, radio tapes, Matthews. It was Schilling's impression that McKnight seemed "dazed." Rierson had told Howe the same thing in their conversations after the battle. It was the impression of the men I interviewed, mostly Rangers, that the experienced Delta operators kept the convoy together, moving, and organized under these hellish conditions. The voices of the commanders in these radio transmissions convey their distress and mounting frustration more compellingly than their words alone. One hears confusion, anger, and disbelief.

20     **"Specialist Spalding was still . . . everything that moved,"** Spalding. **"To make room . . . those still shooting,"** Othic, Hand. **"Many of the vehicles . . . four flat tires,"** Schilling, Gay. **"When the RPG hit Kowalewski . . . out of here ASAP,"** Schilling, radio tapes. **"They weren't home yet . . . another vicious ambush,"** Gay, Spalding, Diemer, Eversmann, Burns, Moore.

## Overrun

1     **"Too many things . . . it would be dark,"** USSOC report, Dave McKnight, operational time line, David. **"Shortly before . . . felt this way,"** Wilkinson, Lamb,

Barton, Belman, Phipps, Mabry, Marsh. Dr. Marsh told me about the battles fought to lug his trauma kits everywhere. The title PJ, for "parajumpers," has recently been upgraded by the air force to the more descriptive "pararescuemen," even though everybody still calls them PJs. Tim asked me if I would consider calling them "pararescuemen" in the book, and I declined. I feel guilty about it, hence this confession. **"As Jollata called back ... upright and intact,"** Wilkinson, battle video, operational time line, radio tapes, *Mogadishu: Heroism and Tragedy!* Phipps insisted that he had remembered to kick out the bags, but I went with Wilkinson's account, which explained *Super Six Eight's* delay in getting up and out. A videotape of the incident shows *Super Six Eight* begin to pull up and away, then settle back into a hover.

2    **"Wilkinson heard the snap ... bodies to cover,"** Wilkinson, Belman, Barton, Lamb, Phipps, Mabry. According to John Burns, Delta sergeant John Macejunas was the only member of that unit who routinely still wore the K-pot. The description of the neighborhood into which *Super Six One* crashed is from my viewing of the videotape, my visit there, and from intelligence photos taken the morning after, which show pieces of the rotors widely scattered. **"Sergeant Fales was at the front end ... bent tail boom,"** Mabry, Wilkinson, *Air Force Magazine* (June 1994), *Night Flyer* (first quarter, 1994), and *Airman* (May 1994). **"The injury to his partner ... to get him out,"** Wilkinson.

3    Abdiaziz Ali Aden.

4    **"Sergeant First Class Al Lamb ... Rob Phipps,"** Lamb, Gould. **"Phipps had roped ... out of the fight,"** Phipps, Lamb, Belman, Gould, Lycopolus. Both Phipps and Gould hold Lycopolus responsible for their injuries. Lycopolus feels he has been unfairly blamed. "I threw six grenades in all," he says. "The first five exploded, so obviously, with all the stress and excitement I was remembering to pull the pin and remove the safety strap correctly. I would have done exactly the same thing with the last one as I did with the first five." Lycopolus believes Somalis behind the wall threw over an American grenade of their own. He attributes the hard feelings about the grenade to the fact that he was new to the Ranger unit, so it was easy for them to blame him—someone they didn't know well. Both Phipps and Gould were shipped out with their injuries immediately after the battle, so Lycopolus never had a chance to address their accusations at the time. By the time Bravo Company flew back to the States, the story of how he'd screwed up was so entrenched he couldn't defend himself against it. That and the friendly fire incident resulted in his being transferred out of the Ranger Regiment. He is still in the army.

5    Goffena, J. Yacone, Matthews, operational event time line, USSOC report, command-net tapes. Colonel David explained that the QRF's roundabout route was necessitated by mines and ambushes his troops had encountered in driving straight through the city in the past. Given the hammering McKnight's convoy was taking at the same time (which David knew nothing about), it would appear to have been prudent.

6    The description in this section, presented mostly through the eyes of Dale Sizemore, is based on dozens of interviews with Rangers, Delta operators, and air force personnel. I asked all of the men who lived in the hangar to tell me about it,

and the various anecdotes emerged from that. Some of the description is also based on the many photographs men sent me of the hangar. **"And even though the ocean had sharks . . ."**—It seems that a big Somali slaughterhouse was located on the waterfront, and for years the remains of butchered carcasses had been dumped in the ocean, feeding happy herds of voracious sharks. Up the beach, the navy hung a big net offshore to provide a safe swimming area, but at least one U.S. soldier was severely injured in a shark attack. This did not, however, deter Rangers from swimming. The guys on vehicles would drive up the beach and post a lookout (for both sharks and officers) while the others frolicked in the surf. **"Right after take-off . . . and racked out,"** P. Howe. **"They taught little tricks . . . absolutely fearless,"** descriptions of the Delta operators are from my interviews with many Rangers. In my initial interviews with Rangers at Fort Benning, which were conducted with a USSOC press officer in attendance, there was no mention of the Delta soldiers who were at the heart of the mission. The Rangers did their best to tell their own stories without mentioning who was actually raiding the target house, although sometimes their own accounts were forced to mention "a soldier from another unit." Even when I started tracking down and interviewing Rangers on my own, working on leads given me by the original group, most were reluctant to discuss the D-boys, whose very existence is, at least officially, secret. Eventually I found some who felt comfortable talking about men who were killed, and would discuss the others without mentioning their names. Those who were out of the army generally were more relaxed about this. Macejunas made such an impression that just about every Ranger I talked to had a story to tell about him, "this unbelievable guy with a blond flattop." I was able to attach a name to the stories when I obtained accounts of the battle written by Delta soldiers and SEALs. **"Specialist John Collett . . . 'I was gasping!'"** Floyd, Collett. **"One of the air force PJs got a blow-up love doll . . ."**—This was mailed by Schilling's wife and a girlfriend of one of the other PJs as a joke. The sex doll was placed on a chair outside the air force's little sector in the hangar with a crude cardboard sign advertising rates. **"Across the road, spooked air force personnel . . ."**—Not to be confused with Schilling, Fales, Wilkinson, Bray, and the other PJs and combat controllers living in the hangar with the task force. These less combat-ready air force folks, male and female, were mostly assigned to medical units. **"Guys always crowded in to watch CNN . . ."**—The Rangers were not the only ones watching CNN. According to Warren Strobel's book *Late Breaking Foreign Policy,* Aidid was a regular viewer and used CNN to communicate to his own people and the world, even after the UN manhunt reached full swing. **"'Black time' . . ."**—The "quote" from the radio is from Othic's diary. I encountered no overt racism among the Rangers I interviewed, but I was surprised to learn that Sergeant Dave Wilson and Specialist Mike Kurth were the only black soldiers in the task force. The Ranger Regiment and Delta, at least as of 1993, seem to have been relatively untouched by the much-heralded integration of the army. The Delta soldiers I interviewed, and there were only a few, all blamed swimming requirements. "Relatively few blacks grow up swimming," one explained. I asked Colin Powell why, and he said he believed the de facto segregation still evident in the army's two most elite units was "a perfect example of what happens where you don't have affirmative action." Given the strenuous qualification requirements for both units—particularly Delta, where fewer than one in ten of those invited to try out successfully complete selection—implementing an affirmative action plan would pose unique difficulties. A few of the Rangers and D-boys I talked to suggested that blacks may not be as inclined as whites to volunteer for dangerous work on behalf of a country and establishment that is primarily white. Still, as Powell pointed out, the relatively high percentage of blacks in other elite army units, like the 82nd Airborne, argues against that. The paucity of blacks suggests to me that there is still something about the culture of the Rangers and Delta that either doesn't welcome or actively excludes black soldiers. Kurth told me he never had any special problems in Somalia, but that Wilson had been taunted as a "traitor" by Somalis for his skin color. **"In the evening they practically wore out the collection of videotapes . . ."**—One of the favorite movies shown in the hangar was *Groundhog Day*, the comedy classic starring Bill Murray, where the hero is trapped in Puxatawney, Pennsylvania, forced to keep living the same day over and over again until he gets it right. Many of the men, frustrated by the long delays between raids and the monotonous long sunny Mogadishu days, saw the film as a metaphor for their mission. **"Listening to the sounds . . . Not now."** Anderson, Sizemore. **"The horror hit home . . . scraped it from the interior,"** Struecker, B. Thomas. **"Sizemore saw all this . . . showed none of this,"** Sizemore, Cash, Anderson. **"Not everyone . . . rest of the men,"** Struecker, Sizemore, Anderson, Cash, B. Thomas. I included the scene with Brad Thomas not to humiliate him, but to illustrate how difficult it was for men who had emerged safely from the intense fighting to drive right back into it. The important part of this anecdote is that Thomas, like Anderson, did his duty despite the terror. There were men in Mogadishu, including Thomas and Anderson, who went back repeatedly.

7      **"You're going to go . . . 'the backseat,'"** Struecker. **"Other volunteers . . . start to move,"** Squeglia. **"As Struecker steered . . . out the back gate,"** Struecker, radio tapes. **"In a Humvee behind . . . a roaring fusillade,"** Cash. **"In another of the rear . . . take a shot,"** Anderson. **"The lead vehicles . . . directly ahead,"** Struecker, radio tapes. **"Durant would say . . . was at hand,"** Durant. **"Box the roadblock . . . hanging by threads,"** Struecker, Cash, Anderson, Sizemore. **"Squeglia saw . . . to get there."** Squeglia, Struecker, Sizemore, Anderson, Cash.

8      **"Up in their Black Hawk . . . ready to go down,"** Goffena, J. Yacone. **"Up in the command bird . . . the downed crew,"** Matthews. Matthews did not tell me Harrell's name. I learned the Delta commander's identity from interviews with Rangers and from battle documents. **"When Goffena's crew chief . . . thumbs-up,"** news accounts quoting Hall. **"There was a small opening . . . began moving that way,"** Goffena, J. Yacone, battle videotape.

9      **"More than a mile . . . had ever shot,"** Yurek, P. Howe, Twombly, DiTomasso. **"Specialist Lance Twombly . . . such a bad shot,"** Twombly. **"Yurek could not believe . . . until nightfall,"** Yurek, Nelson, Barton, Waddell, DiTomasso.

10     Nelson, Barton, Twombly.

11     **"Sergeant Paul Howe and the three . . . *going to be fun*,"** P. Howe. **"Captain Steele saw . . . front and rear positions,"** Steele. **"They hadn't run more . . .**

**ready to roll,"** Perino, M. Goodale, P. Howe, Steele. **"Specialist Stebbins . . . 'Just keep moving,'"** Stebbins. **"Steele, who had a radio . . . robot-Ranger formality,"** Steele. Asked to explain some of the problems he had with Delta soldiers, Steele told me a long story of difficulties he encountered on one the task force's earlier missions with a veteran soldier he identified as a member of the unit. The soldier had ignored Steele's orders on several occasions and, in Steele's opinion, had placed a chalk of Rangers in needless danger before being shipped back to the States. In reality, the soldier in question had been thrown out of Delta long before the Mogadishu mission, and was with the task force as Special Forces medic attached to the Rangers. So at least some of Steele's feelings about the Delta unit were founded on a misunderstanding. **"When Steele cracked down . . . Steele's captaincy,"** Nelson, Diemer, Sizemore, Phipps, M. Goodale, Moore, Burns, Lamb, Watson, etc. The account of the arm-wrestling contest is from my interview with Diemer, and general feelings and perceptions about Steele are garnered from my interviews with dozens of Rangers. **"The disdain was mutual . . . Hoo-ah discipline,"** Steele. Paul Howe feels Steele's characterization of Delta planning sessions is unfair and inaccurate. I suspect it is just a difference in perspective. It points up the culture clash between the Rangers and Delta. It is not surprising that Steele would see the relatively informal give-and-take of a more egalitarian Delta planning session as chaotic. **"Like the time . . . when it was,"** Nelson, P. Howe, Steele. **"In short order . . . getting pinned down,"** P. Howe. **"The Rangers followed . . . he was worth,"** Stebbins. **"Sergeant Mike Goodale who had once . . . This is for keeps,"** Goodale, P. Howe, Perino, Stebbins, Lechner, Watson, radio tapes.

**12**    Mohamed Sheik Ali.

**13**    **"The odor of spent gunpowder . . . out of this alive?"** Floyd. **"He was against the wall . . . other Rangers,"** Floyd, Siegler, Ramaglia, Young, Watson, K. Thomas, Kurth, Collett. **"Watson led the group . . . what-the-fuck!"** Floyd, Ramaglia, Young, K. Thomas, Kurth, Collett. **"Sergeant Keni Thomas was closer . . . like a failure,"** K. Thomas, Watson. **"Collett was feeling good . . . back to the wall,"** Collett, Siegler. **"Rounds poked through . . . resilient men could be,"** Floyd, K. Thomas. **"Specialist Mike Kurth was helping . . . everyone was intact,"** Kurth, Collett, Young. **"Further down the slope . . . pointing at the two Ranger officers,"** Steele, Floyd, Hooten.

**14**    **"What Hooten was trying . . . in that spot,"** Hooten. **"Steele motioned . . . out of this mess,"** Steele. Steele's gesture is based on my interview with Floyd, and the description of what he was doing is from my interviews with him. Steele did not remember seeing Hooten gesturing in the doorway until after the shots hit close. **"Beside Steele, . . . miniguns were blazing,"** Steele, Floyd, Lechner, C. Atwater, K. Thomas, Collett. **"It was just after that . . . the street to help,"** Steele, Atwater, Lechner, Hooten. The circumstances surrounding Lechner's injury became controversial after the battle, with Delta soldiers accusing Steele of abandoning Lechner on the street, a very serious charge, especially to a Ranger, whose code is to never leave a fallen comrade. In my opinion the charge is baseless. Lechner, who was the man supposedly left, said Steele reacted correctly and as anyone would to take cover when rounds started hitting close. He said seconds were all that elapsed between his getting hit, Steele and Atwater scrambling for cover, and Bullock running out to pull him to safety, hardly long enough for Steele or anyone else on the street to take cover, figure out what just happened, and retrieve him. Atwater, who was lying beside both men, confirmed Lechner's and Steele's accounts of the incident in every particular. None of this takes away from Bullock's bravery. He left the safety of the courtyard and moved out into fire in order to drag the lieutenant inside. **"Steele took the radio mike . . .** *Have more casualties, over,"* Steele, radio tapes. Steele's voice in the recording, a kind of gasping shout, shows the extreme duress of the moment. **"Sergeant Goodale . . . pouring from a jug,"** Goodale. According to Lechner, who is now a captain based in Hawaii, the bullet effectively removed a section of bone several inches long from his shin. Doctors were able to stimulate regrowth of the bone, however, and after a long period of recovery and rehab, Lechner has full use of the leg.

**15**     **"At roughly the same time . . . edge of his seat,"** Durant. **"The Black Hawk had flattened . . . face and legs,"** Howa and Bint Abraham Hassan. They still live in a shack alongside the remains of *Super Six Four.* **"The dazed pilots . . . was no rescue team,"** Durant.

**16**     Mo'alim.

**17**     Goffena, J. Yacone, radio tapes. Hallings lost the lower part of his leg, but has reportedly made remarkable progress with a prosthesis and is back with his unit.

**18**     Durant, P. Howe. In Durant's memory and in the official account (including the Medal of Honor citations) Randy Shughart was killed first and Gary Gordon came back around the helicopter, gave Durant a weapon, tried to radio for help, etc. Paul Howe, who knew both men well, convinced me that it was the opposite. He heard Randy's distinctive voice radio twice for help (not Gordon's). Also, Shughart and Gordon carried different customized weapons. The one handed Durant was almost certainly Gordon's, not Shughart's. Shughart carried an M-14, and the weapon handed Durant was, he says, most likely a CAR-15, but certainly not an M-14. Gordon would never have handed Durant his own weapon while he was still capable of using it. Lastly, in his witness statement, Durant said he recognized Gordon because he had frequently attended flight briefings. Actually, says Howe, it was Shughart who routinely attended those briefings. Durant told me while he was reluctant to see the official account altered, he could not be certain which man was which. He did not know either of the men by name.

**19**     **"Hassan Yassin Abokoi had been shot . . . parts of the Americans' bodies,"** Abokoi, who showed up at the Hotel Sahafi with two friends carrying Durant's and Cleveland's helmets (their names were attached with little black stick-strips to the back). They wanted me to buy them for three hundred dollars apiece. I liked the idea of bringing the helmets back and returning them to the 160th, but I was not inclined to reward Abokoi and the others for their war trophies. I told them I wasn't interested. They protested through an interpreter that it was rude of me not to even bargain with them, so I told them if they wanted to leave the helmets I would pay them twenty-five dollars for returning them. They left disgusted, with the helmets, but not before Peter Tobia took pictures of them posing with the trophies on their heads. **"When Mo'alim . . . the layers away,"** Mo'alim, Durant.

20      Durant.

# The Alamo

1      Wilkinson, Mabry, Dowdy.

2      **"A grenade came . . . body of the helicopter,"** Nelson, Barton, Yurek, Twombly, Wilkinson. **"The American forces . . . he wasn't heard,"** P. Howe, Miller, Lamb, Watson, Steele, Perino, DiTomasso, Nelson, Twombly. The "friendly fire" incident was related to me by both Nelson and Howe. In my interview with Twombly, he was still angry about getting hit with the LAW.

3      **"Perino and his men . . . between his legs,"** Perino. **"Across the street, . . . 'I'm hit'!"** Nelson, Perino. **"The lieutenant could tell . . . a doctor, pronto,"** Perino, Stebbins, Nelson, Schmid. **"Perino radioed Captain Steele . . . 'and defend it,'"** Steele, Perino, Schmid, DiTomasso. **"Schmid was still . . . Schmid pleaded,"** Schmid. **"The lieutenant radioed . . . to hang on,"** Perino, Steele, command-net tapes.

4      **"Stebbins shook with fear . . . waiting for him,"** Stebbins, other Rangers. Steele said he never authorized his men to go out on missions without taking their NODs. It was evidently a decision made quickly by the men themselves as they suited up for this mission. The Rangers were most likely imitating the D-boys, who had more flexibility to decide what they did or did not need. It may have been another instance of Steele losing strict control over his men as a result of living in close proximity to Delta. On the other hand, Steele didn't bring his NODs either. The devices were clumsy to have hanging around your neck when doing things like roping out of helicopters and running around, and they were fragile. Once damaged, it wasn't easy to get a replacement. **"The Little Birds . . . unscathed,"** Twombly, Barton, Nelson. **"An old man . . . *loves that donkey*,"** Nelson, Yurek, Floyd, Twombly. **"Closer to the wrecked . . . on the street,"** Belman, Dowdy. It is not mentioned in Captain Coultrop's written account of the battle. **"Then there was . . . woman were gone,"** Yurek, Stebbins, Twombly, Nelson, P. Howe. **"When the sun . . . in fire and light,"** Stebbins, Nelson, Twombly, Yurek, Barton, P. Howe.

5      Wilkinson, *Air Force Magazine, Airman, Night Flyer.*

6      Stebbins, Wilkinson.

7      Floyd, Siegler, Collett.

8      **"Across the city . . . under Kowalewski's skin,"** Marsh, Adams. Adams's written account suggested that the medical team was surprised and somewhat overwhelmed by the volume and severity of casualties, but Marsh, who headed the

team, pointedly differs. He felt the medical response, which he headed, was well-prepared. In Hackworth's *Hazardous Duty*, the celebrated former colonel–cum–military gadfly writes of his postbattle visit to wounded Rangers and Delta soldiers at Walter Reed Hospital: "They were terribly shot up. Many were arm and leg amputation cases. Many had been lying on the ground for hours. 'Why so many amputations?' I asked one of the medics. 'Infections,' he said. Somalia is one of the filthiest places in the world and those guys had been lying out there with bad wounds for hour after hour." In fact, only one soldier lost a limb in the Battle of Mogadishu, and that was Sergeant Brad Hallings, whose leg was shorn off by the RPG explosion that shot down *Super Six Four*. Pilots Goffena and Yacone crash-landed that chopper on friendly ground, and Hallings received immediate medical care. None of the men pinned down overnight around crash site one lost a limb. Ray Dowdy, the crew chief who survived the crash of *Super Six One*, had the tips of two fingers shot off. Medics at crash site one had antibiotics with them and used them throughout the night, a big reason why, according to Marsh, the postwound infection rate was, in fact, "lower than usual." **"While all this . . . force in Mogadishu,"** Goffena, J. Yacone, Matthews, Jones, Dave McKnight, Marsh, radio tapes, battle videotape, Mo'alim. **"Unless they ran out of ammo . . . ammo and water,"** Radio tapes, Dave McKnight. **"Black Hawk *Super Six Six* . . . for the night,"** P. Howe, various Rangers, Matthews, radio tapes.

**9**      **"This ungainly distribution . . . cornered with Steele,"** radio tapes, Steele. **"Then, just before dark . . . to stay down,"** P. Howe.

**10**      **"When Steele and his men . . . further confused matters,"** Steele, Watson, M. Goodale, Lechner, Floyd, Ramaglia, Collett, Kurth, K. Thomas, Siegler. **"At one point . . . sigh of relief,"** Steele, Collett. **"Steele shouted back . . . no back doors,"** Steele, Watson. **"He could talk . . . *anybody out, over,*"** Steele, Perino, command-net tapes. **"Medic Kurt Schmid . . . just barely alive,"** Perino, Schmid, Jim Smith, Jamie Smith (letters). **"When the moon came up . . . to ignore procedure,"** Steele. **"Still, it had seemed . . . 'your night vision?'"** M. Goodale, Young. **"Steele was mortified . . . no one nodded off,"** Steele. **"Miller wasn't sure . . . cover the southern intersection,"** P. Howe. **"The Ranger commander . . . 'all these wounded,'"** Steele, Perino, Watson, radio tapes. Steele's reluctance to move his men up, as Miller wished, became part of the case against him made by some of the Delta soldiers after the battle. To me it seems well advised. The other Rangers with Steele all felt it was the right decision, and all the Delta soldiers I interviewed expressed particular respect for Sergeant Watson, who actually convinced Steele not to make the move. More serious, perhaps, was Steele's refusal to confer with Miller. Paul Howe explained that it was critically important for the whole force on the ground to be in constant communication, even if only for them to keep track of where shots were being fired in order to better appraise the situation at all points on their L-shaped perimeter. My sense of it is that Steele's difficulties with the Delta unit over the previous weeks, and the scorn some of the unit had for him, came to a head under the stress of the battle. There was no clear chain of command on the ground because no one had anticipated the Delta assaulters and the Rangers being thrown together as a fighting force. This would seem to be a significant oversight, and might have created bigger problems if the ground fight had gone a different way, but in fact it had little consequence in this battle. The Little Birds kept the Somalis at bay for the most part, and the two units did what they had to do without the two captains working together. **"This was frustrating news . . . sober satisfaction,"** Steele, Collett, Floyd, radio tapes, Hooten. Miller's determination to move his men north, closer to his position, was to secure the southwestern intersection of the block where most of the force was pinned down. From his position down the block, it was not possible to see what was happening on the east-west alleyway that divided Steele's force from his. Steele and his men were in a courtyard halfway down that block, so they could not see what was going on in the alley either. *"—Hey, Captain, we've got . . . get his people moving!"* Steele, Perino, radio tapes. **"From the commanders' perspective . . . were ready to move,"** Dave McKnight, David. **"Harrell reported . . . ready to attempt it,"** McKnight, Matthews. **"Miller and Steele . . . Steele told him,"** radio tapes, Steele, P. Howe, Perino. **"Not long afterward, . . . He was gone,"** Schmid, Perino. **"Harrell was still . . . 'just been KIA,'"** radio tapes, Steele. **"Medic Schmid . . . gut feeling,"** Schmid. **"Steele, too . . . other guys yet,"** Steele, Watson. **"Goodale was in high spirits . . . *Smitty was dead?*"** Goodale, Ramaglia, Lechner, Atwater, Watson. **"Private George Siegler . . . meant her no harm,"** Siegler. **"It got quieter . . . beat of his heart,"** Kurth.

11　　**"Sergeant Waddell . . . passed around greedily,"** Waddell. *"When are we gonna . . .* sips of water," Phipps. **"When it was clear . . . at the waist,"** Lamb, Yurek, Nelson, Twombly. **"Abdiaziz . . . was not hit,"** Aden. **"Tim Wilkinson . . . 'my health, right?' "** Wilkinson, Stebbins.

12　　Hooten, Floyd, Ramaglia, K. Thomas, Steele, Collett, Watson.

13　　**"From overhead . . . doing his job,"** Battle video, P. Howe, J. Yacone, Goodale, Steele. **"One block up . . . in the world,"** Yurek, P. Howe, Bray (from *Air Force Magazine*), Waddell.


# N.S.D.Q.

1　　**"Michael Durant heard . . . with the chain,"** Durant. **"What Durant didn't know . . . get him back,"** Sharif Ali Mohamed, Firimbi. **"Mo'alim's men . . . given Durant up,"** Mo'alim. **"If the Habr Gidr leader . . . or pay,"** Sharif Ali Mohamed, Firimbi. **"Durant's right leg . . .** *cools down,*" Durant.

2　　**"Word of the big fight . . . speaking tour,"** Downing, Lake, *On the Edge*. **"Garrison's move . . . if necessary,"** USSOC report (p. 10), from Rysewyk's "Experiences of Executive Officer . . ." (p. 12), testimony of Garrison and Montgomery before the Senate Armed Forces Committee (May 12, 1994), Dave McKnight, Matthews, Marsh. **"Lieutenant Colonel Bill David . . . the two crash sites,"** David. **"While the commanders . . . 'do it for him,' "** Marsh, Eversmann, Sizemore, Anderson, Squeglia, B. Thomas. **"It was 9:30 P.M. . . . had to be the priority,"** operational time line, USSOC report, David. **"To the Rangers . . . it was now 11:23 P.M."** Operational time line, Cash, Ahlfinger, Guelzow, Keller, Lepre, David, Meyerowich.

3       Steele, Perino, radio tapes.

4       **"Captain Drew Meyerowich . . . mortally wounded,"** Meyerowich, Rysewski. **"For all his careful planning . . . working his radio,"** Squeglia, details on Lamb's wound from Marsh. **"All of the way out . . . that part of Mogadishu,"** Sizemore, Anderson, Kallman, Struecker.

5       **"Earlier in the day . . . Ismael Ahmed,"** Kassim Sheik Mohamed. After spending the morning touring Kassim's ruined facilities in Mogadishu, Kassim accused me of being an American military officer (I have never served in the military). I denied it, and he rejected my denial, explaining that he had watched how carefully I had placed my feet while touring blasted locations in the city. "It shows you have experience looking for mines," he said. "How much of an expert do you have to be to watch where you put your feet where there might be mines?" I asked. I reiterated that I had never spent a day in the military, at which Kassim said my comment proved I was lying, because "all Americans must spend two years in the military when they finish school." I told him there was no use in my arguing further with a man who obviously knew so much about my own country. Kassim and other Somalis eagerly showed me graves, their scars, and damage to their property, evidently hoping that the information I gathered would help document a case for some kind of damage claim to the UN.

6       **"Half of the rescue convoy . . . returned to the convoy,"** USSOC report, Vega, Dave McKnight. **"Meyerowich's northern half . . . 'Americans get out!' he said,"** Meyerowich, Kaiser, Nearpass, Gay. **"One of those who emerged . . . 'Sorry, man,'"** Lepre.

7       Radio tapes, Steele.

8       USSOC report, Goodale, Rodriguez, Stebbins, Wilkinson, radio tapes, Yurek, P. Howe, Steele, operational time line. Much has been made of how the task force stayed in the city overnight because they would not leave behind Wolcott's body. It is true that American soldiers will go to great lengths to recover the bodies of their fallen brothers, evidenced by the long wait and strenuous effort here to recover Wolcott's body, but the ninety-nine men who fought through the night in Mogadishu were there because they had little choice. A number of commanders forthrightly said they would have sadly but certainly left Wolcott's body if the chance had presented itself to evacuate their wounded and beseiged troops.

9       Steele, Perino, Yurek, Ramaglia, Collett, Nelson, P. Howe, Floyd, Watson.

10      Abdi Mohamed Elmi.

11      Abdi Karim Mohamed, Bashir Haji Yusuf, Hassan Aden Hassan.

12      USSOC report, Marsh, Adams, Dowdy, Young, Siegler, Perino, Nelson, Schilling, Steele, radio tapes, Matthews, Kallman, Goodale, Gould, Rodriguez, Anderson, K. Thomas, Cash, Phipps, Floyd, Stebbins, Watson, Sizemore, Atwater, Ramaglia.

13    P. Howe.

14    Sizemore, Cash, Steele, Floyd, Diemer, Telscher, Nelson, Eversmann, Perino, Watson.

15    **"American awakened . . . by angry crowd,"** *The New York Times* (Oct. 5, 1993), *The Philadelphia Inquirer,* CNN. **"President Clinton . . . he demanded,"** Drew, *On the Edge,* Lake. **"The trickle . . . *One of the guys*,"** S. Shughart. **"In a bedroom . . . wasn't giving up hope,"** W. Frank, B. Yacone. **"At the hangar . . . kind of animals . . . ?"** J. Yacone. **"The D-boys . . . a massacre,"** P. Howe, Goffena, Matthews, McKnight. **"Mace . . . courage and cool,"** Nelson, Sizemore, Goodale, Floyd.

16    **"Mike Durant's captors . . . *feed starving people?*"** Durant, CNN archives. **"Willi Frank . . . off the frame!"** W. Frank. **"Durant felt okay . . . with Aidid,"** Durant, Firimbi, Sharif Ali Mohamed.

17    **"Garrison and the . . . the fight,"** McKnight, P. Howe, J. Howe, Matthews. **"Former U.S. Ambassador . . . Lake asked,"** Oakley, Lake. **"Now they were in trouble . . . released. Now,"** *The New York Times, The Philadelphia Inquirer* (October 5, 1993), *On the Edge,* (pp. 325–326), Lake, Oakley.

18    Durant, Firimbi.

19    Jim Smith, U.S. Army Mailgram.

20    Shughart.

21    D. Beck. DeAnna Joyce has remarried. She is now DeAnna Joyce Beck, and with her husband's blessing actively keeps alive her memories of her first husband.

22    **"Durant's fear . . . out the initials,"** Durant, Firimbi. Durant's hastily scribbled note was painstakingly analyzed by army intelligence officers for hidden messages and possible clues to Durant's whereabouts. The reference to pizza was weighed as a possible hint that the pilot was being held near the Italian compound. The request that prayers be said for him might mean he was being held in or near a mosque. Three references to receiving medical treatment might point to a location near a hospital. It was ultimately decided, correctly, that the note meant nothing more than it said. **"After Hofstadter left . . . had gotten through,"** Durant, Huband. While some have criticized Durant for making these comments, the commanders I interviewed, both on and off the record, unanimously praised the pilot's performance in captivity. "Mike Durant did everything right," said General Wayne A. Downing, who was commander of U.S. Special Operations Command at the time.

23    USSOC report, P. Howe, Marsh, Eversmann, Steele, Perino, Schmid, Rodriguez, Sizemore, Anderson, M. Goodale, K. Goodale, Lechner, Stebbins, Othic, Spalding, Galentine, Burns. Marsh has recovered fully enough from his severe injuries to run a thriving private practice in Virginia, supervise a clinic at the

University of Virginia Hospital, manage (with his wife) a growing family and a large horse farm, and serve as a volunteer firefighter and chief physician at a nearby maximum security prison. I spent a day trying to keep up with the doctor, whose energy and enthusiasm are inspiring. Galentine's thumb was reattached in surgery, but he has never regained much use of it. "It's kind of worthless," he says.

**24**    W. Frank.

**25**    Durant, Firimbi.

**26**    Oakley, Zinni.

**27**    Firimbi, Durant, *The New York Times* (Ocober 15, 1993). Durant met with an emissary from Aidid in a Tennessee hotel lobby in 1996, with Special Forces soldiers staked out nearby to keep an eye on things. It was a perfectly innocuous meeting. The man, who runs an orphanage in Baidoa, brought along various items (among them a T-shirt depicting a white American hand and black Somali hand clasped in friendship) as a goodwill gesture, and delivered a letter from Firimbi, who urged Durant not to harbor bad feelings. The pilot was invited to return to Somalia for a friendly visit. Durant wrote back to Firimbi, but declined the offer of a return trip.

# ACKNOWLEDGMENTS

I would like to thank my friends Max King and Bob Rosenthal at *The Philadelphia Inquirer* for their exceptional vision and support. *Black Hawk Down* began as a newspaper project and is the kind of story no other newspaper in America would have undertaken. Max and Rosey saw the potential for it early on, and enlarged my own ambitions for it. By helping to craft my first draft of this story into an episodic newspaper series, David Zucchino was its first editor and substantially contributed to this book's final shape. I owe a great deal to photographer Peter Tobia, who made the very difficult trip to Mogadishu with me in the summer of 1997, and returned with a stunning collection of work documenting that blasted city.

I have made several friends for life reporting this story. Since I had no military experience of my own, the last two years have been a crash course in martial terminology, tactics, and ethics. I have learned a great deal from Lieutenant Colonel L. H. "Bucky" Burruss, U.S. Army (ret.), a great soldier and fine writer, who was kind enough to seek me out and act as a first reader and expert adviser. Master Sergeant Paul Howe and Dan Schilling, a former air force combat controller, were also early readers and made thoughtful and helpful suggestions. I would not have been able to get started on this story without the help of Jim Smith, a former Ranger captain whose son, Jamie, was killed in Mogadishu. Jim kindly introduced me to some of his son's fellow Rangers. Walt Sokalski and Andy Lucas of the U.S. Special Operations Command public relations office set up the initial interviews with Rangers and 160th SOAR helicopter pilots that launched this project. Thanks to Jack Atwater of the U.S. Army Ordnance Museum for his quick course in Weaponry 101. These are just a few of the hundreds of military people who have generously shared their time and expertise, some of whom have asked me not to name them. I am grateful to Ibrahim Robles Farah for his help in getting Peter and me in and out of Somalia.

Thanks again to my very patient wife, Gail, and our family, Aaron, Anya, B. J., Danny, and Ben, who permit me to live and work in a way that often complicates their own lives. My agent, Rhoda Weyr, has proved her unerring judgment once more by steering me to Morgan Entrekin, whom I feel very lucky to have as an editor, publisher, and friend, and Assistant Editor Amy Hundley. Together with the rest of the very smart and successful team at Grove/Atlantic, they have created one of the finest care and feeding systems for writers currently in existence.

# INDEX